Asian Turtle Trade:
Proceedings of a Workshop on Conservation and Trade of Freshwater Turtles and Tortoises in Asia

EDITED BY
PETER PAUL VAN DIJK, BRYAN L. STUART, AND ANDERS G.J. RHODIN

Asian Turtle Trade:

Proceedings of a Workshop on Conservation and Trade of Freshwater Turtles and Tortoises in Asia.

Phnom Penh, Cambodia, 1– 4 December 1999

EDITED BY

PETER PAUL VAN DIJK[1], BRYAN L. STUART[2],
AND ANDERS G.J. RHODIN[3]

[1]*TRAFFIC Southeast Asia, Petaling Jaya, Selangor, Malaysia;*
[2]*Wildlife Conservation Society Lao Program, Vientiane, Laos;*
[3]*Chelonian Research Foundation, Lunenburg, Massachusetts, USA*

CHELONIAN RESEARCH MONOGRAPHS
Number 2

August 2000
Chelonian Research Foundation

COVER ILLUSTRATIONS

Front Cover: Hundreds of adult Malaysian giant turtles (*Orlitia borneensis*) in a holding pen in Medan, Sumatra, Indonesia, awaiting international export to the food and Traditional Chinese Medicine markets of East Asia, September 1999. Photo by CHRIS R. SHEPHERD/TRAFFIC SOUTHEAST ASIA.

Frontispiece: Turtle dealer in a market in Hong Kong offering live Asian box turtles (genus *Cuora*) for sale for food or Traditional Chinese Medicine, holding up an adult yellow-margined box turtle (*Cuora flavomarginata*), with many Chinese three-striped box turtles, "golden coin turtles" (*Cuora trifasciata*), and other turtle species, eels, and crabs in cages at his feet. Photo by ANDERS G.J. RHODIN.

Back Cover (Upper): Close-up portrait of an adult southeast Asian box turtle (*Cuora amboinensis*) from Uthai Thani, Thailand. This species is heavily exploited by the food and Traditional Chinese Medicine markets of East Asia. Photo by PETER PAUL VAN DIJK.

Back Cover (Lower): Many hundreds of adult southeast Asian box turtles (*Cuora amboinensis*) in a holding pen in Medan, Sumatra, Indonesia, awaiting international export to the food and Traditional Chinese Medicine markets of East Asia, representing an average day's volume in the trade of this species at this site, September 1999. Photo by CHRIS R. SHEPHERD/TRAFFIC SOUTHEAST ASIA.

Asian Turtle Trade: Proceedings of a Workshop on Conservation and Trade of Freshwater Turtles and Tortoises in Asia. Edited by PETER PAUL VAN DIJK, BRYAN L. STUART, AND ANDERS G.J. RHODIN.

CHELONIAN RESEARCH MONOGRAPHS, *Number 2*.

ISSN (monograph series): 1088-7105
ISBN (this volume): 0-9653540-2-4 (hard cover); 0-9653540-3-2 (soft cover)

Published and Copyright © 2000 by Chelonian Research Foundation, Lunenburg, Massachusetts, USA.
Printed by MTC Printing, Inc., Leominster, Massachusetts, USA.

Asian Turtle Trade: Proceedings of a Workshop on Conservation and Trade of Freshwater Turtles and Tortoises in Asia
P.P. van Dijk, B.L. Stuart, and A.G.J. Rhodin, Eds.
Chelonian Research Monographs, Number 2 • © 2000 by Chelonian Research Foundation

TABLE OF CONTENTS

Asian Turtle Trade: Proceedings of a Workshop on Conservation and Trade of Freshwater Turtles and Tortoises in Asia
P.P. van Dijk, B.L. Stuart, and A.G.J. Rhodin, Eds.
Chelonian Research Monographs 2:7 • © 2000 by Chelonian Research Foundation

FOREWORD

The Workshop on Conservation and Trade of Freshwater Turtles and Tortoises in Asia was held in Phnom Penh, Kingdom of Cambodia, from 1 to 4 December 1999. It brought together the people directly involved in regulating and monitoring this trade in the exporting and importing countries and those involved in field status assessments in the turtles' native areas. The Workshop objective was to characterize the trade and assess its impact on the conservation of Asia's freshwater turtles and tortoises. The forty-five delegates from fifteen countries brought with them a wide range of expertise from throughout the region, involving all aspects of the utilization, trade, biology, and conservation of non-marine chelonians, and put together the clearest picture yet of the size and dynamics of the trade and its impacts on native turtle populations. This picture exceeded many of our worst anticipations — the trade is larger and has greater impacts on turtle populations than most knew or feared. But recognition of the scale of the problem is one of the first steps towards improvement, and much of the Workshop was devoted to consideration of realistic conservation actions to address the trade and contribute to the conservation of freshwater turtles and tortoises in their native habitats.

This Proceedings volume is a direct outgrowth of the Workshop, bringing together original contributions from the participants and other colleagues consulted after the Workshop. The volume is structured as was the Workshop, as a series of individual country reports divided into four geographic regions: Northeast Asia (China, Hong Kong, and Taiwan), Indochina (Cambodia, Laos, and Vietnam), South Asia (Bangladesh, India, and Myanmar), and Southeast Asia (Indonesia, Malaysia, Papua New Guinea, and Thailand). For each geographic region an additional summary report brings into focus the results of two-day break-out group discussions held among the representative country delegates. In addition, a two-day special group session evaluating and recommending revisions to the 1996 IUCN Red List status of 90 Asian non-marine turtle species is presented as an Appendix.

This volume is an important step in the process of understanding and evaluating the threats posed to Asia's (and the world's) turtles, especially the effects of both local and international trade for human consumption and utilization. It is also an important landmark in the on-going endeavor of bringing the process of conservation assessment and management planning to a regional scale, involving primarily those people most affected by their loss of regional biodiversity. The synergy created by the open discussions and presentations by these regional and international experts has led to a diverse and encompassing document that should stand as a testament to the value of working together from a variety of perspectives and experiences. The conclusions and recommendations emanating from this synergetic process of evaluation become the next steps necessary in our continuing struggle to bring some semblance of sustainability and preservation to the world's populations of turtles.

The Workshop was organized and funded by Wildlife Conservation Society (WCS), TRAFFIC (the joint wildlife trade monitoring program of WWF and IUCN–The World Conservation Union), and World Wildlife Fund (WWF), and was also supported by the German Federal Agency for Nature Conservation, Federal Ministry for Environment, Nature Conservation and Nuclear Safety; the Office of Scientific Authority, U.S. Fish and Wildlife Service; Chelonian Research Foundation (CRF); Kari and Andrew Sabin; and the Kadoorie Farm & Botanic Garden, Hong Kong. We are most grateful for their significant contributions to conserving Asia's freshwater turtles and tortoises. Special thanks go to Colin Poole, Nhem Sok Heng, Kunthea Ka, Keat Leng, and the other WCS Cambodia staff, James Compton and Craig Hoover of TRAFFIC, and Joshua Ginsberg and John Thorbjarnarson of WCS for organizing what proved to be an exceptionally well-run and inspirational workshop.

PETER PAUL VAN DIJK   BRYAN L. STUART   ANDERS G.J. RHODIN

Asian Turtle Trade: Proceedings of a Workshop on Conservation and Trade of Freshwater Turtles and Tortoises in Asia
P.P. van Dijk, B.L. Stuart, and A.G.J. Rhodin, Eds.
Chelonian Research Monographs 2:9–12 • © 2000 by Chelonian Research Foundation

WORKSHOP PARTICIPANTS
AND PROCEEDINGS CONTRIBUTORS (*)

GARY ADES*
Kadoorie Farm & Botanic Garden
Lam Kam Road
Tai Po, New Territories
HONG KONG
Fax: 852-248-31877
E-mail: kfgarya@kfbg.org.hk

CHRIS B. BANKS*
Melbourne Zoo
P.O. Box 74
Parkville, Victoria 3052
AUSTRALIA
Fax: 61-3-9285-9360
E-mail: Cbanks@zoo.org.au

S. BHUPATHY*
Salim Ali Centre for Ornithology and Natural History
Anaikatti P.O.
Coimbatore 641108
INDIA
E-mail: salimali@vsnl.com

KURT A. BUHLMANN*
Conservation International
c/o Savannah River Ecology Laboratory
P.O. Drawer E
Aiken, SC 29802
USA
E-mail: Buhlmann@srel.edu

BOSCO CHAN*
Department of Ecology & Biodiversity
The University of Hong Kong
Pokfulam Road
HONG KONG
Fax: 852-254-01836
E-mail: bochan@hkusua.hku.hk

HSIEN-CHEH CHANG*
School of Chinese Medicine
China Medical College
91 Hsueh Shih Rd.
Taichung 400, Taiwan
REPUBLIC OF CHINA
E-mail: hcchang@mail.cmc.edu.tw

TIEN-HSI CHEN*
National Museum of Marine Science and Technology
2 Pei-Ning Rd.

Keelung 202, Taiwan
REPUBLIC OF CHINA
Fax: 886-2-2-462-7716
E-mail: thchen@mail.ntou.edu.tw

B.C. CHOUDHURY*
Wildlife Institute of India
Post Bag No. 18
Chandrabani
Dehra Dun 248001
INDIA
E-mail: bcc@wii.gov.in

CHUL THACH*
Fishery Office
Kampong Thom Province
CAMBODIA

CHUN SARETH
Under Secretary of State
(Management Authority for CITES)
MAFF, Norodom Boulevard
Phnom Penh
CAMBODIA
E-mail: cites@forum.org.kh

CHUN SOPHAT*
CITES Office
MAFF, Norodom Boulevard
P.O. Box 582
Phnom Penh
CAMBODIA
Fax: 855-23-215470
E-mail: bigcatch@bigpond.com.kh

JAMES COMPTON*
TRAFFIC Southeast Asia–Vietnam
c/o World Wide Fund For Nature Conservation
  Indochina Programme
7 Yet Kieu Street
Hanoi
VIETNAM
Fax: 84-4-822-0642
Present Address:
TRAFFIC Oceania
GPO Box 528
Sydney, NSW 2001
AUSTRALIA
Fax: 61-2-9212-1794
E-mail: jcompton@traffico.org

CAROL REHM CONROY
Operative Services
Nursing Administration
Boston Medical Center
Boston, MA 02118
USA

PAUL CROW*
Kadoorie Farm & Botanic Garden
Lam Kam Road
Tai Po, New Territories
HONG KONG
Fax: 852-248-31877
E-mail: primate1@kfbg.org.hk

INDRANEIL DAS*
Institute of Biodiversity
Universiti Malaysia Sarawak
94300 Kota Samarahan, Sarawak
MALAYSIA
E-mail: idas@mailhost.unimas.my

VAGI R. GENORUPA*
Department of Environment and Conservation
P.O. Box 6601
Boroko, NCD 111
PAPUA NEW GUINEA
Fax: 675-325-0182

FAHMEEDA HANFEE*
TRAFFIC India
World Wildlife Fund India
172-B Lodi Estate
New Delhi 110003
INDIA
Fax: 91-11-469-1226
E-mail: Trfindia@del3.vsnl.net.in

HEIKO HAUPT*
Ministry for Environment, Nature Conservation
    and Nuclear Safety
German CITES Scientific Authority
Federal Agency for Nature Conservation
Animal Species Conservation
Konstantinstrasse 110
53179 Bonn
GERMANY
Fax: 49-228-8491-119
E-mail: HauptH@bfn.de

DOUGLAS B. HENDRIE*
Cuc Phuong Conservation Project
Fauna & Flora International
P.O. Box 78
Hanoi
VIETNAM
E-mail: cpcp@fpt.vn

HENG KIMCHAY*
Wildlife Protection Office
Forestry Department
40 Norodom Boulevard
Phnom Penh
CAMBODIA
E-mail: wpo@forum.org.kh

ROHAN HOLLOWAY*
Applied Ecology Research Group
University of Canberra
Canberra, ACT 2601
AUSTRALIA

HOUT PISETH*
Protected Areas Office
Department of Nature Conservation and Protection
Ministry of Environment
Sihanouk Boulevard
Phnom Penh
CAMBODIA
E-mail: wwfcam@bigpond.com.kh

JACK HURD
World Wide Fund for Nature Conservation in Cambodia
Ministry of Environment
Sihanouk Boulevard
Phnom Penh
CAMBODIA
Fax: 855-23-218034
E-mail: wwfcam@bigpond.com.kh

DJOKO T. ISKANDAR*
Department of Biology
Bandung Institute of Technology
Jalan Ganesa 10
Bandung 40132 Java
INDONESIA
Fax: 62-22-250-0258
E-mail: Iskandar@bi.itb.ac.id

KALYAR*
Wildlife Conservation Society
Bldg. C-1, Aye Yeik Mon 1st Street
Yadanamon Housing Ave.
Hlaing Township, Yangon
MYANMAR
Fax: 95-1-512838
E-mail: wcs.mm@mptmail.net.mm

RAYMOND KAN*
Kans Trading Co. Ltd.
1508, The Center
99 Queen's Road Central
HONG KONG
Fax: 852-284-52105
E-mail: kanr@netvigator.com

S.M. MUNJURUL HANNAN KHAN*
Ministry of Environment and Forests
House No.50/1, Road No.11A
Dhanmondi, Dhaka-1209
BANGLADESH
E-mail: ncsip@bdcom.com

JO-YEN LAI*
The Herp Rescue Center
30 Sec, 2 Hsin Kuang Road
Taipei, Taiwan
REPUBLIC OF CHINA
Fax: 886-2-2938-2316
E-mail: dwx11@mail.zoo.gov.tw

MICHAEL LAU*
Kadoorie Farm & Botanic Garden
Lam Kam Road
Tai Po, New Territories
HONG KONG
Fax: 852-248-31877
E-mail: mwnlau@kfbg.org.hk

LAY KHIM
Protected Areas Office
Department of Nature Conservation
    and Protection
Ministry of Environment
Sihanouk Boulevard
Phnom Penh
CAMBODIA
E-mail: wwfcam@bigpond.com.kh

LIENG SOPHA*
Fisheries Department
Ministry of Agriculture, Forestry and Fisheries
Norodom Boulevard
Phnom Penh
CAMBODIA
Fax: 855-23-427048

HUA-CHING LIN*
Taipei Zoo
Taipei 110, Taiwan
REPUBLIC OF CHINA
Fax: 886-2-2938-2316·
E-mail: dwx11@mail.zoo.gov.tw

NAO THUOK
Fisheries Department
(Scientific Co-Authority for CITES)
MAFF
Norodom Boulevard
Phnom Penh
CAMBODIA
Fax: 855-23-427048
E-mail: catfish@camnet.com.kh

NHEM SOK HENG
Wildlife Conservation Society
Cambodia Program
P.O. Box 1620
Phnom Penh
CAMBODIA
Fax: 855-23-217205
E-mail: wcs@bigpond.com.kh

HIDETOSHI OTA*
Tropical Biosphere Research Center
Dept. of Biology
University of the Ryukyus
Nishihara, Okinawa 903-0213
JAPAN
Fax: 81-98-895-8966
E-mail: ota@sci.u-ryukyu.ac.jp

THANIT PALASUWAN*
Royal Forest Department
61 Phaholyothin Road, Bangkhen
Bangkok 10900
THAILAND
Fax: 66-2-579-3004
E-mail: wildlifept@hotmail.com

STEVEN G. PLATT*
Wildlife Conservation Society
Cambodia Program
P.O. Box 1620
Phnom Penh
CAMBODIA
Fax: 855-23-217205
E-mail: wcs@bigpond.com.kh

COLIN POOLE
Wildlife Conservation Society
Cambodia Program
P.O. Box 1620
Phnom Penh
CAMBODIA
Fax 855-23-217205
E-mail: wcs@bigpond.com.kh

PRAK LEANG HOUR*
Fishery Office
Kampong Chhnang Province
CAMBODIA

S.M.A. RASHID*
Division of Biology
School of Science
Nanyang Technological University
469 Bukit Timah Road, 259756
SINGAPORE
Fax: 65-469-8928
E-mail: carinam95@hotmail.com

ANDERS G.J. RHODIN*
Chelonian Research Foundation
168 Goodrich Street
Lunenburg, MA 01462
USA
Fax: 1-978-582-6279
E-mail: RhodinCRF@aol.com

SAMEDI*
Protected Wildlife Captive Breeding Section
Directorate General of Nature Protection and Conservation
Ministry of Forest and Estate Crops
Jl. Gatot Subroto, Senayan, Jakarta, Java
INDONESIA
Fax: 62-21-572-0227
E-mail: sam.phpa@dephut.cbn.net.id

SENG TEAK
World Wildlife Fund Cambodia
Ministry of Environment
Sihanouk Boulevard
Phnom Penh
CAMBODIA
Fax: 855-23-218034
E-mail: wwfcam@bigpond.com.kh

DIONYSIUS S.K. SHARMA*
World Wildlife Fund Malaysia
Locked Bag No. 911, Jalan Sultan P.O.
46990 Petaling Jaya
MALAYSIA
Fax: 60-3-703-5157
E-mail: DSharma@wwfnet.org

CHRIS R. SHEPHERD*
TRAFFIC Southeast Asia
M19-B (2nd Floor), Jalan Pasar (1/21)
46000 Petaling Jaya, Selangor
MALAYSIA
Fax: 60-3-7784-7220
E-mail: tsea@po.jaring.my

SHI HAITAO*
Department of Biology
Hainan Normal University
Hainan 571158
PEOPLE'S REPUBLIC OF CHINA
Fax: 898-588-3035
E-mail: sht@aneca.hainnu.edu.cn

BRYAN L. STUART*
Wildlife Conservation Society Lao Program
P.O. Box 6712
Vientiane
LAOS
Fax: 856-2121-5400
E-mail: blstuart@unity.ncsu.edu

SUON PHALLA
Wildlife Protection Office
Forestry Department
40 Norodom Boulevard
Phnom Penh
CAMBODIA
E-mail: wpo@forum.org.kh

ROBERT J. TIMMINS*
World Wide Fund for Nature Conservation Lao Project Office
P.O. Box 7871
Vientiane
LAOS
Fax: 856-2121-7161
E-mail: rob@naturalists.freeserve.co.uk

OSWALD BRAKEN TISEN*
National Parks and Wildlife Office
Sarawak Forest Department
Wisma Sumber Alam, Petra Jaya
93660 Kuching, Sarawak
MALAYSIA
E-mail: oswald@pd.jaring.my

TOUCH SEANG TANA*
Fisheries Department
Ministry of Agriculture, Forestry and Fisheries
Norodom Boulevard
Phnom Penh
CAMBODIA
Fax: 855-23-427048
E-mail: tana@forum.org.kh

PETER PAUL VAN DIJK*
TRAFFIC Southeast Asia
M19-B (2nd Floor), Jalan Pasar (1/21)
46000 Petaling Jaya
Selangor
MALAYSIA
Fax: 60-3-7784-7220
E-mail: pptsea@po.jaring.my

WIN KO KO*
Wildlife Conservation Society
Bldg. C-1, Aye Yeik Mon 1st Street
Yadanamon Housing Ave.
Hlaing Township, Yangon
MYANMAR
Fax: 95-1-512838
E-mail: wcsmm@mptmail.net.mm

YUICHIROU YASUKAWA*
Tropical Biosphere Research Center
University of the Ryukyus
Senbaru 1, Nishihara
Okinawa 903-0213
JAPAN

Asian Turtle Trade: Proceedings of a Workshop on Conservation and Trade of Freshwater Turtles and Tortoises in Asia
P.P. van Dijk, B.L. Stuart, and A.G.J. Rhodin, Eds.
Chelonian Research Monographs 2:13–14 • © 2000 by Chelonian Research Foundation

Asian Turtle Trade:
Proceedings of a Workshop on Conservation and Trade of Freshwater Turtles and Tortoises in Asia

EXECUTIVE SUMMARY

At least 90 species of freshwater turtles and tortoises occur in South Asia, East Asia, Southeast Asia, and New Guinea. Of these species, 33 are recognized in the 1996 IUCN Red List of Threatened Species as Vulnerable, Endangered, or Critically Endangered; updated information indicates that the number of threatened species may be double this number.

Populations of Asian tortoises and freshwater turtles are under threat from a variety of human impacts, including collection for local consumption, collection for regional and international food and pet trade, habitat degradation and loss, and introduced predators and competitors. Collection for trade is currently the most significant threat for most Asian species.

Trade in turtles has probably occurred since historical times. In the past few decades, the international pet trade has developed to involve significant numbers of Asian turtle species exported from Asian range states to meet the interests of pet keepers in Europe, America, and parts of Asia. With the exception of a very small number of exceptionally rare species, every known Asian turtle species has been recorded in the international pet trade in recent years.

Turtle meat is considered a culinary delicacy with perceived health and medicinal benefits in many East Asian cultures. Mass trade in turtles for consumption has developed as the economies of Asian countries have grown in recent decades, along with the purchasing power of people who esteem turtle meat. These consumers are predominantly in East Asia, i.e., China, Hong Kong, Japan, Korea, and Taiwan, as well as Chinese ethnic communities around the world.

Related to the trade in live turtles for consumption is the trade in turtle shells for traditional medicinal purposes. Much of the trade in turtle shell and turtle bone appears to involve animals from the consumption trade, but there are also indications that turtles are occasionally butchered only for their shells and their meat discarded.

Wild turtle populations in East Asia have been depleted by over-collection; consequently the seemingly insatiable demand for turtles for consumption has been met in other ways. Farming of Chinese softshell turtles (*Pelodiscus sinensis*) has expanded within East Asia and spread to several countries in Southeast Asia. However, farming has been unable to meet the recent rise in de-

mand, resulting in a rapid and essentially uncontrolled increase in the collection and trade of wild turtles from South and Southeast Asia.

Until recently, the trade in wild-collected turtles was mainly from agricultural and forested areas to cities within a single country. When Chinese currency became convertible in 1989, it became possible for the Chinese to import wildlife from neighboring counties. This rapidly gave rise to voluminous imports of turtles as well as other wildlife to Hong Kong and mainland China.

Initially the main turtle source countries for China were Vietnam and Bangladesh. As their turtle populations collapsed, these countries began acquiring turtles from neighboring countries and trans-shipping them to East Asia. Thus turtle populations of India, Myanmar, Laos, and Cambodia become exposed to these same intensive collection pressures.

At the same time, new wildlife trade routes were developed from resource-rich countries of Southeast Asia to East Asia, such that at present turtles are exported in vast numbers directly from Indonesia, Malaysia, Cambodia, and Myanmar. Much of the trade in live turtles uses airlines, while transport by truck and ship are also significant. Based on the most recent available data, a minimum of 13,000 metric tons of live turtles are exported from South and Southeast Asia to East Asia each year. At least 5000 tons of wild-collected turtles are exported from Indonesia annually and 1500 tons from Bangladesh, as well as 4000 tons of farm-produced softshells from Thailand and 2500 tons of turtles from wild and farmed sources in Malaysia. The actual amounts may be substantially higher and these numbers do not include amounts exported from Cambodia, Laos, Myanmar, or Vietnam.

Data on imports of turtles to East Asia are very incomplete. The only data available are for Hong Kong where customs records indicate a fairly stable level of local consumption between 2000 to 3000 tons annually. A figure of 13,500 tons imported to Hong Kong in 1998 is substantially higher than usual and likely includes amounts trans-shipped to mainland China.

Many species of Asian turtles are known to be significantly affected by the adverse impacts of trade. Impacts are particularly severe on species that have high value in trade. For example, in the mid-1980s the three-striped box turtle (*Cuora trifasciata*) had no unusually high value in the western pet trade, selling for about US$ 50 to US$ 100 per adult animal. This price was similar to that asked for many other turtle species and much cheaper than most tortoises and snake-necked turtles. Since that time, the species has been marketed in China as having cancer-curing and other medicinal properties, creating an increasing demand for the species with prices steadily rising as the supply of wild-collected animals has declined. Prices of several hundred US dollars per animal in the mid-1990s have risen to about US$ 1500 per kg at present. Even small juveniles are in great demand as they can be raised in captivity and sold later. Large farming or rearing enterprises for this species are believed to exist, but since a mature female only produces a few eggs each year such operations cannot meet the market demand. The value of this turtle has become so famous that it is well known in even the smallest villages in rural Indochina. Consequently, collection pressure is overwhelming and the survival of the species in the wild appears increasingly unlikely.

Other box turtles of the genus *Cuora* are also in demand for consumption for medicinal purposes. The number of *Cuora amboinensis* exported from Indonesia to East Asian food markets can be calculated to approach one million individuals annually. *Cuora galbinifrons* is present in 81% of turtle shipments inspected in northern Vietnam and is the third most numerous species in those shipments. The *Cuora* species endemic to China are additionally in great demand in the international pet trade, commanding prices of hundreds or more US dollars per animal in western countries and Japan.

Softshell turtles (several species of the family Trionychidae) are the most preferred species for food consumption and comprise the greatest proportion of known turtle trade volumes. Many of the animals traded are farmed Chinese softshell turtles (*Pelodiscus sinensis*), but an apparently equivalent volume consists of wild-caught individuals of the Asian softshell turtle (*Amyda cartilaginea*) and other softshell species.

Lack of long-term field studies and population status survey data mean that the effects of intensive collecting on natural populations of tortoises and freshwater turtles are not known in detail. It is generally understood, however, that exploited populations are in decline, and often in serious decline. Field collectors unanimously report that more effort is required now to find a turtle than in the past. Local middlemen and exporters pay increasingly higher prices as supplies to their businesses decline. Official export statistics for specific turtle species from various countries usually show short periods of rapid increases followed by equally rapid declines in total volumes exported over a period of a few years. Regular shifts in known trade routes and the species offered for sale in East Asian food markets demonstrate that new areas to supply the trade are continually developed as existing supply areas are exhausted. All indications are that one area after another in South and South-east Asia is depleted of its native turtle species to supply the demand from East Asia.

A comprehensive strategy is urgently needed to address the threats posed by trade to the survival of Asia's tortoises and freshwater turtles and to ensure the survival of secure populations of all regional turtle species in their natural habitats. This strategy must include:

• Improved legal protection of turtles and adequate enforcement of this protection, including:
   – Implementing existing legal protection of turtles, including CITES regulations.
   – Improvement of legislation where appropriate.
   – Incorporation of IATA airline regulations (for transport of live turtles) into national laws across the region, with resultant implementation and enforcement of these regulations.
   – Placing all Asian freshwater turtle species under CITES trade regulations, either in CITES Appendix I if specifically warranted, or Appendix II for all other species.
   – Developing guidelines and appropriate solutions to deal with confiscated turtles in Asia.
   – Safeguarding viable populations in adequately protected areas of natural habitat in their native range.

• Developing better information and conservation strategies for Asian turtles, including:
   – Quantitative surveys of distribution, status, and trade volumes of Asian turtles.
   – Biological studies of turtles, with emphasis on ecological studies of wild populations.
   – Coordinated captive breeding programs for selected species.

• Elimination or reduction of the demand for wild-collected turtles to possibly sustainable levels, by:
   – Finding alternatives to turtle shell used in traditional medicine, or at least sustainable supplies of turtle shell.
   – Possibly creating incentives for commercial farming of selected species for consumption, to reduce the market share of wild-collected turtles.
   – Promoting public awareness of the plight of turtles to elicit changes in consumer behavior.

The Workshop on Conservation and Trade of Freshwater Turtles and Tortoises in Asia was held in Phnom Penh, Cambodia, during 1-4 December 1999. The workshop was organized by Wildlife Conservation Society (WCS), TRAFFIC, and World Wildlife Fund (WWF), and was also funded by the German Federal Agency for Nature Conservation, Federal Ministry for Environment, Nature Conservation and Nuclear Safety; the Office of Scientific Authority, U.S. Fish and Wildlife Service; Chelonian Research Foundation (CRF); Kari and Andrew Sabin; and the Kadoorie Farm & Botanic Garden.

Asian Turtle Trade: Proceedings of a Workshop on Conservation and Trade of Freshwater Turtles and Tortoises in Asia
P.P. van Dijk, B.L. Stuart, and A.G.J. Rhodin, Eds.
Chelonian Research Monographs 2:15–23 • © 2000 by Chelonian Research Foundation

The Status of Turtles in Asia

PETER PAUL VAN DIJK[1,2,3]

[1]*Biology Department, Science Faculty, Chulalongkorn University, Phaya Thai Road, Bangkok 10330, Thailand;*
[2]*Zoology Department, National University of Ireland, Galway, Ireland;*
[3]*Present Address: TRAFFIC Southeast Asia, M19-B (floor 2), Jalan Pasar (1/21),*
46000 Petaling Jaya, Selangor, Malaysia [E-mail: pptsea@po.jaring.my]

Asia is rich in habitats and biodiversity, and correspondingly rich in turtle species. Asia's highest turtle diversity occurs in four hotspot regions, the Indo-Gangetic Plain, mainland Southeast Asia, the South China coastal region, and New Guinea, but almost any area outside the extreme deserts and the high altitude and latitude regions is home to some turtle species. At least 100 species of tortoises and freshwater turtles are native to Asia (Table 1), and new species continue to be described.

Unfortunately, the survival outlook for many of these turtle species is of real concern. The 1996 IUCN Red List of Threatened Species (IUCN, 1996) included 37 Asian species, including 5 in the Critically Endangered category, 9 considered Endangered, and 23 Vulnerable, as well as 18 species which were Data Deficient but perceived to be under some level of threat (Table 1). At present, a re-evaluation of the threats to Asian tortoises and freshwater turtles considers many more species to fall in the threatened categories (see Appendix, this volume). Details of the status of and threats to individual turtle species in most countries of South, Southeast, and East Asia are given in the country papers in this volume.

The threats faced by the Asian turtle species are as diverse as the species themselves, but broadly fall in two groups: targeted exploitation of the species and degradation or destruction of the habitat to the extent that turtle populations cannot survive.

Turtles, like most natural resources, have long been used for subsistence consumption and other purposes by the humans sharing their habitats. Many Stone Age refuse heaps in caves contain fragments of butchered turtles. As societies developed, barter and trade of turtles, along with other foods and useful items, developed as part of "progress." As transport technology and infrastructure progressed and more people moved over greater distances, trade expanded to meet demand in areas that were previously restricted to using only what was locally produced. Other factors, such as economic purchasing power and cultural traditions, were and are powerful influences on the development of trade and trade routes. In the past decade, we have seen how these factors have come together to result in the large-scale extirpation of Asian turtles and other wildlife to supply the demand in East Asia.

This targeted collection of tortoises and freshwater turtles for trade clearly impacts natural populations by reducing the total numbers of animals. Moreover, trade impacts turtle populations particularly severely because much of the trade involves mature adult animals. The life history of turtles is an evolutionary marvel, a strategy that involves a long time to reach maturity with high losses of eggs, hatchlings, and small juveniles to a wide range of natural predators and unfavorable habitat conditions such as drought, flood, fire, or famine. However, once adult size is reached the animals are invulnerable to most predators and have very high survivorship. A very long adult lifespan permits sustained production of offspring over a very long period; a few of these offspring will find favorable environmental conditions and elude predators, and will thus reach maturity and perpetuate the cycle. With intelligence, perseverance and tools, humans have broken the security of this cycle by elimination of adults and sustained intensive collection of eggs.

What effects this reduction and elimination of turtle populations has on natural and human-dominated ecosystems is almost completely unknown. Ecological interactions among turtles of various sizes and species and other organisms are little studied but may safely be assumed to be complex. Many turtles feed on insect larvae, shrimp, crabs, snails, clams, worms, and other invertebrates, as well as fish and other vertebrates, and many scavenge carrion. By doing so, turtles contribute to balancing populations of these prey species, which include species significant to humans such as the intermediate snail host of *Schistosoma* blood flukes and various agriculturally undesirable species. In turn, turtle eggs, hatchlings, and occasional adults represent food for a variety of large carnivores ranging from storks to leopards. Turtles feed on and distribute the seeds of a wide variety of herbs, shrubs, and trees, and passage through a turtle's digestive system actually helps germination of certain plant seeds. Turtles feeding on particular plant species and using vegetation as shelter can influence the plant community composition and vegetation structure in wetlands and dryland habitats. While poorly known, the ecological role of turtles can be significant in places and the effects of their removal are unpredictable.

As well as targeted collection of turtles for local use and trade, be it for food, medicinal purposes, live pets, stuffed specimens or ornamental materials, populations of tortoises and freshwater turtles are further impacted by human-related habitat disturbance. Fire has a long history of being used to cleanse existing agricultural land, clear non-cultivated land for agricultural expansion, and stimulate growth of herbs and grasses in open forest to benefit grazing mammals, domestic livestock, and hunted wild species of cattle and deer. Forest fires are part of the natural processes in Asian forests, but human influences have made forest fires a much more frequent occurrence in many places. Fires not only directly kill or injure a part of the tortoise and freshwater turtle population in the affected area, but have additional indirect effects such as reducing water quality when the rains eventually wash the ashes into streams and wetlands, and changing the tree species composition and structure of the forest itself. Regular, repeated fires eventually kill many tree species, including ecologically critical fruiting trees, leading to a secondary forest type dominated by fire-resistant tree and bamboo species. Such secondary forest types frequently do not provide the right habitat conditions for species of turtles and other wildlife.

Other human impacts on natural habitats can be even more extreme and destructive. Logging, whether clearcutting or selective logging to extract only the high-value timber species, has effects on tree species composition, canopy closure, and forest structure. More directly, opening an area to loggers leads to greatly increased numbers of hunters and collectors, often followed by settlers and conversion of the land to agricultural use. Similarly, drainage of wetlands for agriculture is a serious loss of natural habitats, followed in many areas by the disappearance of the very best agricultural land under concrete as cities expand and develop sprawling residential and industrial areas. Streams, rivers, and wetlands are often treated as convenient ways to eliminate waste products from agriculture, homes, industry, and mining. Rivers are dammed to create reservoirs to generate electricity and provide water for irrigated agricul-

ture, industry, and domestic use. Reservoir impacts on downstream rivers include a reduction in temperature and oxygen content of the water, increased scouring of the river bed, and coastal erosion. Estuaries are developed for ports, coastal mangroves may be overexploited or eliminated for charcoal and aquaculture operations. Turtles inhabit these habitats, and their degradation has direct and indirect effects on the survival of turtle populations.

Together, exploitation and habitat loss have reduced and sometimes eliminated turtle populations over large areas. At the same time, laws, customs, and practices have more or less effectively protected areas of natural or little-impacted habitats in every country (see MacKinnon et al., 1996; MacKinnon, 1997). In some cases, these protected areas are extensive, vast enough to protect turtle populations that are large enough to survive indefinitely, provided the existing conditions remain stable. The past few decades have seen a very encouraging expansion of the number and size of protected areas in Asia, with a corresponding increase in the dedication to safeguard these areas. The fact that several turtle species are not considered seriously threatened in their survival, even though populations continue to decline in many areas, is mostly due to the security offered by some of these protected areas.

There are ways to improve the effectiveness of Asia's protected areas further. These include further safeguarding existing parks and sanctuaries from encroachment, incursions, and permitted yet detrimental forms of exploitation, and expansion of the system by including more of habitats that remain inadequately represented and areas of particular ecological and biodiversity importance.

Figure 1. Though prized in food markets of East Asia, attempts at commercial breeding of *Amyda cartilaginea*, the Asiatic softshell turtle, have not been very successful. This animal is from Khao Laem, Thailand. Photo by PPvD.

Figure 2. *Cuora trifasciata*, the Chinese three-striped box turtle or "golden coin turtle," perceived to have cancer-curing effects, sells for up to US$ 1000 per animal in East Asian markets. Photo by Lee Kwok Shing.

In the absence of direct exploitation, a number of turtle species are well able to survive in healthy populations in human landscapes, such as areas of irrigated rice culture, plantations, fishponds, and recreational parks. Increased public awareness and appreciation of turtles, combined with social and legal incentives for would-be collectors to leave the animals there, could help turtles' survival as part of these human-modified ecosystems.

Trade has not only removed turtles from various Asian countries; it has also brought two non-native species, the red-eared slider, *Trachemys scripta elegans,* from southern North America to almost the entire region and the Chinese softshell turtle, *Pelodiscus sinensis,* from East Asia to Southeast Asia. Hatchlings of the red-eared slider are widely sold as pets, and numerous individuals that survived, grew, and became less attractive have been released into the wild. Thus reproducing populations have become established in many Asian countries. The spread of the Chinese softshell turtle, in contrast, resulted from aquaculture of the species to meet the demand for softshell meat. Techniques to culture the species in commercial quantities were developed in Japan and Taiwan; softshell farming spread to Southeast Asia to take advantage of the tropical conditions and abundance of cheap food. These factors combine to make farming of Chinese softshell turtles very profitable and economically competitive with softshells cultured in East Asia, even when incorporating the higher transport costs. Efforts have been made to culture native softshell species (mainly *Amyda cartilaginea,* Fig. 1) on a commercial scale in Southeast Asia, but these proved less successful because *A. cartilaginea* grow less rapidly and produce fewer eggs per year.

The establishment and predicted future spread of these two exotic turtle species has led to calls for their elimination from the wild and termination of imports and farming operations of these species. Such calls echo similar sentiments about introduced red-eared sliders in other parts of the world. Both these exotic species have been implicated in the decline of native turtle species by their perceived more aggressive behavior and greater ability to compete for food, space, and other resources. Alternatively, it is argued that Asian turtle species are evolutionarily and ecologically robust enough to have survived numerous species invasions in geological history, and that these exotic species are made scapegoats for declines in native turtle populations that are actually caused by overharvesting and habitat degradation. Indeed, if the Chinese softshell were such an adaptable ecological competitor, one wonders why it did not spread into tropical Southeast Asia by natural means long ago. Clearly, the ecological impacts of these exotic turtle species on native turtle populations and on the ecosystems in general, deserves detailed study.

A similarly contentious issue that requires study is whether farming of turtles increases or decreases exploitation pressures on native turtle populations. The main species of concern in this respect is the Chinese softshell turtle. One view would be that increased supply of farmed turtles meets a large part of the demand for turtle meat, so that a smaller proportion and thus a smaller overall amount of turtles need to be collected from the wild. In addition, the steady supply of farmed turtles would create a stable market and steady price, making exploitation of increasingly scarce wild populations economically less rewarding since their price will increase less than the effort required to collect a wild turtle. The opposite view argues that increased availability of turtles stimulates increasing demand, with a connoisseur's preference being placed on wild-collected animals, leading to higher prices for wild animals and thus increased exploitation pressure. In addition, wild animals of the species being farmed would continue to be collected from the wild to increase farm founder stock and experiment with genetic improvements. Finally, farming a species outside its native range leads to escapes and a potential invasive species problem, while farming within the range contributes to concerns about genetic purity and disease transmittal to the wild population. At least in the case of the three-striped box turtle or golden coin turtle (*Cuora trifasciata*, Fig. 2), its perceived medicinal value has escalated its value to extraordinary heights, and while the species is known to be farmed commercially in China, collection pressure on the remaining wild populations continues to increase.

The discovery and taxonomic description of numerous new species of turtles, and resurrection of previously synonymized species, together involving some 20 species in the past 15 years, has been remarkable. Many of these became known only through the animal trade, and the natural history or even the exact area of occurrence of several species remains unknown despite substantial efforts by scientists and others to find these species in the wild. Such data are urgently required to make informed decisions about a conservation strategy for such species. The absence of reliable field sightings, the very small numbers known for some of these species, the lack of clarity where a species comes from, and the sometimes striking morphological similarities to other species have led to suspicions that some of these newly-discovered species may in fact be natural or intentionally farmed hybrids. Clarification of the taxonomic status and validity of such forms is urgently required: limited conservation resources should not be wasted on hybrids, while these forms represent top conservation priorities if they are valid and extremely rare species.

While much of recent research efforts involving Asian turtles have been concerned with new species descriptions and taxonomic revisions, studies of the natural history and field conservation status of Asian turtle species, rare and common alike, remain regrettably basic, scattered, and incomplete. Several excellent studies exist from across the region, but the overall impression is that a vast amount of field information remains to be collected. The impression is also that time to collect this information is running out very rapidly for many species.

In conclusion, the status of many Asian species of tortoises and freshwater turtles gives cause for grave concern. Trade in turtles represents arguably the greatest source of threat, and is discussed in great detail in this volume. A wide variety of measures are proposed to address this threat, ranging from improved legal protection through improved enforcement and alternative supplies to meet an undeniable demand, to effecting a change in consumer attitudes. Meanwhile, species-specific conservation programs including captive breeding efforts in the country of origin and elsewhere, and habitat-based conservation efforts including

expansion and improvement of Asian protected areas are all essential components in a comprehensive strategy that must be implemented if Asia's diversity of turtles is to survive into the future.

Acknowledgments. — My sincere thanks go to all those people who over the years provided information to help me understand the biology of turtles and some of the conservation issues in Asia. The assistance of TRAFFIC, WCS, and WWF in providing the opportunity to attend the workshop at Phnom Penh and prepare this paper are gratefully acknowledged. The views and opinions expressed here are the ones I developed over a decade in Southeast Asia and do not necessarily reflect the views of these organizations.

LITERATURE CITED

BOURRET, R. 1939. Notes Herpétologiques sur l'Indochine Française. XVI. Tortues de la Collection du Laboratoire des Sciences Naturelles de l'Université. Description d'une espèce nouvelle. Annexe au Bulletin Général de l'Instruction Publique 6:5-12.

FRITZ, U., ANDREAS, B., AND LEHR, E. 1998. Eine neue Unterart der Dreikiel-Scharnierschildkröte, *Pyxidea mouhotii* (Gray, 1862) (Reptilia: Testudines: Bataguridae). Zoologische Abhandlungen Staatliches Museum für Tierkunde Dresden 50(3):34-43.

FRITZ, U., GAULKE, M., AND LEHR, E. 1997. Revision der südostasiatischen Dornschildkröten-Gattung *Cyclemys* Bell, 1834, mit Beschreibung einer neuen Art. Salamandra 33(3):183-212.

FRITZ, U. AND OBST, F.J. 1996. Zur Kenntnis der Celebes-Erdschildkröte, *Heosemys yuwonoi* (McCord, Iverson & Boeadi, 1995). Herpetofauna 18(102):27-34.

FRITZ, U. AND OBST, F.J. 1997. Zum taxonomischen status von *Cuora galbinifrons serrata* Iverson & McCord, 1992, und *Pyxidea mouhotii* (Gray, 1862). Zoologische Abhandlungen, Staatliches Museum für Tierkunde zu Dresden 49(14):261-279.

FRITZ, U. AND OBST, F.J. 1999. Neue Schildkröten aus Südostasien. Teil II. Bataguridae (*Cyclemys, Heosemys, Mauremys, Ocadia, Pyxidea, Sacalia*) und Trionychidae. Sauria (Berlin) 21(1):11-26.

GASPERETTI, J., STIMSON, A.F., MILLER, J.D., ROSS, J.P., AND GASPERETTI, P.R. 1993. Turtles of Arabia. In: Fauna of Saudi Arabia. Vol. 13, pp. 170-367.

GRAY, J.E. 1863. Observations on the box tortoises, with the descriptions of three new Asiatic species. Proceedings of the Zoological Society of London 1863:173-179.

GUO, C.-W., NIE, L.-W., AND WANG, M. 1997. The karyotypes and NORs of two species of *Chinemys*. Sichuan Journal of Zoology 15(Suppl.):97-104.

IUCN (INTERNATIONAL UNION FOR THE CONSERVATION OF NATURE AND NATURAL RESOURCES). 1996. 1996 IUCN Red List of Threatened Animals. IUCN, Gland, Switzerland, 448 pp.

IVERSON, J.B. 1992. A Revised Checklist with Distribution Maps of the Turtles of the World. Privately Printed, Richmond, Indiana, 363 pp.

IVERSON, J.B. AND McCORD, W.P. 1989. The proper taxonomic allocation of *Emys nigricans* Gray, *Emys muticus* Cantor, and *Geoclemys kwantungensis* Pope. Amphibia-Reptilia 10:23-33.

IVERSON, J.B. AND McCORD, W.P. 1992a. A new Chinese eyed turtle of the genus *Sacalia* (Batagurinae: Testudines). Proceedings of the Biological Society of Washington 105(3):426-432.

IVERSON, J.B. AND McCORD, W.P. 1992b A new subspecies of *Cuora galbinifrons* (Testudines: Batagurinae) from Hainan Island, China. Proceedings of the Biological Society of Washington 105(3):433-439.

IVERSON, J.B. AND McCORD, W.P. 1994. Variation in East Asian Turtles of the genus *Mauremys* (Bataguridae: Testudines). Journal of Herpetology 28(2):178-187.

IVERSON, J.B. AND McCORD, W.P. 1997. A new species of *Cyclemys* (Testudines: Bataguridae) from Southeast Asia. Proceedings of the Biological Society of Washington 110(4):629-639.

LEHR, E., FRITZ, U., AND OBST, F.J. 1998. *Cuora galbinifrons picturata* subsp. nov., eine neue Unterart der Hinterindischen Scharnierschildkröte. Herpetofauna 20(119):5-11.

MACKINNON, J., SHA, M., CHEUNG, C., CAREY, G., ZHU, X., AND MELVILLE, D. 1996. A Biodiversity Review of China. WWF International, Hong Kong.

MACKINNON, J. (Ed.). 1997. Protected Areas Systems Review of the Indo-Malayan Realm. Asian Bureau of Conservation and World Conservation Monitoring Centre for the World Bank, 198 pp.

McCORD, W.P. 1998. *Mauremys pritchardi*, a new batagurid turtle from Myanmar and Yunnan, China. Chelonian Conservation and Biology 2(4):555-562.

McCORD, W.P. AND IVERSON, J.B. 1992. A new species of *Ocadia* (Testudines: Bataguridae) from Hainan Island, China. Proceedings of the Biological Society of Washington 105(1):13-18.

McCORD, W.P. AND IVERSON, J.B. 1994. A new species of *Ocadia* (Testudines: Batagurinae) from southwestern China. Proceedings of the Biological Society of Washington 107(1):52-59.

McCORD, W.P. AND PHILIPPEN, H.D. 1998 A new subspecies of box turtle, *Cuora amboinensis lineata*, from northern Myanmar (Burma), with remarks on the distribution and geographic variation of the species. Reptile Hobbyist 1998(March):51-58.

McCORD, W.P., IVERSON, J.B., AND BOEADI. 1995. A new batagurid turtle from northern Sulawesi, Indonesia. Chelonian Conservation and Biology 1(4):311-316.

MEYLAN, P.A. AND WEBB, R.G. 1988. *Rafetus swinhoei* (Gray) 1873, a valid species of living soft-shelled turtle (Family Trionychidae) from China. Journal of Herpetology 22(1):118-119.

NUTPHAND, W. 1986. "Manlai," the world's biggest softshell turtle. Thai Zoological Magazine 1(4):64-70 (in Thai).

OBST, F.J. AND REIMANN, M. 1994. Bemerkenswerte Variabilität bei *Cuora galbinifrons* Bourret 1939, mit Beschreibung einer neuen Unterart: *C. galbinifrons bourreti* subsp. nov. Zoologische Abhandlungen, Museum für Tierkunde Dresden 48:125-137.

PHILIPPEN, H.D. AND GROSSMANN, P. 1990. Eine neue Schlangenhalsschildkröte von Neuguinea: *Chelodina reimanni* sp. n. (Reptilia, Testudines, Pleurodira: Chelidae). Zoologische Abhandlungen Staatliches Museum für Tierkunde Dresden 46(5):95-102.

PRITCHARD, P.C.H. 2000. *Indotestudo travancorica...* a valid species of tortoise? Reptile and Amphibian Hobbyist 5(6):18-28.

PRITCHARD, P.C.H. AND McCORD, W.P. 1991. A new emydid turtle from China. Herpetologica 47(2):139-147.

RHODIN, A.G.J. 1994a. Chelid turtles of the Australasian Archipelago: I. A new species of *Chelodina* from southeastern Papua New Guinea. Breviora 497:1-36.

RHODIN, A.G.J. 1994b. Chelid turtles of the Australasian Archipelago: II. A new species of *Chelodina* from Roti Island, Indonesia. Breviora 498:1-31.

WEBB, R.G. 1995. Redescription and neotype designation of *Pelochelys bibroni* from southern New Guinea (Testudines: Trionychidae). Chelonian Conservation and Biology 1(4):301-310.

YASUKAWA, Y., OTA, H., AND HIKIDA, T. 1992. Taxonomic re-evaluation of the two subspecies of *Geoemyda spengleri* (Gmelin, 1789) (Reptilia: Emydidae). Japanese Journal of Herpetology 14(3):143-159.

YASUKAWA, Y., OTA, H., AND IVERSON, J.B. 1996. Geographic variation and sexual size dimorphism in *Mauremys mutica* (Cantor, 1842) (Reptilia: Bataguridae), with description of a new subspecies from the southern Ryukyus, Japan. Zoological Science 13:303-317.

Table 1. Species diversity of tortoises and freshwater turtles in Asia; distribution is based on a variety of sources, currently recognized subspecies and taxonomic changes and additions published since Iverson (1992) are noted under Remarks.

Species / English name	Distribution	1996 IUCN Red List	Remarks
Suborder Cryptodira			
Family Testudinidae			
Geochelone elegans (Schoepff, 1794)			
Indian star tortoise	IN, LK, PK	—	
Geochelone platynota (Blyth, 1853)			
Burmese star tortoise	MM	CR (A1cd+2cd, C2a)	
Geochelone sulcata (Miller, 1779)			
African spurred tortoise	SA?, YE?, Africa	VU (A1cd)	Occurrence in Arabia discussed by Gasperetti et al., 1993.
Indotestudo elongata (Blyth, 1853)			
Elongated tortoise	BD, CN?, IN, KH, LA, MM, MY, NP, TH, VN	VU (A1acd)	
Indotestudo forstenii (Schlegel and Müller, 1840)			
Sulawesi tortoise	ID	VU (A1cd)	
Indotestudo travancorica (Boulenger, 1907)			
Travancore tortoise	IN	VU (A1cd)	
Manouria emys (Schlegel and Müller, 1844)			
Asian brown tortoise	BD, CN?, ID, IN, KH?, MM, MY, TH	VU (A1cd)	Subspecies: *emys, phayrei*.
Manouria impressa (Günther, 1882)			
Impressed tortoise	CN, KH?, LA, MM, MY, TH, VN	VU (A1acd, B1+2acd)	
Testudo graeca Linnaeus, 1758			
Spur-thighed tortoise	AM, AZ, EG, GE, IL, IQ, IR, JO, LB, RU, SY, TM, TU, Africa, Europe	VU (A1cd)	Several subspecies in the Middle East.
Testudo horsfieldii Gray, 1844			
Central Asian tortoise	AF, CN, IQ, IR, KZ, PK, RU, TM, UZ	VU (A2d)	

Table 1. (*continued*).

Testudo kleinmanni Lortet, 1883			
Egyptian tortoise	EG, IL, LB, Africa	EN (A1abcd)	
Family Bataguridae			
Batagur baska (Gray, 1831)			
River terrapin	BD, ID, IN, KH†, MM†, MY, SG†, TH†, VN†	EN (A1bcd)	
Callagur borneoensis (Schlegel and Müller, 1844)			
Painted terrapin	BN, ID, MY, TH†	CR (A1bcd)	
Chinemys megalocephala Fang, 1934			
Big-headed pond turtle	CN	—	Reinstated as a distinct species by Guo et al. (1997).
Chinemys nigricans (Gray, 1834)			
Red-necked pond turtle	CN	DD	Formerly known as *Chinemys kwantungensis* (see Iverson and McCord, 1989).
Chinemys reevesii (Gray, 1831)			
Reeves' turtle	CN, JP, TW	—	
Cuora amboinensis (Daudin, 1802)			
Southeast Asian box turtle	BD, ID, IN, KH, LA, MM, MY, PH, SG, TH, VN	LR: nt	Subspecies: *amboinensis, couro, kamaroma, lineata* McCord and Philippen, 1998.
Cuora aurocapitata Luo and Zong, 1988			
Yellow-headed box turtle	CN	DD	
Cuora flavomarginata (Gray, 1863)			
Yellow-margined box turtle	CN, JP, TW	VU (A2c)	At times placed in *Cistoclemmys*; subspecies: *evelynae, flavomarginata, sinensis.*
Cuora galbinifrons (Bourret, 1939)			
Indochinese box turtle	CN, KH?, LA, VN	LR: nt	At times placed in *Cistoclemmys*; subspecies: *bourreti* Obst and Reimann, 1994, *galbinifrons, picturata* Lehr et al., 1998; *hainanensis* synonymized with *galbinifrons* by Iverson and McCord, 1992b.
Cuora mccordi Ernst, 1988			
McCord's box turtle	CN	DD	
Cuora pani Song, 1984			
Pan's box turtle	CN	DD	
Cuora serrata Iverson and McCord, 1992b			
Serrate box turtle	CN	—	Elevated from subspecies of *C. galbinifrons* by Fritz and Obst (1997), though validity questioned.
Cuora trifasciata (Bell, 1825)			
Chinese three-striped box turtle	CN, LA?, VN	EN (A2d)	
Cuora yunnanensis (Boulenger, 1906)			
Yunnan box turtle	CN	DD	Not seen since 1906 and likely extinct.
Cuora zhoui Zhao, 1990			
Zhou's box turtle	CN	DD	
Cyclemys atripons Iverson and McCord, 1997			
Black-bridged leaf turtle	KH, TH	—	
Cyclemys dentata (Gray, 1831)			
Asian leaf turtle	BN, ID, TH, MY, PH, SG	—	
Cyclemys oldhamii Gray, 1863			
Oldham's leaf turtle	ID, IN, LA, MM, MY, NP, TH	—	Resurrected from synonymy of *C. dentata* by Fritz et al. (1997).
Cyclemys pulchristriata Fritz, Gaulke, and Lehr, 1997			
Streak-shelled leaf turtle	VN	—	
Cyclemys tcheponensis (Bourret, 1939)			
Indochinese leaf turtle	LA, TH, VN	—	Resurrected from tentative synonymy of *C. dentata* by Fritz et al. (1997).
Geoclemys hamiltonii (Gray, 1831)			
Spotted pond turtle	BD, ID, NP?, PK	LR: nt	
Geoemyda japonica Fan, 1931			
Ryukyu leaf turtle	JP	EN (A1c, B1+2c)	Resurrected from synonymy of *G. spengleri* by Yasukawa et al. (1992).
Geoemyda silvatica Henderson, 1912			
Cochin cane forest turtle	IN	EN (B1+2c)	
Geoemyda spengleri (Gmelin, 1789)			
Black-breasted leaf turtle	CN, VN	—	
Hardella thurjii (Gray, 1831)			
Crowned river turtle	BD, IN, NP, PK	LR: nt	Subspecies: *indi, thurjii.*
Heosemys depressa (Anderson, 1875)			
Arakan forest turtle	MM	CR (A2cd, B1+2c)	
Heosemys grandis (Gray, 1860)			
Giant Asian pond turtle	KH, LA, MM, MY, TH, VN	LR: nt	

Table 1. (*continued*).

Heosemys leytensis Taylor, 1920			
Philippine pond turtle	PH	EN (B1+2c)	
Heosemys spinosa (Bell, 1829)			
Spiny turtle	BN, ID, MM? MY, PH, SG, TH	VU (A1bd)	
Heosemys yuwonoi (McCord, Iverson, and Boeadi, 1995)			
Sulawesi forest turtle	ID	DD	Formerly in genus *Geoemyda* (see Fritz and Obst, 1996).
Hieremys annandalii (Boulenger, 1903)			
Yellow-headed temple turtle	KH, LA, MM?, MY, TH, VN	VU (A1acd+2cd)	
Kachuga dhongoka (Gray, 1835)			
Three-striped roofed turtle	BD, IN, NP?	LR: nt	
Kachuga kachuga (Gray, 1831)			
Red-crowned roofed turtle	BD, IN, NP	EN (A1cd)	
Kachuga smithi (Gray, 1863)			
Brown roofed turtle	BD, IN, PK	—	Subspecies: *pallidipes, smithi.*
Kachuga sylhetensis (Jerdon, 1870)			
Assam roofed turtle	BD, IN	DD	
Kachuga tecta (Gray, 1831)			
Indian Roofed Turtle	BD, IN, NP, PK	—	
Kachuga tentoria (Gray, 1834)			
Indian tent turtle	BD, IN	—	Subspecies: *circumdata, flaviventer, tentoria.*
Kachuga trivittata (Duméril and Bibron, 1835)			
Burmese roofed turtle	MM	EN (A1c)	
Malayemys subtrijuga (Schlegel and Müller, 1844)			
Malayan snail-eating turtle, Ricefield turtle	ID, KH, LA, MY, TH, VN	—	
Mauremys annamensis (Siebenrock, 1903)			
Annam leaf turtle	VN	—	Formerly in genus *Annamemys* (see Iverson and McCord, 1994).
Mauremys caspica (Gmelin, 1774)			
Caspian turtle	AM, AZ, GE, IL, IQ, IR, LB, RU?, SY, TM, TU, Europe	—	
Mauremys iversoni Pritchard and McCord, 1991			
Fujian pond turtle	CN	DD	
Mauremys japonica (Temminck and Schlegel, 1835)			
Japanese pond turtle	JP	—	
Mauremys mutica (Cantor, 1842)			
Yellow pond turtle	CN, JP, TW, VN	—	Subspecies: *kami* Yasukawa, Ota, and Iverson 1996, *mutica.*
Mauremys pritchardi McCord, 1998			
Pritchard's pond turtle	CN, MM?	DD	Suspected hybrid between *M. mutica* and *C. reevesi* (Aoki, in Fritz and Obst, 1999).
Melanochelys tricarinata (Blyth, 1856)			
Tricarinate hill turtle	BD, IN, NP	VU (B1+2c)	
Melanochelys trijuga (Schweigger, 1812)			
Indian black turtle	BD, IN, LK, MM, MV, NP	DD	Subspecies: *coronata, edeniana, indopeninsularis, parkeri, thermalis, trijuga.*
Morenia ocellata (Duméril and Bibron, 1835)			
Burmese eyed turtle	MM	LR: nt	
Morenia petersi (Anderson, 1879)			
Indian eyed turtle	BD, IN	LR: nt	
Notochelys platynota (Gray, 1834)			
Malayan flat-shelled turtle	BN, ID, MY, MM?, TH, SG	DD	
Ocadia glyphistoma McCord and Iverson, 1994			
Notch-mouthed stripe-necked turtle	CN or VN	DD	
Ocadia philippeni McCord and Iverson, 1992			
Philippen's stripe-necked turtle	CN	DD	
Ocadia sinensis (Gray, 1834)			
Chinese stripe-necked turtle	CN, TW, VN	LR: nt	
Orlitia borneensis Gray, 1873			
Malayan giant turtle	ID, MY	LR: nt	
Pyxidea mouhotii (Gray, 1862)			
Keeled box turtle	CN, IN, LA, MM, VN	—	Subspecies: *mouhotii, obsti* Fritz, Andreas, and Lehr, 1997.
Sacalia bealei (Gray, 1831)			
Beal's eyed turtle	CN	VU (B1+2c)	
Sacalia pseudocellata Iverson and McCord, 1992			
Chinese false-eyed turtle	CN	DD	
Sacalia quadriocellata Siebenrock, 1903			
Four-eyed turtle	CN, LA, VN	VU (B1+2c)	

Table 1. (*continued*).

Siebenrockiella crassicollis (Gray, 1831)			
Black marsh turtle	ID, KH, MY, MM, SG, TH, VN	—	
Family Emydidae			
Emys orbicularis (Linnaeus, 1758)			
European pond turtle	AM?, AZ, GE, IR, KZ, RU, SY, TM, TU, UZ?, Africa, Europe	LR: nt	
Trachemys scripta (Schoepff, 1792) *			
Common slider	Widely introduced	[LR: nt]	
Family Platysternidae			
Platysternon megacephalum Gray, 1831			
Big-headed turtle	CN, LA, MM, TH, VN	DD	Subspecies: *megacephalum, peguense, shiui, tristernalis, vogeli.*
Family Trionychidae			
Amyda cartilaginea (Boddaert, 1770)			
Asiatic softshell turtle	BN, ID, IN, KH, LA, MM, MY, SG, TH, VN	VU (A1cd+2cd)	
Aspideretes gangeticus (Cuvier, 1825)			
Indian softshell turtle	BD, IN, NP, PK	—	
Aspideretes hurum (Gray, 1831)			
Indian peacock softshell turtle	BD, IN	—	
Aspideretes leithii (Gray, 1872)			
Leith's softshell turtle	IN	LR: nt	
Aspideretes nigricans (Anderson, 1872)			
Black softshell turtle, Bostami turtle	BD	CR (B1+2a)	
Chitra chitra Nutphand, 1986			
Southeast Asian narrow-headed softshell turtle	ID, MY?, TH	CR (A1cd, B1+2c)	
Chitra indica (Gray, 1831)			
Indian narrow-headed softshell turtle	BD, IN, MM, NP?, PK	VU (A1cd)	
Dogania subplana (Geoffroy St.-Hilaire, 1809)			
Malayan softshell turtle	BN?, ID, MM, MY, SG, TH	—	
Lissemys punctata (Bonnaterre, 1789)			
Indian flapshell turtle	BD, IN, LK, MM, NP, PK	—	Subspecies: *andersoni, punctata.*
Lissemys scutata (Peters, 1868)			
Burmese flapshell turtle	BD? MM, TH?	DD	
Nilssonia formosa (Gray, 1869)			
Burmese peacock softshell turtle	MM	VU (A1acd+2cd, B1+2c)	
Palea steindachneri (Siebenrock, 1906)			
Wattle-necked softshell turtle	CN, VN, MU*, US*	LR: nt	
Pelochelys bibroni (Owen, 1853)			
New Guinea giant softshell turtle	ID, PN	VU (A1cd)	
Pelochelys cantorii Gray, 1864			
Asian giant softshell turtle	BD, CN, ID, IN, KH, LA, MM, MY, PH, PN, TH, VN	VU (A1cd+2cd)	Previously considered synonym of *P. bibroni*, see Webb (1995).
Pelodiscus sinensis (Wiegmann, 1835)			
Chinese softshell turtle	CN, JP, TW, VN, TH*, US*	—	Taxonomy unclear, several taxa may be recognizable.
Rafetus euphraticus (Daudin, 1802)			
Euphrates softshell turtle	IQ, IR, SY, TR	EN (A1ac+2c)	
Rafetus swinhoei (Gray, 1873)			
Yangtze softshell turtle	CN, VN?	—	Resurrected from synonymy by Meylan and Webb (1988).
Trionyx triunguis (Forsskål, 1775)			
African softshell turtle	CY, IL, LB?, TR, Africa	[CR (C2a)]	
Family Carettochelyidae			
Carettochelys insculpta Ramsay, 1886			
Pig-nosed turtle	AU, ID, PN	VU (A1bd)	
Suborder Pleurodira			
Family Chelidae			
Chelodina mccordi Rhodin, 1994b			
Roti snake-necked turtle	ID	VU (D2)	
Chelodina novaeguineae Boulenger, 1888			
New Guinea snake-necked turtle	ID, PN, AU	—	
Chelodina parkeri Rhodin and Mittermeier, 1976			
Parker's snake-necked turtle	ID, PN	VU (D2)	

Table 1. (*continued*).

Chelodina pritchardi Rhodin, 1994a			
Pritchard's snake-necked turtle	PN	VU (D2)	
Chelodina reimanni Philippen and Grossmann, 1990			
Reimann's snake-necked turtle	ID, PN?	DD	
Chelodina siebenrocki Werner, 1901			
Siebenrock's snake-necked turtle	ID, PN	—	
Elseya branderhorstii (Ouwens, 1914)			
White-bellied snapping turtle	ID	—	Previously considered part of *E. novaeguineae*; see Rhodin and Genorupa, this volume.
Elseya novaeguineae (Meyer, 1874)			
New Guinea snapping turtle	ID, PN	—	
Emydura subglobosa (Krefft, 1876)			
Red-bellied short-necked turtle	AU, ID, PN	—	
Family Pelomedusidae			
Pelomedusa subrufa (Bonnaterre, 1789)			
Helmeted turtle	SA, YE, Africa	—	Occurrence in Arabia discussed by Gasperetti et al., 1993.

Common names follow Iverson (1992). Country codes: AF - Afghanistan; AM - Armenia; AU - Australia; AZ - Azerbaijan; BD - Bangladesh; BN - Brunei Darussalam; CN - P.R. China; CY - Cyprus; EG - Egypt; GE - Georgia; ID - Indonesia; IL - Israel; IN - India; IQ - Iraq; IR - Iran; JO - Jordan; KH - Cambodia; KZ - Kazakhstan; LA - Laos; LB - Lebanon; MM - Myanmar; MU - Mauritius; MV - Maldives; MY - Malaysia; NP - Nepal; PH - Philippines; PK - Pakistan; PN - Papua New Guinea; RU - Russian Federation; SA - Saudi Arabia; SG - Singapore; SY - Syria; TH - Thailand; TM - Turkmenistan; TR - Turkey; TW - Taiwan; US - U.S.A.; UZ - Uzbekistan; YE - Yemen; VN - Vietnam.
* = Established exotic species; † = Extinct in the wild in country; ? = Country record questionable, unconfirmed or suspected.

Asian Turtle Trade: Proceedings of a Workshop on Conservation and Trade of Freshwater Turtles and Tortoises in Asia
P.P. van Dijk, B.L. Stuart, and A.G.J. Rhodin, Eds.
Chelonian Research Monographs 2:24–29 • © 2000 by Chelonian Research Foundation

An Overview of Asian Turtle Trade

JAMES COMPTON[1,2]

[1]TRAFFIC Southeast Asia–Vietnam, c/o WWF Indochina Programme, 7 Yet Kieu Street, Hanoi, Vietnam;
[2]Present Address: TRAFFIC Oceania, GPO Box 528, Sydney, NSW 2001, Australia
[Fax: 61-2-9212-1794; E-mail: jcompton@traffico.org]

As the Chairman of the IUCN/SSC Tortoise and Freshwater Turtle Specialist Group, John Behler, remarked a few years ago, "there is no more serious turtle crisis than that which is taking place in Southeast Asia and southern China." From general opinions shared in the lead-up to this workshop — indeed, the very reasons which led to this workshop being organized — the situation has not altered much since then. Perhaps it has even become worse. Some species previously observable in the market in high volumes are less numerous and vastly reduced in size and some others, e.g., *Chinemys reevesii*, have all but disappeared from the food markets in southern China.

The fact that some Asian chelonian species are regarded as "commercially extinct," where populations and densities have been reduced so much that targeted exploitation of these species is no longer economically worthwhile, should be enough to alert even the uninitiated to the threats facing native Asian species. To that same uninitiated ear it prompts the question: why does this trade exist and what drives it to continue? If scientists and conservation groups are to muster the support necessary to ensure that tortoises and freshwater turtles obtain the protection they deserve, answers to such questions need to be communicated clearly and unambiguously to government decision-makers and donors alike.

To accurately assess the impact of turtle trade, herpetologists must play a crucial role in gathering specific field data on wild populations. Some species described from market specimens have never been observed in the wild, e.g., *Cuora mccordi*, *C. zhoui*, and *Ocadia glyphistoma*, and therefore little is known about their habitat and behavior. Similarly, there are many unknowns when describing the dynamics of turtle trade.

To convince governments and regulatory bodies that relatively "non-charismatic" animals such as chelonians deserve heightened protection demands scientific back-up. Therefore, to give trade observations and official import/export statistics the necessary context, baseline survey data are often necessary to make accurate assessments of the impact of trade on wild populations. At present, there are many gaps in official trade data due to non-species specific monitoring, while market observations — although indicative of species in trade — can never provide more than an estimate of actual volumes.

However, consistent observations of Asian box turtles, *Cuora* spp., in trade prompted a proposal (from Germany and the USA) to list the entire genus on Appendix II of CITES. This proposal was considered and adopted at the 11th Conference of the Parties to CITES, held in Nairobi, Kenya, in April 2000.

History of the Trade and Changes Over Time

Although freshwater turtles and tortoises have been targeted for human consumption for centuries (Zhao, 1995), it is only in the past 15 years or so that commercial trade in these species has risen at an alarming rate.

This development has its roots in the economic transformation of the region. Mainland Southeast Asian economies have grown (e.g., Thailand, Malaysia) or have been opened up after long periods of isolation (e.g., Vietnam, Laos, Cambodia) at the same time that the Chinese currency became convertible. The subsequent "open door" trade activities that engaged the world's largest consumer market have been phenomenal on many fronts.

Such is the pervasiveness of this "open door" approach that wildlife, including chelonians, is treated in the same way as any other commodity — sold to the highest bidder or towards the greatest market demand. In the case of tortoises and freshwater turtles, this demand has come from China (now including Hong Kong) and ethnic Chinese communities in other parts of Asia.

It is considered that China's native turtle species have already been hit hard by the trade. Michael Lau is often quoted on the increasing demand from southern Chinese provinces depleting China's own wild populations and leading to a 10-fold increase in imports from Southeast Asian countries since 1977.

Types of Demand

Demand for turtles can be summarized in five main categories: food (turtle meat and eggs) (Fig. 1), Traditional Chinese Medicine (TCM) (Figs. 2 and 3), sometimes referred to as Traditional East Asian Medicine (TEAM), pets and herpetoculture, decoration and the curio market (Fig. 4), and religious release (especially in southeast Asian temple ponds). Of all the sectors of the trade, greatest demand comes from the food markets and TCM, which generally exert the greatest pressure on wild turtle populations. An alarming fact is that overall trade is non-species specific, save for a few highly prized species such as *Cuora trifasciata* (Fig. 5). This indiscriminate trade has led to wholesale harvesting of wild species from South

Figure 1. Softshell turtles being exported from Sumatra, Indonesia, destined for East Asian food markets. Photo by Chris R. Shepherd/ TRAFFIC Southeast Asia.

and Southeast Asia, extending from India to as far east as New Guinea.

Though food and TCM are believed to exert the greatest pressure, it is worth giving some outline of how the pet trade contributes to overall turtle trade dynamics. In Europe and the USA in 1990–91, Southeast Asian species offered for sale were few: primarily *Manouria emys*, *Indotestudo elongata* (Fig. 6), *Heosemys spinosa*, and *Cuora trifasciata*. In November 1999 just a quick browse on the internet showed that the sale and advertisement of Asian turtle species (some claiming to be captive bred) in the West is now extensive, involving large numbers of species. As the economic purchasing power in Asia has increased, native North American species have also been observed in Asian markets, e.g., *Chelydra serpentina* and *Trachemys scripta elegans*, to supply the pet trade within Asia. These species, particularly red-eared sliders, *Trachemys scripta elegans*, have now become so prolific in Asia that introduced wild populations exist on some Indonesian islands, in Singapore, on Taiwan, and in some areas of mainland Southeast Asia.

Indian star tortoises, *Geochelone elegans,* are commercially popular in Kuala Lumpur, Bangkok, and Singapore. The pet trade affords dealers a perfect opportunity to "launder" shipments of turtles and tortoises — e.g., Indian star tortoises smuggled in thousands through the United Arab Emirates (UAE), from where they were re-exported as "captive-bred" specimens with UAE official CITES documentation (Behler, 1997).

Countries Involved and Trade Routes

All South and Southeast Asian countries — from India to Papua New Guinea — are involved in regional turtle trade in some way. This involvement varies between source

countries, consumer markets for domestic and non-native species, trans-shipment points between source and market countries, and simply exporters.

As an example, the countries of Cambodia, Laos, and Vietnam act as source areas and exporters. Vietnam also functions as a small-scale domestic market for farm-bred softshell turtles, and a corridor for chelonian species originating from Laos and Cambodia en route to southern China. The high demand from southern China acts as a magnet for any turtle collected in these three countries, so much so that hunters in remote parts of Cambodia, Vietnam, and Laos are well aware of the ultimate destination of their catches. In this equation, Vietnamese nationals act very much as middlemen traders.

Confiscations in India suggest that eastward trade routes to Bangladesh and Myanmar are connected with Chinese

Figure 2. Traditional Chinese Medicine turtle products sold in Hong Kong. Photo by Anders G.J. Rhodin.

Figure 3. Turtles, mainly *Mauremys mutica*, kept in stock at a turtle jelly restaurant in Hong Kong. Photo by Peter Paul van Dijk.

market demand, as well as direct transport by air to Singapore (F. Hanfee, *pers. comm.*). Reports from Bangladesh indicate there is export of native species and trans-shipment of others originating from neighboring countries to China, Singapore, and the Middle East. Large numbers of Myanmar turtles are believed to be mixed among general wildlife trade into the Chinese province of Yunnan via the town of Ruili (Kuchling, 1995; TRAFFIC, unpubl. data).

The trade out of Indonesia, particularly Sumatra, is known to be massive. The movement of tons of turtles by air directly from Medan in Sumatra into Guangzhou in southern China on a weekly basis (with any excess being transported by sea) is an indicator of how serious a business the turtle trade has become (Shepherd, this volume). Bulk exports of turtles, along with snakes and fish, from Phnom Penh are believed to go to the same

Table 1. Asian turtle species listed in the Appendices of the Convention on International Trade in Endangered Species of Fauna and Flora (CITES), following COP 10 (1997).

Peacock softshell turtle	*Aspideretes hurum*	CITES I
Indian softshell turtle	*Aspideretes gangeticus*	CITES I
Black softshell turtle	*Aspideretes nigricans*	CITES I
River terrapin	*Batagur baska*	CITES I
Indian roofed turtle	*Kachuga tecta*	CITES I
Tricarinate hill turtle	*Melanochelys tricarinata*	CITES I
Burmese eyed turtle	*Morenia ocellata*	CITES I
Spotted pond turtle	*Geoclemys hamiltonii*	CITES I
Indian flapshell turtle (downlisted 1995)	*Lissemys punctata*	CITES II
Painted terrapin	*Callagur borneoensis*	CITES II
Indian star tortoise	*Geochelone elegans*	CITES II
Burmese star tortoise	*Geochelone platynota*	CITES II
Elongated tortoise	*Indotestudo elongata*	CITES II
Sulawesi tortoise	*Indotestudo forstenii*	CITES II
Asian brown tortoise	*Manouria emys*	CITES II
Impressed tortoise	*Manouria impressa*	CITES II
Central Asian tortoise	*Testudo horsfieldii*	CITES II

destination. If the main centers in mainland Southeast Asia are operating in the same fashion — as an alternative to more arduous road routes — then there should be a greater emphasis to monitor and control this air traffic through existing International Air Transport Association (IATA) regulations and increased attention by customs.

Price Hierarchy Example

The exploitation of the Chinese three-striped box turtle, *Cuora trifasciata* (sometimes referred to as the "golden coin turtle") (Fig. 5) is perhaps the best example of the threat posed by attributed medicinal properties — in this case a cure for cancer.

Table 2. Net exports of CITES-listed freshwater turtles and tortoises from Southeast Asia (compiled from CITES WCMC data).

Taxon	Term	Cntry	1985	1986	1987	1988	1989	1990	1991	1992	1993	1994	1995	1996	1997	1998	Total
Batagur baska																	
	live	MY	10	0	0	0	0	5	0	0	0	0	0	0	10	0	25
Callagur borneoensis																	
	live	ID	0	0	0	0	0	0	0	0	0	0	0	0	2	0	2
Geochelone platynota																	
	live	MY	0	26	7	0	0	0	0	500	0	0	0	0	0	0	533
	live	SG	0	0	0	0	0	150	526	0	0	0	38	0	0	0	714
Indotestudo elongata																	
	live	ID	0	0	0	0	21	0	0	0	150	50	0	18	14	25	278
	live	MY	100	945	1402	1716	821	1521	287	928	3342	1244	469	552	700	60	14087
	shells	MY	0	0	3	0	0	0	0	0	0	0	0	0	0	0	3
	skins	MY	0	0	0	352	0	0	0	0	0	0	0	0	0	0	352
	live	SG	0	0	0	0	0	0	0	0	1	0	0	0	0	0	1
	bodies	TH	0	0	0	0	0	0	0	0	0	0	0	1	0	0	1
	live	TH	6	5	149	89	186	0	0	0	0	0	0	0	0	0	435
Indotestudo forstenii																	
	live	ID	40	120	400	500	550	384	135	23	727	232	4	1168	965	15	5263
Manouria emys																	
	live	ID	0	0	0	0	25	39	258	65	741	221	2	561	832	15	2759
	eggs	MY	0	0	4	0	0	0	0	0	0	0	0	0	0	0	4
	live	MY	32	283	785	864	553	965	100	37	127	227	853	170	163	0	5159
	shells	MY	0	0	2	0	0	0	0	0	0	0	0	0	0	0	2
	live	TH	2	9	84	33	63	0	0	0	0	0	0	0	0	0	191
Manouria impressa																	
	live	MY	0	109	148	312	272	706	0	0	122	70	1	82	51	0	1873
	live	TH	2	1	5	0	0	0	0	0	0	0	0	0	0	0	8

Figure 4. Decorated curio mask from Nepal made from *Indotestudo elongata* shell. Photo by Anders G.J. Rhodin.

Price quotes for this species in Laos have ranged from US\$ 300–700/kg and US\$ 250–375 per individual turtle (Tobias, 1997; B.L. Stuart, *in litt.*, 1999; W.G. Robichaud per B.L. Stuart *in litt.*, 1999 – cited in Timmins and Khounboline, 1999). Further on in the market chain, prices for one individual rise to as high as US\$ 1000 in Hong Kong (B. Chan, TRAFFIC East Asia, in prep.) and US\$ 2200 per pair on a US-based website.

In areas of its natural range such as Vietnam (and probably northeast Laos), *C. trifasciata* has become a rarity in observable trade and almost impossible to find in the wild.

Asian Markets

China and expatriate Chinese communities are believed to make up the bulk of the consumer markets for food and traditional medicine. Most turtles offered in Chinese markets are Southeast Asian species. Fewer South Asian turtles were observable and exclusively Chinese species made up only a small proportion of the turtles in the market in observations reported by Kadoorie Farm's South China survey team in recent years. High volume observations of non-native species in China included Southeast Asian box turtle *Cuora amboinensis*, Indian eyed turtle *Morenia petersi*, and Indian flapshell turtle *Lissemys punctata* (Fellowes and Hau Chi-hang, 1997). Many non-native species such as *Heosemys grandis, Orlitia borneensis, Siebenrockiella crassicollis, Batagur baska, Callagur borneoensis, Morenia ocellata,* and *Notochelys platynota* were all observed in markets in Guangdong, Guanxi, and Hainan, along with species ranging into southern China such as *Indotestudo elongata* and *Manouria impressa*. North American turtles *Trachemys scripta elegans* and *Chelydra serpentina* were also present from time to time (M. Lau, *pers. comm.*).

Other non-native species that have been observed in Chinese food markets include CITES Appendix I-listed *Aspideretes gangeticus, A. hurum, Geoclemys hamiltonii,* and *Kachuga tecta*; and CITES Appendix II-listed *Geochelone platynota* and *Manouria emys*.

Until now, these observations have been made in markets in southern China. However, recent newspaper reports have suggested that consumption of turtles as food may be gradually gaining popularity further north in China (M. Lau, *pers. comm.*)

CITES Species in Trade

Only a limited number of Asian chelonians are listed under CITES and are thus afforded some chance of legal protection from over-exploitation in international trade (Table 1). As a result, many other species simply do not appear in any international trade data. In many cases, any recorded (legal) chelonian exports are listed without details of species (e.g., from Thailand and Indonesia).

Available CITES data for the years 1985 to 1998 shows that the Southeast Asian region exported *Batagur baska, Callagur borneoensis, Geochelone platynota, Indotestudo elongata, I. forstenii, Manouria emys,* and *M. impressa* (Table 2).

Indonesia, Malaysia, Singapore, and Thailand are countries that regularly export and import CITES-listed species of freshwater turtles and tortoises. Vietnam and Myanmar report that they only export in small quantities and irregularly. However, observations and government confiscations indicate that in reality *Indotestudo* and *Manouria* tortoises are illegally exported from Vietnam in huge numbers.

Figure 5. Chinese three-striped box turtles (golden coin turtles), *Cuora trifasciata*, for sale in a Hong Kong market. Photo by Anders G.J. Rhodin.

Figure 6. The elongated tortoise, *Indotestudo elongata*, exported in large numbers according to CITES data. Photo by Peter Paul van Dijk.

The CITES species exported live in highest volumes from the region are *Indotestudo elongata* (Fig. 6), *Manouria emys,* and *I. forstenii.* Between 1985 to 1998, the live export totals reported by all range countries to the CITES Secretariat were:

Indotestudo elongata	14,801 individuals
Manouria emys	8,109 individuals
Indotestudo forstenii	5,263 individuals

In addition, Malaysia exported some shells, skins, and eggs of *I. elongata* and *M. emys,* but the numbers were fewer and such exports only occurred before 1989.

The majority of *Indotestudo elongata* in trade came from Malaysia, with a large increase in 1993 (3342 specimens) which has since dropped to less than 700 annually, and down to only 60 in 1998. Prior to 1990, the quantities exported were consistently around 1000 individuals annually. Most of the exported *I. elongata* went to Europe (Denmark, France, Great Britain, Germany, Netherlands), USA, and Japan, with the latter two countries among the highest importers.

Indotestudo forstenii was exported only from Indonesia and the export appears to have moved in cycles with three peaks: 1989 (550 specimens), 1993 (727 specimens), and 1996 (1168 specimens). The numbers exported appear to drop drastically after each peak before reaching a higher export quantity immediately afterwards (Table 2). Exported *I. forstenii* were destined for the same regions as *I. elongata.*

For *Manouria emys,* the export from Indonesia followed a similar trend to *I. forstenii,* with two peaks in 1993 (at 741 specimens) and 1997 (832 specimens), before sharp falls in exports occurred. The export from Malaysia was highest before 1990, peaking at just below 1000 specimens, but has been dropping to less than 200 per year except for 1995 (853 specimens). Thailand does not appear in CITES

trade data after 1990 due to cessation of exports for all CITES-listed turtle species. Europe, USA, and Japan were the main importing countries.

Summary and Discussion Points

Action at national levels clearly needs to be taken in order to achieve some regional impact on the trade. Information compiled from market observations and information gleaned from traders and hunters in the network needs to be analyzed alongside export and monitoring data to present the most reliable conclusions. Only then will any government be likely to consider action to halt this trade.

Monitoring of the trade and enforcement of existing laws are two key points that need to be improved. Listing of turtle and tortoise species on CITES appendices and national protection schedules is another element to an integrated response to this "turtle crisis."

Many Asian countries (of which all are members of CITES except Laos and Bhutan) have limitations relative to under-trained, under-paid border officials and field enforcement staff. When considered alongside the fact that CITES is not a law *per se*, rather it depends on cooperation between member states to make it work, it is unrealistic to expect any reduction in the trade in chelonians as a result of Vietnam (1994), Cambodia (1997), and Myanmar (1997) joining the convention. Neither is it realistic to expect the successful listing of the genus *Cuora* on CITES Appendix II at CoP 11 in April 2000 to suddenly curb trade in those species.

Scientific concern that CITES-listed and non-listed turtles are being systematically extirpated, with one species' commercial extinction following another, argues that conservation measures other than those afforded by CITES must be taken. The Convention must be used as a conservation tool in conjunction with many other protection measures put into place by governments. Coherent strategies designed by national level organizations and international conservation groups will also assist the process. These measures must address priorities to:

• Develop an integrated communications strategy to raise the profile of turtles and tortoises and the trade in these species;

• Raise awareness of the need to control trade under existing legislation among decision-makers at all levels and among the general public;

• Increase enforcement capacity and monitoring techniques;

• Strengthen national legislation to protect chelonian species;

• Develop expertise among the scientific community at national levels;

• Gather baseline data on wild populations;

• Improve habitat protection.

In addition to these short-term (1–3 years) measures, a concurrent long-term strategy to assess the supply/demand nexus should be initiated. This would involve working with source/producer countries to discover why people are collecting and exporting; while at the same time mounting an effort in consumer countries to analyze why consumption is so prolific and what it would take to change this consumptive behavior.

LITERATURE CITED

BEHLER, J.L. 1997. Troubled times for turtles. In: Proceedings: Conservation, Restoration and Management of Tortoises and Turtles - An International Conference. New York Turtle and Tortoise Society.

FELLOWES, J R., AND HAU CHI-HANG. 1997. A Faunal Survey of nine Forest Reserves in Tropical South China, with a Review of Conservation Priorities in the Region. Kadoorie Farm & Botanic Garden, Hong Kong, 167 pp.

KUCHLING, G. 1995. Turtles at a Market in Western Yunnan: Possible Range Extensions for some Southern Asiatic Chelonians in China and Myanmar. Chelonian Conservation and Biology 1(3):223-226.

TIMMINS, R.J. AND KHOUNBOLINE, K. 1999. Occurrence and trade of the golden turtle, *Cuora trifasciata*, in Laos. Chelonian Conservation and Biology 3(3):441-447.

TOBIAS, J. 1997. Environmental and Social Action Plan for the Nakai-Nam Theun Catchment and Corridor Areas - Report of the Wildlife Survey. Wildlife Conservation Society, Laos, Vientiane.

ZHAO, E. 1995. Chelonian Fauna and their Conservation in China. In: Proceedings - International Congress of Chelonian Conservation, Gonfaron, France, 6-10 July 1995 (B. Devaux, ed.). Editions SOPTOM, Gonfaron.

Asian Turtle Trade: Proceedings of a Workshop on Conservation and Trade of Freshwater Turtles and Tortoises in Asia
P.P. van Dijk, B.L. Stuart, and A.G.J. Rhodin, Eds.
Chelonian Research Monographs 2:30–38 • © 2000 by Chelonian Research Foundation

Conservation and Trade of Terrestrial and Freshwater Turtles and Tortoises in the People's Republic of China

Michael Lau[1] and Shi Haitao[2]

[1]*Kadoorie Farm and Botanic Garden, Lam Kam Road, Tai Po, New Territories, Hong Kong Special Administrative Region,*
People's Republic of China [Fax: 852-248-31877; E-mail: mwnlau@kfbg.org.hk];
[2]*Department of Biology, Hainan Normal University, Haikou 571158, People's Republic of China*
[Fax: 86-898-5883035; E-mail: sht@aneca.hainnu.edu.cn]

There has been a long history of using chelonians as food and medicine in China. Softshell turtles were used by the king to reward his army more than 2700 years ago (Zhou and Zhou, 1992). Softshell turtles are regarded as a delicacy and are widely eaten throughout China. In the past, hard-shelled turtles were consumed mainly because of their perceived medicinal or tonic value. However, the eating of hard-shelled turtles has become popular in southern China and there are restaurants in Guangdong that only serve dishes with turtle ingredients. Turtles are often for sale in the food markets in southern China. In big cities such as Guangzhou, Shenzhen, Nanning, and Haikou, numerous hard-shelled and softshell turtles are available in the markets.

During the Ming Dynasty, the medicinal properties of turtles were recorded in detail in the "Compendium of Materia Medica." Dried softshell turtle heads, turtle shells (both hard-shelled and softshell species), and even turtle blood can be used as medicine (Zhou and Zhou, 1992). *Cuora trifasciata* is reported to have additional properties in curing cancer and other hard-to-heal diseases (Zhou and Zhou, 1992). In a recent pharmaceutical study, two out of six plastrons examined were shown to contain selenium, an anti-cancer substance (Zhang and Zhang, 1998). The most commonly used turtle part in Traditional Chinese Medicine (TCM) is the bony shell; bags full of hard-shelled plastrons and softshell carapaces are for sale in TCM markets. Various TCM pills and other medications with turtle ingredients and canned turtle jelly have also been produced.

The keeping of turtles has a long history in mainland China but the commercial trade of turtles solely as pets has just started. Only a small number of *Trachemys scripta elegans*, and occasionally *Indotestudo elongata* and *Manouria impressa*, have been seen in the few pet shops in big cities such as Guangzhou, Nanning, and Haikou.

National Utilization

Although several of the non-marine chelonians in China are protected by national law and individual provinces protect additional species, collecting and trade of native turtles are still widespread. With the exception of *Cuora yunnanensis*, which may already be extinct, all Chinese turtle and tortoise species are exploited whenever they are found. Due to the high market value that live turtles have

commanded in recent years, they are rarely utilized by villagers for subsistence consumption. Rather the turtles are either sold directly to urban restaurants or to food markets in big cities through middlemen (Fig. 1). The most valued species is *Cuora trifasciata* which currently costs up to US$ 1000 per kg in Guangzhou markets. Young individuals of this species would be raised to adulthood before being sold in markets.

There are farms in mainland China producing captive-bred *Pelodiscus sinensis* for food but detailed information on these softshell turtle farms is lacking.

Turtles are not harvested for their shell alone. The dried carapaces and plastrons in the TCM trade are believed to be obtained from turtles also utilized in the food trade.

Legal International Trade

Before the economic reforms in China at the beginning of the 1980s, trade in turtles for food was dominated by Chinese species. Since the opening of borders with other Asian countries and when the Chinese currency became convertible, there has been an increasing influx of Asian turtles into China. The overall trade has probably increased because of the increasingly prosperous human population in southern China, the improved infrastructure and transport links with other Asian countries, and the northward spread of the habit of consuming wildlife. China is the major consumer of freshwater turtles and tortoises in the world and the majority of these are now imported from other Asian countries. However, due to the very large volume of trade and the multitude of trade routes (some direct while others are trans-shipped from other ports) involving different means of transport, control and monitoring of the international trade are far from adequate. In most cases, it is not certain where the turtles originated from nor what the national laws are that apply at the country of origin. Except CITES-listed species which are likely to have been imported illegally, it is difficult to differentiate legal international trade from illegal trade in other species. Statistics of the international trade are also lacking. However, up to 19 tons of turtles passed through three border ports between Guangxi province and Vietnam per day (Li and Li, 1997, 1998) and as much as several hundred tons of turtles were flown to Guangzhou from Indonesia in one day (O. Shiu and R. Kan, *pers. comm.*). A very small number of North American turtles (mainly

Trachemys scripta elegans and *Chelydra serpetina*) were also imported from time to time.

Most of the Asian turtles have been seen for sale in the food markets in south China. Non-CITES species believed to have been imported into China include: *Platysternon megacephalum, Cuora amboinensis, Cuora galbinifrons, Cuora trifasciata, Cyclemys* spp., *Geoemyda spengleri, Hardella thurjii, Heosemys grandis, Heosemys spinosa, Heosemys yuwonoi, Hieremys annandalii, Malayemys subtrijuga, Mauremys annamensis, Mauremys mutica, Morenia petersi, Notochelys platynota, Ocadia sinensis, Orlitia borneensis, Pyxidea mouhotii, Sacalia quadriocellata, Siebenrockiella crassicollis, Amyda cartilaginea, Nilssonia formosa, Palea steindachneri*, and *Pelodiscus sinensis*.

A small number of food turtles (including both Chinese and other Asian species) are also exported from China to Hong Kong for human consumption. Large quantities of plastron and carapace are also exported to Taiwan.

Certain rare or newly described, native Chinese species have been targeted for the international pet trade. These are purchased from food markets or local villagers by Hong Kong pet dealers or their staff. They are transported to Hong Kong and then shipped to other countries such as the USA, Germany, and Japan. Rare or restricted Asian species that turned up in Chinese food markets are also sought for. Species particularly targeted include: *Cuora aurocapitata, Cuora galbinifrons, Cuora mccordi, Cuora pani, Cuora zhoui, Heosemys yuwonoi, Mauremys iversoni, Mauremys pritchardi, Ocadia glyphistoma, Ocadia philippeni*, and *Sacalia pseudocellata*.

Illegal Trade

CITES-listed species that have been observed in south China food markets include: *Batagur baska, Callagur borneoensis, Geoclemys hamiltonii, Kachuga tecta, Morenia ocellata, Indotestudo elongata* (Fig. 1), *Manouria emys, Manouria impressa, Aspideretes gangeticus, Aspideretes hurum*, and *Lissemys punctata*. It is most likely that they were imported into China illegally.

Potential Trade Impacts

With the exception of *Pelodiscus sinensis* in which the vast majority of individuals traded were bred and raised in farms, virtually all Asian chelonians in trade are believed to be wild-caught. Due to the very high price of *Cuora trifasciata*, there are small-scale farms in China breeding and rearing this species. However, the level of production is not enough to meet the demand as indicated by the continual increase in the value of this species. Small numbers of other Chinese turtles have also been produced from the opportunistic breeding of animals in stock, but they occupy an insignificant proportion of the food market. The continual harvest of large numbers of slow-growth, low-fecundity chelonians

Figure 1. Turtle seller at Ching Ping market, Shenzhen, China, with several crates of chelonians, including elongated tortoises, *Indotestudo elongata*, a CITES-listed species probably illegally imported. Photo by ML.

from the wild is clearly unsustainable and must have a deleterious effect. Already Chinese species have declined drastically in the wild and many of them are now endangered (Zhao, 1998). For example, *Chinemys reevesii* used to be very common and widespread and was the principal species in trade. Now, it hardly ever turns up in the food markets. Similar impacts have or are expected to occur to other Asian turtles populations. For example, the recently described *Heosemys yuwonoi,* which is endemic to Sulawesi in Indonesia, has already become commercially extinct in Chinese markets after being observed in those markets in great numbers for a short while.

The trade routes to supply turtles have shifted to more distant countries. The food trade may find new source countries to supply the turtles once the existing stock in Asia is depleted. Already small numbers of North American species are for sale in southern China markets, probably testing the response or just waiting for these trade networks to become connected.

Although the trade in rare turtles only involves a limited number of species in relatively low numbers, trade impact on them is significant because the species concerned are rare and restricted. The very high price offered by the international pet market may provide enough incentive for some poor farmers to turn into full-time turtle collectors. Already species like *Cuora aurocapitata* and *Cuora mccordi* may have become commercially extinct in the wild.

Conservation and Management

Legal Status. — Several freshwater turtles and tortoises are listed in the People's Republic of China Wild Animals Protection Law: *Testudo horsfieldii* and *Pelochelys cantorii* (listed as *P. bibroni*) are state major protected wildlife grade I, while *Cuora trifasciata, Cuora yunnanensis, Geoemyda spengleri, Manouria impressa,* and *Palea steindachneri* are grade II protected. The Wild Animals Protection Law also covers important economic and scientific species, though the actual species are not listed. For terrestrial species, the State Forestry Administration is responsible for the administering and enforcing of this law, while the Fisheries Ministry is responsible for the aquatic species. The collecting of state major protected species is only allowed for scientific research, captive-breeding, exhibition, and other special reasons. Permission from the Forestry or Fisheries Bureau in the central government is needed for the collecting of grade I protected species. For grade II protected species, permission from the Forestry or Fisheries Department in the provincial government is required. The transport of state major protected species across county boundaries needs the permission from the provincial Forestry or Fisheries Department. The import and export of these state major protected species and CITES-listed species need the permission from the Forestry or Fisheries Bureau in the central government and a certificate issued by the Endangered Species of Wild Fauna and Flora Import and Export Administrative Office. The People's Republic of China became a Party to CITES in 1981. Non-native CITES Appendix I species are treated as state major protected wildlife grade I. Similarly, non-native CITES Appendix II species are treated as grade II protected.

In addition to the state-protected species, individual provinces may have a list of provincially protected turtles. The management of these species is formulated by the provincial legislature.

Species Management. — As far as is known, there is no management plan for freshwater turtles and tortoises anywhere in China. In addition to the protected measures offered by the Wild Animals Protection Law outlined above, hunting and collecting of turtles inside the more than 700 reserves are prohibited. However, enforcement is not adequate. Protected species are commonly seen for sale in the markets and illegal collecting of turtles inside reserves occurs regularly.

Habitat Conservation. — There are more than 700 reserves in the People's Republic of China, protecting more than 6% of the total national area (Mackinnon et al., 1996).

One of them is specifically for the protection of *Testudo horsfieldii* in Xinjiang province. The turtle habitats within these reserves are afforded protection according to law. However, illegal logging, liming of streams to collect aquatic animals, and/or conversion to cultivated land occurs in some of the reserves. Some major lowland turtle habitats such as large river and freshwater marshes are under-represented in the existing protected area system and are threatened by pollution and development. Also the habitats of some of the very restricted species like *Cuora aurocapitata* and *Cuora pani* lie outside the reserves and remain unprotected.

Control Measures. — The Forestry Department and Fisheries Department are responsible for enforcing the various conservation laws and regulations protecting tortoises and turtles. Inspections are carried out in markets, restaurants, and ports.

SPECIES ACCOUNTS

Platysternon megacephalum (Fig. 2)

Distribution: Widespread in central and southern China, including Yunnan, Guizhou, Anhui, Jiangsu, Zhejiang, Jiangxi, Hunan, Fujian, Guangdong, Hainan, and Guangxi provinces.

Habitat availability: This species normally lives in unpolluted hill streams and the surrounding riparian habitats. There are still many suitable streams left.

Population status: This species is considered to be "endangered" in China (Zhao, 1998). It is now rarely seen in the wild.

Population trends: Previously common in the food markets but now only low numbers of individuals turn up in the market, indicating that wild populations have declined drastically.

Threats: Main threat is over-collecting for the food trade. Deforestation, the construction of small hydro-electric plants, and the liming of streams within the range of this species cause habitat destruction and degradation.

Chinemys megalocephala

Distribution: Reported from Jiangsu, Anhui, Hubei, and possibly Guangxi provinces in central and southern China (Zhao, 1998). The validity of this species has been in debate (Iverson et al., 1989) but a recent karyotype study indicated that it is a valid species (Guo et al., 1997).

Habitat availability: This species lives in creeks and ponds in low hills. There are still suitable habitats left in China.

Population status: This species is rare and considered to be "endangered" in China (Zhao, 1998).

Population trends: Used to be regularly offered in the food markets but now is rarely found, indicating a decline in wild populations.

Threats: Main threat is over-collecting for the food trade. Urbanization, water pollution, and the increased use of fertilizer and pesticide cause habitat destruction and degradation.

Figure 2. The big-headed turtle, *Platysternon megacephalum*, a species that was previously common in the food markets of southern China, but now only low numbers of individuals turn up in the market, indicating that wild populations have declined drastically. Photo by Peter Paul van Dijk.

Chinemys nigricans

Distribution: Restricted to Guangdong and Guangxi provinces in southern China. There is also a record from Hainan based on market animals (Zhao, 1998).

Habitat availability: This species lives in unpolluted forest streams and suitable habitat is still available.

Population status: Has always been a rare species. Now considered to be "endangered" in China (Zhao, 1998).

Population trends: It has nearly completely disappeared in the food markets, indicating that wild populations have declined.

Threats: Main threat is over-collecting for the food trade. Deforestation, the construction of small hydro-electric plants, and the liming of streams within the range of this species cause habitat destruction and degradation.

Chinemys reevesii

Distribution: Widespread in China including Hebei, Shangdong, Henan, Shaanxi, Gansu, Sichuan, Yunnan, Guizhou, Hubei, Anhui, Jiangsu, Zhejiang, Jiangxi, Hunan, Fujian, Guangdong, and Guangxi provinces.

Habitat availability: This species lives in rivers, lakes, reservoirs, ponds, marshes, and paddy fields. There are still many suitable habitats left in China.

Population status: This species used to be the most common and widespread freshwater turtle in China. It is now considered to be "conservation dependent" in China (Zhao, 1998).

Population trends: Used to be the most common turtle in the Chinese food markets but has virtually disappeared, indicating that wild populations have declined drastically.

Threats: Main threat is over-collecting for the food trade. Urbanization, water pollution, and the increased use of fertilizers and pesticide cause habitat destruction and degradation.

Cuora amboinensis

Distribution: Reported from Guangdong and Guangxi provinces in southern China (Zhang et al., 1998). However, all the records are based on market animals or shells retained by people. So far this species has never been found in the wild in China despite the fact that it is a lowland species that can live in man-made water bodies in other countries. If it is native to China, chances are that it would have been recorded by earlier researchers.

Habitat availability: Reported to live in lowland marshes, ponds, rivers, and paddy fields (Ernst and Barbour, 1989). There are still numerous suitable habitats left in China.

Population status: Unknown. The few specimens recorded were from markets and probably originated from other countries.

Population trends: Not known.

Threats: Not certain as populations may not exist in China.

Cuora aurocapitata

Distribution: Restricted to Nanling, Yixian, Guangde, and Jingxian counties in Anhui province, central China.

Habitat availability: This species lives in unpolluted streams and ponds in the hills. Also ventures into the surrounding riparian habitats. There are still suitable habitats left.

Population status: This is a very rare and restricted turtle. It is considered to be "critically endangered" in China (Zhao, 1998).

Population trends: Used to be available in small numbers for the international pet trade. Now very few specimens, if at all, can be secured by pet dealers, indicating that the wild population has become depleted.

Threats: Main threat is exploitation for the pet and food trade.

Cuora flavomarginata

Distribution: Widespread in central and southern China, including Henan, Hubei, Anhui, Jiangsu, Zhejiang, Hunan, and Fujian provinces. Records from Guangdong and Guangxi provinces probably refer to animals brought in from the north for the food trade (Zhao, 1998).

Habitat availability: This species lives along forest edges and shrubland. Also reported to occur in moist areas near rivers and lakes. There are still numerous suitable habitats left in China.

Population status: This species is now considered to be "endangered" in China (Zhao, 1998).

Population trends: Populations are reported to be in decline (Chen, 1991; Zhao, 1998). Fewer animals turn up in the Chinese food markets, indicating that this species is in decline.

Threats: Main threat is over-collecting for the food trade. Deforestation and urbanization cause habitat destruction and degradation.

Cuora galbinifrons

Distribution: Restricted to Guangxi and Hainan provinces in southern China.

Habitat availability: This species lives in forest streams, ponds, and the surrounding moist terrestrial habitats. There are still suitable habitats left.

Population status: This species is now considered to be "endangered" in China (Zhao, 1998).

Population trends: This turtle is still being collected and trapped in Hainan (de Bruin and Artner, 1999), even within protected areas. The population is believed to be in decline.

Threats: Main threat is over-collecting for the food trade. Deforestation, construction of small hydro-electric plants, and the liming of streams cause habitat destruction and degradation.

Cuora mccordi

Distribution: This species is believed to be restricted to the Bose area in Guangxi province, south China. All the known specimens are either bought from the food markets or supplied by pet dealers, hence the exact area of occurrence is not certain.

Habitat availability: Exact habitat of this species is not known. It probably lives in forest and hill streams in remote hilly areas and hence was not discovered until recently.

Population status: Not certain. Since its discovery, only a small number of individuals have been available in the market despite the very high price commanded by this species. In the last few years, very few specimens could be obtained by animal dealers, indicating a very small extant population. This species is classified as "data deficient" in China (Zhao, 1998).

Population trends: Not certain. The number of individuals available in the international pet market has decreased to a handful (O. Shiu and R. Kan, *pers. comm.*), suggesting that the population is in decline.

Threats: Main threat is over-collecting for the pet and food trade. The habitats of this species may also be affected by deforestation, construction of small hydro-electric plants, and the liming of streams.

Cuora pani

Distribution: The type specimens were collected from Pingli county, Shaanxi province in central China. Some other specimens were also purchased from Yunnan but the exact locality is not known.

Habitat availability: Specimens were obtained in irrigation ditches alongside rice paddies at 420 m elevation. There should not be any shortage of suitable habitats within the range of this species.

Population status: Not certain. Since its discovery, only a small number of individuals have been collected from the wild or seen in the market, indicating a small population size. This species is considered to be "critically endangered" in China (Zhao, 1998).

Population trends: Not certain.

Threats: Main threat is over-collecting for the pet and food trade. The habitat of this turtle may also suffer from urbanization, water pollution, and the increased use of fertilizers and pesticides.

Cuora trifasciata

Distribution: Widely distributed in Guangdong, Hainan, Guangxi, and Fujian provinces in southern China.

Habitat availability: This species lives in hill streams and the surrounding forests or shrubland. There are still numerous suitable habitats left in China.

Population status: This species is classified as "critically endangered" in China (Zhao, 1998). Recent field surveys conducted in suitable habitats in Guangdong, Guangxi, and Hainan provinces failed to find any specimens in the wild. Only a few specimens were found offered for sale in Hainan in 1997 (de Bruin and Artner, 1999).

Population trends: The number of individuals exported from mainland China has decreased sharply (Zhao, 1998) in recent years, suggesting that the population is in decline. Also, according to local villagers in south China, it is now very difficult to collect any individuals in the wild.

Threats: Main threat is over-collecting for the food, traditional medicine, and pet trade. Deforestation, construction of small hydro-electric plants, and the liming of streams cause habitat destruction and degradation.

Cuora yunnanensis

Distribution: Only known from the the two localities of Dongchuan and Kunming, Yunnan Province, in southwest China.

Habitat availability: Specimens were obtained at high altitudes (from 2000 to 2260 m). The exact habitat of this turtle is not known. However, habitat of this species has probably been destroyed in Kunming, which has become a big city. Suitable habitats may still exist at Dongchuan.

Population status: A very rare species that is only known from eight specimens collected in 1906. It is considered to be "probably extinct in the wild" in China (Zhao, 1998).

Population trends: Not certain. Probably extinct.

Threats: Not certain. Habitat destruction and habitat degradation in the Kunming area was probably a serious threat.

Cuora zhoui

Distribution: Exact distribution not known but the type specimens were obtained from markets in Nanning and Pingxiang, Guangxi Province. Additional specimens were reported to be bought from markets in Wuding and Yuanmou in Yunnan Province.

Habitat availability: Exact habitat of this species is not known. It probably lives in forest and hill streams in remote hilly areas and hence was not discovered until recently.

Population status: Not certain. This species is classified as "data deficient" in China (Zhao, 1998). Since its discovery, only a small number of individuals have been available in the market despite the high price commanded, indicating a small extant population.

Population trends: Not certain.

Threats: Main threat is over-collecting for the pet and food trade. The habitats of this species may also be affected by deforestation, construction of small hydro-electric plants, and the liming of streams.

Cyclemys dentata

Distribution: Reported from Yunnan and possibly Guangxi provinces in south China (Zhao, 1998). However, all records are from market animals. So far this species has never been confirmed in the wild in China.

Habitat availability: Reported to live in streams and surrounding terrestrial habitats (Zhang et al., 1998). There are still suitable habitats left in China.

Population status: Is considered "endangered" in China (Zhao, 1998). The few specimens recorded were from markets and might have originated from other countries.

Population trends: Not known.

Threats: Not certain as populations may not exist in China.

Geoemyda spengleri

Distribution: Distributed in Guangdong, Guangxi, Hainan, and Hunan provinces in south and central China.

Habitat availability: This species usually inhabits moist, close-canopy forests. Also occurs in small streams and even pineapple fields. There are still suitable habitats left in China.

Population status: This species is now considered to be "endangered" in China (Zhao, 1998). It is now rarely seen in the wild except in very remote places.

Population trends: According to Zhao (1998), a certain number of individuals were available in Guangxi markets in

the 1950s but virtually disappeared in later years. When China opened its border in the 1980s, many live turtles of this species were imported from Vietnam to supply the market (Zhao, 1998). The population in China is believed to be in drastic decline.

Threats: Main threat is over-collecting for the food and pet trade. Deforestation also threatens this species.

Mauremys iversoni

Distribution: Restricted to Nanping and Jianyang in Fujian Province, and Guiyang in Guizhou Province. Specimens have also been purchased from local people near Nanning, Guangxi Province (Zhao and Adler, 1993).

Habitat availability: This species lives in slow-moving sections and backwaters of hill streams at elevations of about 500 m. There are still suitable habitats left in China.

Population status: This species is considered to be "data deficient" in China (Zhao, 1998). Only a few specimens of this turtle have been recorded since it was discovered, indicating that the wild population is small.

Population trends: Not certain.

Threats: Main threat is over-collecting for the pet and food trade. Deforestation, construction of small hydro-electric plants, and the liming of streams may pose further threats to this species.

Mauremys mutica

Distribution: Widespread in central and southern China, including Yunnan, Hubei, Anhui, Jiangsu, Zhejiang, Jiangxi, Hunan, Fujian, Guangdong, Guangxi, and Hainan provinces.

Habitat availability: This species lives in water bodies in basins and river valleys. There are still many suitable habitats left in China.

Population status: It is now considered to be "endangered" in China (Zhao, 1998).

Population trends: This species used to be one of the commonest turtles for sale in the Chinese food markets but has become uncommon in recent years, indicating that wild populations have declined substantially.

Threats: Main threat is over-collecting for the food trade. Urbanization, water pollution, and the increased use of fertilizers and pesticides cause habitat destruction and degradation.

Mauremys pritchardi

Distribution: Only recently discovered and in China is reported from Chin-hung in Yunnan Province. Specimens were not collected in the wild and the exact distribution is not known (McCord, 1997).

Habitat availability: Exact habitat not known.

Population status: Only a few specimens of this turtle have been recorded since it was discovered, indicating that the wild population is small.

Population trends: Not certain.

Threats: Main threat is over-collecting for the pet and food trade.

Ocadia glyphistoma

Distribution: This species is only known from the types that were purchased in southwest Guangxi near the Vietnam border. However, the specimens were reported to have originated from Vietnam (McCord and Iverson, 1994). The possibility of these turtles being hybrids produced in turtle farms cannot be ruled out.

Habitat availability: Exact habitat is not known.

Population status: This species is considered to be "data deficient" in China (Zhao, 1998). The few specimens recorded were from food markets and they may actually originate from outside China or may be hybrids produced in turtle farms.

Population trends: Not known.

Threats: Main threat is over-collecting for the pet and food trade.

Ocadia philippeni

Distribution: The type specimens were purchased near Dongfang County, west Hainan, in south China (McCord and Iverson, 1992). In 1999, another specimen was bought from the Haikou city market in north Hainan. The possibility of these turtles being hybrids produced in turtle farms cannot be ruled out.

Habitat availability: Exact habitat is not known.

Population status: This species is considered to be "data deficient" in China (Zhao, 1998). The few specimens recorded were from food markets and they may actually be hybrids produced in turtle farms. Specimens could not be located in 1997 in the wild near the type locality in Hainan despite intensive searching (de Bruin and Artner, 1999).

Population trends: Not known.

Threats: Main threat is over-collecting for the pet and food trade.

Ocadia sinensis

Distribution: Distributed in Jiangsu, Zhejiang, Fujian, Guangdong, Guangxi, and Hainan provinces in southeastern China.

Habitat availability: This species lives in low-altitude water bodies such as rivers, canals, and ponds. There are still suitable habitats left in China.

Population status: This species is considered to be "endangered" in China (Zhao, 1998).

Population trends: Its abundance has sharply decreased in the wild (Zhao, 1998). Hainan still has a considerable population of this turtle but trapping and collecting is widespread. The number of animals appearing in the food markets has also decreased.

Threats: Main threat is over-collecting for the food trade. Urbanization, water pollution, and the increased use of fertilizers and pesticides pose further threats to this species.

Pyxidea mouhotii

Distribution: Distributed in Yunnan, Hunan, Guangdong, Guangxi, and Hainan provinces in south and central China.

Habitat availability: This species lives in hill forests. There are still suitable habitats left in China.

Population status: This species is considered to be "endangered" in China and is rarely seen in the wild (Zhao, 1998).

Population trends: Populations have probably declined drastically. Villagers in Hainan reported that this species used to be very common but is now difficult to obtain. Although this species can still be found in Hainan, trapping and collecting is widespread on the island (de Bruin and Artner, 1999).

Threats: Main threat is over-collecting for the food trade. Deforestation poses a further threat to this species.

Sacalia bealei

Distribution: Reported from Guizhou, Anhui, Jiangxi, Fujian, Guangdong, Hainan, and Guangxi provinces in central and south China. However, in the past this species and *Sacalia quadriocellata* were often considered to be conspecific and some of the records might refer to *S. quadriocellata* instead. For instance, this species has been reported from Hainan but recent field surveys and market surveys only found *S. quadriocellata* and not *S. bealei* (de Bruin and Artner, 1999).

Habitat availability: This species lives in hill streams and irrigation ditches; the animals also forage in paddy fields and ponds in the summer. There are still suitable habitats left in China.

Population status: This species is considered to be "endangered" in China (Zhao, 1998).

Population trends: Populations have declined (Zhao, 1998). This species was regularly seen in the market in the past but now is very rarely found, indicating a drastic population decline in the wild.

Threats: Main threat is over-collecting for the food trade. Deforestation, construction of small hydro-electric plants, water pollution, and liming of streams pose further threats to this species.

Sacalia pseudocellata

Distribution: This species is only known from several specimens purchased from villagers in Dongfang County, west Hainan, in south China. The possibility of these turtles being hybrids produced from turtle farms cannot be ruled out.

Habitat availability: Exact habitat is not known.

Population status: This species is considered to be "data deficient" in China (Zhao, 1998). The few specimens recorded were from food markets and they may actually be hybrids produced from turtle farms. No specimens were found on a field survey in Hainan in 1997 (de Bruin and Artner, 1999).

Population trends: Not known.

Threats: Main threat is over-collecting for the pet and food trade.

Sacalia quadriocellata

Distribution: Reported from Jiangxi, Fujian, Guangdong, Hainan, and Guangxi provinces in central and south China.

However, in the past this species and *Sacalia bealei* were often considered to be conspecific and some of the records might refer to *S. bealei* instead. This species has been observed in the wild in Guangdong, Hainan, and Guangxi provinces.

Habitat availability: This species lives in hill streams and there is suitable habitat available in China.

Population status: Zhao (1998) considered this species to be rare and "endangered" in China. However, a fairly healthy population still exists on Hainan but is subject to trapping and collecting (de Bruin and Artner, 1999).

Population trends: According to Zhao (1998), populations have declined.

Threats: Main threats are over-collecting for the food trade and habitat destruction or degradation as a result of deforestation, construction of small hydro-electric plants, water pollution, and liming of streams.

Indotestudo elongata

Distribution: Reported from Yunnan and Guangxi provinces in south China. Records from Yunnan are based on market animals that may have originated from neighboring countries such as Myanmar.

Habitat availability: This species lives in hilly areas and suitable habitat is still available.

Population status: This species is considered to be "endangered" in China (Zhao, 1998).

Population trends: The species is believed to have declined drastically due to its limited range and over-exploitation.

Threats: Main threat is over-collecting for the food trade. Deforestation poses another threat.

Manouria impressa

Distribution: Reported from Yunnan, Hunan, Guangxi, and Hainan provinces in south China (Zhao and Adler, 1993). The Hunan record is based on one specimen found in Shaoyang city (Zhao, 1998) and probably was a market animal. Similarly, this species has never been recorded in the wild in either Guangxi or Hainan, and the market records should be treated with caution due to the extensive cross-border turtle trade.

Habitat availability: This species lives in hill forests and suitable habitat is still available.

Population status: This species is considered to be "endangered" and rare in China (Zhao, 1998).

Population trends: The species is believed to have declined drastically due to its limited range and over-exploitation.

Threats: Main threats are over-collecting for the food trade and deforestation.

Testudo horsfieldii

Distribution: Restricted to the western part of Xinjiang province in northwest China.

Habitat availability: This species lives in semi-desert meadows between 700 and 1000 m elevation, and also occurs in surrounding dry fields. There is still suitable habitat in China.

Population status: This species is considered to be "critically endangered" with about 1000 individuals left in the wild in Xinjiang (Zhao, 1998). The 350 km² Huo Cheng nature reserve was created in 1983 specifically for the protection of this species and its habitat, but the area is heavily cultivated (McKinnon et al., 1996).

Population trends: The Chinese population has declined drastically. In the early 1960s, density could reach more than 4000 animals per km². However, in the early 1990s, density decreased to 6 animals per km². The range of this species also dropped from 500 km² in the early 1960s to 180 km² in the early 1990s (SH, *pers. obs.*)

Threats: Main threats are over-collecting for the food trade and habitat degradation due to the conversion of meadow into dry fields.

Palea steindachneri

Distribution: Distributed in Yunnan, Guizhou, Guangdong, Hainan, and Guangxi provinces in central and south China.

Habitat availability: This species lives in large hill streams, creeks, and small rivers. There are still suitable habitats left in China.

Population status: This species is considered to be "endangered" in China (Zhao, 1998).

Population trends: According to Zhao (1998), populations have declined as indicated by the continual reduction in the number of animals harvested each year.

Threats: Main threat is over-collecting for the food trade. Habitat destruction or degradation as a result of construction of small hydro-electric plants, water pollution, and liming of streams also pose threats to this species.

Pelochelys cantorii

Distribution: Distributed in Yunnan, Jiangsu, Zhejiang, Fujian, Guangdong, Hainan, and Guangxi provinces in central and south China. Historically also occurred in Anhui (Chen, 1991). In the past, the name *Pelochelys bibroni* was used for the Chinese populations, but that name is now restricted to southern New Guinea populations.

Habitat availability: This species normally lives in rivers and lakes, and is also found in reservoirs. There are still suitable habitats left in China.

Population status: This species is considered to be "extinct in the wild" in China (Zhao, 1998).

Population trends: According to Zhao (1998), both the population and range of this species in China have become significantly reduced. The Zhejiang population is close to extinction (Huang et al., 1990).

Threats: Main threats are over-collecting for the food trade and habitat destruction or degradation as a result of urbanization, water pollution, and over-fishing.

Pelodiscus sinensis

Distribution: Widespread in China and has been reported from nearly all provinces except Xinjiang, Qinghai, Xizang (Tibet), and Ningxia.

Habitat availability: This species lives in rivers, creeks, lakes, reservoirs, ponds, and the surrounding ditches and paddy fields. There are still numerous habitats left in China.

Population status: This species is considered to be "vulnerable" in China (Zhao, 1998).

Population trends: Populations have declined rapidly (Chen, 1991; Zhao, 1998).

Threats: Main threat is over-collecting for the food trade. Habitat destruction or degradation as a result of urbanization, water pollution, and the increased use of fertilizers and pesticides also threaten this species. There are numerous farms in China raising this species for commercial exploitation, but detailed information on these softshell turtle farms is lacking.

Rafetus swinhoei

Distribution: Reported from the lower reaches of Chang Jiang and Tai Hu drainage systems in Shanghai and Jiangsu provinces, central China and possibly Yunnan Province in southwest China (Zhao, 1998).

Habitat availability: This species lives in big rivers and lakes. There are still suitable habitats left in China.

Population status: Only known from a small number of specimens. A few specimens are in captivity in zoos and temples. This species is considered to be either "critically endangered" or "extinct in the wild" in China (Zhao, 1998).

Population trends: Not known.

Threats: Not certain. Over-collecting and habitat destruction or degradation probably have been serious impacts.

LITERATURE CITED

CHEN, B. 1991. The Amphibian and Reptilian Fauna of Anhui. Hefei: Anhui Publishing House of Science and Technology.

DE BRUIN, R.W.F. AND ARTNER, H.G. 1999. On the turtles of Hainan Island, southern China. Chelonian Conservation and Biology 3(3):479-486.

ERNST, C.H. AND BARBOUR, R.W. 1989. Turtles of the World. Smithsonian Institution Press, Washington D.C.

GUO, C.-W., NIE, L.-W., AND WANG, M. (1997). The karyotypes and NORs of two species of *Chinemys*. Sichuan Journal of Zoology 15 (Suppl.):97-104.

HUANG, M., CAI, C., JIN, Y., GU, H., ZHANG, S., GUO, H., AND WEI, J. 1990. Fauna of Zhejiang, Amphibia Reptilia. Hangzhou: Zhejiang Science and Technology Publishing House.

IVERSON, J.B., ERNST, C.H., GOTTE, S.W., AND LOVICH, J.E. 1989. The validity of *Chinemys megalocephala* (Testudines: Batagurinae). Copeia 1989(2):494-498.

LI, Y. AND LI, D. 1997. The investigation on wildlife trade across Guangxi borders between China and Vietnam. Conserving China's Biodiversity – Reports of the Biodiversity Working group, China Council for International Cooperation on Environment and Development, pp. 118-127.

LI, Y. AND LI, D. 1998. The dynamics of trade in live wildlife across the Guangxi border between China and Vietnam during 1993-1996 and its control strategies. Biodiversity Conservation 7:895-914.

MACKINNON, J., MENG, S., CHEUNG, C., CAREY, G., ZHU, X., AND MELVILLE, D. 1996. A Biodiversity Review of China. Hong Kong: World Wide Fund for Nature International, WWF China Programme.

MCCORD, W.P. 1997. *Mauremys pritchardi*, a new batagurid turtle from Myanmar and Yunnan, China. Chelonian Conservation and Biology 2(4):555-562.

MCCORD, W.P. AND IVERSON, J.B. 1992. A new species of *Ocadia* (Testudines: Bataguridae) from Hainan Island. Proceedings of the Biological Society of Washington 105(1):13-18.

MCCORD, W.P. AND IVERSON, J.B. 1994. A new species of *Ocadia* (Testudines: Bataguridae) from southwestern China. Proceedings of the Biological Society of Washington 107(1):52-59.

ZHANG, H. AND ZHANG, C. 1998. Turtle plastron extract's nutritional value and its effect on dividing cancer cells. Hong Kong Pharmaceutical Journal 7:104-107.

ZHANG, M., ZONG, Y., AND MA, J. 1998. Fauna Sinica, Reptilia Vol. 1. Beijing: Science Press.

ZHAO, E. 1998. China Red Data Book of Endangered Animals: Amphibia and Reptilia. Beijing: Science Press.

ZHAO, E. AND ADLER, K. 1993. Herpetology of China. Soc. Study Amphib. Reptiles, Contr. Herpetol. No. 10, 522 pp.

ZHOU, J. AND ZHOU, T. 1992. Chinese Chelonians Illustrated. Nanjing: Jiangsu Science and Technology Publishing House.

Asian Turtle Trade: Proceedings of a Workshop on Conservation and Trade of Freshwater Turtles and Tortoises in Asia
P.P. van Dijk, B.L. Stuart, and A.G.J. Rhodin, Eds.
Chelonian Research Monographs 2:39–44 • © 2000 by Chelonian Research Foundation

Trade and Conservation of Turtles and Tortoises in the Hong Kong Special Administrative Region, People's Republic of China

MICHAEL LAU[1], BOSCO CHAN[2], PAUL CROW[1], AND GARY ADES[1]

[1]*Kadoorie Farm & Botanic Garden, Lam Kam Road, Tai Po, New Territories, Hong Kong*
[Fax: 852-248-31877; E-mail: mwlau@kfbg.org.hk];
[2]*TRAFFIC East Asia, Room 2001, Double Building, 22 Stanley Street, Central, Hong Kong*

Hong Kong Special Administrative Region, People's Republic of China, is situated 320 km south of the Tropic of Cancer on the coast of Guangdong Province. The total land area is 1095 sq. km. It includes Kowloon and the New Territories on the Chinese mainland and more than 100 islands, the largest of which are Lantau and Hong Kong. The topography is very rugged and the highest peak is Tai Mo Shan (957 m) in the central New Territories. The climate is under monsoonal influence and is strongly seasonal with cool dry winters and hot wet summers. The annual rainfall averages 2124 mm.

Hong Kong was formerly a self-administered British Dependent Territory but reverted to the People's Republic of China in 1997. There are over six million people with 95% of the population living and working on less than 20% of the land. There has been a long history of human influence and the original broad-leaved forests were almost completely cut down by the seventeenth century (Dudgeon and Corlett, 1994). Forests were re-established through reforestation and regeneration. The freshwater habitats are also diverse and Hong Kong supports at least five species of southern Chinese turtles. Due to the extensive protected areas system, the protection afforded by law to local turtles, and the economically well-off human population, there are still healthy populations of turtles in the wild.

Turtles have long been utilized by the Chinese for food, medicine, and as pets. In addition to being a consumer, Hong Kong also functions as an important transit center for turtles due to its good port and airport facilities, free trade practice, and convertible currency. Although the trade in CITES-listed species is regulated and controlled, the majority of Asian turtles are not listed and their trade is legal.

Legal Status

All wild chelonians are legally protected in Hong Kong by the Wild Animals Protection Ordinance which prevents the collection, removal, destruction, disturbance, and possession of any wild turtle or possession of any hunting or trapping equipment. The Agriculture, Fisheries and Conservation Department (AFCD) of the Hong Kong Special Administrative Region Government, being the Management Authority of CITES in Hong Kong, is also responsible for administering and enforcing the Animals and Plants (Protection of Endangered Species) Ordinance which gives effect to CITES. Import, export, trade, and possession of

listed species, whether native or exotic, is only allowed with permission from the AFCD. The maximum penalty for breaking this ordinance is HK$ 5,000,000 (ca. US$ 62,500) and two years imprisonment. In addition, all animals including turtles are protected within the Country Parks in accordance with the Country Parks Ordinance.

Utilization and Trade

Use of chelonians as medicine, food, and pets has a long history in China. In Hong Kong, turtle consumption is largely restricted to turtle jelly and turtle soup; the latter is only consumed during winter when wildlife meat is supposed to warm the consumer's blood. Turtle jelly (Fig. 1) has become very popular locally in recent years, and chain stores specializing in turtle jelly can be found around Hong Kong. The dark brown turtle jelly is traditionally prepared with various medicinal herbs and the plastron of *Cuora trifasciata* — although *Mauremys mutica* and *Notochelys platynota* seem to be the species commonly used now, due to their availability and large size, respectively. This jelly is widely believed to have cancer-healing properties as well as serving to detoxify the body. Food dishes with turtle ingredients are often prepared with *Pelodiscus sinensis*, which is bred in captivity in large numbers and farm-raised in Thailand and China (Fig. 2). However, about half a dozen Asian hard-shelled turtle species are readily available in local markets for home preparation of turtle soup. The cooking of turtle soup appears to be common judging from the availability of live turtles in almost all food markets. Chelonian eggs are not commonly eaten, although eggs of *Cyclemys dentata* and *N. platynota* have been seen for sale on rare occasions. These eggs were laid by gravid females in stock in food stores and are generally eaten as a novelty. Freshwater turtles, particularly *Chinemys reevesii*, *C. trifasciata*, and numerous overseas species are commonly kept as pets, mainly for their reputation as undemanding pets but also for *feng shui* reasons because turtles are long-lived. *Cuora trifasciata* is often kept because the Chinese name for this species is golden coin turtle and is thus believed by some people to bring good fortune.

National Utilization

Hong Kong has five species of native non-marine turtles. Although local laws afford protection to all chelonians, illegal collecting and trade still occur regularly. *Cuora trifasciata* and *P. sinensis* are in general the targeted species; the former is sold to food and pet stores because of its high price and the latter is collected for food.

Legal International Trade

The trade in turtles in Hong Kong is big business. In 1997, based on official statistics, the trade in live chelonians into Hong Kong was worth over HK$ 3 billion (US$ 38.7 million). The vast majority of the turtles in trade were imported from other countries. In 1998 alone, over 13.5 million kg of live chelonians were imported into Hong Kong. Comparison with the 1992 trade statistics revealed that the trade in live turtles has increased about 28-fold during these 7 years. Exports from Thailand to Hong Kong have increased 74-fold since 1979. Using a conservative conversion based on the estimated average weight of the commonly-seen food turtles (ca. 1.5 kg per adult), over 9 million live chelonians were imported into Hong Kong in 1998 alone. It is likely that the majority of these animals were re-exported to China for food. In 1998, the vast majority of imports into Hong Kong (> 99%) were live turtles destined for the food trade. Since 1992, imports of live turtles into Hong Kong originated from Bangladesh, China, India, Indonesia, Japan, Malaysia, Pakistan, Singapore, Taiwan, Thailand, USA, and Vietnam. The greatest volume of imports into Hong Kong originated from Indonesia and Thailand, respectively. Together these two countries accounted for 81.5% (about 11 million kg, or over 7 million live turtles) of total imports into Hong Kong. The USA regularly exports live chelonians to Hong Kong but in much

Table 1. The ten most heavily traded chelonian species, in descending order, in trade in Hong Kong during the period May 1998 to May 1999 (excluding farmed *Pelodiscus sinensis* and *Trachemys scripta elegans*).

Species	Type of Trade
Mauremys mutica	Food / Pets
Cuora amboinensis	Food / Pets
Chinemys reevesii	Pets
Cuora flavomarginata	Food / Pets
Cuora galbinifrons	Food / Pets
Chelydra serpentina	Pets
Cuora trifasciata	Food / Pets
Ocadia sinensis	Pets
Graptemys pseudogeographica	Pets
Notochelys platynota	Food

smaller volumes — the highest annual export from USA to Hong Kong was in 1994 with 29,533 kg of live turtles (many of which were hatchlings of *Trachemys scripta elegans*).

In 1998, imports of chelonians into Hong Kong peaked in August, possibly due to the large number of readily available captive-bred species as well as wild-caught adults during the warmer months of the year. This seasonal trend is similar to that found in a previous survey conducted in southern China, including Hong Kong (Lau et al., 1996), in which a similar peak was observed for the importation of live turtles from Indonesia in 1993–94.

A year-long survey conducted by TRAFFIC East Asia in 1998–99 (Chan, in press) recorded a total of 84 species of chelonians, both for food and pets, from twelve representative market sites in Hong Kong. Excluding *Pelodiscus sinensis* and *Trachemys scripta elegans*, which are produced in large quantity from farms, the ten most heavily traded species, in descending order, are listed in Table 1.

Eight of the top ten most heavily-traded species in 1998–99 were of Asian origin. Of the 84 species encountered, 30 were Asian species and the remaining 54 species, destined mainly for the pet trade, originated mainly from the USA. Chinese species were still readily available with 18 species seen during the survey — although some species also occur in Southeast Asia and thus individuals encountered in the markets may have originated from China or Southeast Asia. This represents over half of the 31 species of non-marine chelonian fauna in China.

Thirteen species were recorded as being used both as food and as pets. These were *Chelydra serpentina*, *Chinemys reevesii*, *Cuora amboinensis*, *Cuora flavomarginata*, *Cuora galbinifrons*, *Cuora trifasciata*, *Cyclemys dentata*, *Heosemys grandis*, *Mauremys annamensis*, *Mauremys mutica*, *Platysternon megacephalum*, *Pyxidea mouhotii*, and *Siebenrockiella crassicollis*. Of these species, *M. annamensis*, *C. serpentina*, *C. reevesii*, and *H. grandis* were only recorded in the food trade once, *M. annamensis* and *C. reevesii* were misidentified and mixed together with the superficially similar *M. mutica*. Eight Asian species were consistently present in the food trade: *C.

Figure 1. Herbal tortoise jelly sold in Hong Kong for use as Traditional Chinese Medicine. Photo by Anders G.J. Rhodin.

Figure 2. Small softshell turtles, *Pelodiscus sinensis*, for sale in Hong Kong market. Photo by Anders G.J. Rhodin.

amboinensis, C. flavomarginata, C. galbinifrons, C. trifasciata, M. mutica, N. platynota, P. megacephalum, and *P. mouhotii.* Of these species, *C. trifasciata* is by far the most expensive species in trade; a large adult usually sells at retail for about HK$ 8000 or over US$ 1000 in the food market.

A survey conducted in 1993–94 in Hong Kong, Macau, and southern China recorded only 58 chelonian species in trade (Lau et al., 1996), while 84 species of traded chelonians were encountered during the TRAFFIC survey five years later (Chan, in press). The percentage of species increase was 31%. However, some of the CITES-listed and highly endangered species, such as *Geoclemys hamiltoni,* recorded during the 1994 survey were not seen in the more recent survey. Reasons for this may be three-fold: 1) better law enforcement both locally and internationally, 2) direct trading routes from the country of origin to the main consumer area (south China), and 3) indication of population crashes for these species.

Illegal Trade

One species (*Kachuga tecta*) listed on Appendix I of CITES and 15 CITES II species were recorded during the recent market survey (Chan, in press). Although trade in CITES-listed chelonians is regulated by Hong Kong's CITES-implementing legislation, certain CITES-listed specimens were evidently imported illegally and lacked the required possession licenses. Such cases were reported to AFCD for follow-up actions.

Potential Trade Impacts

With the exception of *Pelodiscus sinensis* and juveniles of *Chinemys reevesii, Cuora flavomarginata, Mauremys mutica, Ocadia sinensis,* and the North American species,

all chelonians in trade in Hong Kong are believed to be wild caught. Hatchling and juvenile turtles enter the pet trade while adults supply the food market. The food species composition has changed markedly over the last two decades; the Chinese native *C. reevesii,* one of the most numerous species in food markets up until 1994, is at present totally absent from the food trade. The same is also true for the southeast Asian *Malayemys subtrijuga,* which has completely disappeared from the food trade within the last 5 years. This trend may indicate a drastic decline in wild populations for these two species. Rare or restricted species (e.g., *Cuora pani* and *Geoemyda japonica*) are targeted by the pet trade and any level of commercial exploitation may be detrimental to their survival. For many widespread and presumably common Asian turtles (e.g., *Cuora amboinensis* and *Pyxidea mouhotii*), the large-scale exploitation for the food trade is most likely unsustainable and efforts should be directed towards detailed *in situ* conservation measures and ecological studies of such species. Asian turtles are of particular concern because many of them are not included in the present international assessment and regulation systems due to a lack of baseline ecological information. Criteria for selecting species for inclusion on CITES appendices and IUCN Red Lists seem to reflect research efforts in certain regions rather than reviewing threats and conservation status of all species in the world. For example, *Cuora galbinifrons* has a very restricted global distribution and is being heavily traded for food, yet trade in this species is not yet regulated under CITES [now regulated as of April 2000 CITES meeting].

There is a trend for the importation of captive-bred hatchlings of several Asian species, some in large farm-scale numbers: *Chinemys reevesii, Cuora flavomarginata, Mauremys mutica,* and *Ocadia sinensis.* There are also small numbers of yearlings of *Mauremys annamensis, Cuora amboinensis, C. galbinifrons, Pyxidea mouhotii,* and *Geoemyda spengleri* for sale in pet shops. Although the latter group of turtles are believed to be the result of opportunistic hatching of eggs laid by gravid females held in stock, it reflects that dealers are aware of the financial benefits of captive breeding. Captive breeding and/or farming has the potential to produce healthy hatchlings (including rare and protected species) to meet the demand from the pet trade. However, the present level of turtle farming, with the exception of *Pelodiscus sinensis*, is far from adequate to satisfy demands of the food trade. Future conservation measures should include the dissemination of species-specific breeding techniques and implementation of licensed breeders for commercially important species.

Conservation and Management

Approximately 75% of Hong Kong's surface area can be described as countryside in various stages of recovery or degradation, all of which may provide potential habitat for local turtle species. However, suitable turtle habitats are probably confined to wetlands and the surrounding areas since no tortoise is native to Hong Kong. Over half of these areas (more than 40% of Hong Kong's total land mass) are legally protected as Country Parks or Special Areas. There are currently 23 Country Parks which amount to approximately 41,500 ha and provide relatively safe habitats for turtles. Man-made reservoirs (about 20) associated with these Country Parks may prove to be important habitat for marsh and pond species, although many reservoirs are currently inhabited by invasive species. A further 14 areas are given special protection, though not specifically for turtles, and may provide potential refuge for native turtles. These areas are under the management and protection of the Agriculture, Fisheries and Conservation Department (AFCD) of the Hong Kong Special Administrative Region Government.

Some major lowland turtle habitats fall outside the protected area system and as such are under threat from drainage improvement, pollution, and development. For example, many areas of abandoned agricultural fields in the lowlands revert into marshes which support species like *Chinemys reevesii*. However, many of these lowland sites are privately owned and are vulnerable to urban development.

Kadoorie Farm & Botanic Garden (KFBG), with an area of 148 ha, is a privately-run wildlife sanctuary. Its well-established secondary forests and hill streams support populations of *Platysternon megacephalum* and *Cuora trifasciata*. KFBG also has a wild animal rescue center in which a growing number of Asian turtles are currently being maintained (70 individuals of 16 species). These animals were received as public donations of unwanted pets or "stray" animals from the Society for the Prevention of Cruelty to Animals (SPCA) as well as being illegal imports confiscated by the AFCD. Currently there are 5 main outdoor turtle holding facilities and many multipurpose reptile-holding areas of varying sizes. The center is planning to construct a further series of outdoor breeding units and will continue to

accept turtle stock and incorporate them into suitable captive breeding programs both locally and internationally where possible. Development of some of these areas awaits clarification of the international and regional role KFBG will play in the conservation of east Asian chelonians. The KFBG wild animal rescue center continues to refine the husbandry methods and veterinary procedures suitable to rehabilitate turtles. With its fully equipped veterinary hospital, fairly complex and unique procedures can be carried out on a regular basis.

In accordance with the mission of KFBG, the center's work is incorporated into the extensive education program which targets all ages and in particular school children. An awareness campaign has been run with the support of the SPCA and The Hong Kong Buddhist Association to highlight the problems associated with the turtle trade and to dispel popular misconceptions about releasing exotic turtles into the wild.

Certain Chinese CITES-listed species confiscated by the AFCD are passed onto Chinese authorities for release back to the wild. In 1997, KFBG in collaboration with the Malaysian and Hong Kong governments, returned eight large *Orlitia borneensis* to the wild in Malaysia after rehabilitation and quarantine. These turtles had reached Hong Kong as a result of the turtle trade.

Species Management. — There is no management plan for freshwater turtles in the wild but all wild turtles are protected in Hong Kong and Agriculture, Fisheries and Conservation Department is responsible for enforcing the relevant ordinances for their protection.

Control Measures. — Agriculture, Fisheries and Conservation Department enforces the various conservation laws and regulations protecting wildlife. They carry out inspections of pet shops and local markets and conduct investigations of suspected illegal trade in CITES-listed species, including turtles. They also take prompt enforcement action against such trade in response to reports and collected intelligence. Recently, the enforcement officers of AFCD began compiling an identification manual on CITES-listed chelonians to specifically deal with the illegal trade of these animals. Hong Kong has very high maximum penalties for the illegal wildlife trade but the actual fine levied is usually much smaller.

National Trade and Use. — Illegal turtle traps (believed to be targeting *Cuora trifasciata*) have recently been found both outside and within protected areas in Hong Kong. One local dealer has claimed that over 200 *C. trifasciata* are purchased from local villagers every year. However, it is not possible to assess what level of damage is actually being caused to wild turtle populations due to the lack of long-term monitoring. Trade in turtles and turtle parts is locally widespread. However, the vast majority of turtles in the food and pet trade originate from outside Hong Kong.

International Trade. — According to an animal dealer, some of the illegally-trapped *Cuora trifasciata* in

Hong Kong are exported to developed countries, such as USA, to meet demand for the pet market.

SPECIES ACCOUNTS

Native Species

Platysternon megacephalum. — Big-headed turtle.

Distribution: Fairly widespread in the central and eastern part of the New Territories. Also occurs at Sunset Peak on Lantau Island.

Habitat availability: This species lives in unpolluted forest streams and there are many suitable streams in Hong Kong.

Population status: Data not available. However, this species is regularly recorded in some of the stream systems in central New Territories indicating that fairly stable populations exist.

Population trends: Data lacking.

Threats: Low-altitude streams outside country parks may be affected by development projects. Illegal trapping and collecting targeted at *Cuora trifasciata* may also remove a small number of this species from the wild.

Chinemys reevesii. — Reeves' turtle.

Distribution: Widely recorded in the New Territories, Lantau Island, Hong Kong Island, and some smaller islands such as Cheung Chau and Peng Chau.

Habitat availability: This species lives in reservoirs, ponds, rivers, and slow-flowing streams and there are still many suitable habitats left. However, the spread of urban development to lowland areas in the New Territories and some islands has caused a significant decrease in available habitats.

Population status: Data not available. The species was previously considered Hong Kong's most common freshwater turtle but has been infrequently recorded in recent years.

Population trends: This species appears to be less frequently recorded in recent years.

Threats: Certain lowland habitats such as rivers, marshes, wet agricultural fields, and fish ponds are subject to development or urban encroachment. Illegal trapping and collecting may also remove a small number of this species from the wild. Release of exotic pet turtles, *Trachemys scripta elegans*, into the wild may cause competition. The introduction of conspecifics from further north may also cause outbreeding depression.

Cuora trifasciata. — Three-striped box turtle (Fig. 3).

Distribution: Known from scattered localities in the New Territories, Lantau Island, Hong Kong Island, and Lamma Island.

Habitat availability: This species lives in unpolluted forest streams and may venture to the surrounding areas. There are a good number of suitable streams in Hong Kong.

Population status: Data not available. A fair number of recent records including one hatchling and several

Figure 3. The three-striped box turtle, *Cuora trifasciata*, or golden coin turtle, in its native habitat in Hong Kong . Photo by ML.

juveniles from different localities indicate that breeding populations still exist.

Population trends: Data lacking. However the discovery of illegal traps containing *C. trifasciata* both outside and within protected areas, together with a report that hundreds of individuals are taken from the wild every year would lead to a conclusion that the population of this species is in decline.

Threats: Due to the high price commanded by this species in the market, illegal trapping and collecting seems to have intensified in recent years. Low-altitude streams outside country parks may also be affected by development projects.

Sacalia bealei. — Beale's terrapin.

Distribution: Known only from three localities in the New Territories. One of these has been heavily degraded by water pollution and will be channelized in the future.

Habitat availability: This species lives in streams from low to high altitude. There appear to be several suitable streams inside protected areas in Hong Kong.

Population status: The species is believed to be rare in Hong Kong as only six specimens are known to date, including two fairly old records.

Population trends: Data lacking but recent visits to the site where four specimens were found in early 1980s failed to yield any animals.

Threats: Former habitats outside protected areas have been degraded. Illegal trapping and collecting may also remove some individuals from the wild.

Pelodiscus sinensis. — Chinese softshell turtle.

Distribution: Occurs localized in Hong Kong, with its stronghold in the Inner Deep Bay fish ponds of the northwestern New Territories. Also recorded in some reservoirs but the animals concerned were probably released.

Habitat availability: The main habitat for this species, fish ponds, is on the decrease due to recent urban development.

Population status: Data not available, but a fairly healthy population is believed to exist in the Inner Deep Bay area.

Population trends: Data deficient. In view of the reduction in size of suitable habitat, the population is believed to have decreased.

Threats: Habitat destruction is the main threat as the vast majority of fish ponds in Hong Kong are on private land. Although a lot of the Inner Deep Bay fish ponds are zoned Conservation Area as buffer to the Mai Po and Deep Bay Ramsar site, there is still a lot of pressure for development. Illegal collecting when the fish ponds are drained for fish-harvesting and when animals venture onto the roads may also remove a small number of this species from the wild.

Species of Uncertain Status in Hong Kong

Cuora flavomarginata. — Yellow-margined box turtle.

Distribution: Known from three widely-separated localities in the New Territories (central and northeastern part) and Lantau Island.

Habitat availability: This is reported to be a forest species that also lives around forest streams. There are quite a number of suitable habitats left in Hong Kong.

Population status: The few specimens found so far are almost certainly released animals. It is uncertain whether a breeding population exists in Hong Kong.

Population trends: No observed trend.

Threats: Not known.

Mauremys mutica. — Chinese pond turtle.

Distribution: Known from several localities in the New Territories, Hong Kong Island, and Cheung Chau.

Habitat availability: This is reported to be an aquatic species that lives in lowland wetlands. There are quite a number of suitable habitats left in Hong Kong.

Population status: The few specimens found so far are almost certainly released animals. It is unclear whether a breeding population exists in Hong Kong.

Population trends: More specimens have been found in recent years, probably reflecting an increase in the practice of releasing turtles into the wild.

Threats: Not known.

Ocadia sinensis. — Chinese stripe-necked turtle.

Distribution: Known with certainty from only one locality on Hong Kong Island.

Habitat availability: This is reported to be an aquatic species that lives in large lowland wetlands. Most suitable habitats in Hong Kong have been destroyed or degraded.

Population status: The only specimen known from Hong Kong was dug up from a dried pond during the Second World War. Probably no viable population exists in Hong Kong.

Population trends: No observed trend.

Threats: Not known.

Palea steindachneri. — Steindachner's softshelled turtle.

Distribution: Known from only one locality in the New Territories.

Habitat availability: This species is reported to live in large hill streams and rivers. Suitable habitats do not exist in Hong Kong.

Population status: The only specimen known from Hong Kong was found in a reservoir and was probably released. A viable population probably does not exist in Hong Kong.

Population trends: No observed trend.

Threats: Not known.

Established Exotic Species

Trachemys scripta elegans. — Red-eared slider.

Distribution: Established in local reservoirs, large marshes, and fish ponds in the New Territories, Lantau Island, and Hong Kong Island.

Habitat availability: Some habitats of this species, such as marshes and fish ponds, are on the decrease due to recent urban development.

Population status: Established in Hong Kong around the 1980s; the population seems to be thriving and expanding into new areas. Reproduction in the wild has been recently confirmed.

Population trends: Population seems to be increasing and expanding into new areas. However, it is uncertain whether this is due to active introduction or population growth.

Threats: Habitat destruction of lowland wetlands limits the size of the potential habitats for this exotic species.

In addition, individuals of *Cuora amboinensis, Cuora galbinifrons, Pyxidea mouhotii, Chelydra serpentina,* and *Amyda cartilaginea* have been found in the wild but these were clearly released by people and these species do not appear to have become established in Hong Kong.

Acknowledgments. — The authors would like to thank Agriculture, Fisheries and Conservation Department for their valuable input and comments.

LITERATURE CITED

CHAN, P.L.B. In press. An Overview of the Trade in Freshwater Turtles, Tortoises, and other Wildlife in Hong Kong. TRAFFIC East Asia.

DUDGEON, D. AND CORLETT, R. 1994. Hills and Streams. An Ecology of Hong Kong. Hong Kong University Press, Hong Kong.

IUCN. 1996. IUCN Red List of Threatened Animals. IUCN, Gland, Switzerland, 448 pp.

LAU, M.W.N., ADES, G., GOODYER, N., AND ZOU, F.S. 1996. Wildlife Trade in Southern China including Hong Kong and Macao. Report to Biodiversity Working Group, China Council for International Cooperation on Environment and Development project, Hong Kong.

Asian Turtle Trade: Proceedings of a Workshop on Conservation and Trade of Freshwater Turtles and Tortoises in Asia
P.P. van Dijk, B.L. Stuart, and A.G.J. Rhodin, Eds.
Chelonian Research Monographs 2:45–51 • © 2000 by Chelonian Research Foundation

Current Status and Utilization of Chelonians in Taiwan

TIEN-HSI CHEN[1], HUA-CHING LIN[2], AND HSIEN-CHEH CHANG[3]

[1]*National Museum of Marine Science and Technology, Keelung 202, Taiwan [E-mail: thchen@mail.ntou.edu.tw];*
[2]*Taipei Zoo, Taipei 110, Taiwan [E-mail: dwx11@mail.zoo.gov.tw];*
[3]*China Medical College, Taichung 400, Taiwan [E-mail: hcchang@mail.cmc.edu.tw]*

ABSTRACT. – We present an overview of the current status of freshwater turtles and of the trade and utilization of chelonians in Taiwan. With the lack of basic ecological information, several studies on the freshwater turtles have been conducted in recent years. Farming of softshell turtles is a common practice in Taiwan, and the annual production has increased greatly for domestic demand and export. The production of softshell turtles reached 2237 tons in 1998. The trade and usage of turtle shells for Traditional Chinese Medicine has occurred in huge volumes for a long time. More than 1186 tons of hard-shelled and softshell turtle shells were imported from China and Southeast Asia to Taiwan in 1992–98. Clear policies are urgently needed to regulate the medicinal trade. Much of the trade in native and imported turtles and tortoises is for pets and release in religious ceremonies. There were at least 38 species of chelonians recorded in the pet trade, including many endangered species. Recommendations are given for the future conservation of native turtles and regulation of the live turtle trade and the traditional Chinese medicinal market.

There are five freshwater turtles native to Taiwan: the Chinese stripe-necked turtle (*Ocadia sinensis*), the yellow pond turtle (*Mauremys mutica*), the Reeves' turtle (*Chinemys reevesii*), the yellow-margined box turtle (*Cuora flavomarginata*), and the Chinese softshell turtle (*Pelodiscus sinensis*). Under the Wildlife Conservation Law, all marine species are designated as endangered and three freshwater turtles (*C. flavomarginata, M. mutica, C. reevesii*) as rare and valuable species. However, little has been published about the basic ecological information of the turtles for their conservation and management.

Due to over-exploitation, as well as rapid habitat loss and degradation, most of the populations of freshwater turtles in Taiwan are believed to have been declining in recent decades. Additionally, some exotic species have been introduced in recent years, especially red-eared sliders (*Trachemys scripta elegans*). Their status and probable impacts on native fauna on Taiwan need further detailed studies and monitoring.

Historically, turtles have been utilized for a long time by the Chinese people for meat, shells, and to keep in temple ponds. In Taiwan, turtle shells are heavily used as an important ingredient in traditional medicines. As the economy continues to grow rapidly, the demand for turtle shell increases in the Traditional Chinese Medicine market. Little of this turtle shell is supplied from domestic sources; the supply depends mainly on import from China and Southeast Asia. If the burgeoning trade is left uncontrolled, it will undoubtedly pose negative impacts on the populations of turtles in these areas.

As the Chinese softshell turtle yields high aquaculture profits, farming of this turtle is common in Taiwan. The annual production of this turtle has reached very high numbers in recent years. Recently softshell turtles have also been exported to Hong Kong, Macau, and China. Because of the excellent market value of its meat, it is the most exploited species among all turtles occurring in Taiwan. Meanwhile, the current status of the wild populations is unclear.

Most of the native turtles in Taiwan, like many other Asian species, are facing an uncertain future. In this report, we concentrate on the status and trade of freshwater turtles and discuss some probable threats to the chelonians in Taiwan.

In Taiwan, there are various kinds of protected areas designated under local or central laws, including 6 national parks (3222 km^2), 18 nature reserves (633 km^2), 11 wildlife refuges (117 km^2), and 35 forest protected areas (837 km^2). They cover 4520 km^2, or 12.6% of the total land area. Among the protected areas, only one refuge is designated for the nesting habitat of green turtles on an offshore island. Most of the protected habitats are located in middle- or high-altitude areas, or coastal areas. Only very limited areas cover the critical habitats of freshwater turtles, especially for aquatic species.

Current Status and Biological Characteristics

Ocadia sinensis. — Chinese stripe-necked turtle.

The Chinese stripe-necked turtle is abundant and widespread in low-altitude freshwater habitats of Taiwan. This species is highly aquatic, inhabiting still and slow-moving water bodies, such as middle and lower reaches of rivers, ponds, lakes, and reservoirs. Previously, *O. sinensis* was regarded as herbivorous, but recent studies have shown that it is omnivorous and that its dietary habits change with the seasons and body size and differ between sexes (Chen and Lue, 1998a, 1999a). This turtle consumes many plant items and various animal food types.

In the populations of northern Taiwan, the body size of gravid females ranges from 19 to 25 cm in carapace length (CL), whereas males are seldom larger than 18 cm CL. The body sizes seem to be larger in the populations of central and southern Taiwan. Most females lay only one clutch in a nesting season, and clutch size in the northern Taiwan populations varies from 7 to 17.

Although this turtle is still common in Taiwan, intensive collection for pets or release in religious rituals will inevitably pose threats to its survival. Additionally, water pollution in some important habitats will contribute to its decline.

Chinemys reevesii. — Reeves' turtle.

In Taiwan, this turtle was first recorded near Taipei in 1931 (Horikawa, 1934), from very limited collection localities. Mao (1971) collected this turtle from Taipei and Nantou, whereas only very few individuals were found near Tainan and I-Lan in recent years (Chen, pers. obs.). In a preliminary survey in 1997, this turtle was found to still be common on Kimmen, an island near mainland China (Chen, unpubl. data). There are few available data on the current status of this turtle in Taiwan. Few detailed studies have been carried out on the status of the Kimmen population, but judging from the known distribution, it is believed that *C. reevesii* is rare on this island. The species is protected under the Wildlife Conservation Law as a rare and valuable species.

Mauremys mutica. — Yellow pond turtle.

The yellow pond turtle is more common in the central and northern parts of Taiwan, but the populations have been declining because of extensive habitat loss. This turtle inhabits mainly still water bodies such as old ponds, lakes, drainage ditches, and rice paddies, and occasionally is found far from aquatic habitats. At present this species can be found in some remote montane ponds in low densities. This turtle occurs in somewhat scattered and small populations subject to the natural environmental stress associated with human disturbances. It is omnivorous, and is known to feed on various plant and animal materials, including roots and shoots of plants, aquatic invertebrates such as insects, sewage worms, and leeches. Based on limited data, the nesting season extends from May to July, and clutch size ranges from 4 to 7 eggs.

Few studies have been carried out on the current status and ecology of this turtle. Based on the rapid reduction of suitable aquatic habitat in Taiwan, it is probable that populations have been dramatically declining. *Mauremy mutica* is considered a rare and valuable species and is protected under the Wildlife Conservation Law.

Cuora flavomarginata. — Yellow-margined box turtle.

The yellow-margined box turtle was described by Gray (1863) on the basis of a specimen collected by Swinhoe from Tamsui, northwestern Taiwan. In the original description, this species was reported to be abundant in ponds near rice paddies, occasionally basking on stones. Actually, this turtle is highly terrestrial, and is presently found in and around primary and well-developed secondary forests of Taiwan (Chen and Lue, 1999b; Lue and Chen, 1999). The nesting season of this species extends from May to July. Clutch size ranges from 1 to 3 eggs in the populations of northern Taiwan. It can lay as many as 4 eggs in a clutch in southern Taiwanese populations. Females sometimes produce two nests in a nesting season.

Habitat loss and degradation caused by land development seem to be the primary factors that could cause population declines of the yellow-margined box turtle. Deforestation and habitat fragmentation in low altitude evergreen forests may be serious threats to this turtle. *Cuora flavomarginata* is protected under the Wildlife Conservation Law as a rare and valuable species, but until now, no effective action for the conservation of this turtle has been carried out.

The yellow-margined box turtle was noted to be imported from Taiwan into the U.S. in large numbers for the pet trade (Connor and Wheeler, 1998). It is known that this turtle has been intensively collected for the pet trade and for stuffed specimens, but no solid data could be used to estimate the actual number. The commercial exploitation must have diminished or completely ceased as populations declined and protective legislation was implemented in Taiwan.

Pelodiscus sinensis. — Chinese softshell turtle.

The Chinese people believe that meat and blood of softshell turtles are extremely tonic and beneficial for their health. Because breeding the species yields high commercial profit, there are many turtle farms in Taiwan raising this species as a side-line business. Natural populations of this turtle inhabit ponds, lakes, and slow-moving rivers, and are widely distributed in Taiwan. The nesting season extends from late March to early November in Taiwan. A female can lay 5 to 6 clutches in a nesting season. Clutch size ranges from 10 to 35 eggs. There is a lack of data concerning the status of Chinese softshell turtles in the wild, but probably they are facing the same stresses as their freshwater hardshelled counterparts.

Trachemys scripta elegans. — Red-eared slider.

The introduced red-eared slider is now abundant in low altitude aquatic habitats of Taiwan (Shao and Tzeng, 1993; Chen and Lue, 1998b). This turtle is known to have already established breeding colonies on Taiwan (Chen and Lue, 1998b). They were observed in various habitats, including estuaries, rivers, reservoirs, and montane streams and ponds. To elucidate the probable impacts on native fauna, this turtle should be closely monitored.

Other Introduced Turtles

Besides the red-eared slider, several other non-native turtles have been found in the wild in Taiwan. They include the common snapping turtle (*Chelydra serpentina*), the alligator snapping turtle (*Macroclemys temminckii*), the

Table 1. Trade records of hard-shelled turtle shells (in weight, kg) imported into Taiwan for Traditional Chinese Medicine market from different areas or countries in 1992–98.

Year	Bangladesh	Cambodia	China	Indonesia	Laos	Malaysia	Pakistan	Singapore	Thailand	Vietnam	Total
1992	0	0	33,731	13,740	0	1,830	2,500	59,947	804	0	112,552
1993	0	0	154,594	51,920	0	0	4,750	34,580	3,480	0	249,324
1994	1,790	0	50,626	56,511	446	2,850	0	900	413	735	114,271
1995	4,920	0	7,460	65,253	0	0	0	6,331	0	0	83,964
1996	2,700	7,659	14,137	90,566	0	0	0	1,400	0	210	116,672
1997	0	8,050	8,366	88,278	0	0	0	0	0	19,942	124,636
1998	0	14,740	93,764	37,315	0	1,100	0	0	0	9,605	156,524
Total	9,410	30,449	362,678	403,583	446	5,780	7,250	103,158	4,697	30,492	957,943

matamata (*Chelus fimbriatus*), map turtles (*Graptemys* spp.), the black-breasted leaf turtle (*Geoemyda spengleri*), the Chinese three-striped box turtle (*Cuora trifasciata*), and the big-headed turtle (*Platysternon megacephalum*). Their current status in Taiwan remains unclear, but these turtles should be closely monitored.

Utilization and Trade of Turtles

Traditional Chinese Medicine (TCM). — Turtle shells have been consumed for medical purposes since historical times in the Chinese culture, including the societies of China, Taiwan, Hong Kong, Japan, and South Korea. According to the traditional medicinal text, the raw materials — shells of hardshelled and softshell turtles — came chiefly from mainland China (Yen, 1992). According to the statistics of the Board of Foreign Trade for 1992 to 1998, as much as 958 tons of hardshelled turtle shells were imported from China and Southeast Asia into Taiwan (Table 1), and the amount of softshell turtle shells was 228 tons (Table 2). Indonesia has become the main supplier of turtle shell to the traditional Chinese medicinal market in Taiwan, representing 42.1% and 51.4% of hardshelled and softshell turtle shell products, respectively, in 1992–98 (Tables 1-2). Meanwhile China and Singapore also contributed a great deal to the turtle shell demand in Taiwan. The amount of turtle shell imported into Taiwan usually exceeded 100,000 kg per annum in 1992–98, with 249,324 kg in 1993 alone (Figs. 1 and 2). The monetary figures are also astounding. According to the records of the Board of Foreign Trade for 1992–98, the total value of turtle shell markets exceeded NT 100 million (US$ 3.2 million). Although the exact number of turtles slaughtered to meet the needs of the medicinal market is impossible to estimate, it must be a huge number.

To collect reliable data to evaluate the possible impacts on the turtles in the areas of origin, more detailed investigations should be conducted. Chang (1997) has pointed out that at least 20 species of turtles could be found in the medicinal trade (Table 3). Among them, *Cuora amboinensis*, *Malayemys subtrijuga*, and *Siebenrockiella crassicollis* were the most common species traded in the markets, usually representing more than 75% of the total amount. *Chinemys reevesii* was the most common species imported from China, and *Cuora amboinensis* and *Malayemys subtrijuga* from Indonesia and Singapore. Some turtles listed on the Appendices of CITES could frequently be found among the raw materials.

Meat (Softshell Turtles). — Although softshell turtles have long been popular in Taiwanese cooking, the meat of other turtles has never been consumed much in Taiwan. Most of the residents on the island do not eat hardshelled turtle meat because of religious sentiments. The Chinese softshell turtle (*Pelodiscus sinensis*) is frequently consumed as food and medicine in Taiwan and has a good market value.

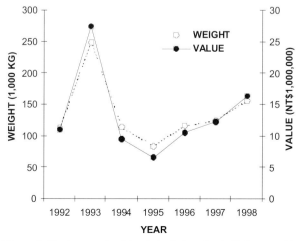

Figure 1. Trade records of hard-shelled turtle shells imported into Taiwan for Traditional Chinese Medicine market from 1992 to 1998.

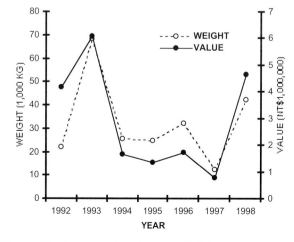

Figure 2. Trade records of softshell turtle shells imported into Taiwan for Traditional Chinese Medicine market from 1992 to 1998.

Table 2. Trade records of imported turtle shells (in weight, kg) imported into Taiwan for the Traditional Chinese Medicine market from different areas or countries in 1992–98.

Year	Bangladesh	China	Indonesia	Laos	Malaysia	Singapore	Total
1992	0	14,689	7,118	0	70	69	21,946
1993	16,560	32,339	18,184	0	282	880	68,245
1994	2,300	5,367	17,149	82	0	700	25,598
1995	6,750	930	16,040	0	0	1,250	24,970
1996	0	0	32,337	0	0	0	32,337
1997	0	1,245	11,213	0	0	0	12,458
1998	22,000	5,249	15,064	0	0	0	42,313
Total	47,610	59,819	117,105	82	352	2,899	227,867

Table 3. Turtle species known in the Traditional Chinese Medicine market and their prevailing occurrence in the Taiwan market.

Species	Occurrence	CITES Status
Cuora amboinensis	Abundant	
Siebenrockiella crassicollis	Abundant	
Chinemys reevesii	Common	
Indotestudo elongata	Common	II
Cuora flavomarginata	Occasional	
Geochelone elegans	Occasional	II
Geoemyda spengleri	Occasional	
Hardella thurji	Occasional	
Heosemys grandis	Occasional	
Hieremys annandalii	Occasional	
Kachuga tecta	Occasional	I
Malayemys subtrijuga	Occasional	
Manouria emys	Occasional	II
Manouria impressa	Occasional	II
Mauremys mutica	Occasional	
Morenia ocellata	Occasional	I
Pyxidea mouhotii	Occasional	
Cyclemys dentata	Rare	
Ocadia sinensis	Rare	
Platysternon megacephalum	Rare	

Because of the economic value, farming softshell turtles is an important industry in Taiwan. At the beginning of this century, small scale turtle farming was documented in Taiwan. The total production was 50,999 kg in 1920–25 (Tzeng and Hsu, 1998). According to statistics in the *Bulletin of Fisheries of Taiwan*, more than 100 million hatchlings were propagated from 1966 to 1997 in Taiwan alone (Fig. 3). In recent years, the production of turtle hatchlings has increased year by year, with 1.1 million in 1994 and increasing to 32.7 million in 1997 (Fig. 3). Turtle hatchlings were also exported to other countries and areas, including Hong Kong, Macau, China, and Malaysia from 1995 onwards. The amount increased rapidly in recent years, reaching more than 249 tons in 1998 (Table 4). The exportation of non-hatchling softshell turtles has also increased greatly in these few years, reaching 2237 tons in 1997 (Fig. 4). Since 1995, live softshell turtles have been exported to Hong Kong, Macau, China, and Malaysia (Table 4). More than 3336 tons of live animals have been transported to these areas. Recently, some softshell turtle hatchlings were imported from the USA, Indonesia, and Bangladesh, but the species were not recorded in the trade statistics. In addition to turtle farming, *Pelodiscus sinensis* is also collected extensively from the wild. The price of wild-caught softshell turtles is much higher than that of farmed animals.

Some other hardshelled turtles were also exported from Taiwan for various purposes. The total amount was modest, with only 554 kg exported from 1992 to 1998 (Table 5).

Eggs of Softshell Turtles. — The consumption of softshell turtle eggs is common in Taiwan, but few data are available to determine the domestic market size. According to the trade statistics, 95,311 kg of softshell turtle eggs were exported to Hong Kong, Macau, Japan, Thailand, and some other countries in 1995–98 (Table 6). The demand for softshell turtle eggs has been increasing year by year.

Pet Markets. — Because of the lack of trade records, it is impossible to estimate the actual numbers of exotic chelonians imported into Taiwan. It is reported that at least 182,200 *Trachemys scripta elegans* were imported from the U.S. into Taiwan during 1994–98 (Salzberg, 1998). Meanwhile only 309 kg of live turtle imports were recorded formally by the Taiwan Board of Customs in 1998. In a preliminary survey conducted in 1995–96, at least 24 species of turtles and tortoises could be seen in pet stores in

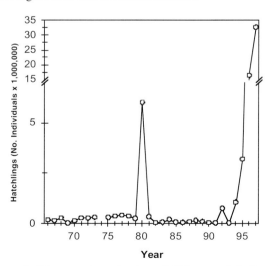

Figure 3. The annual production of Chinese softshell turtle (*Pelodiscus sinensis*) hatchlings in Taiwan in 1966–97.

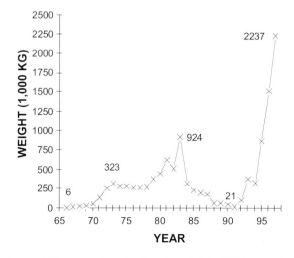

Figure 4. The annual production (in weight) of Chinese softshell turtles (*Pelodiscus sinensis*) in Taiwan in 1966–97.

Table 4. Trade records of exported live softshell turtles (*Pelodiscus sinensis*) in weight (kg) from Taiwan to different areas or countries in 1995–98 (hatchlings in parentheses).

Country	1995	1996	1997	1998	Total
China	0	2,400	0	25,316	27,716
		(38,429)	(15,610)	(378)	(54,417)
Hong Kong	0	108,860	458,685	166,037	733,582
		(1,249)	(12,090)	(96,030)	(109,369)
Italy	0	0	0	5	5
Japan	0	0	0	0	0
		(89)			(89)
Korea	0	0	1,920	0	1,920
Macau	0	155,204	1,113,674	1,276,320	2,545,198
		(29,391)	(152,967)	(150,829)	(333,187)
Malaysia	27,480	0	0	0	27,480
	(12,434)	(2,625)		(1,654)	(16,713)
Mauritius	0	200	0	0	200
Mexico	0	0	0	5	5
Philippines	0	0	0	0	0
			(90)		(90)
Singapore	0	0	0	0	0
		(5)	(1,300)		(1,305)
Thailand	0	0	0	0	0
		(88)		(513)	(601)
Vietnam	0	0	0	0	0
			(150)		(150)
Total	27,480	266,664	1,574,279	1,467,683	3,336,106
	(12,434)	(71,876)	(182,207)	(249,404)	(515,921)

Table 5. Trade records of exported live hard-shelled turtles in weight (kg) from Taiwan to different areas or countries in 1993–98.

Country	1993	1994	1995	1996	1997	1998	Total
Brunei	0	0	0	0	3	0	3
Germany	0	0	0	0	2	4	6
Greece	0	0	0	0	0	3	3
Italy	0	0	0	0	0	10	10
Japan	49	9	73	123	94	79	427
Korea	0	0	0	0	2	0	2
Mexico	0	0	0	0	0	1	1
Philippines	0	0	0	0	26	12	38
Spain	0	0	0	0	0	7	7
U. A. Emirates	0	0	0	3	0	0	3
UK	0	0	0	2	0	0	2
USA	0	0	0	0	0	52	52
Total	49	9	73	128	127	168	554

Because investigating officers seldom have sufficient background to be able to accurately identify most species of turtles, it is impossible to estimate the amount traded in pet stores and on the black market. According to the records of Taipei Zoo, a shelter for confiscated live animals, more protected turtles than expected are traded on the black market, including *Geochelone carbonaria*, *Geochelone denticulata*, *Geochelone radiata*, *Testudo horsfieldii*, and *Testudo hermanni*. Taipei Zoo alone has accepted several hundred protected turtles which were confiscated from pet dealers in recent years.

A potentially harmful byproduct of the prevailing pet trade is the release of captive turtles into the wild. Most pet owners are unaware of the aggressive behavior and adult body size of some turtle species. Grown *Trachemys scripta elegans* are often released into local ponds and streams. These introduced turtles may compete for limited resources with the native species.

Release of Turtles for Religious Ceremonies. — In Oriental popular religion and superstition, the turtle is regarded as the symbol of long life and a creature of supernatural powers. In Taiwan, people think that hardshelled turtles are sacred and the Buddhists believe that showing mercy by releasing live animals will be rewarded by blessing with good fortune in return. Thus releasing turtles has been a popular activity. Of all animals, the turtle is the one that the Taiwanese most like to set free. Turtles were occasionally released into temple ponds or wild aquatic areas as a meritorious act. Some shops near temples in Taipei sold turtles entirely for releasing in mercy practices. The most common species sold for the mercy act were *O. sinensis*, *T. s. elegans*, and occasionally *M. mutica* (Table 7). Recently, there have been considerably high ratios of turtles with carved inscriptions caught in the wild (Chen and Lue, 1998b), especially in remote montane areas. The inscriptions are believed to be associated with the act of releasing.

Taipei alone (Table 7). Many of these were species protected by the Wildlife Conservation Law or regulated by CITES. Since statistics on importation of live turtles and tortoises usually were combined with those for tropical fish, there is no way to calculate the actual numbers involved. Moreover, *T. s. elegans* can be easily bred in Taiwan and some farms have artificially bred this species for pet markets for several years (Lu et al., 1996). There are at least five turtle farms operating in central and southern Taiwan that supply the demand from the pet trade. *Ocadia sinensis* and *T. s. elegans* are the two most common turtles propagated for the growing demand from the pet trade, a part of which supplies the market for release in religious ceremonies. Interviews with owners of turtle farms indicate that more than 30,000 hatchlings per year could be propagated in a turtle farm. Meanwhile the turtle farms depend almost completely on wild-caught adult or subadult turtles for use as breeding stock. There are almost no data available on the actual number of turtles collected directly from the wild for captive propagation.

Although releasing exotic turtles can pose impacts on native fauna, as mentioned above, the translocation of native species could cause problems to the environment. It is reported that some diseases have been spreading to wild populations via release of pet animals. Moreover the genetic

Table 6. Trade record of exported softshell turtle eggs (*Pelodiscus sinensis*) in weight (kg) from Taiwan to different areas or countries in 1995–98.

Country	1995	1996	1997	1998	Total
Hong Kong	0	0	3,175	1,704	4,879
Japan	0	0	0	312	312
Macau	0	0	29,129	60,879	90,008
Malaysia	47	0	0	0	47
Thailand	0	0	0	45	45
Vietnam	0	0	20	0	20
Total	47	0	32,324	62,940	95,311

variation among turtle populations would be mixed through the release act. In temple ponds, the released turtles usually receive no additional attention thereafter. Most temple ponds are not suitable for turtles, surrounded by steep cement banks and containing scarce food resources. Turtles usually are kept in high density and poor water quality. In preliminary studies, the mortality rate was found to be high, and the population structure was skewed towards large individuals, with very few small animals (Chen, unpubl. data), indicating that the recruitment rate is very low.

Although releasing pet animals to the wild is completely prohibited under the Animal Protection Law in Taiwan, this legislation has never been enforced.

Threats to Freshwater Turtles in Taiwan

Taiwan has experienced a human population explosion in the past 50 years. The rapid population growth, along with virtually unchecked land development policies, has contributed to the severe degradation of wildlife habitat. It is believed to be a causal factor in the wide-spread declines of turtles in various areas around the island. The aquatic habitats in urban areas, including ponds, drainage ditches, and reservoirs have been drained or filled, thus depriving turtles of critical habitats, such as basking sites and nesting areas, and food sources. The ongoing construction of streambank and channel dredging has severely modified the river channel and riparian corridor of many major rivers in Taiwan. Habitat fragmentation accompanying the habitat alteration also certainly impacts the native turtles. Water pollution

Table 7. Turtle species and numbers observed in the pet market of Taipei in a survey conducted in October 1995 to January 1996. Values in parentheses indicate the numbers sold in stores near temples.

Species	No. Individuals
Asia	
Carettochelys insculpta	36 (0)
Chelodina novaeguineae	14 (0)
Cuora flavomarginata	1 (0)
Cuora amboinensis	1 (0)
Cuora galbinifrons	3 (0)
Cyclemys dentata	15 (0)
Geochelone elegans	33 (0)
Heosemys spinosa	23 (0)
Mauremys mutica	10 (6)
Ocadia sinensis	1242 (1183)
Pelodiscus sinensis	20 (20)
Sacalia bealei	1 (0)
North America	
Apalone ferox	18 (0)
Apalone spinifera	6 (0)
Chelydra serpentina	17 (0)
Graptemys spp.	214 (0)
Macroclemys temminckii	61 (0)
Malaclemys terrapin	11 (0)
Pseudemys spp.	101 (0)
Sternotherus carinatus	21 (0)
Terrapene carolina	32 (0)
Trachemys scripta elegans	809 (450)
South America	
Chelus fimbriatus	11 (0)
Africa	
Geochelone sulcata	1 (0)

from sewage and industrial discharge is another threat to the turtle fauna in Taiwan, and is suspected to be the major cause of high mortality rate in the *O. sinensis* population in the Keelung River (Chen and Lue, 1998a).

Habitat loss has been blamed as a major cause of rapid decline of terrestrial box turtle populations. Large-scale deforestation of low-altitude evergreen forests has deprived the terrestrial *C. flavomarginata* of many of its essential habitats in Taiwan. It has been shown that stable habitats in the forest are critical to this turtle as shelter for overwintering and during the non-reproductive season (Lue and Chen, 1999). The extensive collection and release of native or exotic turtles will also pose serious impacts to the natural populations.

In Taiwan, all marine turtles and three freshwater turtle species (*C. flavomarginata, M. mutica, C. reevesii*) are designated as vulnerable species by the Wildlife Conservation Law validated in 1988. The Division of Conservation, Council of Agriculture, is the authority responsible for implementing this law. Although these turtles are protected through legislation, the laws are not enforced effectively in the field. Exploitation of turtles, especially freshwater species, still occurs in considerable numbers.

Recommendations for Turtle Conservation and Management

More Research and Status Surveys. — Basic information on the life history of Taiwanese turtle populations is lacking, and no effective management plans for their conservation have yet been carried out. The most urgent and essential measure for the conservation of native turtles in Taiwan is to secure and preserve the natural habitats of turtles. With the lack of essential ecological information for many species, we must first identify their various needs to sustain stable populations, including habitat requirements, food habits, growth, population structure, reproduction, and recruitment. As the status of many turtles is still unclear, detailed research on their life history and general surveys of their distribution are strongly needed. Since 1995, a number of studies on the current status of native turtle species, monitoring of introduced species, and the impact of habitat degradation on aquatic turtles have been funded by the Council of Agriculture and the National Science Council. More detailed and long-term studies on their ecology are still needed.

Regulating International and Domestic Trade of Live Turtles. — Although Taiwan is not a signatory to the Convention on International Trade in Endangered Species of Wild Fauna and Flora (CITES), all turtle species listed on the Appendices have been protected under the Wildlife Protection Law. Commercial trade of wild-caught turtles is also prohibited in Taiwan because they are protected by the Animal Protection Law. Meanwhile the trade of live turtles is still common and left unregulated in Taiwan. Many of the traded species are endangered and protected or regulated by local laws and international agreements. The legislation should be effectively enforced to halt the illegal trade of live turtles in the market. The fact that central and local governments do not have proper staff and trained enforcement officers have hindered the enforcement efforts. More training programs should be developed for the front-line officers responsible for the enforcement of wildlife law. The monitoring and inspecting systems should be improved, as live turtles have been smuggled across Taiwan's borders in huge numbers. Additionally, the live turtle trade should be discouraged, especially that in rare and endangered species.

In addition to regulating the market, the final destination of the live turtles should be closely monitored. Because releasing captive turtles to the wild is detrimental to the natural environment, it must be strictly prohibited.

Regulating the Traditional Chinese Medicinal Market. — Although molecular tools could be helpful to identify the various sources of turtle shells in the market (Chang, 1997), some easy-to-use identification guides should be developed and designed to help customs officers and medicinal dealers dealing with turtle shell specimens, so that they could more easily identify and control trade of protected species. To develop clearer control policies, the responsible agencies need to cooperate closely with scientists, exporting countries, and medicinal dealers and markets to achieve reasonable and sustainable usage of turtle shell products.

Public Education. — The key to success of any conservation effort is wide public support and cooperation. Through the public media, the green turtle *Chelonia mydas* has become a symbolic animal for conservation in Taiwan, but most freshwater turtles are still left unaffected. First of all, the needs for conservation should be understood, especially by the policy makers for land development. Land-use planning decisions need to address cumulative impacts to riparian ecosystems, although there are conflicts between conservation and development motives. It is necessary to make the public aware of the problems for turtle conservation, and the fact that positive actions are needed, especially concerning the improper release of exotic species into the wild.

Close cooperation with local societies is also important for conserving turtles, especially in terms of financial and manpower support. With the burgeoning awareness of wildlife conservation, one temple in southern Taiwan is planning an ecological garden and education center displaying native turtles. Some people on this island have begun to consider the problems of turtles in temple ponds and the future of native turtle species.

Acknowledgments. — We wish to express our sincere thanks to TRAFFIC Taipei for providing the domestic trade data, K.-Y. Lue for comments on this manuscript, and L.-L. Lee for drawing our attention to the valuable information of this workshop.

LITERATURE CITED

CHANG, H.-C. 1997. Study on Carapax Testudinis in the Taiwan market for the origin, morphologic, DNA PCR identification and classic literature. Report to Department of Health, Republic of China.

CHEN, T.-H., AND LUE, K.-Y. 1998a. Ecology of the Chinese stripe-necked turtle, *Ocadia sinensis* (Testudines: Emydidae), in the Keelung River, northern Taiwan. Copeia 1998:944-952.

CHEN, T.-H., AND LUE, K.-Y. 1998b. Ecological notes on feral populations of *Trachemys scripta elegans* in northern Taiwan. Chelonian Conservation and Biology 3:87-90.

CHEN, T.-H., AND LUE, K.-Y. 1999a. Food habits of the Chinese stripe-necked turtle, *Ocadia sinensis* (Testudines: Bataguridae), in the Keelung River, northern Taiwan. Journal of Herpetology 33:463-471.

CHEN, T.-H., AND LUE, K.-Y. 1999b. Population characteristics and egg production of the yellow-margined box turtle, *Cuora flavomarginata flavomarginata*, in northern Taiwan. Herpetologica 55:487-498.

CONNOR, M.J., AND WHEELER, V. 1998. The Chinese box turtle *Cistoclemmys flavomarginata* Gray 1863. Tortuga Gazette 34(10):1-7.

GRAY, J.E. 1863. Observations on the box tortoises, with the descriptions of three new Asiatic species. Proceedings of the Zoological Society of London 1863:173-179.

HORIKAWA, Y. 1934. Turtles of Taiwan. The Taiwan Jiho 181:7-16. (in Japanese)

LU, D.-J., CHEN, T.-H., AND WU, S.-H. 1996. The trade collection of freshwater turtles and tortoises in domestic market. Council of Agriculture, R.O.C., Taipei. (in Chinese)

LUE, K.-Y. AND CHEN, T.-H. 1999. Activity, movement patterns, and home range of the yellow-margined box turtles (*Cuora flavomarginata*) in northern Taiwan. Journal of Herpetology 33:590-600.

MAO, S.H. 1971. Turtles of Taiwan. The Commercial Press, Taipei.

SALZBERG, A. 1998. Chelonian conservation news. Chelonian Conservation and Biology 3:147-150.

SHAO, K.T. AND TZENG, C.S. 1993. Revision on the checklist of admitting import of aquarium fishes of Taiwan (II). Council of Agriculture, R.O.C., Taipei.

TZENG, L.-L. AND HSU, C.-Y. (Eds.). 1998. Statistics Collection for the Fisheries History of Taiwan. Bureau of Fisheries, Taiwan.

YEN, K.-Y. 1992. The Illustrated Chinese Materia Medica. SMC Publishing Inc., Taipei.

Asian Turtle Trade: Proceedings of a Workshop on Conservation and Trade of Freshwater Turtles and Tortoises in Asia
P.P. van Dijk, B.L. Stuart, and A.G.J. Rhodin, Eds.
Chelonian Research Monographs 2:52–54 • © 2000 by Chelonian Research Foundation

Turtle Trade in Northeast Asia: Regional Summary
(China, Hong Kong, and Taiwan)

GARY ADES[1], CHRIS B. BANKS[2], KURT A. BUHLMANN[3], BOSCO CHAN[4],
HSIEN-CHEH CHANG[5], TIEN-HSI CHEN[6], PAUL CROW[7], HEIKO HAUPT[8], RAYMOND KAN[9],
JO-YEN LAI[10], MICHAEL LAU[11], HUA-CHING LIN[12], AND SHI HAITAO[13]

[1]*Kadoorie Farm & Botanic Garden, Lam Kam Road, Tai Po, New Territories, Hong Kong*
[Fax: 852-248-31877; E-mail: kfgarya@kfbg.org.hk];
[2]*Melbourne Zoo, P.O. Box 74, Parkville, Victoria 3052, Australia [Fax: 61-3-9285-9360; E-mail: Cbanks@zoo.org.au];*
[3]*Conservation International, c/o Savannah River Ecology Laboratory, P.O. Drawer E, Aiken, SC 29802 USA [E-mail: Buhlmann@srel.edu];*
[4]*Department of Ecology & Biodiversity, The University of Hong Kong, Pokfulam Road, Hong Kong*
[Fax: 852-254-01836; E-mail: bochan@hkusua.hku.hk];
[5]*School of Chinese Medicine, China Medical College, 91 Hsueh Shih Rd., Tichung, Taiwan 404, Republic of China*
[E-mail: hcchang@mail.cmc.edu.tw];
[6]*National Marine Science Museum, 2 Pei-Ning Rd., Keelung 202, Taiwan, Republic of China*
[Fax: 886-2-2-462-7716; E-mail: thchen@mail.ntou.edu.tw];
[7]*Kadoorie Farm & Botanic Garden, Lam Kam Road, Tai Po, New Territories, Hong Kong[*]*
[Fax: 852-248-31877; E-mail: primate1@kfbg.org.hk];
[8]*German CITES Scientific Authority, Federal Agency for Nature Conservation, Animal Species Conservation,*
Konstantinstrasse 110, 53179 Bonn, Germany [Fax: 49-228-8491-119; E-mail: HauptH@bfn.de];
[9]*Kans Trading Co. Ltd., 1508 The Center, 99 Queen's Road Central, Hong Kong*
[Fax: 852-284-52105; E-mail: kanr@netvigator.com];
[10]*The Herp Rescue Center, 30 Sec, 2 Hsin Kuang Road, Taipei, Taiwan, Republic of China*
[Fax: 886-2-2938-2316; E-mail: dwx11@mail.zoo.gov.tw];
[11]*Kadoorie Farm & Botanic Garden, Lam Kam Road, Tai Po, New Territories, Hong Kong*
[Fax: 852-248-31877; E-mail: mwnlau@kfbg.org.hk];
[12]*Taipei City Zoo, Taipei 110, Taiwan, Republic of China*
[Fax: 886-2-2938-2316; E-mail: dwx11@mail.zoo.gov.tw];
[13]*Department of Biology, Hainan Teachers College, Hainan 571158, People's Republic of China*
[Fax: 898-588-3035; E-mail: sht@aneca.hainnu.edu.cn]

Patterns of Trade

In the Northeast Asian subregion, consumption of turtles can be separated into three main areas: (1) live turtles for food, (2) shells for Traditional Chinese Medicine, and (3) live turtles as pets, including those for Buddhists' release. The food trade involves by far the largest quantities of turtles.

Softshell turtles are widely eaten by the Chinese as a delicacy. Hence, the sale of softshell turtles is widespread in China, Hong Kong, and Taiwan. The vast majority of these are farm-bred Chinese softshell turtles, *Pelodiscus sinensis*, either raised locally or imported from neighboring countries such as Thailand. A smaller number of wild-caught softshells (both within the countries or imported from Southeast Asian or South Asian countries) are also traded. Hardshelled turtles are also widely consumed in southern China and Hong Kong, but not in Taiwan due to cultural sentiments. There are unconfirmed reports that some cities in North China also import hardshelled turtles for food. Nearly all hardshelled turtles seen in Chinese food markets are wild-caught and most of these are imported from Indochina, Southeast Asia, and South Asia.

Due to the large number of source countries involved, there are many different trade routes for the food chelonians,
but nearly all of them end up in large cities in South China (such as Guangzhou) and Hong Kong. All means of transport are used depending on their availability and the distance between the source countries and South China. Land-based transport is used to deliver turtles from neighboring countries (such as Vietnam and Myanmar) to southern provinces in China. Turtles are also flown from countries further away (such as Indonesia) either directly or via some major ports to South China. The extent of sea transport used is not certain. The major ports involved in the freight of turtles are Bangkok, Guangzhou, Hong Kong, Kuala Lumpur, Singapore, and Taiwan. As indicated by the frequent change in species composition of the turtles observed in the food markets, the source areas shift regularly. Hence, there are no fixed routes and the routes used depend on the source markets at the time, the availability of freights, and the restrictions imposed by different ports. However, it seems that there are more turtles being directly shipped to South China than previously.

Although some species command a much higher price than others, the food turtle trade in South China is indiscriminate in that all available chelonian species are consumed. Most of the Asian species have been observed in food markets in South China and recently small numbers of North American turtles have also been seen. It is likely that some of the traders are exploring new sources, such as North and South America, to supply food turtles.

The shells of turtles (usually plastrons from hardshelled species and carapaces from softshells) are widely used in Traditional Chinese Medicine. No data are available for the turtle shell trade in China and Hong Kong, although bags of plastrons and carapaces can be found in Chinese medicine markets in South China. Turtle jelly, in which one of the main ingredients is turtle shell, has become popular in Hong Kong and there are chain stores specializing in this "health food." From 1992–98, Taiwan imported more than 1186 tons of turtle shell (both hardshelled and softshell species) from mainland China and Southeast Asian countries such as Indonesia and Singapore.

Keeping turtles as pets is quite popular in both Hong Kong and Taiwan, but has just started in mainland China where the present pet trade is insignificant. The bulk of the pet market is comprised of a handful of North American species, of which vast numbers of captive-bred hatchlings are imported from the United States and Japan. Small numbers of exotic turtles and tortoises also turn up in pet shops in Hong Kong and Taiwan. There is, however, a global market for rare species. Hong Kong and Taiwan re-export a small number of rare Asian turtle species to USA, Europe, and Japan. Some of these species are of Chinese origin, while others arrive in China or Hong Kong from other Asian countries with shipments of food turtles, but are picked out by the pet dealers. Recently, a dealer in Shanghai has started a business exporting turtles directly to western countries and Japan.

Species in Trade

Nearly all species of Asian chelonians are consumed in South China. The primary species in the food trade are *Pelodiscus sinensis*, *Cuora amboinensis*, *Malayemys subtrijuga*, *Siebenrockiella crassicollis*, *Cyclemys* spp., *Orlitia borneensis*, *Notochelys platynota*, *Indotestudo elongata*, and *Amyda cartilaginea*. Species composition in the food market changes frequently. For instance, *Geoemyda yuwonoi*, *Morenia petersi*, and *Lissemys punctata* were common in the market a few years ago, but have now more or less disappeared. *Chinemys reevesii* and *Mauremys mutica* were the commonest species in the 1970s and early 1980s before the influx of turtles from other Asian countries. Now *C. reevesii* appears to have disappeared completely from the food markets.

The primary species identified in the Taiwan plastron trade are *C. amboinensis*, *M. subtrijuga*, and *S. crassicollis*. Many *C. reevesii* plastrons are also imported. The primary species used in the plastron trade in Hong Kong and China markets are not known.

The pet trade can be separated into species for sale in the Northeast Asia subregion and those leaving the Northeast Asian subregion. The local pet market is dominated by hatchlings of captive-bred North American turtles (*Trachemys scripta elegans*, *Graptemys* spp., and *Pseudemys* spp.), and *Ocadia sinensis*. A small number of turtles are also exported from Northeast Asia for the pet trade. This trade normally targets a multitude of rare or new species or varieties.

Effects of Trade on Native Turtle Populations

Due to the long history of consuming chelonians in mainland China, particularly in the southern part, wild populations of the once common chelonian species have long been affected and are believed to have declined drastically. Some of the highly restricted species that were only discovered in the last 15 years are particularly sought after by dealers to supply overseas collectors and researchers. Species like *Cuora aurocapitata* and *C. mccordi* are further threatened by the food trade because they resemble *C. trifasciata* and command a very high price in food markets.

In Hong Kong, nearly all the turtles consumed are imported from mainland China or other Asian countries. Hence, with the exception of *C. trifasciata*, the collecting pressure is not intense. *Cuora trifasciata* commands a very high price in both food markets and the pet trade. Illegal turtle traps have been found in both protected and unprotected areas in Hong Kong. The impact of such trapping on the local population of *C. trifasciata* is not yet known.

In Taiwan, *Pelodiscus sinensis* is the only turtle consumed and much of this demand is met by animals produced from local turtle farms. The impact of trade on wild populations of *P. sinensis* is not considered to be serious. There are several farms that produce hatchlings of *Ocadia sinensis* for the pet trade and for release. Often, adults from the wild are collected to supplement the breeding stock. This small scale collecting does not appear to have a major negative impact on *O. sinensis* in Taiwan.

In both Hong Kong and Taiwan, large numbers of hatchling *Trachemys scripta elegans* are sold as pets. When these hatchlings grow up, the owners often release them into the wild and this species has become established in lowland water bodies in both countries. The impact of this exotic turtle on the local chelonian fauna is unclear, but it may have caused or contributed to the decline in the sympatric populations of *Chinemys reevesii* in Hong Kong.

Current Regulations and Controls

The Northeast Asia subregion has laws in place to protect both the native chelonians and CITES-listed species. In China, *Testudo horsfieldii* and *Pelochelys bibroni* (current name = *P. cantorii*) are listed as Class I National Protected Wild Animals. *Cuora trifasciata*, *C. yunnanensis*, *Geoemyda spengleri*, *Manouria impressa*, and *Trionyx steindachneri* (current name = *Palea steindachneri*) are in Class II. Collecting of and trade in Class I protected species is only allowed with the permission from the central government. For Class II species, permission from the provincial government is required. CITES Appendix I species are treated as Class I National Protected Wild Animals and similarly, CITES Appendix II species are regarded as Class II National Protected.

In Hong Kong, all native chelonians are protected. The trade and possession of CITES-listed species is only allowed with permission from the Agriculture, Fisheries and Conservation Department. In Taiwan, local populations of *C. reevesii*, *C. flavomarginata*, and *M. mutica* are protected, as are all CITES-listed species.

However, some of the laws are not clearly defined and subject to different interpretations. Enforcement is not adequate due to the following:

• identification problems and lack of holding facilities;
• general lack of well-trained staff;
• inadequate inspection of the content and labeling of imported and trans-shipped turtles (some are labeled as seafood);
• lack of understanding of the seriousness of this issue among officials;
• enforcement responsibility is often divided and unclear between departments.

Priority Projects

1. Produce identification guides and develop identification skills and networks for law enforcement staff.

2. Shipments of live turtles should adhere to the International Air Transport Association (IATA) regulations and guidelines on the transport of live turtles.

3. Live turtles coming into the subregion should be inspected to verify the labeled contents of the shipments and to check the health certificates (in the case of Hong Kong and Taiwan).

4. Sources of funding to undertake adequate enforcement need to be identified. The possibility of having a tax (certain portion of which has to go back to the law enforcement department) on the import and export of live turtles can be explored.

5. Trade volume, species composition, consumption centers, and trends should be monitored.

6. Existing laws and regulations should be reviewed using the most up-to-date information.

7. Conservation programs, particularly *ex-situ* breeding for *Cuora aurocapitata*, *C. mccordi*, and *C. zhoui*, and also *in-situ* conservation measures should be established for priority species.

8. Herbal medicine alternatives to turtle shell should be explored.

9. The exact medicinal and/or tonic properties of turtle shells and hard-shelled turtles should be examined.

10. Findings and recommendations of this workshop should be presented to all the governments involved, particularly China, and all relevant non-government organizations.

11. Promote education projects and materials to raise the profile of turtles with school groups, Buddhists, and the general public.

12. Utilize media coverage and launch a global marketing campaign.

13. Possibility of farming native hard-shelled turtles, together with an accreditation system should be explored.

14. Placement of confiscated animals, such as for use in educational programs for schools and communities, founder stocks for *ex-situ* breeding programs, release back to the wild, and possible commercial use, should be addressed and a network of recognized placement centers be established.

15. Field research and inventory studies should be encouraged.

16. A gene bank of Asian turtles should be established.

Asian Turtle Trade: Proceedings of a Workshop on Conservation and Trade of Freshwater Turtles and Tortoises in Asia
P.P. van Dijk, B.L. Stuart, and A.G.J. Rhodin, Eds.
Chelonian Research Monographs 2:55–57 • © 2000 by Chelonian Research Foundation

Overview of Turtle Trade in Cambodia

Touch Seang Tana[1], Prak Leang Hour[2], Chul Thach[3], and Lieng Sopha[1]
with contributions from
Chun Sophat[4], Hout Piseth[5], and Heng Kimchay[6]

[1]*Fisheries Department, Ministry of Agriculture, Forestry and Fisheries, Norodom Boulevard, Phnom Penh, Cambodia*
[Fax: 855-23-427048; E-mail: tana@forum.org.kh];
[2]*Fishery Office, Kampong Chhnang Province, Cambodia;*
[3]*Fishery Office, Kampong Thom Province, Cambodia;*
[4]*CITES Office, MAFF, Norodom Boulevard, P.O. Box 582, Phnom Penh, Cambodia*
[Fax: 855-23-215470; E-mail: bigcatch@bigpond.com.kh];
[5]*Protected Areas Office, Department of Nature Conservation and Protection, Ministry of Environment,*
Sihanouk Boulevard, Phnom Penh, Cambodia [E-mail: wwfcam@bigpond.com.kh];
[6]*Wildlife Protection Office, Forestry Department, 40 Norodom Boulevard, Phnom Penh, Cambodia*
[E-mail: wpo@forum.org.kh]

Patterns of Trade

Local subsistence use of turtles is widespread in Cambodia, and probably not species-specific.

There is a domestic trade in turtles, which are used for meat, eggs, Khmer and Chinese medicine, decoration, pets, and Buddhist release. However, the domestic trade is considered minor when compared to the much larger international trade.

A legal international trade is run through KAMFIMEX, a government export agency for aquatic products, whereby turtles are shipped by air from Phnom Penh directly to Guangzhou or Hong Kong, China. This trade is restricted by an annual quota and by the size of individual turtles, which must be larger than 1 kg to be legally exported. China Group Company Ltd. under KAMFIMEX's license carried out the first legal international export of live reptiles (turtles, water snakes, and venomous snakes) in the fishing season of 1998–99. Reportedly the total exported quantity of reptiles was 200 tons, in which turtles were estimated to comprise 50%. In the fishing season 1999–2000, the same live reptile quantity has already been approved for export to China through the same legal procedure.

The illegal international trade of Cambodian turtles to Vietnam is much larger. Approximately one or two major middlemen in each province accumulate turtles from hunters, and about four or five major middlemen work in Phnom Penh. Turtles are sent to middlemen in Phnom Penh, and from there transported across the Vietnamese border via river or road through Kaam Sam Nor and Chrey Thom, or via the main road through Kompong Cham or Svay Rieng.

Few data exist on illegal trade of turtles to Thailand, although without further information it is presumed to be much less significant than the trade to Vietnam.

Species in Trade

Turtles are usually collected by using bamboo traps, hunting dogs, and by burning brush. Hunters apparently collect all species, and the vast majority of collected turtles are probably sold. Turtles that are harvested but not sold because of a lack of demand from traders are probably consumed by the hunters. Table 1 reviews the status of species that are known or suspected to occur in Cambodia.

Current Regulations and Controls Concerning Tortoises and Freshwater Turtles

• Law No. 33 (Department of Fisheries): main law on use of aquatic animals.
• Law No. 35 (Department of Forestry): main law on use of land animals.
• Declaration No. 359 (Ministry of Agriculture, Forestry and Fisheries): protect "nationally threatened" wild animal species. No turtles are currently listed, but could be added in the future if they are shown to be threatened.
• Joint Declaration (Ministry of Agriculture, Forestry and Fisheries and Ministry of Environment) No. 1563: wild animals cannot be hunted with traps, explosive materials, or poison, nor can wild animals or their products be sold, commercialized, exploited, or transported, nor can wild animals or their products be served in restaurants.
• Government Decision 01 (Department of Forestry): to end illegal trade in land animals.
• Government Decision 02 (Department of Fisheries): to end illegal trade in aquatic animals.
• Tortoises, specifically *Indotestudo elongata* and *Manouria impressa* (if it occurs in Cambodia), are listed in CITES Appendix II. Cambodia has been a signatory member of the CITES convention since 1997.

Recommendations to Improve Turtle Conservation in Cambodia

1. Studies are needed to determine trade volumes of turtles in order to set regulations for controlling the trade. Likewise, studies are needed to determine which species in Cambodia should be protected.

Figure 1. *Hieremys annandalii*, the yellow-headed temple turtle, a species for which the Cambodian population is probably the most important in the Indochina region. Photo by Peter Paul van Dijk.

2. Programs and funds are needed to strengthen the capacity of inspectors and other trade enforcers.

3. Trade enforcers should initially focus their attention on the middlemen working through Phnom Penh.

4. Education and awareness programs are needed. Programs using the influence of Buddhism or the support of the King or Prime Minister in protecting turtles and other wildlife would probably be the most successful campaigns.

5. Facilities for quarantining and rehabilitating confiscated turtles are needed.

6. An identification guide to Cambodian turtles in Khmer language is needed; one is currently in preparation.

7. Important habitats for turtles need to be identified and the protection of those habitats needs to be improved.

LITERATURE CITED

ERNST, C.H., AND BARBOUR, R.W. 1989. Turtles of the World. Smithsonian Institution Press, Washington DC, 313 pp.

IVERSON, J.B. 1992. A Revised Checklist with Distribution Maps of the Turtles of the World. Privately printed, 363 pp.

Table 1. The status of turtle species known or suspected to occur in Cambodia. Global distributions summarized from Ernst and Barbour (1989) and Iverson (1992), and status of species in Thailand, Laos, and Vietnam summarized from Indochina subregional group discussions at the conference. UR = Uncertain species identification; UT = Uncertain if species is traded; Trade = tentative assessment of relative trade levels in Cambodia based on the numbers in trade rather than an assessment of the impact on wild populations – identifications that went towards this assessment were very tentative, and very few data are available for most of Cambodia; Population = suspected importance of the Cambodian population relative to Thai, Lao, and Vietnamese populations in relation to its size and likely value for conservation of the species in the region; Habitat and Occurrence = habitat and preferences in Indochina and likelihood of occurrence in Cambodia. Country Codes: BD = Bangladesh; CN = China / S.CN = southern China; ID = Indonesia; IN = India; JP = Japan; KH = Cambodia; LA = Laos; MM = Myanmar; MY = Malaysia / W.MY = Peninsular (West) Malaysia; PN = Papua New Guinea; NP = Nepal; PH = Philippines; SG = Singapore; TH = Thailand; VN = Vietnam / N.VN = northern Vietnam.

Trade	Population	Global Distribution	Habitat and Occurrence
Platysternon megacephalum			
UR	Low	LA, VN, KH?, CN, TH, MM	Probably in mountains in northeastern Cambodia, but would be a small population because of limited habitat.
Batagur baska			
UT	High	VN, KH, IN, MY, ID	Extinct in Vietnam and Thailand, and probably very rare or extinct in Cambodia.
Cuora amboinensis			
High	High	LA, VN, KH, TH, MM, SG, MY, IN, PH, ID	Widespread in lowlands, both in water and land. Cambodia has a large lowland area with a low density of people, and so probably has the largest population of this species in Indochina.
Cuora galbinifrons			
UR-High	—	LA, VN, S.CN	Central Laos, central and northern Vietnam, and southern China. Unlikely to occur in Cambodia.
Cuora trifasciata			
UR-Low	—	LA, VN, S.CN	Known from mountains of northern Vietnam and southern China, probably also in mountains of northern Laos. Unlikely to occur in Cambodia.
Cyclemys dentata complex			
Low	Medium	LA, VN, KH, TH, MY, ID	Widespread in hills, forested streams and some lowlands in Indochina, including

Table 1. (*continued*).

			Cambodia. Probably a large population in Cambodia, but such habitat still remains extensive in Laos, Vietnam, and Thailand.
Geoemyda spengleri			
—	—	VN, S.CN	Known from mountains of northern Vietnam and southern China. Unlikely to occur in Cambodia.
Heosemys grandis			
Medium	Medium	LA, VN, KH, TH, W.MY	Wetlands from lowlands to low hill terrain, thus extensive habitat remains in Cambodia. Thai population similar or larger than Cambodian population, but Cambodian population probably larger than Lao or Vietnamese populations.
Hieremys annandalii (Fig. 1)			
Medium	High	LA, VN, KH, TH, W.MY	Predominantly lowland wetlands, not hill areas and fast flowing streams or rivers. Such habitat correlates closely with where people live, so exploitation is likely to be even higher than *Heosemys*. Population probably nearing extinction in Vietnam, greatly reduced in Laos, and low in Thailand. Cambodian population probably most important in the region.
Malayemys subtrijuga			
High	Medium	LA, VN, KH, TH, MY, ID	Probably the most abundant turtle species in Cambodia. Lowland species, so plenty of habitat in Cambodia. Vietnamese population very low, Lao population still widespread but undoubtedly declining, and Thai population large.
Mauremys annamensis			
—	—	VN	Known only from central Vietnam. Unlikely to occur in Cambodia.
Mauremys mutica			
UR-High	—	VN, S.CN, JP	Known from mountains of northern Vietnam and southern China. Unlikely to occur in Cambodia.
Ocadia sinensis			
—	—	VN, S.CN	Known from mountains of northern Vietnam and southern China. Unlikely to occur in Cambodia.
Pyxidea mouhotii			
UR-Low	—	LA, VN, MM, CN, IN	Central Laos, north and central Vietnam, China, and Myanmar in low hills and limestone karst. Unlikely in Cambodia because of little available habitat.
Sacalia quadriocellata			
—	—	LA, VN, S.CN	Known from mountains of northern and central Vietnam and southern China, and a limited area of eastern Laos. Unlikely to occur in Cambodia.
Siebenrockiella crassicollis			
Low	High	LA, VN, KH, TH, MM, MY, SG, ID	Lowland species. Lao population has not yet been found, Vietnamese population probably almost extinct, Thai population thriving but under threat. Cambodian population potentially large, and might be most important population in the region. Best global populations in Malaysia and Indonesia.
Indotestudo elongata			
Medium	High	IN, NP, MM, CN?, TH, LA, VN, KH, MY	Lowland species of open forest habitats. Probably the second most common species in Cambodia. Vietnamese population very low, Lao and Thai populations still reasonably large. Cambodian population probably very large.
Manouria emys			
UR-Low	—	IN, BD, MM, TH, MY, ID	Found in the region only in peninsular, western, and northern Thailand, and is unlikely to occur in Cambodia.
Manouria impressa			
Low	Low	LA, VN, CN, W.MY, KH?	Probably in mountains of eastern Cambodia, but population small because of limited habitat.
Amyda cartilaginea			
Medium	Medium	LA, VN, KH, TH, MM, MY, SG, ID	Widespread in many habitats, from lowlands to mid elevations. Thai population good, Lao population widespread and still numerous, Vietnamese population probably very low. Cambodian populations likely to be very good.
Dogania subplana			
—	—	TH, MM, MY, SG, ID	Found in the region only in peninsular and western Thailand. Unlikely to occur in Cambodia.
Palea steindachneri			
—	—	N.VN, S.CN	Known from mountains of northern Vietnam and southern China. Unlikely to occur in Cambodia.
Pelodiscus sinensis			
UR-Low	Low	VN, CN, JP, RU	Species found in northern Vietnam and China. Farmed in Vietnam, Thailand, and other Southeast Asian countries, and now many escaped populations in non-native areas. Unlikely to be found in Cambodia unless introduced from Thailand, Vietnam, or China for farming.
Pelochelys cantorii			
Low	High	IN, BD, MM, TH, LA, KH, VN, CN, MY, ID, PH, PN	Large lowland rivers. Vietnamese population probably extinct, Lao and Thai populations very small and nearing extinction. Cambodia suspected to have a good population, and might be the most important population in the region.

Asian Turtle Trade: Proceedings of a Workshop on Conservation and Trade of Freshwater Turtles and Tortoises in Asia
P.P. van Dijk, B.L. Stuart, and A.G.J. Rhodin, Eds.
Chelonian Research Monographs 2:58–62 • © 2000 by Chelonian Research Foundation

Conservation Status and Trade of Turtles in Laos

BRYAN L. STUART[1] AND ROBERT J. TIMMINS[2]

[1]*Wildlife Conservation Society Lao Program, P.O. Box 6712, Vientiane, Laos*
[Fax: 856-21-215400; E-mail: blstuart@unity.ncsu.edu];
[2]*25 Cradley Road, Cradley Heath, West Midlands, B64 6AG, United Kingdom*
[E-mail: rob@naturalists.freeserve.co.uk]

The turtle fauna of Laos (Lao PDR) has long remained poorly known. General wildlife and herpetological field surveys by several non-governmental organizations, particularly Wildlife Conservation Society (WCS), from 1993 to present have now confirmed the occurrence (Table 1) and general distributions of 13 species of turtles in Laos, and have also provided inferences on their conservation status. It was learned during these efforts that all species of turtles in Laos are threatened by varying levels of hunting for local subsistence, domestic consumption, and especially for international trade to Vietnam and China.

General Status of Turtles

A contingent of turtle species continue to survive in appropriate habitat throughout Laos, although their populations are probably quite reduced: *Platysternon megacephalum*, *Cyclemys dentata* complex, *Malayemys subtrijuga*, *Indotestudo elongata*, *Manouria impressa*, and *Amyda cartilaginea*.

A second suite of species are considered more susceptible to exploitation than the first, including *Cuora amboinensis*, *C. galbinifrons*, *Heosemys grandis*, and *Pyxidea mouhotii*. This higher level of threat is probably attributable to *P. mouhotii* and *C. galbinifrons* having naturally restricted ranges in the country prior to being threatened by collecting, and *C. amboinensis* and *H. grandis* being associated with habitat highly utilized by humans.

Hieremys annandalii and *Pelochelys cantorii* are very reduced in numbers from collection pressure, both because they are large-sized species and because they are associated with large river lowland habitat which also contain high densities of people. Only a few records exist in the country for both species, and they are presumed to be relatively rare.

Sacalia quadriocellata seems to have a restricted natural distribution in Laos, and so its status is unclear. There may be other species in this category which have not yet been recorded in Laos, such as *Mauremys mutica* and *Palea steindachneri*.

Lastly, there is a highly-prized and sought-after turtle for the international trade that is believed to be *Cuora trifasciata*, based on descriptions by villagers and by individuals of this species that turned up in the Vientiane Zoo in 1996 and bore the same, almost legendary, local name

(Timmins and Khounboline, 1999). This turtle is very affected by collecting and is nearing extirpation in the country, although the identification of this reported species as *Cuora trifasciata* remains to be confirmed by examination of a specimen of known Lao provenance.

Conservation and Management

Legal Status. — The Division of Forest Resource Conservation (DFRC) within the Department of Forestry, Vientiane, is responsible for writing and enforcing legislation protecting wildlife, specifically by allocating species to one of three Lao Wildlife Management Categories. DFRC is also responsible for central level management of the national protected areas (National Biodiversity Conservation Areas or NBCAs, see below).

All trade in turtles is legal, as no turtles are truly protected in Laos. Three local names of turtle are listed in the Lao Wildlife Management Categories, with the intention of protecting them from collection and trade. However, local names are often incongruent with scientific taxonomy (for example, juveniles and adults of the same species sometimes bear different names) and most local names vary regionally. Therefore, the local names listed in the legislation are unlikely to be recognized throughout the species' range in the country, nor are the names likely to protect the scientific taxon as a whole. In reality, no scientific species are truly protected by law in Laos. This legislation is currently under review by the Lao government. Laos is not party to the CITES convention.

Species Management. — No species management programs exist for turtles in Laos.

Habitat Conservation and Control Measures. — Since 1993, the government of Laos has officially designated 20 areas as National Biodiversity Conservation Areas (NBCAs), which cover approximately 12.5% of the country's surface. Most of the NBCAs were designated on the basis of forest cover and indirect evidence of wildlife populations, and many maintain large areas of intact forest. However, the NBCAs are "multiple use areas," and continue to support villages within their boundaries. In reality, little to no protection exists in most of these areas because of considerable confusion and ignorance of the laws and boundaries, as well as a lack of training, resources, manpower, and infrastructure by governing and enforcing bodies. The international borders of Vietnam and China with Laos are porous, so

Table 1. List of scientific and common names of turtle species known and suspected to occur in Laos.

Scientific Name	Common Name
Confirmed Species	
Platysternon megacephalum	Big-headed turtle
Cuora amboinensis	Southeast Asian box turtle
Cuora galbinifrons	Indochinese box turtle
Cyclemys dentata complex	Asian leaf turtles
Heosemys grandis	Asian giant pond turtle
Hieremys annandalii	Yellow-headed temple turtle
Malayemys subtrijuga	Malayan snail-eating turtle
Pyxidea mouhotii	Keeled box turtle
Sacalia quadriocellata	Four-eyed turtle
Amyda cartilaginea	Southeast Asian softshell
Pelochelys cantorii	Asian giant softshell
Indotestudo elongata	Elongated tortoise
Manouria impressa	Impressed tortoise
Unconfirmed But Suspected Species	
Cuora trifasciata	Chinese three-striped box turtle
Siebenrockiella crassicollis	Black marsh turtle
Introduced Exotic Species	
None recorded	

transboundary wildlife trading and poaching continues mostly unchecked. Despite the lack of protection within these areas, their vastness in combination with the relatively low density of people within them probably provides the best protection afforded to Lao turtles by keeping populations inaccessible to collectors. Unfortunately some of the richest and least accessible areas lie along the Lao-Vietnam border, and these are close to the major wildlife trade routes. Also very few of the lowland large river habitats fall within NBCA boundaries, and those that do continue to maintain high densities of people and subsequently wildlife populations there suffer from heavy hunting pressure.

An upsurge in efforts to control wildlife trading in recent years by officials has resulted in fewer turtles being openly seen in most markets, including the major wildlife markets at Ban Lak (52) in Vientiane Municipality and at Ban Lak (20) in Bolikhamxai Province. It is unclear whether trading in these markets has been actually reduced, or if the trade has only been driven underground and less visible. The latter scenario seems more likely.

Use and Trade of Lao Turtles

No data are available on domestic or international trade volumes of turtles in Laos, as no trade monitoring studies have been conducted. Rather, trade records of turtles represent brief visits to markets and villages. Data were collected on wild turtles in the field, captive turtles found in local markets and villages, and remains of turtles found in villages during the course of general wildlife and herpetological field surveys by several non-governmental organizations, particularly WCS, from 1993 to present. These data were used to confirm occurrence (Table 1) and general distributions of Lao turtles, and they also provide the baseline for inferences on their conservation status.

Additional data on collection and trade of turtles were compiled from interviewing residents of 23 villages from 8 sites during the course of herpetological surveys. These interviews usually involved older hunters that had lived most of their lives in the area. Earlier in these studies, the interviewees were asked to select the species they knew to occur in their area from a series of color photographs of the regional turtles, which included some photographs of distinct species that do not occur in the region. This method was abandoned after it became apparent that the villagers had considerable difficulty in recognizing turtles from photographs, perhaps because they were not used to seeing turtles in only two dimensions, or because the characters which they use for distinguishing the turtles were not always apparent in the photographs. Interviewees were also asked the following basic questions:

1. How many different kinds of turtles live around here, and what are their names?

For each name presented:

2. Do you catch this turtle for food or for sale?

3. Compared to ten years ago, today do you find as many of these turtles, fewer of these turtles, or more of these turtles?

In some cases, scientific names could be assigned to the provided local names when live turtles or parts were encountered and recognized by the interviewees. However, folk taxonomy of turtles in Laos is not always congruent with scientific taxonomy, as sometimes juveniles and adults of the same species have different local names, and sometimes more than one species shares the same local name. For these reasons, the results of the interviewees are not reported below by suspected scientific name, but rather by treating each reported name simply as a "kind" of turtle, recognizing that each "kind" does not necessarily relate to a scientific taxon.

Records of collection by local people were obtained during the surveys for every species of turtle now known to occur in Laos. Additional evidence that every species of turtle in Laos is involved in collection comes from summarizing the answers of villagers asked whether each kind of turtle they recognize is collected for food, for sale or trade, or not collected. This question was asked of 92 reported kinds of turtles during interviews. Of the 92 kinds, 90 (98%) were reported to be collected for food or for sale or trade. The remaining 2% may not even represent legitimate taxa, for example, they may refer to juveniles of a species. These answers support the recorded evidence that every species of turtle in Laos has value as a food or trade commodity.

Three outcomes for turtles collected by local people in Laos have been identified, and these are illustrated in Fig. 1.

Local subsistence, where turtles are not sold or traded but rather consumed directly by the collectors or their community for food and/or medicinal purposes. Local subsistence use of wild-collected turtles is widespread throughout the country, and is not species-specific. This use has most certainly been practiced for a very long time, and

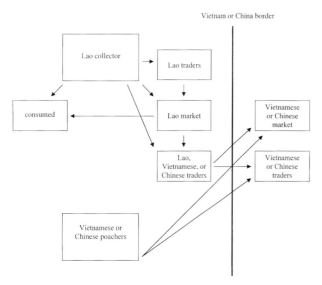

Vietnam or China border

Figure 1. Generalized movements of collected turtles in Laos. Arrows indicate the direction of movement of the turtles or their parts. Transfer of turtles between parties can be a result of direct purchase and sale, or from a trade of wares.

probably has had long-term effects in depressing populations throughout most of the country prior to any domestic or international trade.

Domestic consumption trade refers to the purchase, sale, or trade of Lao turtles for food and/or medicinal purposes, where the turtles or their products are consumed or utilized within the country. This use is more species-specific than local subsistence. Softshell turtles (*Amyda cartilaginea* and probably *Pelochelys cantorii*) are highly valued for their meat, and *Malayemys subtrijuga* and *Indotestudo elongata* are frequently seen in markets, probably because they remain relatively two of the most common species in the country. Such turtles are sold in markets directly by collectors or via Lao traders who transport them from villages. In the markets they are sold to semi-rural and urban Lao people, although some of these turtles are probably purchased in the markets by traders for the international trade in Vietnam and China. In many cases, middlemen may sell animals directly to end-users such as restaurants. This domestic consumption trade usually involves live turtles. Sometimes shells of *Manouria impressa* are sold to Lao traders and turn up in specialty shops in the vicinity of Louangphabang, and shells of turtles (mostly *Heosemys grandis*) were reported by villagers in the vicinity of Thakhek to be sold to traders in the market there. The eventual destination and use of these shells is unclear, although villagers have reported that the *Manouria* shells are eventually exported to China.

International consumption trade refers to the purchase, sale, trade, or transboundary incursionist poaching of Lao turtles for food and/or medicinal purposes, where the turtles or their products are consumed or utilized outside of the country. This international trade is the major outcome for most collected turtles in the country. Some species have been identified as being very valuable to the international trade, for example, *Cuora galbinifrons* (Fig. 2) and *Platysternon megacephalum* (Fig. 3), and notably a very

high-priced turtle that is probably *Cuora trifasciata*. Most traded turtles originating in Laos pass into Vietnam, and to an unknown extent, directly into China, via an extensive trade network which has been developed throughout the country by Lao, Vietnamese, and Chinese traders (Fig. 4). There is also direct collecting by Vietnamese and Chinese poachers within the borders of Laos. It seems that more turtles move from Laos into Vietnam than into China, but this conclusion may be an artifact of more extensive field investigations in central and southern Laos than in northern Laos. There appears to be some demand for turtles from Thai traders, although the influence of Chinese and especially Vietnamese traders is far greater. Lao villagers consistently report that a demand for turtles from Vietnamese traders developed about 10 years ago, and since then turtles have been collected at much higher levels than before; previously turtles were collected mostly for local subsistence or for trade in local markets. Live adults, sometimes juveniles, and to a lesser extent shells of post-consumed animals, are either sold by villagers to traders or are traded for wares such as monosodium glutamate (MSG), salt, clothing, shoes, batteries, cutlery, gasoline, machetes, and so forth. Without question, the unregulated export of turtles to Vietnam and China is the greatest threat to these species in Laos.

There is some evidence that processing plants for other wildlife products occur in Laos, although little information is available on this, and any processing of turtles in the country for the medicinal trade is currently unknown.

Figure 2. Special hunting dog owned by a turtle hunter locating *Cuora galbinifrons* in leaf litter in the field. Photo by BLS.

Figure 3. Big-headed turtle, *Platysternon megacephalum*. Photo by Peter Paul van Dijk.

Major routes of wildlife trade into Vietnam include Route 7 from Xiangkhouang to Nghe An, Route 8 through Ban Lak (20), Route 9 through Lao Bao to Dong Ha, and Route 12 in Khammouan Province. Residents of villages along the Lao-Vietnamese border, particularly those close to these major exit points, are very aware of the value of turtles in the international trade, but the effects of trade probably lessen moving westward and further from these exit points. Routes of wildlife traded into China are unclear, but Phongsali and Louang-Namtha are suspected to be significant outlets.

Although there are three main outcomes for collected turtles in Laos, the factors which determine whether they will be consumed, traded domestically, or traded internationally are complex, and certainly involve a number of factors, including the proximity of the collector to trade routes as well as the value of that species on the international market.

No pet trade of turtles exists in Laos other than occasional hatchling red-eared sliders (*Trachemys scripta elegans*) being offered for sale in aquarium shops in Vientiane. No farming operations of turtles are known to exist in Laos.

Population Trends

Wildlife inventories of Laos resumed in 1993; these have been limited to short-term studies that have covered many areas. No long-term monitoring programs based in a single area have been initiated for turtles, or any other wildlife species. However, evidence that turtle populations have declined considerably in Laos comes from an extreme paucity of field records during those 6 years of surveys by wildlife biologists. Only approximately 20 records of turtles incidentally encountered in the field were accumulated during 35 man-months of general bird and mammal surveys by 5 international wildlife biologists. During 12 man-months of herpetofaunal surveys by one person (BLS), only 4 records of turtles incidentally encountered in the field (not counting those found on two occasions with a special hunt-

ing dog) were accumulated during active searches for general herpetofauna. However, passive methods such as traps were not used during any of these surveys, nor were the highly effective hunting dogs regularly used. Certainly more records would have been accumulated with these methods; for example, three days that were spent with a hunter using a hunting dog during the herpetofaunal surveys accumulated 4 additional field records of turtles (one individual of the *C. dentata* complex and three *C. galbinifrons*). Regardless, considering the amount of time that these field workers spent in remote forested areas in Laos, the paucity of incidental records is strong evidence that turtle populations have been reduced to low levels throughout the country.

Additional evidence that turtle populations have declined considerably comes from asking villagers whether each kind of turtle they recognize is perceived to be easier to find, of the same abundance, or harder to find when compared to 10 years ago. This question was asked for 61 reported "kinds" of turtles during the course of the interviews. Of the 61 kinds, 37 (60%) were reported to be rarer today than 10 years ago, 23 (38%) were reported to be of the same abundance today as 10 years ago, and 1 (2%) was reported to be more abundant today than 10 years ago (Fig. 5). These perceptions of villagers also suggest that populations of turtles in Laos have declined in recent years.

Figure 4. Large sack of *Platysternon megacephalum* being transported by a cross-border Vietnamese trader coming from a Lao village in Nakay-Nam Theun National Biodiversity Conservation Area, November 1998. Photo by BLS.

Suggestions for Improving
Turtle Conservation in Laos

1. Revision of the national wildlife laws of Laos to afford protection to all turtles, and dissemination of these laws in a format useable to provincial and district Forestry staff, border police, and local people. A useable format will require photographs that can be linked with scientific names and standardized Lao names; a Lao language photographic guide to the native turtle fauna is currently in preparation. Wildlife laws are currently under revision in Laos.

2. Greater understanding, closer monitoring, and measures based on appropriate legislation to reduce trade and its routes are essential.

3. Increased security measures preventing the entry of illegal Vietnamese and Chinese poachers into the country. Foreign traders do provide benefits for Lao villagers, and this increased security measure is not intended to exclude those who enter and exit the country with supervision.

4. Education and awareness programs on the importance of and threats to turtles.

5. Furthering efforts to protect NBCAs from development and exploitation, namely by reworking and enforcing legislation which prevents building roads into protected areas or in any similar way making these vast, remote areas more accessible to collectors.

6. Captive breeding needs to be encouraged in the international zoo community for at least the Chinese three-striped box turtle, *Cuora trifasciata*. The species is likely to be very soon extirpated in Laos, and possibly throughout

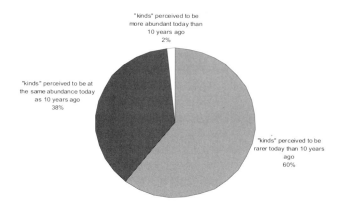

Figure 5. Cumulative perceptions of residents of 15 villages throughout Laos when asked about the present abundance of each "kind" of turtle they recognize in their area compared to its abundance ten years ago.

its entire range. Sufficient intact habitat probably remains in its suspected range in Laos, and captive populations of this species could form a basis for future reintroduction programs. Any captive breeding activity of *C. trifasciata* in Laos would have to circumvent the high risk of theft of the stock. Other species might also warrant captive breeding to ensure long-term conservation of Lao populations.

LITERATURE CITED

TIMMINS, R.J. AND KHOUNBOLINE, K. 1999. Occurrence and trade of the golden turtle, *Cuora trifasciata*, in Laos. Chelonian Conservation and Biology 3(3):441-447.

Asian Turtle Trade: Proceedings of a Workshop on Conservation and Trade of Freshwater Turtles and Tortoises in Asia
P.P. van Dijk, B.L. Stuart, and A.G.J. Rhodin, Eds.
Chelonian Research Monographs 2:63–73 • © 2000 by Chelonian Research Foundation

Status and Conservation of Tortoises and Freshwater Turtles in Vietnam

Douglas B. Hendrie[1]

[1]*Cuc Phuong Conservation Project,*
Fauna & Flora International, P.O. Box 78, Hanoi, Vietnam
[Fax: 844-943-2254; E-mail: cpcp@fpt.vn]

Vietnam stretches over 1500 km from north to south, covers an area of 332,000 km² and is inhabited by approximately 80 million people. Vietnam encompasses a wide variety of habitats, ranging from the tropical lowlands of the Mekong delta to the temperate mountain areas of the northwest. More than 100 established plus proposed protected areas cover about 20,000 km² or about 6% of the country's surface; about half this area represents natural habitat (MacKinnon, 1997). Related to this diversity of habitat types and the presence of several distinct mountain areas, Vietnam harbors a wide diversity of animal and plant species, including 23 species of tortoises and freshwater turtles (Table 1).

Conservation and Management

Wildlife Protection Agencies. — Responsibility for monitoring and enforcing legal protection of wildlife species rests with the Forest Protection Department (FPD), which is under the Ministry of Agriculture and Rural Development. The FPD includes the National Parks and Protected Area Management division which implements forest protection, and the CITES management authority office.

Research Institutions. — Recent wildlife research concerning turtle biology, conservation, and trade has been carried out by a variety of persons and institutes. These include Le Xuan Canh, Deputy Director, and Nguyen Van Sang, Herpetologist, at the Institute of Ecology and Biological Resources (IEBR), and Le Dien Duc at the Center for Natural Resources Management and Environmental Studies (CRES). The Cuc Phuong Conservation Project, administered by Fauna & Flora International, runs an active turtle conservation and research project in cooperation with Cuc Phuong National Park and the National Forest Protection Department.

Legal Status. — Generally, turtles receive little protection in Vietnam. Although nine species are listed in the Vietnam Red Data Book of Endangered Wildlife, none of these species except *Indotestudo elongata* and *Pelochelys cantorii* (as *P. bibroni*) are specifically protected under Vietnamese law.

Decree 18 (17 January 1992) affords protection to 60 animal species in Vietnam including two turtle species (*Indotestudo elongata* and *Pelochelys cantorii*). Both turtles are listed under category II which limits trade to scientific research, establishing breeding populations, and international exchange. Category II species require a collection permit issued by the Ministry of Agriculture and Rural Development (MARD). Directive 359 (1996) restricts trade in wildlife and animal parts, including prohibiting the sale of wildlife in restaurants.

Commerce and trade regulations require a permit issued at the provincial level for trade in any commodity, including wildlife. These regulations provide the legal basis for most trade seizures. Forest protection laws restrict hunting in National Parks and Protected Areas.

Species Management. — Very few conservation programs are aimed at protecting Vietnam's turtles within their habitat or from trade. The Cuc Phuong Conservation Project, in cooperation with Cuc Phuong National Park and the Forest Protection Department (both under the Ministry of Agriculture and Rural Development), established a Turtle Conservation and Ecology Project in 1998. The project is aimed at receiving and translocating turtles confiscated from the wildlife trade, carrying out research, increasing public awareness and education, and training of regional authorities.

The Institute for Ecology and Biological Resources (IEBR) is involved with an attempt to establish softshell turtle breeding farms, though details are not available. Softshell farming is relatively common in some regions of the country with small-time farmers receiving hatchlings from regional traders. It is unknown to what extent captive breeding has reduced (if at all) hunting of softshells from the wild. The success of such small-scale farming initiatives is unknown.

A recent trend in Vietnam is to establish "breeding farms" for animals confiscated from the trade. Unfortunately, these facilities have little expertise or knowledge about the requirements, maintenance, and care of animals confiscated from the trade. These new centers also tend to be poorly funded, and have limited conservation aims aside from "breeding" animals in captivity, or providing viewing opportunities for visitors.

Additionally, lack of understanding about the life history and ecology of chelonians often results in the mistaken perception that breeding turtles requires only a limited investment in time and will counterbalance the decline in wild populations. There are no known successful breeding projects for hard-shelled chelonians in operation in Vietnam.

Habitat Conservation. — Vietnam presently has designated 11 National Parks and 91 Protected Areas, together covering 13,425 km² or 4.1% of the country (MacKinnon, 1997). According to MacKinnon, Vietnam has sustained a serious and devastating loss of forests since 1945 when approximately 43% of the country remained forested. War, timber exploitation, conversion to agriculture, and subsis-

Table 1. List of turtle species found in Vietnam.

Indotestudo elongata	Elongated tortoise, Yellow tortoise
Manouria impressa	Impressed tortoise
Cuora amboinensis	Southeast Asian box turtle
Cuora galbinifrons	Indochinese box turtle
Cuora trifasciata	Chinese three-striped box turtle
Cyclemys tcheponensis;	
C. pulchristriata	Vietnamese leaf turtle
Geoemyda spengleri	Black-breasted leaf turtle
Heosemys grandis	Asian giant pond turtle
Hieremys annandalii	Yellow-headed temple turtle
Malayemys subtrijuga	Snail-eating turtle
Mauremys annamensis	Vietnamese pond turtle
Mauremys mutica	Vietnamese yellow pond turtle
Ocadia sinensis	Chinese striped-necked turtle
Pyxidea mouhotii	Keeled box turtle
Sacalia quadriocellata	Four-eyed turtle
Siebenrockiella crassicollis	Black marsh turtle
Platysternon megacephalum	Big-headed turtle
Amyda cartilaginea	Southeast Asian softshell
Palea steindachneri	Wattle-necked softshell turtle
Pelochelys cantorii	Asian giant softshell
Pelodiscus sinensis	Chinese softshell
Rafetus sp.	East Asian giant softshell turtle
Trachemys scripta	
(established exotic?)*	Red-eared slider

* No record of established populations of *Trachemys* in the wild, however, this turtle is present in the pet trade and found in Ho Chi Minh temple ponds and Hanoi markets.

tence use have reduced the nation's natural forests to less than 10% of the country. This would suggest a level and rate of habitat loss with substantial impacts upon the populations of forest-dwelling species, even without the added pressures of the wildlife trade.

Control Measures. — Enforcement of national wildlife protection laws is generally marginal and inconsistent. The National Forest Protection Department continues to invest in training of its rangers and increasing enforcement activities on the ground, however, the process is slow and unlikely to achieve the results needed to meet the substantial threat posed by the illegal wildlife trade in the near future.

Official records would suggest that trade confiscations account for only a small fraction of the trade in turtles if compared with trade figures estimated at border crossings and during market and other surveys carried out by TRAFFIC and other sources.

As evident in the figures presented in Table 2, these records do not indicate the species traded, a problem stemming from the limited knowledge and capacity of enforcement authorities to identify turtle species after trade seizures. Subsequently, monitoring activities by authorities do not produce meaningful data that can be used to direct enforcement efforts or respond to species conservation needs. This problem is compounded by lack of associated information pertaining to trade seizures that would pinpoint problem areas, identify significant traders, and provide information to other FPD regions that would enhance enforcement efforts.

CITES Enforcement. — Although Vietnam became a signatory of CITES in 1994, Vietnam has yet to pass legislation that would incorporate CITES provisions into national law. *Indotestudo elongata* and *Manouria impressa*, both CITES Appendix II listed species, are readily traded

both in regional markets and across border with China without permits as would be required under CITES.

National Trade and Use

Subsistence use of turtles has probably been reduced in recent years, as market values in the wildlife trade with China have provided a local incentive to sell turtles to traders rather than consume them locally. This change has not been widely studied, though regional surveys have shown that nearly all turtles that are collected are sold, rather than consumed locally.

Additionally, in some areas (e.g., Muong minority communities), encountering a turtle was considered bad luck in the past and turtles were largely left alone. However, the prospects of income have overshadowed any notion of superstition in many areas where turtles were previously avoided or left alone. Hunters using dogs or deliberately setting out after rain to find turtles now report a significant decline in the number of turtles found. Most turtles are now found opportunistically while collecting other forest product such as snails, mushrooms, bamboo, and banana trees.

The extent of use of turtles in traditional medicine in Vietnam is unknown, though Jenkins (1995) and others have reported shops in Hanoi offering medicinal products with turtle parts as an ingredient. It is possible that economic factors prevent the widespread use of turtle-based traditional medicines. If this is true, Vietnamese demand for traditional medicines with turtle ingredients is likely to increase as the economy continues to develop and the population acquires the financial means to buy expensive traditional medicines.

Maintaining turtles as pets is not widespread in Vietnam, though some people do keep turtles, both in urban

Table 2. Declared figures for volumes of hard-shelled and softshelled turtles in trade seized during 1998, by province. Source: Forest Protection Department.

	No. of Turtles	Weight (kg)
Testudinidae		
Bac Can	3	
Binh Dinh		20
Binh Phuoc	2	
Can Tho		380
Hoa Binh		242
TP Ho Chi Minh		229
Hanoi		1647
Lao Cai	32	
Nghe An		784
Thua Thien Hue	39	
Vinh Phuc	2	
Yen Bai	40	
TP Da Nang	65	
Gia Lai	142	
Trionychidae		
Binh Dinh		18
Bac Ninh		19
Hoa Binh		2.4
Ha Tinh		35
Kon Tum	6	
Nghe An		90
TP Da Nang	23	

centers like Hanoi as well as in rural areas. Dong Xuan market is the principal pet market in Hanoi and carries a variety of turtle species, sold mainly as pets. Most turtles in the pet trade tend to be juveniles or species of smaller size (like *Geoemyda spengleri*) that weigh little and therefore probably bring a higher price on the pet market than they would in the cross-border food and medicine trade.

Ho Chi Minh's Cau Mong market, which is now closed, was reported to have a much larger selection of turtles, including adults. Although there has been no detailed study of the market, nor its principal patrons, the availability of turtles in Ho Chi Minh markets is sharply in contrast with most other areas in the country where turtles are observed mainly in the trade pipeline to China. This may in part be attributed to the generally higher standard of living in HCM City, or related to different interests and values associated with turtles by people in the HCM region.

Softshell turtles are readily eaten by Vietnamese, and can be found on menus in restaurants throughout the country. Their high price limits local consumption, and like other turtles, provides an incentive for farmers and fishermen to sell them to local traders. Hard-shelled chelonians have not been observed as a food source in the north, though it is also possible that the apparent absence of significant domestic consumption results from the high trade value of turtles in the export market to China. Further study is warranted on the domestic consumption of hard-shelled chelonians in Vietnam.

International Trade

International trade in certain turtle species is permitted under certain conditions in Vietnam, which include licensing of exports. These export data are compiled by the CITES

Figure 1. Part of an illegal shipment of of at least six different species of hard-shelled turtles being transported from Ninh Binh Province, Vietnam, bound for Hanoi and eventual export. Confiscated in October 1999; total shipment ca. 36 kg. Photo by DBH.

office in the Forest Protection Department, even though many traded species are not listed in the CITES appendices. The numbers of turtles declared as exported from Vietnam from 1994 to 1999 are presented in Table 3.

There are no official records available for illegal cross-border trade (Fig. 1). Most references to volumes in trade originate from the Chinese side of the border (Li et al., 1996). Various figures have been used to describe the volume of trade in recent years, including unlikely estimates of 18 tons daily (Li and Li, 1997). While Vietnam's turtles are indeed being shipped across the border to China in large numbers, the country's native turtles are already depleted to well below the ability to sustain these daily export volumes, based upon the limited remaining natural habitat and historic human pressures upon most of these areas.

Other Comments

The composite picture of trade in Vietnam is far from complete. The absence of trade monitoring and lack of baseline information about distribution, population status, and other factors make it difficult to provide even a reasonably clear picture of the situation in Vietnam. However, from a series of "snapshots" it becomes painfully obvious that Vietnam's turtles are in trouble. It is clear that the level of trade, whether it is 18 tons a day or per year, threatens all but the most remote and remnant populations of turtle

Table 3. Numbers of turtles legally exported from Vietnam during the period 1994–99, by species. Source: FPD CITES office.

Species	1994	1995	1996	1997	1998	1999	Total
Manouria impressa	60	355	60	155	10	0	640
Cuora galbinifrons	300	1300	1410	1296	490	310	5106
Cuora amboinensis	550	3330	2390	2540	3760	870	13440
Pyxidea mouhotii	550	1465	1580	1290	630	1045	6560
Heosemys grandis	0	180	740	626	235	190	1971
Cyclemys tcheponensis	0	200	840	1155	160	800	3155
Malayemys subtrijuga	0	330	0	620	400	1270	2620
Sacalia quadriocellata	0	0	260	370	0	0	630
Platysternon megacephalum	0	0	50	0	0	0	50
Geoemyda spengleri	0	0	0	12	0	0	12
Siebenrockiella crassicollis	0	0	0	0	385	1130	1515
Total	1460	7160	7350	8064	6070	5615	35719

species in Vietnam. The combined effects of habitat loss and wildlife trade will not afford Vietnam the time to develop effective protection for natural areas, nor survive the development of a modern economy in which the luxury of conservation can be transferred into government planning and decision making. Vietnam's 23 turtle species require immediate and substantial intervention from both inside and outside the country if they are to survive in the wild.

Constraints and Opportunities for Conservation Action

Weaknesses

(1) Low capacity of enforcement and protection authorities, specifically:
  • Lack of knowledge about life history and ecology of turtles.
  • Lack of understanding of the law.
  • Inability to identify species.
  • Misperceptions about turtle trade and sustainability of exploitation.
(2) Lack of national scientific interest in turtles.
  • Subsequently, turtle conservation lacks a strong voice in wildlife protection, scientific research, and conservation from within the Vietnamese community.
(3) What to do with confiscated turtles?
  • Breeding farms and "rescue centers" are the present trend, though these facilities are poorly planned, managed, and funded, as well as lacking conservation goals.
  • Release in parks and protected areas is common in some areas, however, there are few considerations for habitat requirements, natural distribution, impacts on existing populations, or health and welfare of animals released.
  • Usually, turtle traders are fined and the turtles are put back into the trade. This practice may in part provide a source of supplemental income for some protection authorities and should not be overlooked as a major economic consideration in resolving what should be done with confiscated animals.
(4) Lack of information on the distribution and status of wild populations.
  • Very little formal field work has been done on natural distribution of species within Vietnam. Most current field records are incidental.
(5) Low public and national concern for turtles and the impacts of trade.
  • There is little public understanding about the threat of trade to the country's native turtles. Nor is there a generally high level of appreciation for turtles, regarded by many as an abundant resource to be exploited, and likened to the status afforded to fish.
  • There is also little public will to become involved in helping protect wildlife resources from exploitation for the trade.

(6) Low level of protection for natural habitat.
  • Low pay, poor morale and motivation, lack of effective supervision, inadequate training, and lack of incentives result in generally low levels of effective protection in most National Parks and Protected Areas. However, National FPD continues to move forward with training aimed at improving ranger performance in the field.
(7) Lack of data on the trade.
  • Most trade data comprise brief glimpses of various segments of the trade. The true extent and volume of the turtle trade is unknown and the country lacks an established monitoring system that would provide useful information.

Recommendations

(1) Training and capacity building of enforcement and protection agencies.
  • Establish protection methods and guidelines.
  • Provide resources for identification of turtles.
  • Conduct workshops for authorities on turtle ecology, conservation, and protection.
(2) Improve habitat protection.
(3) Conduct field surveys on the natural distribution and status for specific species.
(4) Invest in developing national expertise.
(5) Support the establishment of well-managed facilities for confiscated turtles and conservation-focused breeding centers.
  • Repatriate (translocate) confiscated animals into suitable habitat.
(6) Establish captive breeding programs for specific species threatened by trade.
  • Explore head-start programs.
  • Ensure genetic preservation.
(7) Initiate a national and regionally focused public awareness program. Conduct focused educational programs in target areas.
(8) Develop an effective trade monitoring program.
(9) Cross-border cooperation with states of origin and market states.

Species Conservation Assessments

Indotestudo elongata. — Elongated tortoise, Yellow tortoise.
  Distribution (Vietnam): Forested upland areas. North, central, and south Vietnam. May have once occupied lowland savannas and forests.
  Habitat availability: Probably limited to remaining forests, National Parks, and Protected Areas.
  Population status: Unknown.
  Population trends: Uncommon in field survey reports. Common in the wildlife trade. Vietnamese populations, threatened by hunting and habitat loss, are undoubtedly in decline.
  Threats: Habitat loss and the illegal wildlife trade.

National utilization: Unknown. Some collection may be for local consumption in remote areas, though most hunting appears to be for export to China. Exceptions possibly include turtles observed in Ho Chi Minh markets. Smaller individuals are occasionally sold as pets.

Legal trade: Official figures do not indicate any CITES permits being issued for export of *Indotestudo* between 1994 and 1999.

Illegal trade: *Indotestudo elongata* is listed under category II of Vietnam's Decree 18 that restricts trade to scientific research, establishing breeding populations, and international exchange. *Indotestudo elongata* is common in the illegal trade and has been documented in roughly 60% of all observed trade seizures by Ninh Binh Provincial authorities since 1998. Often observed in the trade in large numbers during certain times of the year. A large portion of the present trade volume may include tortoises brought into Vietnam from Cambodia or Laos. Le Dien Duc and Broad (1995) estimated that as much as 500 kg of *I. elongata* were being sold each day in Chau Mong market in Ho Chi Minh. Trade seizure records since 1997 have documented several large shipments including a confiscation of ca. 1000 kg in Hanoi and a second seizure of 800 kg in Ninh Binh.

Potential trade impacts: Depletion of wild populations and compromised viability of surviving populations.

Manouria impressa. — Impressed tortoise.

Distribution (Vietnam): Tropical and subtropical evergreen forests in mountainous areas of northern and central Vietnam. Possibly mountainous regions in southern Vietnam (trade specimen observed in Nha Trang, September 1999).

Habitat availability: Limited to remaining forests, National Parks, and Protected Areas.

Population status: Unknown.

Population trends: Surveys in communities bordering remaining natural areas (where conducted) suggest that there are far fewer of this species in the wild at present than in the past.

Threats: Hunting and collection for the illegal trade and habitat loss.

National utilization: Juveniles observed with frequency in the Hanoi pet market. *Manouria impressa* may have been consumed locally in the past, but recent reports suggest that most individuals captured are sold to traders and exported to China.

Legal international trade: National CITES records show that permits were issued for export of 640 individuals between 1994 and late 1999.

Illegal trade: *Manouria impressa* is observed fairly frequently in the trade in small numbers, with 55% of observed shipments containing at least one *M. impressa*. Many of the trade specimens observed in 1998–99 were large adults. Most often observed in trade shipments during June to September. This corresponds with pet market occurrence.

Potential trade impacts: Depletion of wild populations and compromised viability of surviving populations.

Cuora amboinensis. — Malayan box turtle, Asian box turtle.

Distribution (Vietnam): Streams and marshes in lowland forest and rice paddies. Central lowlands and southern Vietnam.

Habitat availability: Limited to remaining natural forests and wetlands within its range.

Population status: Unknown.

Population trends: Based on agricultural conversion of wetlands and marshes into rice fields and overall reduction of riparian forest habitat, in addition to hunting pressures, few if any viable populations of *C. amboinensis* are likely to exist in Vietnam.

Threats: Habitat loss and hunting for the wildlife trade.

National utilization: Unknown, though Le Dien Duc and Broad (1995) documented this species for sale in Ho Chi Minh in large numbers. This species may have been consumed locally in some rural areas in the past.

Legal international trade: Official CITES office records show that 13,440 individuals were exported between 1994 and late 1999. The origin of these turtles is unknown and may include Cambodia.

Illegal trade: In contrast with national CITES permit records, *C. amboinensis* has been fairly uncommon in Ninh Binh provincial trade seizures with only five individuals observed since 1998. This may simply be a result of alternative trade routes (air, sea, train) for many southern species that bypass the principal northern ground transport routes, or may result from confusion between *Cuora* species (e.g., *C. amboinensis* and *C. galbinifrons*).

Potential trade impacts: Depletion of wild populations and compromised viability of surviving populations.

Cuora galbinifrons. — Indochinese box turtle (Fig. 2).

Distribution (Vietnam): Evergreen forests on hillsides and in mountainous regions. Northern and central Vietnam, though a subspecies has been reported for southern Vietnam (*C. g. picturata*).

Habitat availability: Limited to remaining forests, National Parks, and Protected Areas.

Population status: Unknown.

Population trends: Wild populations in decline due to heavy harvesting for the wildlife trade with China.

Threats: Habitat loss and collection.

National utilization: Unknown. May have been consumed locally in the past but presently most turtles are likely to be sold to traders for export.

Legal international trade: Official CITES office records indicate that 5106 turtles of this species were legally exported between 1994 and late 1999.

Illegal trade: *Cuora galbinifrons* is the most frequently

Figure 2. *Cuora galbinifrons*, Indochinese box turtle. Specimen from Hue, Vietnam, confiscated from illegal trade. Photo by DBH.

observed turtle in the wildlife trade based on seizures in Ninh Binh Province, appearing in 81% of all trade seizures where turtles were present. The volume (number of individuals) in the trade ranks third behind *I. elongata* and *M. subtrijuga*. However, it should be noted that Ninh Binh seizures represent only a sampling of the wildlife trade in the country. Smaller individuals are commonly sold as pets. Most commonly observed in the trade during the late summer through October.

Potential trade impacts: Depletion of wild populations and compromised viability of surviving populations.

Cuora trifasciata. — Chinese three-striped box turtle, Golden turtle.

Distribution (Vietnam): Mountainous evergreen forest. Northern and central Vietnam.

Habitat availability: Limited to remaining natural forests, parks, and protected areas.

Population status: Unknown.

Population trends: Based on the commercial value of *C. trifasciata*, remaining native populations are likely to be under severe pressure from hunting. In three years of observed trade seizures in Ninh Binh Province, only one *C. trifasciata* has been observed.

Threats: Collection and habitat loss.

National utilization: May have been consumed locally in the past. However, exceptionally high market values derived from trade with China have probably led to a reduction in local use with the prospects of immediate wealth luring collectors to sell *C. trifasciata* to traders. *Cuora trifasciata* has not been observed in the Hanoi pet trade in recent years, though they were present or available in the past, as reported by Le Dien Duc and Broad (1995) and Lehr (1997).

Legal international trade: Official CITES office records

show no permits issued for export of this species between 1994 and 1999.

Illegal trade: Extremely rare in the wildlife trade, possibly due to small remaining numbers available in the wild. Alternatively, the value of this species may lead traders to separate this species from other shipments and transport *C. trifasciata* in smaller numbers where there are reduced chances of being caught.

Potential trade impacts: Extirpation of wild populations and compromised viability of surviving populations.

Cyclemys tcheponensis, C. pulchristriata. — Asian leaf turtles.

Distribution (Vietnam): Forested uplands and streams in mountainous regions. Northern and central Vietnam.

Habitat availability: Limited to remaining natural forests, parks, and protected areas.

Population status: Unknown.

Population trends: Unknown. However, like most other turtles, *Cyclemys* is readily sought for the wildlife trade, and wild populations are likely declining.

Threats: Collection and habitat loss.

National utilization: In the past, *Cyclemys* may have been collected for local consumption. Most present collecting appears to be for the wildlife trade. Smaller individuals are observed with some frequency within the domestic pet trade.

Legal international trade: Official CITES office records indicate that 3155 turtles of these two species (all identified as *C. dentata*) were exported with permits between 1994 and late 1999.

Illegal trade: Seizures along northern land routes show *C. tcheponensis* appearing in 66% of all trade seizures and representing the fourth highest traded species after *M. subtrijuga*, *I. elongata*, and *C. galbinifrons* in terms of numbers of individuals.

Potential trade impacts: Depletion of wild populations and compromised viability of surviving populations.

Geoemyda spengleri. — Black-breasted leaf turtle.

Distribution (Vietnam): Forested hillsides and mountains. Northern and central Vietnam.

Habitat availability: Limited to remaining natural forests, parks, and protected areas.

Population status: Unknown.

Population trends: Unknown. As with other species in Vietnam, natural populations arc unlikcly to susten present levels of collection.

Threats: Collection and habitat loss.

National utilization: Common species in the domestic pet trade.

Legal international trade: Official CITES office records indicate that only 12 of this species were legally exported between 1994 and late 1999.

Illegal trade: Trade appears to be mainly for the domestic pet market. Only one reported case of an individual being observed in a mixed trade shipment to China. This is possibly related to the small size of adults that are unlikely to bring the same profits to Chinese traders based on their low relative weight.

Potential trade impacts: Depletion of wild populations and compromised viability of surviving populations

Heosemys grandis. — Orange-headed temple turtle, Giant Asian pond turtle.

Distribution (Vietnam): Streams, rivers, and freshwater marshes. Lowlands of central and southern Vietnam.

Habitat availability: Unknown. Probably reduced due to agricultural conversion of wetlands and riparian forests.

Population status: Unknown.

Population trends: Unknown. As with other species in Vietnam, natural populations are unlikely to sustain present levels of collection.

Threats: Collection and habitat loss.

National utilization: This species is apparently common in Buddhist temple ponds. In the past, consumption may have been local, however, the value of such large turtles in the export trade probably results in most wild-caught *H. grandis* being sold to traders. Le Dien Duc and Broad (1995) documented *H. grandis* in Cau Mong market in Ho Chi Minh.

Legal international trade: Official CITES office records indicate that 1971 turtles of this species were legally exported between 1994 and late 1999.

Illegal trade: Fairly common trade species observed in seizures along the principal ground transport route to China. Seizures may include specimens entering into the trade from Cambodia. Rarely seen in the pet markets of Hanoi.

Potential trade impacts: Depletion of wild populations and compromised viability of surviving populations

Hieremys annandalii. — Yellow-headed temple turtle.

Distribution (Vietnam): Rivers and freshwater marshes, possibly estuaries. Lowlands of southern Vietnam.

Habitat availability: Unknown. Probably reduced due to agricultural conversion and loss of riparian wetlands and forest.

Population status: Unknown.

Population trends: Unknown. As with other species in Vietnam, natural populations are unlikely to sustain present levels of collection.

Threats: Collection and habitat loss.

National utilization: Similar to *H. grandis*, *H. annandalii* is apparently common in Buddhist temple ponds. In the past, consumption may have been local, however the value of such large turtles in the export trade probably results in most wild-caught *H. annandalii* now being sold to traders. Le Dien Duc and Broad (1995) documented *H. annandalii* in Cau Mong market in Ho Chi Minh.

Legal international trade: Official CITES office records do not indicate any legal exports of this species. However, based on possible confusion between this species and *H. grandis*, it is possible that *H. annandalii* were exported under *H. grandis* permits.

Illegal trade: *H. annandalii* is fairly uncommon in trade seizures along northern land routes to China. Seizures may include specimens entering into the trade from Cambodia. Rarely seen in the pet trade in Hanoi.

Potential trade impacts: Depletion of wild populations and compromised viability of surviving populations.

Malayemys subtrijuga. — Malayan snail-eating turtle.

Distribution (Vietnam): Wetlands and marshes, canals, and rice fields. Lowlands of southern Vietnam.

Habitat availability: Unknown. Reduced natural wetlands due to agricultural conversion would suggest that the availability of natural habitat has been severely reduced, though this species is known to inhabit rice fields and irrigation ditches as well.

Population status: Unknown.

Population trends: Unknown. *Malayemys subtrijuga* is heavily collected for the wildlife trade.

Threats: Collection and habitat loss. As with other species in Vietnam, natural populations are unlikely to sustain present rates of collection.

National utilization: In addition to the wildlife trade, *M. subtrijuga* is believed to be one of the most common turtles released as part of Buddhist religious rituals. *Malayemys subtrijuga* is fairly uncommon in the Hanoi pet market, but was documented as the most common species sold in Cau Mong market in Ho Chi Minh City (Le Dien Duc and Broad, 1995).

Legal international trade: Official CITES office records indicate that 2620 turtles of this species were legally exported between 1994 and late 1999.

Illegal trade: *Malayemys subtrijuga* is common in the wildlife trade with large numbers transported along ground routes each year. Although less frequently observed in Ninh

Binh provincial trade seizures, *M. subtrijuga* represents the most heavily traded species (in terms of number of individuals) based on accounts of a few large shipments that have been confiscated in Hanoi and Ninh Binh in 1996 and 1998.

Potential trade impacts: Depletion of wild populations and compromised viability of surviving populations.

Mauremys annamensis. — Vietnamese pond turtle (Fig. 3).

Distribution (Vietnam): Marshes, streams, and ponds. Lowlands of central Vietnam.

Habitat availability: This species is endemic to the lowlands of central Vietnam and only known from trade surveys in a few provinces. Agricultural conversion is likely to be a factor resulting in severe reduction in natural habitat.

Population status: Unknown.

Population trends: Unknown. Where once this species was observed more frequently in trade seizures, only a few specimens have been observed in 1998 and 1999. This reduction in observed occurrence within the trade, combined with loss in habitat and continued hunting pressures within its extremely limited known range, would suggest that *M. annamensis* is under serious threat of extirpation.

Threats: Collection and habitat loss.

National utilization: Unknown. In the past, *M. annamensis* might have been hunted for local consumption, however at present it is likely that most turtles encountered are sold to traders.

Legal international trade: Official CITES office records indicate no legal exports of this species between 1994 and late 1999.

Illegal trade: *Mauremys annamensis* is uncommon in northern ground route trade seizures and is seldom seen in Hanoi pet markets. Le Dien Duc and Broad (1995) reported its occurrence in Cau Mau markets south of Hanoi which might suggest that this species' natural range may extend southward from central Vietnam. Specimens continue to appear occasionally in the regional and western pet trade.

Potential trade impacts: Extirpation of wild populations and compromised viability of surviving populations

Mauremys mutica. — Asian yellow pond turtle.

Distribution (Vietnam): Marshes, ponds, and slow-moving streams in lowland regions of northern and north-central Vietnam.

Habitat availability: Unknown. Reduced habitat resulting from agricultural conversion of wetlands and marshes.

Population status: Unknown.

Population trends: Unknown. Likely to be in decline due to hunting and habitat loss.

Threats: Collection and habitat loss.

National utilization: Unknown. In the past, *M. mutica* might have been hunted for local consumption, however, at present it is likely that most turtles encountered are sold to traders. Not observed in Hanoi pet market in recent years.

Legal international trade: Official CITES office records indicate that none of this species were legally exported between 1994 and late 1999.

Illegal trade: This author has only observed this species in the wildlife trade on a few occasions. Additionally, there has been only one observation of this species in the Hanoi domestic pet market. Its relative absence in the trade is unexplained, unless most northern populations of the species

Figure 3. *Mauremys annamensis,* Vietnamese pond turtle, the only endemic Vietnamese chelonian, now quite rare; specimen confiscated from illegal trade. Photo by DBH.

have been severely depleted due to hunting and habitat loss.

Potential trade impacts: Depletion of wild populations or compromised viability of surviving populations

Notochelys platynota. — Malayan flat-shelled turtle.

Distribution (Vietnam): Reported to occur in Vietnam, possibly based on continuous repetition of a nineteenth-century record, but there are no current field or trade records to indicate the presence of this species in Vietnam.

Ocadia sinensis. — Chinese striped-necked turtle.

Distribution (Vietnam): Wetlands, marshes, ponds, and rivers. Lowlands of northern and central Vietnam.

Habitat availability: Unknown. Reduced habitat available from agricultural conversion of wetlands and marshes. Limitations on nesting areas may influence populations that have adapted to aquatic habitats with substantial human presence.

Population status: Unknown.

Population trends: Unknown. As with other species in Vietnam, natural populations are unlikely to sustain present levels of collection.

Threats: Collection and habitat loss.

National utilization: In the past, it is likely that turtles were consumed locally, however most turtles encountered presently are probably sold to traders. *Ocadia sinensis* is relatively common in Hanoi's pet market.

Legal international trade: Official CITES office records indicate that none of this species were legally exported between 1994 and late 1999.

Illegal trade: Relatively uncommon within the wildlife trade, though in 1999 two shipments were observed with large adults present.

Potential trade impacts: Depletion of wild populations and compromised viability of surviving populations.

Pyxidea mouhotii. — Keeled box turtle.

Distribution (Vietnam): Forested regions of northern and central Vietnam.

Habitat availability: Limited to remaining natural forests, parks, and protected areas.

Population status: Unknown.

Population trends: Unknown. As with other species in Vietnam, natural populations are unlikely to sustain present levels of collection.

Threats: Collection and habitat loss.

National utilization: In the past, it is likely that these turtles were consumed locally, however most individuals encountered presently are probably sold to traders. *Pyxidea mouhotii* is common in the domestic pet trade. Smaller individuals are also kept as pets in rural areas.

Legal international trade: Official CITES office records indicate that 6560 turtles of this species were legally exported between 1994 and late 1999.

Illegal trade: Common in wildlife trade seizures along northern ground routes, particularly during the spring.

Potential trade impacts: Depletion of wild populations and compromised viability of surviving populations

Sacalia quadriocellata. — Four-eyed turtle.

Distribution (Vietnam): Streams in mountainous evergreen forests. Northern and central Vietnam.

Habitat availability: Limited to remaining natural forests, parks, and protected areas.

Population status: Unknown.

Population trends: Unknown. As with other species in Vietnam, natural populations are unlikely to sustain present rates of collection.

Threats: Collection and habitat loss.

National utilization: Primarily collected for the domestic pet trade. Common in Hanoi pet markets. In the past, it is likely that turtles were consumed locally, however most turtles encountered presently are probably sold to traders.

Legal international trade: Official CITES office records indicate that 630 turtles of this species were legally exported between 1994 and late 1999.

Illegal trade: Rare in wildlife trade seizures along northern ground transport routes.

Potential trade impacts: Depletion of wild populations and compromised viability of surviving populations.

Siebenrockiella crassicollis. — Black marsh turtle.

Distribution (Vietnam): Wetlands, marshes, ponds, canals, and other slow-moving bodies of water. Lowlands of southern Vietnam.

Habitat availability: Reduced habitat resulting from agricultural conversion of wetlands and marshes to rice fields.

Population status: Unknown.

Population trends: Unknown. As with other species in Vietnam, natural populations are unlikely to sustain present levels of collection.

Threats: Collection and habitat loss.

National utilization: Unknown. In the past, it is likely that this species was consumed locally, however most encountered presently are probably sold to traders.

Legal international trade: Official CITES office records indicate that 1515 turtles of this species were legally exported in the past two years, but none in the period 1994–97.

Illegal trade: Unknown. Inspections of trade seizures along northern ground routes have resulted in only one observation of this species. Market surveys by Le Dien Duc and Broad (1995) and Lehr (1996) also failed to observe this species. Since trade in turtles includes virtually all species, whether domestic markets or Chinese markets are the end destination, either *S. crassicollis* is presently absent from the trade (perhaps no longer readily found in the wild), or is shipped by alternative routes (sea, air, rail) from southern Vietnam.

Potential trade impacts: Depletion of wild populations and compromised viability of surviving populations

Platysternon megacephalum. — Big-headed turtle.

Distribution (Vietnam): Mountainous streams and small

rivers in forested regions. Northern and central Vietnam.

Habitat availability: Limited to remaining natural forests, parks, and protected areas.

Population status: Unknown.

Population trends: Unknown. As with other species in Vietnam, natural populations are unlikely to sustain present levels of collection.

Threats: Collection and habitat loss.

National utilization: Seldom observed in the Hanoi pet market. In the past, it is likely that turtles were consumed locally, however most turtles encountered presently are probably sold to traders.

Legal international trade: Official CITES office records indicate that 50 turtles of this species were legally exported between 1994 and late 1999.

Illegal trade: Relatively common in wildlife trade seizures along ground transport routes in the north, particularly during the spring and early summer months.

Potential trade impacts: Depletion of wild populations and compromised viability of surviving populations.

Amyda cartilaginea. — Asiatic softshell turtle.

Distribution (Vietnam): Most water bodies including marshes, estuaries, streams, rivers, ponds, and canals. Central and southern Vietnam.

Habitat availability: Unknown. Availability of nesting sites is presumed to be a factor affecting the potential survivorship of wild populations in areas under heavy human influence.

Population status: Unknown.

Population trends: Unknown. As with other species in Vietnam, natural populations are unlikely to sustain present levels of hunting.

Threats: Hunting for local and domestic consumption, as well as the wildlife trade. Habitat loss.

National utilization: Softshell turtles are available on the menus of many restaurants throughout Vietnam. Smaller individuals are sometimes available in pet markets.

Legal international trade: National export records do not list any figures for trade in any softshell species.

Illegal trade: *Amyda cartilaginea* is uncommon in trade seizures along the wildlife trade ground transport routes in the north. Trade in softshell turtles may involve an entirely separate network, based on domestic consumption.

Potential trade impacts: Unknown. Trade volumes for domestic consumption are poorly documented.

Palea steindachneri. — Wattle-necked softshell turtle.

Distribution (Vietnam): Streams, rivers, and other water bodies in northern and central Vietnam.

Habitat availability: Unknown. Availability of nesting sites is presumed to be a factor affecting the potential survivorship of wild populations in areas under heavy human influence.

Population status: Unknown.

Population trends: Unknown. As with other species in Vietnam, natural populations are unlikely to sustain present levels of hunting.

Threats: Hunting for local and domestic consumption, as well as the wildlife trade. Habitat loss.

National utilization: Softshell turtles are available on the menus of many restaurants throughout Vietnam.

Legal international trade: National export records do not list any figures for trade in any softshell species.

Illegal trade: *Palea steindachneri* is uncommon in trade seizures along transport routes in the north. Trade in softshell turtles may involve an entirely separate network, destined for domestic consumption.

Potential trade impacts: Unknown. Trade volumes for domestic consumption are poorly documented.

Pelochelys cantorii. — Asian giant softshell turtle.

Distribution (Vietnam): Lowland rivers, estuaries, and coastal areas. Central and southern Vietnam.

Habitat availability: Unknown. Availability of nesting sites is presumed to be a factor affecting the potential survivorship of wild populations in areas under heavy human influence.

Population status: Unknown.

Population trends: Unknown. As with other species in Vietnam, natural populations are unlikely to sustain present levels of hunting.

Threats: Hunting for local and domestic consumption, as well as the wildlife trade. Habitat loss.

National utilization: Softshell turtles are available on the menus of many restaurants throughout Vietnam.

Legal international trade: National export records do not list any figures for trade in any softshell species.

Illegal trade: *Pelochelys cantorii* is uncommon in trade seizures along ground transport routes in the north (no observations recorded). Trade in softshell turtles may involve an entirely separate network, destined for domestic consumption. *Pelochelys cantorii* is restricted from trade under Decree 18.

Potential trade impacts: Unknown. Trade volumes for domestic consumption are poorly documented. Based on lack of observations of this species in the trade or domestic market, *P. cantorii* may be extremely rare in Vietnam.

Pelodiscus sinensis. — Chinese softshell turtle.

Distribution (Vietnam): Most water bodies including marshes, estuaries, streams, rivers, ponds, and canals. Throughout northern, central, and southern Vietnam.

Habitat availability: Unknown. Availability of nesting sites is presumed to be a factor affecting the potential survivorship of wild populations in areas under heavy human influence.

Population status: Unknown.

Population trends: Unknown. Since *P. sinensis* is the principal aquaculture softshell species, it is difficult to assess wild populations based on domestic consumption

Figure 4. *Rafetus* sp., East Asian giant softshell turtle, from Hoan Kiem Lake, Hanoi, possibly *R. swinhoei* or an undescribed species, in either case extremely rare and critically endangered. Photo by unknown photographer, obtained from public internet source from Vietnam.

or trade. Wild populations may be supplemented or introduced to some areas as a result of escapes from aquaculture farms, particularly in areas where flooding occurs.

Threats: Hunting for local and domestic consumption, as well as the wildlife trade. Habitat loss.

National utilization: Softshell turtles are available on the menus of many restaurants throughout Vietnam. Smaller individuals of *P. sinensis* are sometimes available in pet markets.

Legal international trade: National export records do not list any figures for trade in any softshell species.

Illegal trade: *Pelodiscus sinensis* is uncommon in trade seizures along ground transport routes in the north. Trade in softshell turtles may involve an entirely separate network, destined for domestic consumption.

Potential trade impacts: Unknown. Trade volumes for domestic consumption are poorly documented.

Rafetus sp. — East Asian giant softshell turtle (Fig. 4).

Distribution (Vietnam): Known to occur in Hoan Kiem Lake in central Hanoi and possibly still occurs in other wetlands in the Red River floodplain.

Habitat availability: Unknown, as its habitat requirements are unknown.

Population status: Extremely rare and presumably on the verge of extinction.

Population trends: Unknown.

Threats: Capture for consumption and trade. Drainage of wetlands and conversion to agricultural lands. Elimination of nesting sites. Pollution.

National utilization: Any animals encountered and caught outside Hoan Kiem Lake will be consumed or sold.

Legal international trade: National export records do not list any figures for trade in any softshell species.

Illegal trade: Specimens purported to be *Rafetus* have been confiscated from traders, suggesting at least some illegal trade.

Potential trade impacts: Depletion and extirpation of the population and species.

Note: The taxonomic status of the giant softshells of the Red River basin and Hoan Kiem Lake remains poorly known; whether these populations are referable to *R. swinhoei* or represent a separate undescribed species is currently under study (Ha Dinh Duc, in prep.). Its attribution to *Rafetus* is reasonably certain (Ha Dinh Duc, P. Pritchard, *pers. comm.*).

LITERATURE CITED

JENKINS, M.D. 1995. Tortoises and Freshwater Turtles: The Trade in Southeast Asia. TRAFFIC International, United Kingdom, 48 pp.

LE DIEN DUC AND BROAD, S. 1995. Investigations into Tortoise and Freshwater Turtle Trade in Vietnam. IUCN Species Survival Commission. IUCN, Gland, Switzerland and Cambridge, UK.

LEHR, E. 1997. Untersuchungen zum Schildkrötenhandel in Vietnam zwischen 1993 und 1996. Mitteilungen der Zoologischen Gesellschaft für Arten- und Populationsschutz 13(2):12-16,19.

LI, W., FULLER, T.K., AND WANG, S. 1996. A survey of wildlife trade in Guangxi and Guangdong, China. TRAFFIC Bulletin 16(1):9-16.

LI, Y. AND LI, D. 1997. The investigation on live wildlife trade across Guangxi borders between China and Vietnam. In: Conserving China's Biodiversity - Reports of the Biodiversity Working Group. China Council for International Cooperation on Environment and Development (CCICED), Beijing, pp. 118-127.

MACKINNON, J. (Ed.). 1997. Protected Areas Systems Review of the Indo-Malayan Realm. Asian Bureau of Conservation and World Conservation Monitoring Centre for the World Bank, 198 pp.

Asian Turtle Trade: Proceedings of a Workshop on Conservation and Trade of Freshwater Turtles and Tortoises in Asia
P.P. van Dijk, B.L. Stuart, and A.G.J. Rhodin, Eds.
Chelonian Research Monographs 2:74–76 • © 2000 by Chelonian Research Foundation

Turtle Trade in Indochina: Regional Summary
(Cambodia, Laos, and Vietnam)

BRYAN L. STUART[1], ROBERT J. TIMMINS[2], DOUGLAS B. HENDRIE[3], LIENG SOPHA[4],
CHUN SOPHAT[5], HOUT PISETH[6], HENG KIMCHAY[7], TOUCH SEANG TANA[8],
PRAK LEANG HOUR[9], CHUL THACH[10], JAMES COMPTON[11], AND ROHAN HOLLOWAY[12]

[1]*WCS Lao Program, P.O. Box 6712, Vientiane, Laos [Fax: 856-21-215400; E-mail: blstuart@unity.ncsu.edu];*
[2]*WWF Lao Projects Office, P.O. Box 7871, Vientiane, Laos*
[Fax: 856-2121-7161; E-mail: rob@naturalists.freeserve.co.uk];
[3]*Cuc Phuong Conservation Project, Fauna & Flora International, P.O. Box 78, Hanoi, Vietnam*
[E-mail: cpcp@fpt.vn];
[4]*Fisheries Dept., Ministry of Agriculture, Forestry and Fisheries, Norodom Boulevard, Phnom Penh, Cambodia*
[Fax: 855-23-427048];
[5]*CITES Office, MAFF, Norodom Boulevard, P.O. Box 582, Phnom Penh, Cambodia*
[Fax: 855-23-215470; E-mail: bigcatch@bigpond.com.kh];
[6]*Protected Areas Office, Department of Nature Conservation and Protection, Ministry of Environment, Sihanouk*
Boulevard, Phnom Penh, Cambodia [E-mail: wwfcam@bigpond.com.kh];
[7]*Wildlife Protection Office, Forestry Dept., 40 Norodom Boulevard, Phnom Penh, Cambodia*
[E-mail: wpo@forum.org.kh];
[8]*Fisheries Dept., Ministry of Agriculture, Forestry and Fisheries, Norodom Boulevard, Phnom Penh, Cambodia*
[Fax: 855-23-427048; E-mail: tana@forum.org.kh];
[9]*Phnom Penh, Cambodia;*
[10]*Phnom Penh, Cambodia;*
[11]*TRAFFIC Southeast Asia–Vietnam, c/o WWF Indochina Programme, 7 Yet Kieu Street, Hanoi, Vietnam*
[Fax: 84-4-822-0642; E-mail: jcompton@traffico.org];
[12]*Applied Ecology Research Group, University of Canberra, Canberra, ACT 2601, Australia*

Patterns of Trade

Consumption of turtles for local subsistence seems widespread and not species-specific in Cambodia and Laos. This use has most certainly been practiced for a very long time, and probably has had long-term effects, at least in Laos, in depressing populations prior to any domestic or international trade. Local subsistence use of turtles in Vietnam was probably much more significant in the past, but today probably relatively few are consumed rather than traded, considering the well-established trade networks and heavy demands for turtles in the trade.

A minor domestic consumption trade persists in all three countries. In Cambodia, turtles and eggs are sold as food, and turtles are sold for Khmer and Chinese medicinal purposes, as decoration, as pets, and for Buddhist release. It remains unclear which species are primarily used in the Cambodian domestic trade. In Laos, the domestic trade is somewhat more species-specific than local subsistence use, at present mostly involving softshells (*Amyda cartilaginea* and probably *Pelochelys cantorii*), *Malayemys subtrijuga*, and *Indotestudo elongata*. In Vietnam softshells are a favored species in the domestic consumption trade, but also some domestic trade targets selling turtles for Buddhist release or selling

small species such as *Geoemyda spengleri* and *Sacalia quadriocellata* for pets. However, in all three countries, the domestic consumption trade is considered minor when compared with the international trade of Indochinese turtles to China.

The majority of turtles originating in Cambodia and Laos are transported to Vietnam, where they join with Vietnamese turtles on northward trade routes to China. Some Cambodian turtles are transported directly by air from Phnom Penh to Hong Kong and Guangzhou, China, but the majority of Cambodian turtles travel overland or by boat to the Vietnam border. Some Lao turtles in the northern parts of the country are transported directly to China, but the usual trade routes first go through an overland network into Vietnam. Turtles are transported to China from Vietnam by road, air, rail, or ship. There is some trade of turtles from Cambodia and Laos to Thailand, but this trade, pending further investigation, is considered minimal when compared with the trade volumes to Vietnam and China.

Species in Trade and
Effects of Trade on Native Turtle Populations

It appears that all species of turtles in Cambodia, Laos, and Vietnam are harvested and traded. Some species in Cambodia and Laos are more likely to be utilized for local subsistence and domestic trade than others, while some species command higher prices on the international market and are more sought after by traders for export to Vietnam and China. In Cambodia and Laos, the factors which determine whether a harvested turtle will be consumed for subsistence or sold into the trade probably depends on a number of factors, such as proximity of the harvester to trade networks and the value of the species in the trade.

Little is known about the specific volume of trade emanating from these three countries because of a lack of an effective system for monitoring the trade. Most trade records sporadically represent captive animals in villages awaiting sale to traders, in markets, or after seizure by officials. Although monitoring studies of wild turtle populations are nonexistent in all three countries, recent surveys in these countries have produced surprisingly few field records of turtles. Hunters in at least Laos and Vietnam consistently report that turtles have become much rarer in recent years.

Inferring from the paucity of field records, hunter interview data, observations along trade routes and border posts, and species composition of Chinese markets, it appears that the current levels of harvest and trade threaten most populations of turtles in Indochina.

Current Regulations and Controls

All three countries have legislation intended to control wildlife trade, including turtles. However, the current legislation is limited, primarily due to misperceptions about the sustainability of turtle trade and a lack of national scientific interest in turtles. As identified particularly in Vietnam, a low national interest has resulted in turtles lacking a strong advocacy in wildlife protection, scientific research, and conservation from within the Vietnamese community.

Despite what legislation is in effect, relatively little implementation seems to take place in any of the three countries for a number of reasons. Confusion over the laws, low enforcement capacity, and species identification problems are the primary obstacles to implementation in all three countries. In Cambodia there additionally remains a lack of data on status and trade levels to conclude which species should be protected, although inferences can be made from the regional status of these species.

When legislation is enforced, there remains the problem of disposition of turtles confiscated from the trade. Depositing confiscated animals in breeding farms and "rescue centers" are a present trend in Vietnam, although these facilities tend to be poorly planned, managed, and funded, and usually lack conservation goals. Sometimes confiscated animals in Cambodia and Vietnam are released in parks and protected areas, however there are few considerations for habitat requirements, natural dis-

tribution, impacts on existing populations, and health and welfare of animals released. Presently in Vietnam, apprehended turtle traders are fined, but without alternative solutions the animals are usually returned to the apprehended traders.

Cambodia has legislation that is intended to prevent destroying or trading wild animals (terrestrial and aquatic), and which protects nationally threatened species. These wildlife laws are currently under revision by the Cambodian government; many turtles are likely to be included as nationally threatened species.

Laos has legislation that intends to protect three "kinds" of turtles from harvest and trade, although it remains unclear which scientific species these are. These wildlife laws are also currently under revision by the Lao government.

Vietnam has legislation that specifically protects two turtles, *Indotestudo elongata* and *Pelochelys cantorii*, as well as legislation that generally restricts trade and export of wildlife. Additionally, commerce regulations prevent traders from operating businesses without a license, and this seems to be the most regularly enforced of any legislation relating to trade of turtles. However, the official Forestry Protection Department annual figures of confiscated turtles represent a miniscule fraction of the number of turtles estimated to cross the border into China every year, and so clearly very little enforcement of trade regulations currently occurs in Vietnam.

Cambodia and Vietnam are both signatory members of the CITES convention, while Laos is not.

Priority Projects

1. Review and modification of existing national legislation to better protect turtles from excessive trade.

2. Strengthen capacity of inspectors and other enforcers, particularly in regard to identifying turtles and understanding legislation, as well as building national expertise.

3. Greater understanding, closer monitoring, and stiffer measures (based on appropriate legislation) to break the patterns and routes of trade are essential. Specific consideration should be given to the following lines of investigation (note this list is not exhaustive):
• Investigating if turtles are exported from Vientiane by air.
• Investigating if factories for processing turtles for the medicinal trade exist in any of the three countries.
• Investigating the significance of air and rail traffic in exporting turtles out of Vietnam.
• Focus trade investigations in Cambodia on the middlemen in Phnom Penh.

4. Studies of trade volume for prioritizing species for protection and setting regulations.

5. Education and awareness programs on the importance of and threats to turtles.

6. Investigation of the options available for confiscated turtles, such as supporting the establishment of well-managed facilities for confiscated turtles as well as methods for repatriating confiscated animals into suitable habitat without jeopardizing the health or genetic integrity of existing populations.

7. Identifying important habitats and improving habitat protection for turtles, especially by securing and protecting remote areas of turtle habitat and maintaining their relative inaccessibility to collectors.

8. Establishment of conservation-oriented captive breeding programs for highly vulnerable Indochinese species. Specifically, captive breeding needs to be encouraged in the international zoo community for the highly valuable Chinese three-striped box turtle *Cuora trifasciata* and the endemic Vietnamese pond turtle *Mauremys annamensis*. *Cuora trifasciata* is very soon (if not already) likely to be extirpated from the wild in Laos and Vietnam, and possibly throughout the remainder of its range in southern China. Sufficient intact habitat probably remains in its suspected range in Laos, and captive populations of this species will be needed for future reintroduction programs. Any captive breeding activity for the species in Laos and Vietnam would have to work around the high risk of theft of the stock. Although of much lower trade value, the entire global distribution of *Mauremys annamensis* is restricted to lowland central Vietnam, an area in which any population of turtle is under extreme threat from the high density of people and well-developed trade networks. Captive breeding will be required to maintain the species in existence beyond its predicted very near-future extirpation from the wild.

Asian Turtle Trade: Proceedings of a Workshop on Conservation and Trade of Freshwater Turtles and Tortoises in Asia
P.P. van Dijk, B.L. Stuart, and A.G.J. Rhodin, Eds.
Chelonian Research Monographs 2:77–85 • © 2000 by Chelonian Research Foundation

Trade and Conservation Status of Freshwater Turtles and Tortoises in Bangladesh

S.M.A. RASHID[1,3] AND S.M. MUNJURUL HANNAN KHAN[2]

[1]*Centre for Advanced Research in Natural Resources and Management (CARINAM), Mohammadpur, Dhaka 1207, Bangladesh;*
[2]*National Conservation Strategy Implementation Project-1 (NCSIP-1), Ministry of Environment and Forest,*
House # 50/1, Road # 11A, Dhanmondi, Dhaka, 1209, Bangladesh [E-mail: ncsip@bdcom.com];
[3]*Present Address: Division of Biology, School of Science, Nanyang Technological University,*
469 Bukit Timah Road, 259756 Singapore [Fax: 65-469-8928; E-mail: carinam95@hotmail.com]

Bangladesh, located between 20°34' and 26°33'N and 88°01' and 92°41'E, is almost entirely surrounded by India, except the southeast where it shares borders with Myanmar. The Bay of Bengal lies to the south. The total land area is 147,570 km². The country enjoys a tropical monsoon climate with distinct seasonal variations. Plenty of rainfall occurs during the monsoon (July – September), a brief autumn during October followed by cool winter (November – February), brief spring during mid-February through mid-March and then the hot dry summer (mid-March through June). During summer the average maximum temperature is 34°C and the average minimum is 21°C, whereas in winter the average maximum temperature is 29°C and the average minimum is 11°C. Approximately 70–80% of the rainfall occurs during the monsoon, which varies from about 1100 mm in the western part to 5690 mm in the northeastern part of the country. Three of the largest rivers (among the 700 or more rivers and tributaries) — the Padma (= the Ganges), the Brahmaputra, and the Meghna drain a vast water catchment area extending over Bhutan (4%), Nepal (8%), India (62%), and China (18%).

In terms of chelonian species diversity, Bangladesh supports about 10% of the total world species. A total of 27 species (including 15 subspecies) of turtles and tortoises occur in Bangladesh, which includes 5 marine turtles, 14 batagurids (hard-shelled freshwater or estuarine turtles), 2 testudinids (land tortoises), and 6 trionychids (soft-shelled freshwater or estuarine turtles) (Khan, 1982b, 1987; Sarker and Sarker, 1988; Das, 1991; Rashid and Swingland, 1997). All of these species are exploited in Bangladesh for local and international trade and are losing their ground. According to the IUCN-Bangladesh 1999 Red Data Book (in press), 8 species are Critically Endangered, 15 species are Endangered, 2 species are Vulnerable, and 1 species Data Deficient (in the country).

Turtles have long been associated with humans either in myths, as a food source, as ornaments, as pets, or as medicinal ingredients. Because of this association they deserve some love or respect from humans and are not feared or loathed like their fellow reptilians — the snakes, lizards, and crocodiles. On the other hand, being utilized for multiple purposes and lacking defense, they have been indiscriminately over-exploited to such an extent that it has become impossible for some populations to survive. What is more disturbing is that turtles have lived for almost 200 million years and have survived the major natural catastrophes which eliminated the dinosaurs, but are now being extirpated by humans through unregulated trade, habitat loss, and other threats.

In Bangladesh freshwater turtles became extensively involved in local trade only after the country's independence in 1971, when more opportunities became available to the local people for exploiting the natural renewable resources, and businessmen seized the opportunity to commercially exploit these resources. Turtles became a major commodity for export in the mid-1970s but prior to independence there were a few instances when they were exported on a commercial basis. Local trade, which fulfilled the local demand, was significantly smaller than the commercial exploitation and had little known impact on turtle populations. With increased commercialization, which has involved massive collection throughout the year all over the country, an abrupt decline of turtle populations has been noticed.

Several other factors such as the human population boom, urbanization, water pollution, loss of wetlands, sediment accumulation in rivers, sand mining, etc., have also contributed to the decline of turtles. Alarmingly, forest cover in the country has been reduced from 50% in 1970 to < 6% in 1990. There are 15 protected areas, which occupy 1.5 % of the country.

The President's Order No. 23 of 1973 was subsequently promulgated and enacted as the Bangladesh Wildlife Preservation (Amendment) Act (BWPA) 1974. This Act is the legal arm for the conservation and management of the wildlife of the country. The Act has several articles and clauses, which describe the responsibilities and duties of the relevant government office(r), punitive measures for the offenders, and also includes three Schedules as an appendix, which consists of a list of animals. Schedule I animals are not protected and can be hunted, trapped, and traded with a permit issued by the relevant government office. Schedule II contains a list of animals, which though protected, may be captured or shot subject to the approval of the relevant office. Included on the list are man-eating tigers and rogue elephants. In addition, species which are otherwise not protected fall under Schedule II if they show any signs of pregnancy, suckling an infant, etc., in which case they may not be captured or hunted. Schedule III consists of animals which are protected and may not be hunted, captured, or traded. Revision of the BWPA Schedules is an immediate priority, as many endangered species are not on the protected list, and the status of many species has changed drastically since 1974.

Under the Act, the Forest Department (under the Ministry of Environment and Forest [MOEF]) is the responsible office for the deployment and enforcement of this Act. However, other offices such as the Customs, Police, Bangladesh Rifles, etc., render assistance for enforcement. Bangladesh is a signatory to CITES and acceded it in November 1981. The Forest Department is the management authority to CITES, however, the scientific authority to CITES has still not been designated.

UTILIZATION AND TRADE

The major uses of turtles and turtle products, prior to the recent commercial trade, were consumption as food, use in traditional medicines, and turtle eggs as delicacies. Local trade and subsistence consumption of such species as *Morenia petersi, Lissemys punctata, Kachuga tecta,* and *Cuora amboinensis* was carried out on a relatively sustainable basis. However, the whole scenario changed after the independence of Bangladesh in 1971. Prior to independence there was little commercial trade in turtles. In the late 1970s commercial exploitation started to gain momentum, which continued for more than a decade, bringing some turtle populations to a vulnerable stage. The exploitation continued without any respect for the breeding season of the species concerned and with no foresight or long-term plan. As a result, the businessmen involved took advantage of loopholes in existing laws and continued their business, disregarding the laws governing trade in wildlife and their products. Moreover, exploitation of renewable natural resources on a commercial basis was relatively new for the recently independent country, and the relevant government departments had to learn more about handling this huge volume of trade. Pressure from the business community demanded infrastructure from the government to facilitate trade. Since a considerable amount of foreign exchange was earned through the export of live turtles, the Export Promotion Bureau (EPB) and other government departments acted to facilitate the trade rather than attempting to regulate trade on a long-term basis. With mounting pressures from international and national conservation organizations this process was slowed in the mid-1980s and the government began to look into problems with the trade. This was a period when large volumes of trade were going on simultaneously involving monitor lizard skins, frog legs, shrimp, turtles, and crabs.

Around the mid-1980s, existing regulations tightened and new regulations were imposed (related to export of monitor lizard skins and frog legs). International conventions and treaties like CITES started to play a notable, visible role in controlling the trade. Existing national laws were reviewed or revised, giving blanket protection to the species involved and monitoring the trade to bring it under control.

This process, however, did not last long as many influential parties were involved and the economic stakes were very high. During the early 1990s, an increased demand for turtles for commercial exploitation expanded to almost every corner of the country and virtually any specimen that collectors could lay their hands on was collected. The trade momentum was also boosted by the recent restoration of land transport communications between India and Bangladesh after almost fifty years. Moreover, new trade routes developed to meet the demand for an uninterrupted supply of turtles to the exporters.

Local Consumption and Trade

Turtles form an important source of meat protein for some low-income non-Muslims, as well as tribal peoples living in or near remote forested areas. These people have collected turtles mostly for consumption, primarily *Lissemys punctata, Kachuga tecta, Cuora amboinensis, Morenia petersi,* and occasionally *Indotestudo elongata.* Some of them may have also sold turtles in local markets. However, as word spread that turtles fetch good money, and with the increase in demand and local prices of turtles, subsistence consumption of turtles has now become mostly directed towards local trade. The local trade network for collection of turtles has even reached remote areas.

Local trade involves almost all of the species occurring in Bangladesh, which are caught by fishermen, subsistence collectors, traditional hunters, and professional collectors. This involves capture by fishing net, hook lines, diving, muddling, harpooning, and other methods. Usually a hunter or collector can collect 5–8 turtles per day by muddling or using a harpoon. The major species involved are *Geoclemys hamiltoni, Hardella thurjii, Kachuga tecta, Morenia petersi, Aspideretes hurum,* and *Lissemys punctata.* Ahamed (1958) mentioned that about eight species were involved in local trade, however, a later study showed that about 17 species of freshwater turtles were involved in trade and consumed by local people (Rashid and Swingland, 1990).

The reason for the increased number of species involved in local trade may be attributed to the greatly increased efforts in collecting turtles for commercial exploitation. It is estimated that more than 50,000 people are involved full-time for this purpose all over the country. Selected species are involved in international trade, which leaves the other species for local utilization. Sometimes when an exporter has depleted stock of a species intended for export, other species involved in local trade may be substituted for that species. Species used as substitute species include *Lissemys punctata, Kachuga smithii, K. tentoria, K. tecta,* and *Morenia petersi.*

International Trade

The 1980s and early 1990s were the peak periods for commercial exploitation and export of turtles. Despite listing of several species on CITES Appendix I as well as on

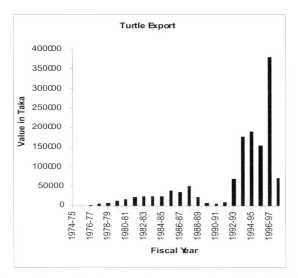

Figure 1. Annual freshwater turtle export earnings in Bangladesh. Source: Export Promotion Bureau, 1998b.

BWPA Schedule III, species such as *A. hurum* and *L. punctata* were exported unabated during that period. On average, Bangladesh earned about US$ 600,000 per annum for turtle exports between 1981 and 1990 (EPB, 1992). Most of these exports were destined for Far East countries like Japan, China, Thailand, Korea, Hong Kong, Singapore, and Malaysia, with some to the UK and USA. This trade involved export of live animals. The magnitude and volume of exports of live turtles decreased to some extent in the early 1990s because of stricter measures adopted by the government and increased awareness among the people. However, trade levels later increased, and from 1995–98 the trade volume (indicated by the annual earnings, Table 1, Fig. 1) surpassed previous records for the whole decade (EPB, 1998b). There are reports that the trade strategy has changed to export of frozen turtle meat under different labels, which needs to be further investigated.

Some of the problems with enforcement of international turtle trade in Bangladesh include:

1. Lack of adequate species identification knowledge among government staff.

2. Intentional misidentification of species by authorities. For example, the CITES Appendix I-listed *A. hurum* is

sometimes identified in export certificates as the non-CITES species *A. leithii* or *Amyda cartilaginea*, even though no records of occurrence of either *A. leithii* or *A. cartilaginea* in Bangladesh are known.

3. Issuance of export certificates without physical verification of the consignment and no checking either at the point of loading or at the port of exit by Forest Department (FD) personnel (FD is responsible for the management and regulation of trade). However, Customs Officers at the port of exit are often trained and have adequate knowledge on this subject.

4. Issuance of health certificates without verification of the turtle consignment.

5. Unhygienic holding conditions in turtle pens at export centers.

6. Injurious and inhumane methods of packing live turtles in wicker baskets for shipment at export centers.

7. Export of gravid females and sometimes under-weight (less than 1 kg) specimens. Turtles weighing less than 1 kg are not allowed to be exported.

The volume of trade is very high during the winter months and early summer (October – April) because water levels are low at that time and turtles are easier to catch. Most adult females are also gravid during that time and removing these gravid turtles from local turtle populations prevents new recruitment, resulting in future population declines.

Trade Routes

The metropolitan capital city, Dhaka, is the major collection center for the export of live turtles. Turtles collected all over the country reach the holding pens of exporters through middlemen located within and in the suburbs of the city. Apart from Dhaka, the port cities of Chittagong and Khulna also have turtle collection centers for export. According to the Export Promotion Bureau (1998a) there are 20 registered agencies involved in turtle export, eight of which also deal with frozen seafood. Among these 20 agencies, 10 are located in Dhaka, 4 in Chittagong, 2 in Khulna, and one each in Barisal, Brahmanbaria, Chandpur, and Mymensingh. The number and geographic distribution of collection centers demonstrates the intensive countrywide collection of turtles, which is also clearly reflected by the trade volume figures. Recently there were unconfirmed reports of exported frozen turtle meat, mostly from the port cities of Khulna and Chittagong, which were labeled as seafood. There are many more unregistered agencies dealing with live turtle export and frozen food. Frozen turtle meat is of recent origin and reported to be exported along with other frozen seafood items, such as shrimp and fish, but usually under a different trade label. These are mainly shipped by sea from the two ports, Chittagong and Mongla.

Bangladesh exports huge volume of live turtles and also acts as a trans-shipment port for turtles which are smuggled in from neighboring India or Myanmar. Previously, it was

Table 1. Annual export earnings in Bangladesh from freshwater turtles and tortoises. Source: Export Promotion Bureau, 1998b.

Year	Amount (Tk.)	Year	Amount (Tk.)
1974–75	1,000	1986–87	34,485,000
1975–76	17,000	1987–88	50,798,000
1976–77	1,187,000	1988–89	22,162,000
1977–78	5,520,000	1989–90	9,190,000
1978–79	6,914,000	1990–91	5,110,000
1979–80	12,948,000	1991–92	9,533,000
1980–81	16,326,000	1992–93	69,070,000
1981–82	22,506,000	1993–94	176,285,000
1982–83	22,884,000	1994–95	190,187,000
1983–84	24,251,000	1995–96	155,145,000
1984–85	23,247,000	1996–97	379,152,000
1985–86	41,135,000	1997–98	72,260,000

assumed that turtles were smuggled into India through the southwestern land border, Benapole (Rashid and Swingland, 1990), but now it appears to be a two-way traffic. This seems to be a recent development with the opening of direct land transport between the two countries. Species such as *L. punctata*, *K. tecta*, and *M. petersi* are smuggled from Bangladesh to India (mainly Calcutta) for consumption, while species such as *A. hurum* and *A. gangeticus* are smuggled from India into Bangladesh for continued export mainly to Far Eastern countries. There are also indications of well-established land trade routes on the eastern side between Comilla (Bangladesh) and Tripura (India) and in the northwest between Dinajpur (Bangladesh) and West Bengal/Assam (India). Trade in small volumes, mostly for consumption, also occurs between Zukiganj (Bangladesh) and Karimganj (India) in the northeast; Durgapur (Bangladesh) and Baliganj, Shiliguri (India) in the north. These routes might be the links for turtle smuggling to China, which shares borders with India. In southeastern Bangladesh, turtles come in from Myanmar in the local tribal markets, usually for local consumption.

Live turtles are mostly transported to the airport at night or early morning and shipped by air before dawn. This is the time when there is comparatively less vigilance and manpower. Moreover, less people are involved in the dealings, which allow safe shipment of the consignments. Most of the shipments are destined for China, Hong Kong, Singapore, and Taiwan. Some consignments are also sent to Europe, the Middle East, and USA along with processed and frozen seafood (Table 2).

Recommendations

1. Creation of a law-enforcement division within the Forest Department to manage and regulate trade in wildlife and other forest products.

2. Booklets, pamphlets, and other educational materials, training sessions on species identification, and various laws governing the trade need to be organized and made available to the personnel carrying out these responsibilities.

3. Review and revision of the BWPA 1974 and other laws pertaining to wildlife trade.

4. Implementation and enforcement of a quota system to limit the volume and seasons for the collection and export of live animals, preferably after the nesting season. The quantity, either in total weight or number of live specimens for each of the species, should be determined every year by the relevant government department, i.e., Forest Department. This calls for an independent and strong Wildlife Department within the Ministry of Environment and Forest. For the time being the present wildlife research officers can provide up-to-date information on the status of the concerned species.

5. CITES export certificates (with country of origin) to be issued only upon physical examination of the consignment by the representatives of the relevant authorities, which include Forest Department and Customs personnel.

Table 2. Destination countries for turtles exported from Bangladesh in 1996–97 vs. 1995–96. Source: Export Promotion Bureau, Export Statistics, 1997.

Country	1996–97		1995–96	
	US$ Amount	%	US$ Amount	%
China	5,558,000	62.42	2,384,000	62.85
Hong Kong	3,060,000	34.37	1,262,000	33.27
UK	75,000	0.84	2,000	0.05
Taiwan	59,000	0.66	38,000	1.00
Italy	42,000	0.47	-	-
Japan	24,000	0.27	45,000	1.19
India	16,000	0.18	-	-
USA	15,000	0.17	3,000	0.08
Thailand	11,000	0.12	44,000	1.16
Bahrain	10,000	0.11	-	-
Singapore	9,000	0.10	-	-
Saudi Arabia	9,000	0.10	-	-
Germany	7,000	0.08	-	-
Canada	2,000	0.02	-	-
Malaysia	2,000	0.02	-	-
Czech Republic	2,000	0.02	-	-
France	1,000	0.01	-	-
Spain	1,000	0.01	-	-
Pakistan	1,000	0.01	-	-
Slovakia	1,000	0.01	-	-
Netherlands	1,000	0.01	-	-
Oman	-	-	15,000	0.40

6. Scientific authority for CITES should be formed immediately to help the management authority in regulating trade in turtles, other wildlife, and their products.

7. Update records of all turtle exports in the past, review them and plan for an export strategy. This should be done in conjunction with the Export Promotion Bureau. Until then all export of wildlife and their products should be temporarily suspended.

8. Cooperation and coordination between the various government departments to facilitate implementation of government plans to curb illegal wildlife trade and over-exploitation of wildlife resources.

9. Setting up national regulations and standards to improve packing materials and methods for transportation of live turtles and animals.

SPECIES ACCOUNTS

We now provide a listing of the 22 species of freshwater turtles and tortoises known to occur in Bangladesh, along with information on distribution, habitat, status, conservation, and trade. This information is also summarized in Table 3.

Family Bataguridae

Batagur baska. — River terrapin.

This species has been recorded from the Sunderbans in India and Bangladesh, southeastward to the Ayeyarwady River in Myanmar, and then south to Thailand, southern Vietnam, and through Malaysia to Sumatra, but it is now extirpated in much of its range. In Bangladesh, it inhabits the mangrove estuaries of Sunderbans and eastwards, possibly to Borguna. Unconfirmed reports exist from some upstream areas as far north as Aricha, more than 200 km north of the coastline, as well as reports of previous occurrences in the mangroves of Chokoria Sunderbans in the southeast and Nijhumdweep in the south (Khan, *pers. comm.*). This species has been seen in local trade in markets in the periphery of the Sunderbans. Reports from upper river reaches need to be checked since this species is involved in local trade and animals may have been transported there. It is also possible that animals could have traveled upstream for nesting, as Moll (1978) reported nesting females moved up to 100 km upstream in Malaysia.

Batagur baska is an endangered species, threatened with extirpation in Bangladesh. It is included in the IUCN 1996 Red List as Endangered and is listed in CITES Appendix I. The main threat to this species is local exploitation and habitat degradation. It is sought mostly for its meat, which is highly prized for some traditional Hindu rituals and believed to have aphrodisiac properties. Proposed as Critically Endangered in the IUCN-Bangladesh 1999 Red Data Book.

Cuora amboinensis kamaroma. — Malayan box turtle.

A semi-aquatic species first reported by Khan (1982a) from the Teknaf Peninsula, in southeastern Bangladesh. Later also found in wetlands in Sylhet and Maulvibazar districts in the northeast in areas adjoining the forests and tea gardens (NERP, 1994). An uncommon species often exploited locally for consumption as food. Not listed by CITES [now listed in CITES Appendix II as of April 2000] and not in BWPA 1974. Included in the Lower Risk: near threatened category in the IUCN 1996 Red List. Listed as Endangered in the IUCN-Bangladesh 1999 Red Data Book.

Cyclemys dentata. — Asian leaf turtle.

A little-known species, first recorded for Bangladesh in 1983 from a forest stream in Thainkhali, Cox's Bazar. Later recorded from Chunati forest, Chittagong in the southeast, and from Lawachera forest, Sri Mangal in Maulvibazar district in northeastern Bangladesh. Status in the wild not known but with loss and fragmentation of forests its habitat is also shrinking and presumably the population is declining. Not listed in the IUCN 1996 Red List. Listed as Data Deficient in the IUCN-Bangladesh 1999 Red Data Book.

Geoclemys hamiltoni. — Spotted pond turtle.

A rare turtle with shrinking habitat countrywide. Its populations have declined abruptly in the last 20 years primarily due to commercial exploitation for meat and, to some extent, habitat loss. Locally extirpated from some of its previous range, particularly in the southwest. Even though it was widely distributed in the past, present distribution is mostly confined to the districts of Pabna, Faridpur, Barisal, Patuakhali, Bakerhat, and Noakhali. Also found in the wetlands of Mymensingh and Sylhet but the numbers are extremely low. Protected under BWPA 1974 and CITES Appendix I. Also listed in the IUCN 1996 Red List as Lower Risk: near threatened. Listed as Endangered in the IUCN-Bangladesh 1999 Red Data Book.

Hardella thurjii thurjii. — Crowned river turtle.

This species is relatively common in Bangladesh. It is found in almost all the major rivers and large wetlands (*haor*, *baor*, *beel*) which retain water throughout the year. It is principally found in the river Brahmaputra and Dholeswari in the greater district of Tangail, the Surma and Kushiyara in the greater district of Sylhet, the Dakatia River in Noakhali, the Gumti and Titas in the greater districts of Comilla, Brahmanbaria, the Dholeswari, Burigonga, and Sitalakkah in the districts of Dhaka, Narayanganj, and Munshiganj, and the Kirtankhola in Barisal District. Occasionally found in small rivers, canals, other wetlands with little, if any current, but also in stagnant, enclosed water bodies, particularly during the dry season. Mostly traded locally but hatchlings are exported for the commercial pet trade. Included in BWPA I, which allows capture and trade. Listed in the IUCN 1996 Red List as Lower Risk: near threatened, and Endangered in the IUCN-Bangladesh 1999 Red Data Book.

Kachuga dhongoka. — Three-striped roofed turtle.

This uncommon species usually inhabits deep, clean, and clear freshwater rivers and large wetlands. Mostly distributed in the south-central and southern wetlands. Population declining mostly due to exploitation for consumption as food and habitat degradation due to river pollution. Protected under the BWPA, 1974 and also included for monitoring in the IUCN/SSC/TFWTSG Conservation Action Plan (1989). Listed in the Lower Risk: near threatened category of the IUCN 1996 Red List and Critically Endangered in the IUCN-Bangladesh 1999 Red Data Book.

Kachuga kachuga. — Red-crowned roofed turtle.

Little-known species with records from only the southern region of Bangladesh. There is a recent unconfirmed record from the Kangsha River, Netrokona District in the north. It may be possible that the specimen recorded from a market in Netrokona was procured from somewhere else because of the local trade involved (Akonda, *pers. comm.*). The status of this species is unknown. As the species is usually restricted to deep rivers with clean water, it may have suffered from river pollution as well as exploitation. Protected under the BWPA 1974 and also included in the IUCN/SSC/TFWTSG Conservation Action Plan (1989). Listed as Endangered in both the IUCN 1996 Red List and the IUCN-Bangladesh 1999 Red Data Book.

Kachuga smithii. — Brown roofed turtle.

Relatively common in the tributaries and distributaries of the old Brahmaputra River, with shallow waters and slow current. Two subspecies are known to occur in Bangladesh (Rashid and Swingland, 1997) — *K. s. smithii* is distributed in the central, northern, and north-central areas while *K. s. pallidipes* is found in the central, south-central, and southern areas of Bangladesh. This species is involved in local trade as well as being substituted for other species for export along with *K. tecta* or other hard-shelled batagurids. Protected under the BWPA 1974, but not included in the IUCN 1996 Red List. Listed as Endangered in the IUCN-Bangladesh 1999 Red Data Book.

Kachuga sylhetensis. — Sylhet roofed turtle.

A rare species known only from a few specimens. Restricted to the hill streams of northeastern Bangladesh and India. Uddin (1983) reported it based on a shell collected from an unknown locality in Sylhet district. Recent records also from Assam, India (Das, 1991). Protected under the BWPA 1974 and also included in the IUCN/SSC/TFWTSG Conservation Action Plan (1989). Listed under Data Deficient category of the IUCN 1996 Red List and proposed as Endangered in the IUCN-Bangladesh 1999 Red Data Book.

Kachuga tecta. — Common roofed turtle.

Locally common and widely distributed freshwater turtle. Inhabits all kind of freshwater wetlands and also the tidally-influenced estuarine waters of the southern district (Rashid, 1991). Exploited mostly for food in local trade as well as for export. The colorful hatchlings were also exported in the past for the pet trade. Because of the high volume of trade in this species, it has already become locally rare within parts of its range, particularly Fulbaria, Mymensingh. Because of local trade it is seen in large quantities in the markets, but its actual population in the wild needs evaluation and trade needs to be closely monitored. Protected under the BWPA 1974 and also included in CITES Appendix I. Suggestions to downgrade this species to CITES Appendix II have not been formalized. Not listed in either the IUCN 1996 Red List or the IUCN-Bangladesh 1999 Red Data Book.

Kachuga tentoria. — Tent turtle.

Associated with the rivers in the north, central, and some parts of the south. Found in the Padma, Brahmaputra, and the upper Meghna rivers and adjacent areas, sometimes along with *K. tecta* in slow current or stagnant wetlands. Two subspecies recognized in Bangladesh, with *K. t. tentoria* distributed in the Padma and Brahmaputra in northern areas as well as extending to central areas, while *K. t. flaviventer* ranges from the old Brahmaputra in central Bangladesh south to Greater Noakhali and adjacent districts. Apparent intergrade specimens of *K. tentoria* x *flaviventer* have also been collected from the old Brahmaputra River at Char Algi, Gaffargaon, Mymensingh (Rashid and Swingland, 1997). Protected under the BWPA 1974. Not listed in the IUCN 1996 Red List but recently proposed as Endangered in the IUCN-Bangladesh 1999 Red Data Book. This species certainly needs further evaluation.

Melanochelys tricarinata. — Tricarinate hill turtle.

Known to be distributed in northern Bangladesh at the foothills of the Garo and Meghalaya hills in India. Only a couple of specimens have been collected in the recent past (Khan, 1982a, 1987). Further studies are needed to determine its distribution within the country. Protected under the BWPA 1974 and included in CITES Appendix I. Listed as Vulnerable in the IUCN 1996 Red List and Endangered in the IUCN-Bangladesh 1999 Red Data Book.

Melanochelys trijuga indopeninsularis. — Black hill turtle.

Little or scant information available on its status and distribution in the wild. Apparently seems restricted only to hill streams. Recorded from hill streams of Cox's Bazar forests (Khan, 1982b). May also occur in the Chittagong Hill Tracts and northeastern forested areas. Protected under the BWPA 1974. Listed as Data Deficient in the IUCN 1996 Red List and Endangered in the IUCN-Bangladesh 1999 Red Data Book.

Morenia petersi. — Bengal eyed turtle.

Initially thought to be endemic to Bangladesh (Khan, 1982a) but later also reported from India (Das, 1985). An uncommon species widely distributed throughout the country and a major constituent of domestic trade. Distributed in the districts of Pabna, Rajshahi, Faridpur, Comilla, Noakhali, Brahmanbaria, Barisal, Bakerhat, Manikganj, Jessore, Dhaka, Sylhet, Sunamganj, Netrokona, and Mymensingh. Regularly seen in markets where turtles are traded. Population declining steadily because of the huge volume of trade. The size, between 1–2 kg, and affordable price makes it one of the species in high demand among people with low income (Rashid and Swingland, 1990). Population and trade need to be closely monitored. Protected under the BWPA 1974. Listed under Lower Risk: near threatened category of the IUCN 1996 Red List and proposed as Vulnerable in the IUCN-Bangladesh 1999 Red Data Book.

Family Testudinidae

Indotestudo elongata. — Elongated tortoise.

Widely distributed in the forested areas of northeastern and southeastern Bangladesh (Hussain, 1979; NERP, 1994). Populations have declined tremendously due to exploitation, habitat loss, and fragmentation of forested areas. Slash-and-burn techniques for clearing forested areas have contributed to its population decline. Protected by BWPA 1974, CITES Appendix II and listed as Vulnerable in the IUCN 1996 Red List and Critically Endangered in the IUCN-Bangladesh 1999 Red Data Book. Also listed in the IUCN/SSC/TFWTSG Conservation Action Plan (1989).

Manouria emys phayrei. — Asian brown tortoise.

A rare species found only in the forested areas of Chittagong Hill Tracts. Only a few records exist of its occurrence (Hussain, 1979). Exploitation and habitat loss are the main reasons suggested for its decline. A recent sighting was in 1988 based on a photograph by a member of the Bangladesh Armed Forces deployed in the CHT (Brigadier Shahjahan, *pers. comm.*). Included in CITES Appendix II. Listed as Vulnerable in the IUCN 1996 Red List and Critically Endangered in the IUCN-Bangladesh 1999 Red Data Book, also included in the IUCN/SSC/TFWTSG Conservation Action Plan (1989).

Family Trionychidae

Aspideretes gangeticus. — Ganges softshell turtle (Fig. 2).

One of the major species traded commercially and captured in large volumes for export. It was fairly common 10–20 years ago, but numbers have been greatly reduced by unregulated commercial exploitation. It occurred in all the major rivers and their tributaries but presently is confined to the deeper areas of large rivers — the Padma, Brahmaputra, and Jamuna — and their tributaries and also in the estuaries of the Lower Meghna in the districts of Noakhali, Barisal, Patuakhali, and Chandpur. The occurrence of this species in the Karnaphuli river system, Chittagong, is still not confirmed. Considerable variation has been observed between specimens from the northern and southern regions (Rashid and Swingland, 1997). Further investigation is needed to document the possible existence of two distinct subspecies. Protected by the BWPA 1974, listed in CITES Appendix I, but not listed in the IUCN 1996 Red List. Listed as Endangered in the IUCN-Bangladesh 1999 Red Data Book.

Aspideretes hurum. — Peacock softshell turtle.

This is one of the common species found throughout Bangladesh. It is found in almost all the river systems, including the Karnaphuli River (Rashid, 1991), large wetlands, including Tanguar Haor in the northeast (NERP, 1994; Rashid and Giesen, 1997). It is more abundant in the large ponds, natural lakes, man-made water reservoirs and estuaries of the southern region in the districts of Barisal, Borguna, Chandpur, Noakhali, and Patuakhali. It has also been recorded from ponds on the offshore islands of Sandweep, Moheskhali, Hatiya, and Kutubdia.

This is one of the major species involved in the turtle trade, both internationally and locally. A large number of individuals were exported between 1985 and 1992, estimated to be in the range of 10,000 metric tons per annum (Fugler, 1984; Barua and Islam, 1986; Rashid and Swingland, 1990) mainly to Japan, Hong Kong, and Singapore for consumption as food. Listed in CITES Appendix I and also in BWPA Schedule III. Recently listed as Endangered in the IUCN-Bangladesh 1999 Red Data Book.

Aspideretes nigricans. — Bostami softshell turtle.

Endemic to Bangladesh, currently known only from a shrine pond and some adjacent ponds in Chittagong. The estimated population is between 200–300 individuals, but these are overcrowded in the small ponds. Most of the animals are suffering from fungal diseases and there is a high chance of the population being lost to an epidemic. Inbreeding depression may also cause the population to collapse (Ahsan, 1997). Local devotees are very protective of these sacred turtles, and this has hindered attempts to relocate some animals. Listed as Critically Endangered in the IUCN 1996 Red List and also as Critically Endangered in the IUCN-Bangladesh 1999 Red Data Book. Included in CITES Appendix II.

Chitra indica. — Narrow-headed softshell turtle.

Distributed in all the major rivers of Bangladesh, i.e., the Padma, Jamuna, Meghna, Brahmaputra, Dholeswari rivers and their major tributaries. It is the largest freshwater turtle in Bangladesh and has become rarer in the northeast, northwest, and central regions while uncommon in the southern districts.

This species was caught in large numbers for the local trade in the late 1970s and early 1980s. Fugler (1984) and Barua and Islam (1986) reported it to be exported, however, Rashid and Swingland (1990) did not observe it in the local

Figure 2. *Aspideretes gangeticus*, the Ganges softshell, one of the most traded freshwater turtles in Bangladesh. Photo by B.C. Choudhury.

Table 3. Summary of distribution and status of freshwater turtles and tortoises of Bangladesh. Format: scientific name, English name, vernacular name, status, distribution.

Family: Bataguridae

Batagur baska — river terrapin, *boro kaitta*   Uncommon
     Sunderbans, south central (?), southeast (?)

Cuora amboinensis kamaroma— Malayan box turtle, *dibba kochhop*   Uncommon
     Northeast and southeast areas adjoining forest and wetlands – Sylhet, Maulvi Bazaar, Chittagong, Cox's Bazar, Chittagong Hill Tracts (?)

Cyclemys dentata — Asian leaf turtle, *chora kochhop*   Rare
     Hilly streams of southeast Chittagong, Chittagong Hill Tracts, Cox's Bazar and northeast-Sylhet, Maulvibazaar

Geoclemys hamiltonii — spotted pond turtle, *pura, bhuna kaitta*   Uncommon/Rare
     Major wetlands, distribution shrank largely in the northwest, southwest, north-central, northeast, and southeast

Hardella thurjii thurjii — crowned river turtle, *kali kaitta*   Common
     Major wetlands throughout the country

Kachuga dhongoka — three-striped roofed turtle, *dura kaitta*   Uncommon
     South and south central, Noakhali, Barisal, Patuakhali districts

Kachuga kachuga — red-crowned roofed turtle   Rare
     South-central and north, north-central – Noakhali, Barisal, Netrokona (?)

Kachuga smithii smithii — brown roofed turtle, *majhari kaitta*   Common
     In river systems, mostly in the north-central, south, and south-central parts of the country

Kachuga smithii pallidipes — brown roofed turtle, *majhari kaitta*   Common
     In river systems north-central, north, northwest

Kachuga sylhetensis — Sylhet roofed turtle, *sylheti kaitta*   Rare
     Northeastern Bangladesh, hill streams – Sylhet, Jukiganj

Kachuga tecta — roofed turtle, *kori kaitta*   Very Common
     Throughout the country in most water bodies, habitat shrinking

Kachuga tentoria tentoria — tent turtle, *vaitthal kaitta*   Common
     Most of the major rivers and tributaries, north, northwest, north-central, south-central – Padma, Brahmaputra rivers and tributaries

Kachuga tentoria flaviventer — tent turtle, *vaitthal kaitta*   Common
     North-central, south, southwest – Old Brahmaputra river, Noakhali

Melanochelys tricarinata — tricarinate hill turtle, *trishira kochhop*   Rare
     North and northeast – Mymensingh, Netrokona, Sylhet

Melanochelys trijuga indopeninsularis — black turtle, *shila kaitta*   Uncommon
     Hilly streams in southeast, Chittagong, Chittagong Hill Tracts, Cox's Bazar

Morenia petersi — Bengal eyed turtle, *halud kochhop*   Common
     Widely distributed, major wetlands. Population declining steadily

Family: Testudinidae

Indotestudo elongata — elongated tortoise, *halud pahari kochhop*   Uncommon
     Hilly areas in the northeast and southeast

Manouria emys phayrei — Asian brown tortoise, *pahari kochhop*   Rare
     Chittagong Hill Tracts, no records in the last 15 years

Family: Trionychidae

Aspideretes gangeticus — Ganges softshell turtle, *khalua, kocha kasim*   Common
     Major river systems including Lower Meghna estuary

Aspideretes hurum — peacock softshell turtle, *jat, dhum kasim*   Very Common
     Major rivers and wetlands throughout the country, including estuary in south and southwest, Dubla Island (Sunderbans)

Aspideretes nigricans — Bostami softshell turtle, *gazari, mandari*   Rare/Restricted
     Found only in a shrine pond and some adjacent ponds in Chittagong

Chitra indica — Narrow-headed softshell turtle, *shim, thal kasim*   Uncommon
     Major rivers – Padma, Jamuna, Meghna, Brahmaputra and estuary. Rare or nearly extinct from Surma, Kushiyara and Karnaphuli river systems

Lissemys punctata andersoni — spotted flapshell turtle, *sundhi, futi kasim*   Very Common
     Throughout the country, including southeastern and northeastern areas adjoining hilly forests

Lissemys punctata punctata — spotted flapshell turtle, *sundhi, dhur*   Uncommon
     Southern Bangladesh, particularly Noakhali, Barisal

Pelochelys cantorii — giant softshell turtle, *shuwa kasim, jata kasim*   Uncommon
     Mostly in the estuaries of the major rivers, Lower Meghna estuary, south and southwest – Patuakhali, Barisal, Khulna

---

and export markets, possibly because of significant population declines. Its large size makes it difficult to transport and local traders prefer to slaughter it to sell the fresh meat. *Chitra* populations are declining rapidly because of excessive exploitation to meet the demand for its meat in local markets, and collectors now complain of its scarcity. *Chitra* individuals from the northern and central areas of Bangladesh are lighter in color than those from the south. Listed as Vulnerable in the IUCN 1996 Red List and Critically Endangered in the IUCN-Bangladesh 1999 Red Data Book.

Lissemys punctata. — Spotted flapshell turtle.

     The spotted flapshell is found throughout the country, although it is most abundant in the southern districts. In the

northern districts it is relatively scarce and its presence in the hill districts of the Chittagong Hill Tracts needs confirmation, however, it has been recorded from the Teknaf Peninsula in the southeast bordering Myanmar. Two subspecies are found in Bangladesh, of which *L. p. andersoni* is more abundant than *L. p. scutata*, which is mostly restricted to the south.

     This species is included in BWPA Schedule I, which allows hunting and capture by permission from the relevant authorities. It is one of the major species involved in local trade mostly for consumption as food. Large numbers are also smuggled into neighboring India. It is also listed in Appendix II of CITES but not in the IUCN 1996 Red List. However, it is proposed as Vulnerable in the IUCN-Bangladesh 1999 Red Data Book.

Pelochelys cantorii. — Asian giant softshell turtle.

Distribution restricted to the estuaries and mouths of the large rivers in the southern districts of Bangladesh. Presumably more common than previously thought. During a survey in 1989 at least 30 specimens were seen in two weeks, slaughtered in the various local markets in the districts of Khulna, Barisal, Patuakhali, and Bagerhat. The meat is highly prized by consumers. Local collectors usually catch them by line hooks (*hazari borshi*) and fishing nets, and occasionally by diving. Moreover, its large size causes problems in transportation. So traders slaughter it to sell the meat in local markets and do not bring it to export centers. Listed as Vulnerable in the IUCN 1996 Red List and proposed as Critically Endangered in the IUCN-Bangladesh 1999 Red Data Book.

LITERATURE CITED

AHAMED, N. 1958. On edible turtles and tortoises of East Pakistan. East Pakistan Directorate of Fisheries, Dhaka, 18 pp.

AHSAN, M.F. 1997. The Bostami or black softshell turtle, *Aspideretes nigricans*: problems and proposed conservation measures. In: Van Abbema, J. (Ed.). Proceedings: Conservation, Restoration, and Management of Tortoises and Turtles – An International Conference. N.Y. Turtle and Tortoise Society, pp. 287-289.

ANONYMOUS. 1974. Wildlife Preservation (Amendment) Act, 1974. Government of the People's Republic of Bangladesh, 50 pp

BARUA, G. AND ISLAM, M.A. 1986. Status of the edible chelonian export from Bangladesh. Bangladesh J. of Fish 9(1-2):33-38.

DAS, I. 1985. Indian Turtles: A Field Guide. World Wildlife Fund-India (Eastern Region). WWF, Calcutta, 119 pp.

DAS, I. 1990. The trade in freshwater turtles from Bangladesh. Oryx 24(3):163-166.

DAS, I. 1991. Color Guide to the Turtles and Tortoises of the Indian Subcontinent. Portishead, UK: R and A Publishing Ltd., 133 pp.

EXPORT PROMOTION BUREAU. 1992. Bangladesh Export Statistics 1985-1991. Government of the People's Republic of Bangladesh, 30 pp.

EXPORT PROMOTION BUREAU. 1997. Bangladesh Export Statistics 1996-97. Government of the People's Republic of Bangladesh, 44 pp.

EXPORT PROMOTION BUREAU. 1998a. Export Directory - Bangladesh. Government of the People's Republic of Bangladesh, pp. 255-256.

EXPORT PROMOTION BUREAU. 1998b. Export from Bangladesh 1972-73 to 1997-98. Government of the People's Republic of Bangladesh, pp. 4-15.

FUGLER, C.M. 1984. The commercially exploited Chelonia of Bangladesh: taxonomy, ecology, reproductive biology and ontogeny. Bangladesh Fisheries Information Bulletin 2(1): 52 pp.

HUSSAIN, K.Z. 1979. Bangladesher bonnya jontu swampad o tar sangraskhan. (In Bangla). Bangla Acad. Biggnan Patrica 5(3):29-31.

IUCN. 1996. 1996 IUCN Red List of Threatened Animals. Gland, Switzerland, 448 pp.

IUCN-BANGLADESH. In press. The 1999 Bangladesh Red Data Book of Threatened Animals. Part 3: Amphibians and Reptiles. IUCN-Bangladesh, Dhaka, Bangladesh.

IUCN/SSC TORTOISE AND FRESHWATER TURTLE SPECIALIST GROUP. 1989. Tortoises and Freshwater Turtles. An Action Plan for their Conservation. Gland, Switzerland: IUCN, 48 pp.

KHAN, M.A.R. 1982a. Chelonians of Bangladesh and their conservation. J. Bombay Nat. Hist. Soc. 79(1):110-116.

KHAN, M.A.R. 1982b. Wildlife of Bangladesh - A Checklist. University of Dhaka, Dhaka, 170 pp.

KHAN, M.A.R. 1987. Bangladesher Bannya Prani. (In Bangla). Vol. 1 (Amphibians and Reptiles). Bangla Academy, Dhaka, 168 pp.

MOLL, E.O. 1978. Drumming along the Perak. Natural History 87:36-43.

MOLL, E.O. 1987. Survey of freshwater turtles in India. Part II: The genus *Kachuga*. J. Bombay Nat. Hist. Soc. 84(1):7-25.

NORTHEAST REGIONAL PROJECT. 1994. Wetland Resources: Utilization and Management. Flood Action Plan-6. Bangladesh Water Development Board/CIDA/SLC, 190 pp.

RASHID, S.M.A. 1991. On the occurrence of common roof turtle, *Kachuga tecta* in saline water in southern Bangladesh. British Herpetological Bulletin 36:39.

RASHID, S.M.A. AND GIESEN, W. 1997. Management Plan of Tanguar Haor: Sustainable use of wetland resources through community participation. National Conservation Strategy Implementation Project-1, Ministry Of Environment and Forest, Government of the People's Republic of Bangladesh, 210 pp.

RASHID, S.M.A. AND SWINGLAND, I.R. 1990. Interim report on freshwater turtle trade in Bangladesh. Asiatic Herpetological Research 3:123-128.

RASHID, S.M.A. AND SWINGLAND, I.R. 1997. On the ecology of some freshwater turtles in Bangladesh. In: Van Abbema, J. (Ed.). Proceedings: Conservation, Restoration, and Management of Tortoises and Turtles – An International Conference. N.Y. Turtle and Tortoise Society, pp. 225-242.

SARKER, S.U. AND SARKER, N.J. 1988. A Systematic List of Wildlife of Bangladesh. Privately published, 50 pp.

UDDIN, K. 1983. Turtles of several districts of Bangladesh. M.Sc. Thesis, Department of Zoology, University of Dhaka.

Asian Turtle Trade: Proceedings of a Workshop on Conservation and Trade of Freshwater Turtles and Tortoises in Asia
P.P. van Dijk, B.L. Stuart, and A.G.J. Rhodin, Eds.
Chelonian Research Monographs 2:86–94 • © 2000 by Chelonian Research Foundation

Status Information on the Tortoises and Freshwater Turtles of India

B.C. Choudhury[1], S. Bhupathy[2], and Fahmeeda Hanfee[3]

[1]Wildlife Institute of India, Post Bag No. 18, Chandrabani, Dehra Dun, India [Fax: 91-135-640117; E-mail: bcc@wii.gov.in];
[2]Salim Ali Centre for Ornithology and Natural History, Anaikatti P.O.,
Coimbatore, 641108, India [E-mail: salimali@vsnl.com];
[3]TRAFFIC India, WWF India, 172-B Lodi Estate, New Delhi, 110003, India
[Fax: 0091-11-4691226; E-mail: Trfindia@del3.vsnl.net.in]

We here provide a listing of the 27 freshwater turtle and tortoise species known to occur in India along with information on their distribution, status, conservation, and trade. The following abbreviations have been used in this report: CITES = Convention on International Trade in Endangered Species of Wild Fauna and Flora; IWPA = Indian Wildlife (Protection) Act 1972; NP = National Park; TR = Tiger Reserve; WII = Wildlife Institute of India; WS = Wildlife Sanctuary. For definitions of Schedules of IWPA, see Bhupathy et al. (this volume).

Bataguridae

Batagur baska (Fig. 1)

Common names: River terrapin; Bengali *pora katha*; *bali katha*; *sona katha* (Das, 1991)

Distribution (India): Sunderbans area of West Bengal, and possibly Orissa coast. Currently, it is restricted to the Sunderbans of West Bengal (Bhupathy 1997); its occurrence in the estuaries of Brahamani–Baitarani–Mahanadi rivers is doubtful (Bhupathy et al., 1994).

Habitat availability: Deltaic mangroves of Ganga and Brahmaputra in West Bengal, Subarnarekha, and Brahmini–Baitarini, Mahanadi in Orissa provide suitable habitat.

Population status: Exploitation has essentially eliminated the species from its distribution range in India (Choudhury and Bhupathy, 1993). It is extremely rare, and an estimated 10 breeding females survive in the Indian Sunderbans (Bhupathy, 1995, 1997). Populations have declined considerably and cannot continue to support sustained exploitation. Habitat loss is also a serious threat to survival (Das, 1997b).

Population trends: Apparently declining further.

Threats: Illegal capture for food and egg collection in the Sundarbans and habitat destruction.

National utilization: For subsistence.

Legal international trade: None.

Illegal trade: Local trade occurs between India and Bangladesh.

Potential trade impacts: Drastic population decline, possibly local extinction.

Legal status: Schedule I of IWPA, CITES Appendix I.

Species management: Continuing captive rearing (headstart) program in Sundarbans, West Bengal, for reintroduction since mid-1980s. About 40 captive raised 2–4 year old *Batagur* were released in the Indian Sunderbans (Bhupathy, 1997).

Habitat conservation: All existing habitats are in protected areas.

Control measures: Fish market raids by West Bengal State Wildlife Department have been so effective that even the subsistence level trade has now gone underground.

Note: Males develop breeding coloration during the mating season. Moll (1978) reported that the skin of head, neck, and legs of males from Malaysia turns black, and the irises change from yellow cream to white during the breeding season, while the skin of males from India and Myanmar instead turns to bright red (Das, 1991). Bhupathy (1995, 1997) observed male *Batagur* with black head and yellow-cream eyes in the Indian parts of the Sunderbans during March, suggesting further investigations.

Cuora amboinensis

Common name: Southeast Asian box turtle or Malayan box turtle. Assamese *jap dura*; Bengali *diba kochop, chapa katha* (Das, 1991).

Distribution (India): Northeastern India, along the Brahmaputra floodplains of Assam, Arunachal Pradesh and Nagaland, also Nicobar Islands.

Habitat availability: Vast stretches of wet grasslands exist in the Brahmaputra flood plains.

Population status: Kaziranga NP, Manas TR, Orang WS, and D'Ering WS hold considerable populations of this species (Bhupathy et al., 1994).

Population trends: No data.

Threats: Suspected pet trade; collection for food (A. Choudhury, *pers. comm.*).

National utilization: Subsistence use at local level.

Legal international trade: None.

Illegal trade: To be assessed.

Potential trade impacts: Drastic decline in population, localized extinction.

Legal status: Not legally protected [now CITES Appendix II].

Species management: None.

Habitat conservation: Inhabits 5 or 6 protected areas in northeastern India.

Control measures: None.

Cyclemys dentata

Common names: Asian leaf turtle; Nepali *thateru* (Das,

Figure 1. *Batagur baska*, considered critically endangered throughout its range, including India. Photo by Anders G.J. Rhodin.

1991); Mizo *tui-satel té*; Rhiâng *atangkrai* (Pawar and Choudhury, in prep.).

Distribution (India): East and northeast India, including West Bengal, Meghalaya, Assam, Arunachal Pradesh (Das, 1991), the North Cachar hills, and Mizoram (Pawar and Choudhury, in prep).

Habitat availability: *Cyclemys dentata* inhabits forest streams and forest floors of semi-evergreen and evergreen forests (Das, 1991; Bhupathy et al., 1999; Pawar and Choudhury, in prep.).

Population status: In northeastern India, it is widespread and common (Bhupathy et al., 1999); not uncommon in forested areas in South Mizoram (Pawar and Choudhury, in prep.).

Population trends: Unknown.

Threats: In Mizoram, collected when encountered incidentally, rarely for food, often as pets locally. Habitat loss in some areas.

National utilization: No records.

Legal international trade: None.

Illegal trade: Not known to be traded from India; to be assessed.

Potential trade impacts: Unknown.

Legal status: Not protected.

Species management: None.

Habitat conservation: Distributed in almost all protected areas of the hill forests of northeastern India, including Nameri WS (Assam), Namdapha TR, Pakhui WS, Itanagar WS (Arunachal Pradesh), Buxa TR, Jaldapara WS, Gorumara WS, and Mahananda WS (West Bengal), and the North Cachar hills (Bhupathy et al., 1999).

Control measures: None.

Geoclemys hamiltonii

Common names: Spotted pond turtle; Assamese *naldura*, Bengali *bhutkatha, kalokatha, bagkathwa* (Das, 1991).

Distribution (India): Brahmaputra and Ganga floodplains of northern and northeastern India.

Habitat availability: Limited in the Ganga floodplains; optimum habitat in Brahmaputra floodplains (Bhupathy and Choudhury, in prep.).

Population status: Common in the Brahmaputra floodplains, rare elsewhere.

Population trends: Apparently stable.

Threats: Local consumption and trade.

National utilization: Localized in northeastern India.

Legal international trade: None.

Illegal trade: To be assessed.

Potential trade impacts: Population decline and local extinction in northwestern limits of its range.

Legal status: Listed in Schedule I of IWPA and CITES Appendix I.

Species management: None.

Habitat conservation: Only in existing protected areas within its range. Known to inhabit Harike WS (Punjab), Keoladeo NP (Rajasthan), Kaziranga NP, and Orang WS (Assam).

Control measures: Local market raids are carried out by wildlife authorities.

Geoemyda silvatica

Common name: Cochin forest cane turtle; Kannada *bettada aame*, Katumaran *churel amai, sevapu talai amai*, Thulu *kunde aame*, Tamil *vengal amai* (Das, 1991).

Distribution (India): From Neria in Karnataka, south to Neyyar, Kerala; patchily distributed in between (Das, 1991).

Habitat availability: Restricted to moist Western Ghats forests, in the range of 400–800 m above sea leavel, may persist in suitable fragments.

Population status: Sparsely distributed.

Population trends: Unknown.

Threats: Mainly habitat loss to forest clearance and agricultural development.

National utilization: Localized, small scale at most by tribal people.

Legal international trade: None.

Illegal trade: To be assessed.

Potential trade impacts: Extinction.

Legal status: Schedule I of IWPA.

Species management: Captive breeding being attempted at Madras Crocodile Bank, Chennai.

Habitat conservation: Most existing records are from protected areas: Neyyar WS, Peppara WS, Peechi-Vazhani WS, Parambiculam WS, Indira Gandhi WS, and Mundanthurai-Kalakkad TR.

Control measures: None.

Hardella thurjii

Common name: Crowned river turtle; Bengali *kalo katha, boro kothoa* (Das, 1991).

Distribution (India): Plains of the Indus and Ganga-Brahmaputra river systems in northern India.

Habitat availability: Appropriate habitat remains available mainly in the Brahmaputra floodplains but also in the Ganga.

Population status: Common locally.

Population trends: Unknown.

Threats: Threatened by over-exploitation of adults and eggs as food and by habitat destruction (Tikader and Sharma, 1985).

National utilization: Occasionally found for sale in Indian markets (Choudhury and Bhupathy, 1993).

Legal international trade: None.

Illegal trade: To be assessed.

Potential trade impacts: Population decline.

Legal status: Not protected.

Species management: Captive breeding attempts in Lucknow Turtle breeding center (D. Basu, *pers. comm.*).

Habitat conservation: No specific efforts; inhabits Harike WS, Keoladeo NP, and Kaziranga NP.

Control measures: Conservation measures are not effective in many areas (Tikader and Sharma, 1985).

Kachuga dhongoka

Common name: Three-striped roofed turtle; Bengali *sada katha*, Hindi *dhoor* (Das, 1991).

Distribution (India): Ganga-Brahmaputra river basins of northern India. However, no recent records indicate its presence in the Brahmaputra.

Habitat availability: Main Ganga river and large tributaries.

Population status: Rare throughout its range (Bhupathy et al., 1999).

Population trends: Declining, based on market records (Choudhury and Bhupathy, 1993).

Threats: Commercial and subsistence utilization for meat.

National utilization: Widespread subsistence use throughout its range.

Legal international trade: None.

Illegal trade: To be assessed.

Potential trade impacts: Local extinction from many areas.

Legal status: Not protected.

Species management: Artificial incubation and hatchery at Morena, Madhya Pradesh, using eggs collected from captives at the Chambal NP (Rao, 1991).

Habitat conservation: No specific efforts.

Control measures: None.

Kachuga kachuga

Common name: Red-crowned roofed turtle; Bengali *adikori katha*; Hindi *lal tilakvala kachua* (Das, 1991).

Distribution (India): Found in the Ganga river basin in northern India. Reports from the Brahmaputra, Godavari, and Kristina river basins are doubtful.

Habitat availability: Large tributaries of Ganga with sandy bottom.

Population status: Undetermined; an elusive species.

Population trends: Reports of severe decline (BCPP, 1997) need to be verified.

Threats: Exploitation as well as pollution of the Ganga river (Das, 1997b).

National utilization: Undetermined.

Legal international trade: None.

Illegal trade: To be assessed; international trade unlikely.

Potential trade impacts: Unknown.

Legal status: Schedule I of IWPA.

Species management: Captive breeding attempts in Morena, Madhya Pradesh (R.J. Rao, *pers. comm.*), and Lucknow, Uttar Pradesh (D. Basu, *pers. comm.*).

Habitat conservation: River sanctuaries exist in the Gangetic river system.

Control measures: Unknown.

Kachuga smithi

Common name: Brown roofed turtle; Bengali *vaittal katha*; Hindi *chapant, chapatua* (Das, 1991).

Distribution (India): Ganga and Brahmaputra river systems (Iverson, 1992), Indus (Jammu) (Frazier and Das, 1994), and Punjab (Bhupathy et al., 1999).

Habitat availability: Substantial areas of appropriate habitat remain.

Population status: Common in the Ganga (Rao, 1995) and in Harike WS, Punjab (Bhupathy et al., 1999).

Population trends: Unknown.

Threats: Exploitation for meat; Rao (1995) found 203 shells on the Ganga river bank in Narora, Uttar Pradesh.

National utilization: Local exploitation.

Legal international trade: None.

Illegal trade: To be assessed.

Potential trade impacts: Unknown.

Legal status: Not protected.

Species management: Small-scale captive hatching and rearing at Narora (Rao, 1995).

Habitat conservation: No specific efforts.

Control measures: None.

Kachuga sylhetensis

Common name: Assam roofed turtle; Bengali *kath kathua, sylhet kori kathua* (Das, 1991); Mizo *tui-satel?*; Rhiâng *tetu-singmanakong* (Pawar and Choudhury, in prep.).

Distribution (India): *Kachuga sylhetensis* is restricted to the hill streams of northeastern India and Bengal (Das, 1997a). In the northeast, it has been recorded from Assam, Arunachal Pradesh, Nagaland, and Meghalaya (Bhupathy et al., 1999). Now reported from Mizoram, extending its range all along the hill states (Pawar and Choudhury, in prep.).

Habitat availability: Silty low elevation hill streams in Ngengpui, Mizoram (Pawar and Choudhury, in prep.).

Population status: Reported to be rare in part of its range; very rare in Ngengpui, Mizoram.

Population trends: Unknown.

Threats: There are unconfirmed reports of some trade involving *K. sylhetensis* (Das, 1991). Small in size and rarely found, but specimens have been taken within protected reserves for human consumption. Habitat loss may be a serious threat.

National utilization: Consumed by native people throughout its range.

Legal international trade: None.

Illegal trade: Not known.

Potential trade impacts: Unknown.

Legal status: Listed in Schedule I of IWPA.

Species management: None attempted.

Habitat conservation: Present in protected areas in northeastern India.

Control measures: None.

Kachuga tecta

Common name: Indian roofed turtle; Bengali *kori katha,* Gujarati *rangeen kachabo,* Hindi *chandan kachhua* (Das, 1991).

Distribution (India): Very widely distributed in north central and northeastern India.

Habitat availability: Occupies a wide range of aquatic habitats.

Population status: Generally abundant.

Population trends: Probably stable.

Threats: Pet trade to a limited extent. Seldom exploited for meat.

National utilization: Widespread in the domestic pet trade.

Legal international trade: None.

Illegal trade: To be assessed; suspected to be traded into the international pet trade (FH, pers. obs.).

Potential trade impacts: Unknown.

Legal status: Schedule I of IWPA; CITES Appendix I.

Species management: None.

Habitat conservation: No specific attempt.

Control measures: Raids of pet traders by enforcement authorities.

Kachuga tentoria (3 subspp.)

Common name: Indian tent turtle; Assamese *halika dura*; Bengali *majhari katha*; Gujarati *rangin kachubo;* Oriya *pani kaicha, andeicha kaichha* (Das, 1991).

Distribution (India): Northeastern and peninsular India.

Habitat availability: Rivers of north India; *K. tentoria* largely prefers the rivers, in contrast to *K. tecta* which prefers stagnant water bodies (Bhupathy and Vijayan, 1991).

Population status: Common in many area in its range.

Population trends: Presumed stable.

Threats: Seldom exploited for its flesh.

National utilization: No specific data available.

Legal international trade: None.

Illegal trade: None.

Potential trade impacts: Unknown.

Legal status: Unprotected.

Species management: None.

Habitat conservation: No specific measures needed or attempted.

Control measures: None.

Melanochelys tricarinata

Common name: Tricarinate hill turtle.

Distribution (India): Western Uttar Pradesh to Arunachal Pradesh, all along the Himalayan foot hills, and the whole of northeastern India.

Habitat availability: Along the moist deciduous tropical forest belt in its range and marshy grasslands.

Population status: Locally abundant in some parts, especially in Dehra Dun, Uttar Pradesh.

Population trends: Unknown.

Threats: Habitat destruction and some level of exploitation in the eastern limit of its range. Great numbers of shells of *M. tricarinata* are used to make decorated artifact masks, which are widely sold in tourist and craft markets.

National utilization: Localized.

Legal international trade: None.

Illegal trade: To be assessed.

Potential trade impacts: Unknown.

Legal status: Included in Schedule I of IWPA and Appendix I of CITES.

Species management: None.

Habitat conservation: Much of its range is covered by protected areas.

Control measures: None.

Melanochelys trijuga (4 subspp.)

Common name: Indian black turtle; Gujarati *kalarangano kachaboI*; Hindi *talab kachhua*; Kannada *kare aame*; Tamil *kal aamai, kareppu aamai*; Telugu *nuiye tabelu* (Das, 1991); Mizo *tui-satel*; Rhiâng *tetu* (Pawar and Choudhury, in prep.).

Distribution (India): Everywhere except the arid northwest and north-central regions; this species is widely distributed over seven biogeographic zones and in at least 11 states. Recently reported from Mizoram (Pawar and Choudhury, in prep.).

Habitat availability: Widespread in all kinds of lotic and lentic water bodies. It inhabits a variety of habitats, including rivers, reservoirs, ponds, streams, wet grasslands, and hill forests (Bhupathy et al., 1999).

Population status: This species is common in many localities; quite common in Mizoram (Ngengpui) at lower altitudes (Pawar and Choudhury, in prep.). The subspecies *M. t. coronata* has an indeterminate, possibly vulnerable status (Tikader and Sharma, 1985).

Population trends: Stable in most areas, though may be threatened in some areas in northeastern India, such as Mizoram, due to regular collection (Pawar and Choudhury, in prep.).

Threats: Subsistence exploitation for food and localized trade exist. Recently, this species entered the pet trade (Choudhury and Bhupathy, 1993).

National utilization: Widespread local exploitation of eggs and adults for food occurs (Tikader and Sharma, 1985). Recently entered markets for local pet demand in India (Choudhury and Bhupathy, 1993).

Legal international trade: None.

Figure 2. *Geochelone elegans*, the Indian star tortoise, is heavily exploited illegally for the pet market. Photo by Peter Paul van Dijk.

Illegal trade: To be assessed.

Potential trade impacts: Unknown.

Legal status: Not protected.

Species management: Has been bred in many zoos.

Habitat conservation: No specific measures, but occurs in many protected areas.

Control measures: No suitable conservation measures have been implemented.

Morenia petersi

Common name: Indian eyed turtle; Bengali *haldey katha* (Das, 1991).

Distribution (India): Eastern part of Ganga and western part of Brahmaputra (Das, 1991). This species was observed in Bettiah in northwestern Bihar (Moll and Vijaya, 1986) and Sunderbans TR (Bhupathy et al., 1994).

Habitat availability: Slow-flowing rivers and standing water bodies (Das, 1991).

Population status: Uncertain.

Population trends: Unknown.

Threats: Probably local consumption and export; in Bangladesh this is the major concern (Das, 1991).

National utilization: Unknown.

Legal international trade: None.

Illegal trade: To be assessed.

Potential trade impacts: Unknown.

Legal status: Unprotected.

Species management: None.

Habitat conservation: Present in some protected areas within its range.

Control measures: None reported.

Pyxidea mouhotii

Common name: Keeled box turtle (Ernst and Barbour, 1989; Iverson, 1992).

Distribution (India): Meghalaya, Assam, Arunachal Pradesh, and possibly also in Mizoram (Bhupathy et al., 1994).

Habitat availability: Forests continue to exist in its range.

Population status: It appears to be common in the North Cachar Hills, Assam, and Namdapha TR (Bhupathy et al., 1999).

Population trends: Unknown.

Threats: Collection for consumption and trade; possibly habitat loss and alteration due to shifting cultivation and logging (Das, 1991).

Potential trade impacts: Unknown.

National utilization: Unknown.

Legal international trade: None.

Illegal trade: To be assessed.

Legal status: Unprotected.

Species management: None reported.

Habitat conservation: At least some of its range is in protected areas.

Control measures: None reported.

Testudinidae

Geochelone elegans (Fig. 2)

Common name: Indian star tortoise; Gujarati *suraj kachhua, jamino kachabo, khadno kachba*; Marwari *khar kachhibo*; Tamil *katu amai, katu pota aamai*; Telugu *metatabelu*; Urdu *tariwalla kachhua* (Das, 1991).

Distribution (India): Peninsular India, from Orissa to Sind and Kutch and to the Tamil Nadu – Kerala border.

Habitat availability: Associated with xeric environments, including scrub-thorn and dry deciduous forest, up to an elevation of about 450 m above sea level.

Population status: Common in its range.

Population trends: Declining.

Threats: Pet trade; consumed in some places throughout its range.

National utilization: Widespread consumption.

Legal international trade: None.

Illegal trade: Well-documented as the primary species in both the Indian export and domestic pet trade. Annual export estimated to be over 5000 individuals (Choudhury and Bhupathy, 1993).

Potential trade impacts: Population decline.

Legal status: Schedule IV of IWPA; CITES Appendix II.

Habitat conservation: Present in many protected areas in its range.

Control measures: Market raids and confiscations.

Indotestudo elongata

Common name: Elongated tortoise; Bengali *pahari haldi kochchop, bon kochchop, shial chekouria, gecho kochop*; Hindi *suryamukhi*; Ho *horo*; Khasia *hunro* (Das, 1991); Mizo *telang*; Rhiâng *kerangkormo* (Pawar and Choudhury, in prep.).

Distribution (India): Northeastern India to Bihar and Uttar Pradesh.

Habitat: Evergreen and deciduous forests; found also in bamboo forest in Mizoram.

Population status: In northern and northeastern India, including Mizoram, the species is reported as rare.

Population trends: Possibly declining.

Threats: Local consumption; habitat degradation.

National utilization: Collected by tribal people all over northeastern India for local consumption (Das, 1991). Much in demand for local consumption by tribal people in Mizoram, who stockpile them to be eaten or sold later (Pawar and Choudhury, in prep.).

Legal international trade: None.

Illegal trade: Not well documented.

Potential trade impacts: Threatened in India; drastic decline in populations locally.

Legal status: Protected under Schedule IV of IWPA; India banned the export of the species in 1979 (Tikader and Sharma, 1985). The species is listed in Appendix II of CITES.

Species management: No attempts reported from India.

Habitat conservation: Present in many protected areas, including Saranda RF, Chaibassa in Bihar; Simlipal TR in Orissa; Gorumara WS and Jaldapara WS, West Bengal; Rajaji NP and Corbett TR in Uttar Pradesh; Meghalaya (Das, 1991; Bhupathy et al., 1999); Ngengpui WS, Mizoram (Pawar and Choudhury, in prep.).

Control measures: No specific measures reported.

Indotestudo travancorica

Common name: Travancore tortoise.

Distribution (India): This species is endemic to the Western Ghats of Tamil Nadu, Kerala, and Karnataka.

Habitat availability: Semi-evergreen to evergreen forest areas still exist in the Western Ghats.

Population status: Locally common in some areas, but generally considered rare (Das, 1991; Bhupathy et al., 1999).

Population trends: Unknown.

Threats: Habitat degradation and human exploitation.

National utilization: Localized subsistence use by local people.

Legal international trade: None.

Illegal trade: Unknown.

Potential trade impacts: A species with restricted range: possibly local extinction.

Legal status: Listed under Schedule IV of IWPA, and in Appendix II of CITES.

Species management: A single report of captive breeding success exists (Bhupathy et al., 1999).

Habitat conservation: Much of its range is in protected areas of the Western Ghats. The species is known to inhabit Kothaiyar RF (Tamil Nadu); Peppara-Neyyar WS, Peechi-Vazhani WS, Parambikulam WS (Kerala), and Neria forest, Sharavati WS (Karnataka) (Bhupathy and Choudhury, 1995).

Control measures: No specific measures taken.

Note: This species has recently been treated as part of *Indotestudo forstenii* of Sulawesi, following Hoogmoed and Crumly (1984). Pritchard (2000) separated the two forms as full species and reinstated *I. travancorica* as a full species endemic to southwestern India.

Manouria emys

Common name: Asian brown tortoise; Bengali *pahari kochchop*; Chakma *mon duri*; Khasia *phrau* (Das, 1991); Mizo *telpui*; Rhiâng *pepui* (Pawar and Choudhury, in prep.).

Distribution (India): Northeast India, including Meghalaya, Assam, Nagaland (Das, 1991; Choudhury, 1996; Bhupathy et al., 1999) and Mizoram (Pawar and Choudhury, in prep.). Likely to occur in all northeastern Indian hill states (Das, 1991; Pawar and Choudhury, in prep.).

Habitat availability: Inhabits primary broadleaf evergreen and bamboo forest, often resting in moist nullahs (gullies in the rainforest and bamboo forest) (Das, 1991; Pawar and Choudhury, in prep.).

Population status: In northeastern India the species seems to be rare.

Population trends: Possibly declining.

Threats: Habitat destruction and human exploitation as a food source.

National utilization: Localized, but may be serious in some tribal areas.

Legal international trade: None.

Illegal trade: Documented, but to be further assessed. In Mizoram, mainly consumed locally by tribal people and much in demand.

Potential trade impacts: Drastic population decline and local extinction.

Legal status: Schedule IV of IWPA, Appendix II of CITES.

Species management: None reported from India.

Habitat conservation: No specific actions, but is present in Nongkyllem Reserve Forest in Meghalaya, Kabri-Anlong in Assam (Choudhury, 1996), Ngengpui WS in Mizoram, and possibly also in other protected areas, including in the states of Arunachal Pradesh and Nagaland (Pawar and Choudhury, in prep.).

Control measures: None.

Note: Two subspecies, *M. emys phayrei* (northern subspecies) and *M. e. emys* (southern subspecies) are generally recognized (Moll, 1989; Das, 1991), though animals showing intermediate morphological characteristics are well known from northeastern India (Anderson, 1872; Das, 1991; Bhupathy, 1994).

Trionychidae

Amyda cartilaginea

Common name: Asiatic softshell turtle; Mizo *sumsi*; Rhiâng *tuimui* (Pawar and Choudhury, in prep.).

Distribution (India): At present reported only from Ngengpui and Mizoram, northeastern India (Pawar and Choudhury, in prep.). Possibly also in neighboring hill tracts in Bangladesh, Myanmar, and northeast Indian hill states.

Habitat availability: Found in hill streams with sandy or silty bottom, probably ascends these forest streams from nearby rivers in the monsoons. Found throughout the area surveyed in Ngengpui area.

Population status: Not uncommon in Ngengpui area; elsewhere unknown.

Population trends: Unknown.

Threats: Hill-stream habitat degradation and loss due to shifting cultivation, and maybe over-exploitation by tribal people.

National utilization: Local subsistence consumption and local trade, sold surreptitiously for Rs 40–50 (ca. US$ 1) per kg of meat.

Legal international trade: None.

Illegal trade: To be properly assessed.

Potential trade impacts: Local extinction.

Legal status: Only now recorded from India, therefore not formally assessed.

Species management: None.

Habitat conservation: At present known only from Ngengpui WS in Mizoram.

Control measures: None.

Aspideretes gangeticus

Common name: Indian softshell turtle; Bengali *ganga-kachim*; Gujarati *moti-kachab*; Hindi *patal*; Oriya *chabeda kaichha* (Das, 1991).

Distribution (India): Drainages of the Indus, Ganga, Mahanadi, Tapi, Mahi, Luni, Narnada (Das, 1991), and Brahmaputra rivers (Bhupathy et al., 1999).

Habitat availability: This widespread species inhabits a variety of aquatic habitats.

Population status: Common throughout range.

Population trends: Possibly in decline.

Threats: Meat trade, local and regional; egg collection.

National utilization: Widespread.

Legal international trade: None.

Illegal trade: Recorded, magnitude to be assessed, including illegal exports.

Potential trade impacts: Population decline.

Legal status: Fully protected under Schedule I of IWPA.

Species management: Headstart program in Ganges River since mid-1980s.

Habitat conservation: Various protected areas exist in the species' range.

Control measures: Protected species.

Aspideretes hurum

Common name: Peacock softshell turtle; Assamese *borkosso*; Bengali *dhalua kachim* (Das, 1991).

Distribution (India): Ganga-Brahmaputra river basins in northern and eastern India, Subarnarekha in peninsular India (Rao, 1991).

Habitat availability: Substantial areas of habitat remain available.

Population status: Nowhere common.

Population trends: Unknown.

Threats: Meat trade.

National utilization: Regional use, mainly in eastern India.

Legal international trade: None.

Illegal trade: To be assessed; illegal exports suspected.

Potential trade impacts: Local decline in population.

Legal status: Protected under Schedule I of IWPA and CITES Appendix I.

Species management: Headstart program was in operation in the Ganges River until the mid-1990s.

Habitat conservation: Inhabits several protected areas, e.g., Keoladeo NP, Varanasi, Kaziranga TR, Dibru-Saikowah, Manas TR, D'Ering WS, Mehao WS, Namdapha TR.

Control measures: Protected species.

Aspideretes leithii

Common name: Leith's softshell turtle; Kannada *pale-poo*; Telugu *nadi tabelu* (Das, 1991).

Distribution (India): Rivers and reservoirs of peninsular India, in the states of Madhya Pradesh, Maharashtra, Karnataka, Andhra Pradesh, Orissa, Tamil Nadu, and Kerala (Das, 1991).

Habitat availability: Inhabits various available aquatic habitats.

Population status: Relatively common.

Population trends: Declining.

Threats: Large-scale local consumption and meat trade (Choudhury and Bhupathy, 1993) continues in recent years (FH, pers obs.).

National utilization: Regional utilization heavy and sporadic nationally.

Legal international trade: None.

Illegal trade: To be assessed; no exports reported.

Potential trade impacts: Local extinction.

Legal status: Schedule IV of IWPA.

Species management: None.

Habitat conservation: Occurs in protected areas with riverine habitats, such as Nagarjunsagar Srisailam TR,

Papikomda, Sivaram Sanctuary in Godavari River, Manjira Sanctuary in Andhra Pradesh.

Control measures: Control of trade.

Chitra indica

Common name: Narrow-headed softshell turtle; Bengali and Hindi *chitra*.

Distribution (India): Indus, Ganga, Mahanadi, Godavari, Krishna, and Cauveri river systems (Das, 1991).

Habitat availability: Inhabits numerous riverine habitats.

Population status: Seriously threatened.

Population trends: Serious decline; very rare in the main Ganga now.

Threats: Exploitation for meat in trade; local consumption of eggs.

National utilization: Widespread.

Legal international trade: None.

Illegal trade: To be assessed; some illegal exports suspected.

Potential trade impacts: Local extinction.

Legal status: Protected under Schedule IV of IWPA

Species management: Headstart captive rearing program and reintroduction at Varanasi, along the Ganga.

Habitat conservation: Turtle sanctuaries exists in Varanasi (Ganga) and in the Chambal River, as well as in Satkosia in Orissa. Also, Harike is a Ramsar site. Known to inhabit Kaziranga NP and Nameri WS, Assam (Bhupathy et al., 1999).

Control measures: Market raids to control trade.

Lissemys punctata (2 subspp.)

Common name: Indian flapshell turtle; vernacular names have been reported from almost every region (Das, 1991).

Distribution (India): Almost whole of Indian peninsula, Brahmaputra and Ganga basin, excluding primary Western Ghat habitats, and hill tracts of northeastern India. Introduced in the desert regions.

Habitat availability: Inhabits practically all freshwater bodies.

Population status: Common.

Population trends: Stable.

Threats: The most common softshell in the meat trade. Habitat loss is not a major concern.

National utilization: Throughout the country, to varying degrees.

Legal international trade: None.

Illegal trade: This is one of the principal species for sale in Indian markets; 50 to 60% of turtles confiscated in Calcutta markets are *L. punctata* (Choudhury and Bhupathy, 1993). Illegal exports occur (FH, pers. obs.).

Potential trade impacts: Unknown.

Legal status: Included in Schedule I of IWPA and CITES Appendix II.

Species management: None.

Habitat conservation: Present in almost all protected areas with freshwater wetlands.

Control measures: Legally Protected.

Pelochelys cantorii

Common name: Asian giant softshell turtle; Bengali *jata kachim* (Das, 1991).

Distribution (India): Most reports from the Orissa coast.

Habitat availability: Known from mangrove creeks of the Sunderbans and Bhitarkanika until the early 1990s.

Population status: Has been practically eliminated from India due to exploitation (Choudhury and Bhupathy, 1993).

Population trends: Severely declining.

Threats: Mainly exploitation for local flesh trade. Possibly nest poaching also.

National utilization: Large numbers are used for human consumption in northern Orissa (Das, 1991)

Legal international trade: None permitted.

Illegal trade: To be assessed. Not known to be traded from India, though trans-boundary exchange between India and Bangladesh may exist.

Potential trade impacts: May result in local extinction.

Legal status: Protected under Schedule I of IWPA.

Species management: None.

Habitat conservation: All mangrove habitats in India are protected.

Control measures: Protected species, thus subject to enforcement of existing laws.

Note: The name *Pelochelys cantorii* was reinstated by Webb (1995) for the *Pelochelys* populations inhabiting the Indomalayan region; the name previously used, *P. bibroni*, is now restricted to the species of southern New Guinea.

LITERATURE CITED

ANDERSON, J. 1872. On *Manouria* and *Scapia*, two genera of land tortoises. Proceedings of the Zoological Society of London 1872:132-144.

BCPP. 1997. Taxon data sheets: *Kachuga kachuga, Kachuga smithii smithii, Kachuga smithii pallidipes, Kachuga sylhetensis, Kachuga tentoria circumdata, Kachuga tentoria flaviventer, Kachuga tentoria tentoria*. BCPP Reptile CAMP Report.

BHUPATHY, S. 1994. The distribution of Asian brown tortoise (*Manouria emys*) in India and the taxonomic status of subspecies. J. Bombay Nat. Hist. Soc. 91:147-149.

BHUPATHY, S. 1995. Status and distribution of the river terrapin *Batagur baska* in the Sunderban of India. Coimbatoire, India: Final Report, Salim Ali Centre for Ornithology and Natural History.

BHUPATHY, S. 1997. Conservation of the endangered river terrapin *Batagur baska* in the Sunderban of West Bengal, India. J. Bombay Nat. Hist. Soc. 94:27-35.

BHUPATHY, S. AND CHOUDHURY, B.C. 1995. Status, distribution and conservation of the Travancore tortoise, *Indotestudo forstenii* in Western Ghats. J. Bombay Nat. Hist. Soc. 92:16-21.

BHUPATHY, S., CHOUDHURY, B.C., AND MOLL, E.O. 1999. Conservation and management of freshwater turtles and land tortoises of India. Wildlife Institute of India, draft report.

BHUPATHY, S., SILORI, C.S., AND WESLEY SUNDERRAJ, S.F. 1994. Additional locality records for two Indian tortoise species. J. Bombay Nat. Hist. Soc. 91:149-150.

CHOUDHURY, A. 1996. New localities for brown hill tortoise *Manouria emys* (Schlegel and Mueller) from Karbi Anglong, Assam. J. Bombay Nat. Hist. Soc. 93:590.

CHOUDHURY, B.C. AND BHUPATHY, S. 1993. Turtle trade in India: A study of tortoises and freshwater turtles. New Delhi, TRAFFIC & WWF-India.

DAS, I. 1991. Colour Guide to the Turtles and Tortoises of the Indian Subcontinent. Portishead, Avon, England: R. & A. Publishing Limited.

DAS, I. 1997a. *Kachuga sylhetensis* recorded from northern Bengal, with notes on turtles of Gorumara National Park, eastern India. Chelonian Conservation and Biology 2(4):616-617.

DAS, I. 1997b. Conservation problems of tropical Asia's most-threatened turtles. In: Van Abbema, J. (Ed.). Proceedings: Conservation, Restoration, and Management of Tortoises and Turtles – An International Conference. N.Y. Turtle and Tortoise Society, pp. 295-301.

ERNST, C.H. AND BARBOUR, R.W. 1989. Turtles of the World. Washington, DC: Smithsonian Institution Press.

FRAZIER, J.G. AND DAS, I. 1994. Some notable records of Testudines from the Indian and Burmese subregions. Hamadryad 19:47-66.

HOOGMOED, M.S. AND CRUMLY, C.R. 1984. Land tortoise types in the Rijksmuseum van Natuurlijke Historie with comments on nomenclature and systematics (Reptilia: Testudines: Testudinidae).

Zoologische Mededelingen 58(15):214-259.

IVERSON, J.B. 1992. A Revised Checklist with Distribution Maps of the Turtles of the World. Richmond, IN, Privately Printed.

MOLL, E.O. 1978. Drumming along the Perak. Natural History 87(5):36-43.

MOLL, E.O. 1989. *Manouria emys* Asian Brown Tortoise. In: Swingland, I.R. and Klemens, M.W. (Eds.). The Conservation Biology of Tortoises. Occ. Pap. IUCN Spec. Surv. Comm. pp. 119-120.

MOLL, E.O. AND VIJAYA, J. 1986. Distributional records for some Indian turtles. J. Bombay Nat. Hist. Soc. 83:57-62.

PRITCHARD, P.C.H. 2000. *Indotestudo travancorica*... a valid species of tortoise? Reptile and Amphibian Hobbyist 5(6):18-28.

RAO, R.J. 1991. Ecological relationships among freshwater turtles in the Chambal Sanctuary. Study report, Wildlife Institute of India.

RAO, R.J. 1995. Studies in biological restoration of Ganga river in Uttar Pradesh: an indicator species approach. Final Technical Report, School of Zoology, Jiwaji University, Gwalior.

TIKADER, B.K. AND SHARMA, R.C. 1985. Handbook of Indian Testudines. Zoological Survey of India, Calcutta.

WEBB, R.G. 1995. Redescription and neotype designation of *Pelochelys bibroni* from southern New Guinea (Testudines: Trionychidae). Chelonian Conservation and Biology 1(4):301-310.

Asian Turtle Trade: Proceedings of a Workshop on Conservation and Trade of Freshwater Turtles and Tortoises in Asia
P.P. van Dijk, B.L. Stuart, and A.G.J. Rhodin, Eds.
Chelonian Research Monographs 2:95–100 • © 2000 by Chelonian Research Foundation

Exploitation and Conservation Status of Tortoises and Freshwater Turtles in Myanmar

Steven G. Platt[1,2], Kalyar[1], and Win Ko Ko[1]

[1]*Wildlife Conservation Society, Bldg. C-1, Aye Yeik Mon 1st Street, Yadanamon Housing Ave., Hlaing Township, Yangon, Myanmar;*
[2]*Present Address: Wildlife Conservation Society, P.O. Box 1620, Phnom Penh, Cambodia*

Myanmar is the largest country in mainland Southeast Asia (677,855 km^2), and contains a variety of ecosystems ranging from tropical forests and coral reefs of the Malay Peninsula to montane forests of the eastern Himalayas (Blower, 1985). The dominant topographical features are the relatively densely populated central basin of the Ayeyarwady-Chindwin river drainage, and the peripheral mountain ranges in the eastern, northern, and western regions of the country (Blower, 1985). The political landscape of the Union of Myanmar is composed of seven States (Kachin, Shan, Rakhine, Chin, Kayah, Mon, Kayin) and seven Divisions (Sagaing, Mandalay, Magwe, Bago, Yangon, Ayeyarwady, Tanintharyi).

At least 23 species of non-marine chelonians occur in Myanmar, including 6 which are endemic (Table 1). However, the chelonian fauna of Myanmar is one of the least known in Asia (McCord, 1997), and fragmentary observations remain the principal source of information (van Dijk, 1993, 1994, 1997; Kuchling, 1995). Most data originated prior to 1900, and even basic studies on distribution, status, and life history have yet to be undertaken (van Dijk, 1997). Furthermore, although large numbers of turtles are currently being exported to markets in southern China, this trade remains largely unquantified and its effect on wild populations unknown. While historical information suggests that turtles were at one time widespread and relatively common, all currently available evidence indicates that populations are now severely depleted, and some species may be on the verge of extirpation. This situation is particularly alarming given the high degree of chelonian diversity and endemism in the country. We herein summarize the existing information and present new data on the exploitation and conservation status of non-marine chelonians in Myanmar.

SPECIES ACCOUNTS

It is likely that all species of turtles occurring in Myanmar are exploited for either food or local and export markets, although trade records for many are lacking. Below we provide accounts for only those species recorded in markets or otherwise known to be exploited. Our summary reflects the general paucity of currently available information on the chelonian fauna of Myanmar.

Family Trionychidae

Amyda cartilaginea

The Asiatic softshell appears to be rare in Myanmar and its distribution remains ill defined. According to Annandale

(1912), the species is restricted in Myanmar to the Arakan (Rakhine) Hills, and mountainous areas of eastern and peninsular Myanmar. However, we recently examined two living adults held by a trader and captured in the Min Tone Chaung (Magwe Division) of west central Myanmar. Kuchling (1995) also reported five *Amyda cartilaginea* in the Ruili market (Table 2), which likely originated in Myanmar. This species is apparently in great demand and commands a relatively high price (Saw Tun Khaing, *pers. comm.*). According to one trader, his average monthly purchase of *A. cartilaginea* has steadily declined from approximately 480 kg in 1999 to 110 kg in 2000. Such a decline is highly suggestive of local over-harvesting.

Lissemys scutata (Fig. 1)

The endemic Burmese flapshell turtle occurs in a variety of natural and anthropogenic habitats throughout much of Myanmar (van Dijk, 1993). Large numbers are captured for both local consumption and export to southern China (Fig. 1) (van Dijk, 1993; Kuchling, 1995; Platt, 1999). However, the available accounts suggest this species remains common (van Dijk, 1993; Platt, 1999). Rapid growth, relatively large clutch size, and the ability to live in ruderal habitats probably allows *L. scutata* to sustain a higher level of harvest than other species of chelonians in Myanmar.

Nilssonia formosa (Fig. 2)

The Burmese peacock softshell is endemic to Myanmar and restricted to the Ayeyarwady, Sittang, and Salween rivers (Ernst and Barbour, 1989). Annandale (1912) reported *N. formosa* from as far north as the Chinese border. Few recent records are available, although van Dijk (1993) found the species at several temple ponds and the Mandalay Zoo (Fig. 2). We examined a photograph of a juvenile found at a fish market in Lontone Village, along the western shore of Indawgyi Lake (Myint Shwe, *in litt.*). The species is harvested for local consumption and sold for export, and has been found in food markets of southern China (H. Artner, unpubl. data), but the extent of this trade or its impact on wild populations has not been determined.

Family Bataguridae

Batagur baska and *Kachuga trivittata*

Two large estuarine turtles occur in Myanmar, the river terrapin (*Batagur baska*) and Burmese roofed turtle (*Kachuga trivittata*). *Batagur baska* has been reported from the Ayeyarwady, Salween, and Sittang rivers (Iverson, 1992).

Table 1. Checklist of non-marine chelonians that occur or potentially occur in Myanmar, based on comparisons with distributions presented in Ernst and Barbour (1989) and Iverson (1992). Additional information from Pritchard (1979), van Dijk (1993), Iverson and McCord (1997), and McCord (1997). Nomenclature follows Iverson (1992). Conservation status from 1996 IUCN Red List: CR = Critically Endangered; EN = Endangered; VU = Vulnerable; LR:nt = Lower Risk, Near Threatened; DD = Data Deficient.

Common Name	Scientific Name	Conservation Status
Endemic Species (6)		
Burmese star tortoise	*Geochelone platynota*	EN
Arakan forest turtle	*Heosemys depressa*	CR
Burmese roofed turtle	*Kachuga trivittata*	EN
Burmese-eyed turtle	*Morenia ocellata*	LR:nt
Burmese flapshell	*Lissemys scutata*	DD
Burmese peacock softshell	*Nilssonia formosa*	VU
Non-endemic Species (20)		
Mangrove terrapin	*Batagur baska*	EN
Malayan box turtle	*Cuora amboinensis*	LR:nt
Asian leaf turtle	*Cyclemys dentata*	
Crowned river turtle	*Hardella thurjii*[1]	
Giant Asian pond turtle	*Heosemys grandis*	
Spiny turtle	*Heosemys spinosa*[2]	VU
Pritchard's turtle	*Mauremys pritchardi*	
Indian black turtle	*Melanochelys trijuga*	DD
Malayan snail-eating turtle	*Malayemys subtrijuga*[2]	
Keeled box turtle	*Pyxidea mouhotii*	
Black marsh turtle	*Siebnrockiella crassicollis*	
Big-headed turtle	*Platysternon megacephalum*	DD
Yellow tortoise	*Indotestudo elongata*	VU
Asian brown tortoise	*Manouria emys*	VU
Impressed tortoise	*Manouria impressa*	VU
Indian flapshell turtle	*Lissemys punctata*	
Asiatic softshell turtle	*Amyda cartilaginea*	VU
Narrow-headed softshell	*Chitra indica*[3]	VU
Malayan softshell turtle	*Dogania subplana*	
Asian giant softshell turtle	*Pelochelys bibroni*	VU
Introduced Species (1)		
Red-eared slider turtle	*Trachemys scripta*[4]	

[1] Not yet recorded; may occur in extreme western Myanmar.
[2] Not yet recorded; possibly occurs in Tenasserim.
[3] No definite records, but likely present in rivers of northern and central Myanmar.
[4] Native to southeastern United States; present in temple ponds and possibly established.

Figure 1. Burmese flapshell turtle, *Lissemys scutata*, from Myanmar being sold at market in Ruili, Yunnan, China, just across the border. Photo by Gerald Kuchling.

Kachuga trivittata is endemic to Myanmar, being found only in the Ayeyarwady and Salween rivers (Ernst and Barbour, 1989). Historic accounts suggest both were common in the Ayeyarwady Delta (Theobald, 1868), and based on egg harvests, Maxwell (1911) estimated a nesting population of 1175 *B. baska* and 225 *K. trivittata*. However, a recent survey found no evidence of extant populations of *B. baska* or *K. trivittata* in the lower Ayeyarwady Delta (Thorbjarnarson et al., 1999). Extinction was attributed to long-term, chronic over-harvesting of eggs and adult turtles, and upstream deforestation which resulted in excessive silt deposition over nesting beaches (Thorbjarnarson et al., 1999). The status of these species elsewhere in Myanmar is unknown, but exploitation of *K. trivittata* populations in the upper Ayeyarwady and Salween is continuing and populations are probably declining (van Dijk, 1993).

Cyclemys dentata

This species probably occurs in hill streams throughout Myanmar (van Dijk, 1993), but little information is available on current status or exploitation. According to van Dijk (1993), *C. dentata* is collected for local consumption, but some living turtles are exported, as Kuchling (1995) found several in the Ruili markets (Table 2). We examined three living specimens destined for export at a trading establishment in Padan Village (Magwe Division) in west-central Myanmar. We also examined numerous living turtles and shells in Rakhine State, where *C. dentata* is widely consumed and plastrons are sold to traders for export. However, our preliminary survey data indicates *C. dentata* remains common in this region of Myanmar. *Cyclemys dentata* is captured with the aid of dogs, and also in elaborate traps consisting of bamboo fences and pitfalls constructed near fruiting trees along riverbanks.

Heosemys depressa

The Arakan forest turtle is endemic to Rakhine (formerly known as Arakan) State in western Myanmar (Ernst and Barbour, 1989). According to Myint Maung (1976) *H. depressa* also occurs in Kayah State, but the basis for this report is unclear and remains to be confirmed. Until recently only eight specimens of *H. depressa* were known (Iverson and McCord, 1997), but during an expedition to central Rakhine State in January 2000 we examined 17 additional specimens, including a living turtle (Platt, 2000). *Heosemys depressa* is captured opportunistically by hunters searching for tortoises, but owing to the low price received from traders, few hunters deliberately seek this species and the annual harvest appears relatively minor. *Heosemys depressa* is consumed locally and plastrons are sold to traders who periodically visit villages. Plastrons are later exported and have been found in Taiwanese medicinal markets (Hsien-cheh Chang, *pers. comm.*). Despite the paucity of records, we do not currently regard *H. depressa* as endangered, as market demand is low, harvest levels appear minimal,

Figure 2. Burmese peacock softshell turtle, *Nilssonia formosa*, from Myanmar. Photo by Peter Paul van Dijk.

extensive tracts of intact habitat remain, and Rakhine State is one of the most sparsely populated regions in Southeast Asia (Salter, 1983). However, we urge caution as populations could become threatened if harvest levels increase in response to changing market demands. Furthermore, plans to construct a large paper mill in Rakhine State and to begin commercial harvesting of bamboo forests could also negatively impact *H. depressa* populations.

Mauremys pritchardi

This species was recently described from 20 specimens obtained from markets in southern China and northern Myanmar (McCord, 1997). The origin of these animals remains speculative, but they were probably collected locally (McCord, 1997). The distribution, life history, and current status of *M. pritchardi* remain unknown.

Melanochelys trijuga edeniana

This endemic subspecies does not appear to be common anywhere in Myanmar. The scant data available suggest this species is consumed locally, and living turtles and plastrons are exported. We examined five shells in western Myanmar,

Table 2. Turtles recorded in markets of Ruili, Yunnan Province, China, on Myanmar border, during a three-day monitoring period in May 1993 (Kuchling, 1995).

Species	Number observed	Percent
Morenia ocellata	81	61.3
Lissemys scutata	32	24.2
Indotestudo elongata	9	6.8
Amyda cartilaginea	5	3.8
Cyclemys dentata	4	3.0
Melanochelys trijuga	1	0.8
Total	132	

van Dijk (1994) obtained a shell from Shwe Settaw Wildlife Sanctuary, and Kuchling (1995) reported a single specimen in the Ruili market (Table 2). It is unclear whether the paucity of records reflects relative abundance or market preferences.

Morenia ocellata (Fig. 3)

This species is endemic to southern Myanmar (Ernst and Barbour, 1989; Iverson, 1992). Historically, these turtles have been exploited for food, and Theobald (1868) stated that "incredible numbers" were harvested in the wake of dry season grass fires. Van Dijk (1993) believed *M. ocellata* was common based on the large numbers found in temple ponds and markets.

Morenia ocellata was the only species of non-marine turtle found during a survey of the lower Ayeyarwady Delta (Thorbjarnarson et al., 1999). The shells of five adults were obtained and most villagers were familiar with the species, although perceptions of abundance varied (Thorbjarnarson et al., 1999). At one village about 100 turtles are harvested annually. This harvest seems to be largely opportunistic, and most are collected from agricultural habitats during routine farming operations. *Morenia ocellata* are usually collected during the wet season (June to November), when gravid females containing 10 to 15 eggs are occasionally found. According to villagers, many of the turtles are consumed locally rather than being sold, and plastrons are purchased by traders.

Living *Morenia ocellata* are also exported to turtle markets in southern China, although the extent of this trade is difficult to quantify. A 1997 videotape taken in Guangzhou, China, showed large numbers of *M. ocellata* being offered for sale (W.P. McCord, *pers. comm.*), and the majority of turtles found during a three-day survey of the Ruili market

Figure 3. Burmese eyed turtles, *Morenia ocellata*, from Myanmar being sold at market in Ruili, Yunnan, China, just across the border. Photo by Gerald Kuchling.

were *M. ocellata* (Fig. 3; Table 2) (Kuchling, 1995). The impact of this trade on wild populations has not been assessed.

Pyxidea mouhotii

Few records of the keeled box turtle are available from Myanmar (van Dijk, 1993). A turtle photographed by Alan Rabinowitz in 1998 at a local market in north-central Myanmar, and shells we obtained from Rakhine and Kayah States are the only recent records. According to hunters, *P. mouhotii* inhabits rocky slopes and ridgelines, and appears to be uncommon throughout its ill defined range in Myanmar. *Pyxidea mouhotii* is consumed locally and plastrons are sold to traders.

Family Testudinidae

Geochelone platynota

The Burmese star tortoise is endemic to Myanmar and considered one of the least known of all living tortoises (Moll, 1989). *Geochelone platynota* occurs within the dry zone of central Myanmar, but its distribution remains ill defined. The species has been recorded from Shwe Settaw Wildlife Sanctuary (van Dijk, 1994; Platt, 1999), Minzon Taung Wildlife Sanctuary (Platt et al., unpubl. data), and the hills near Mandalay (van Dijk, 1993). However, *Geochelone platynota* has not been found in Chattin Wildlife Sanctuary despite an intensive search of apparently suitable habitat (Zug et al., 1998). The results of a recent survey (Platt, 1999) strongly suggests *G. platynota* populations have dramatically declined and this species should be regarded as critically endangered. Large numbers are collected opportunistically for food, and exploitation has recently been accelerated by commercial demands of the pet trade. Over-harvesting is believed to be the single most important threat to the continued viability of *G. platynota* populations, although habitat destruction and fragmentation have further exacerbated demographic problems. *Geochelone platynota* have been observed in markets in southern China (Saw Tun Khaing, *in litt.*), but little quantitative trade data is available.

Indotestudo elongata

The yellow tortoise probably occurs throughout Myanmar in a variety of habitats, including those altered by human activities (van Dijk, 1993). *Indotestudo elongata* is the most commonly traded turtle species and over-exploitation has resulted in widespread population declines (van Dijk, 1993; Platt, 1999). For example, only 6 *I. elongata* were located during an intensive search of the Shwe Settaw Wildlife Sanctuary (Platt, 1999), and Zug et al. (1998) found only one juvenile in 46 weeks of collecting in Chattin Wildlife Sanctuary. Large numbers of *I. elongata* are apparently being harvested for local consumption and export, and much hunting is done with trained dogs, an extremely efficient technique that is likely to overlook few tortoises. Both living tortoises and plastrons are exported to markets in southern China (Kuchling, 1995; Platt, 1999).

Manouria emys

Few records exist for the Asian brown tortoise in Myanmar. Theobald (1876) reported *M. emys* from Arakan (Rakhine) and Moulmain (Mawlamyaing), and other old records are available from Tenasserim (Tanintharyi) and the vicinity of Yangon (Iverson, 1992). We recently examined the carapace of an adult consumed by villagers, and found two plastrons at a trading establishment in west-central Myanmar; the latter almost certainly originated in Rakhine. These specimens constitute the only recent records of *M. emys* from Myanmar. Furthermore, villagers regarded *M. emys* as extremely rare and few had ever observed this species. Given the dense human population and intensive hunting pressure, we consider *M. emys* critically endangered throughout Myanmar.

Family Platysternidae

Platysternon megacephalum

The big-headed turtle is reported to occur in the hill streams of the Sittang and Salween drainages, although nothing is known concerning abundance or exploitation (van Dijk, 1993). A single turtle was photographed in 1998 at a market in central Myanmar (Saw Tun Khaing, *pers. comm.*).

TURTLE TRADE IN MYANMAR

The existence of a large illegal turtle trade from Myanmar into China has long been suspected (Jenkins, 1995). Hunters and villagers throughout Myanmar collect turtles by a variety of methods. Aquatic species are taken with nets, and specially constructed bamboo traps are used to harvest *Lissemys scutata* and *Cyclemys dentata*. Tortoises are taken with the aid of trained hunting dogs, a highly effective technique that leads to rapid decimation of local populations (Platt, 1999). Other turtles are taken opportunistically, but the collecting techniques for the majority of species have not been adequately documented. Turtle hunting is generally a part-time occupation to provide supplemental income, although some professional hunters earn the majority of their livelihood by this means.

Many turtles are collected for local consumption, but among some ethnic groups eating turtle flesh is discouraged by the belief that this practice is responsible for skin disorders, particularly among women. However, the majority of turtles collected are destined for the export market. Turtles are sold to traders who travel to rural villages specifically to purchase living turtles and plastrons. Traders hold living turtles until enough have been gathered to justify shipping. Mortality at this stage can be quite high given the generally inadequate facilities of the traders. In the more remote regions of Myanmar roads are poor or non-existent making it impractical to transport large numbers of living turtles to distant markets. In these areas turtles are consumed locally and only the plastrons are sold to traders. Traders ship living turtles and plastrons to buyers in Mandalay or directly to markets in northeastern Myanmar and southern China. Turtles from lower Myanmar are often smuggled north amidst crab-filled boxes. Much of the trade enters southern China along the old Burma Road (Thorbjarnarson et al., 1999), a traditional smuggling route into Yunnan Province (Hickey, 1992). Additionally, some living turtles destined for the pet trade are smuggled into Thailand through Tachilek, Myawadi and Mae Sot, and Three Pagoda Pass (P.P. van Dijk, *pers. comm.*). Similarly, a limited number of turtles from western Myanmar are reportedly smuggled into Bangladesh (S.M.A. Rashid, *pers. comm.*).

Statistics are currently unavailable, but the large number of Myanmar endemics that have been found in Chinese markets is suggestive of an extensive trade (Kuchling, 1995; W.P. McCord, *pers. comm.*). Kuchling (1995) visited turtle markets in Ruili, a frontier town in Yunnan Province, China, and found *Morenia ocellata* and *Lissemys scutata* composed the majority of turtles being offered for sale (Table 2). Other species, including *Geochelone platynota,* have also been found in this market (Saw Tun Khaing, *pers. comm.*). Market surveys have yet to be conducted in Myanmar, but large numbers of living turtles have been observed at trading establishments in Mandalay (A. Rabinowitz, Saw Tun Khaing, and C. Shepherd, *pers. comm.*). We found lesser numbers of living turtles and plastrons at trading establishments in Rakhine State and Magwe Division during fieldwork in 1999–2000. Significantly, nearly every village we visited seemed to have at least one individual who purchased turtles regularly.

This trade, while extensive, is illegal under Myanmar law. Furthermore, much of the export trade to China is in violation of CITES, which Myanmar became a signatory to on 13 June 1997. Turtles are protected by both Fisheries and Forestry laws, and all wildlife is protected in wildlife sanctuaries and national parks. Protective legislation is enforced by the Wildlife Division of the Forest Department and the Department of Fisheries. The Department of Fisheries does not issue permits for the harvest of turtles and Law 34 provides stiff penalties for those engaged in turtle trading. Some people have received prison sentences of up to two years for violations. However, the trade is so extensive that enforcement measures appear largely ineffectual.

Myanmar is currently expanding its system of protected areas in representative eco-regions throughout the country. Wildlife is legally protected in these areas, but in practice anti-poaching enforcement is minimal. During recent surveys of the Shwe Settaw Wildlife Sanctuary, we found collection by local villagers had resulted in drastic reductions of *Indotestudo elongata* and *Geochelone platynota* populations. Likewise, Thorbjarnarson et al. (1999) found illegal net fishing and crab collecting was commonplace in Meinmahla Kyun Wildlife Sanctuary. Other protected sites in Myanmar have not been evaluated, but the illegal harvest of turtles in these areas almost certainly occurs.

It remains difficult to assess the status of turtle populations in Myanmar given the lack of survey data; however, the available evidence suggests declines have occurred as a result of over-harvesting for both local consumption and to meet the demands of export markets. With the exception of *Lissemys scutata*, all chelonian species in Myanmar should be regarded as threatened by levels of harvest that are almost certainly unsustainable. Rigorous measures must be instituted by conservation authorities in Myanmar and China to regulate the trans-border wildlife trade between the two countries. Regardless of legal protection, as long as these markets are in operation, turtle hunting will remain a lucrative economic proposition for rural inhabitants and exploitation will continue. Without rapid implementation of protective measures, turtle populations may disappear before even basic ecological studies can be undertaken.

Acknowledgments. — Fieldwork in Myanmar was funded by grants from the Walt Disney Company Foundation. The assistance of U Saw Tun Khaing and U Thanh Myint, of the WCS Myanmar Program in Yangon was instrumental in ensuring the success of our field projects. Field assistance was provided by U Myint Shwe, U Soe Lwin, Daw Thin Thin Yu, Daw Lay Lay Khine, Daw Myo Myo, U Nyunt Hlaing, U Kyaw Tun Saung, U Aung Kyaw Soe, U Tun Kyaing, Bill Holmstrom, Bill Zovickian, and John Behler. U Maung Maung Tint, Park Warden of Shwe Settaw Wildlife Sanctuary deserves special thanks for his efforts to make our 1999 survey a success. The Department of Forestry is thanked for granting us permission to conduct surveys of protected areas. U Uga, U Hla Win, Alan Rabinowitz, Michael Klemens, John Thorbjarnarson, Peter Paul van Dijk, Thomas Rainwater, Stephen Johnson, John Iverson, and Thomas Rhott are thanked for providing references, information, and comments. Editorial comments by Peter Paul van Dijk and Bryan Stuart greatly improved this manuscript.

LITERATURE CITED

ANNANDALE, N. 1912. The Indian mud-turtles (Trionychidae). Records Indian Museum 7:151-180.
BLOWER, J. 1985. Conservation priorities in Burma. Oryx 19:79-85.

ERNST, C.H. AND BARBOUR, R.W. 1989. Turtles of the World. Smithsonian Institution Press, Washington, DC, 310 pp.

HICKEY, M. 1992. The Unforgettable Army: Slim's XIV Army in Burma. Spellmount Ltd., Kent, 318 pp.

IVERSON, J.B. 1992. A revised checklist with distribution maps of the turtles of the world. Privately printed, Richmond, Indiana, 363 pp.

IVERSON, J.B. AND McCORD, W.P. 1997. Redescription of the Arakan forest turtle *Geoemyda depressa* Anderson 1875 (Testudines: Bataguridae). Chelonian Conserv. Biol. 2:384-389.

JENKINS, M.D. 1995. Tortoises and Freshwater Turtles: The Trade in Southeast Asia. TRAFFIC International, Cambridge, UK, 48 pp.

KUCHLING, G. 1995. Turtles at a market in western Yunnan: possible range extensions for some Asiatic chelonians in China and Myanmar. Chelonian Conserv. Biol. 1:223-226.

MAXWELL, F.D. 1911. Reports on inland and sea fisheries in the Thongwa, Myaungmya, and Bassein Districts and the turtle-banks of the Irrawaddy Division. Government Printing Office, Rangoon, 57 pp.

McCORD, W.P. 1997. *Mauremys pritchardi*, a new batagurid turtle from Myanmar and Yunnan, China. Chelonian Conserv. Biol. 2:555-562.

MOLL, E.O. 1989. *Geochelone platynota*, Burmese star tortoise. In: Swingland, I.R. and Klemens, M.W. (Eds.). The Conservation Biology of Tortoises. Occ. Pap. IUCN Spec. Surv. Comm, p. 115.

MYINT MAUNG. 1976. The taxonomy of some turtles of Burma. Masters Thesis, Arts and Science University, Mandalay.

PLATT, S.G. 1999. A tortoise survey of the Shwe Settaw Wildlife Sanctuary, Myanmar. Report to Wildlife Conservation Society, New York, 42 pp.

PLATT, S.G. 2000. An expedition into central Rakhine State, Myanmar. Report to Wildlife Conservation Society, New York, 64 pp.

PRITCHARD, P.C.H. 1979. Encyclopedia of Turtles. T.F.H. Publications, Inc., Neptune, New Jersey, 895 pp.

SALTER, J.A. 1983. Wildlife in the southern Arakan Yomas. Survey report and interim conservation plan. FO:BUR/80/006, Field Report 17/83. FAO, Rome, 24 pp.

THEOBALD, W. 1868. Catalogue of reptiles of British Birma, embracing the provinces of Pegu, Martaban, and Tenasserim; with descriptions of new or little-known species. J. Linn. Soc. Zool. 10:4-67.

THEOBALD, W. 1876. Descriptive catalogue of the reptiles of British India. Thacher, Spink and Co., Calcutta.

THORBJARNARSON, J., PLATT, S.G. AND KHAING, S.T. 1999. Ecological reconnaissance of Meinmahla Kyun Wildlife Sanctuary and vicinity, southern Ayeyarwady Delta, Myanmar. Report to Wildlife Conservation Society, 55 pp.

VAN DIJK, P.P. 1993. Myanmar turtles: report on a preliminary survey of the Testudines of the Ayeyarwady Basin. Unpubl. Rep. to Turtle Recovery Program, The World Conservation Union-IUCN/SSC Tortoise and Freshwater Turtle Specialist Group, 34 pp.

VAN DIJK, P.P. 1994. Report on a visit to Myanmar, 18-28 January 1994. Unpubl. Rep. to Turtle Recovery Program, The World Conservation Union-IUCN/SSC Tortoise and Freshwater Turtle Specialist Group, 23 pp.

VAN DIJK, P.P. 1997. Turtle conservation in Myanmar: past, present, and future. In: Van Abbema, J. (Ed.). Proceedings: Conservation, Restoration, and Management of Tortoises and Turtles – An International Conference. N.Y. Turtle and Tortoise Society, pp. 265-271.

ZUG, G.H., HTUN WIN, THIN THIN, THAN ZAW MIN, WIN ZAW LHON, AND KYAW KYAW. 1998. Herpetofauna of the Chattin Wildlife Sanctuary, north-central Myanmar, with preliminary observations of their natural history. Hamadryad 23:111-120.

Asian Turtle Trade: Proceedings of a Workshop on Conservation and Trade of Freshwater Turtles and Tortoises in Asia
P.P. van Dijk, B.L. Stuart, and A.G.J. Rhodin, Eds.
Chelonian Research Monographs 2:101–105 • © 2000 by Chelonian Research Foundation

Turtle Trade in South Asia: Regional Summary
(Bangladesh, India, and Myanmar)

S. Bhupathy[1], B.C. Choudhury[2], Fahmeeda Hanfee[3], Kalyar[4],
S.M. Munjurul Hannan Khan[5], Steven G. Platt[6], and S.M.A. Rashid[7]

[1]*Salim Ali Centre for Ornithology and Natural History, Anaikatti P.O.,*
Coimbatore, 641108, India [E-mail: salimali@vsnl.com];
[2]*Wildlife Institute of India, Post Bag No. 18, Chandrabani, Dehra Dun, India [E-mail: bcc@wii.gov.in];*
[3]*TRAFFIC India, WWF India, 172-B Lodi Estate, New Delhi, 11003, India [E-mail: Trindia@del3.vsnl.net.in];*
[4]*Wildlife Conservation Society, Bldg. C-3, 2nd Fl., Aye Yeik Mon 1st Street, Yadanamon Housing Ave.,*
Hlaing Township, Yangon, Myanmar [E-mail: wcsmm@mptmail.net.mm];
[5]*National Conservation Strategy Implementation Project-1, Ministry of Environment and Forest,*
House no. 50/1, Road No. 11A, Dhanmondi, Dhaka, 1209, Bangladesh [E-mail: munjurul@hotmail.com];
[6]*Wildlife Conservation Society Cambodia Program, P.O. Box 1620, Phnom Penh, Cambodia [E-mail: Plattwcs@aol.com];*
[7]*Division of Biology, School of Science, Nanyang Technological University,*
469 Bukit Timah Road, 259756 Singapore [E-mail: carinam95@hotmail.com]

Trade Patterns and Routes

Bangladesh. — The center of the turtle trade on the Indian subcontinent is Bangladesh. Turtles are collected within the country and Bangladesh also serves as a regional collection center and trans-shipment point for turtles gathered in neighboring countries (principally India, but also western Myanmar and probably Nepal). Previously, most exports consisted of living turtles. However, in 1995–96 this pattern changed in response to a ban on the export of froglegs. The meat packing industry began processing turtles, and now most are exported as frozen meat. Likewise, the shrimp industry also processes and exports large amounts of turtle meat. Most turtle meat is shipped via air from Dhaka, and lesser amounts are exported from the seaports of Chittagong and Mongla. The majority of turtle exports are destined for China, although a lesser amount is shipped to India. There is also an undetermined amount of illegal smuggling of turtle products by ship. Additionally, there is a significant local consumption of turtles in Bangladesh.

India. — Three major trade routes are known to exist in India. The trade in *Geochelone elegans*, primarily for foreign pet markets, is centered in Bombay. Most tortoises are collected in western India, and smuggled from Bombay to the Middle East by boat. From the Middle East, tortoises are provided with false certification stating they are the offspring of captives, and then shipped by air to Europe. Turtles collected in southern India for both pet and food markets are moved overland to Madras and then shipped by air to Singapore. Softshells are the principal species supplied to food markets. Some turtles are also shipped from Madras to Colombo, Sri Lanka, and then to Singapore. Colombo also appears to be the center of the turtle trade in Sri Lanka, although the extent of this trade remains to be determined. In central and northern India, turtles are shipped overland to Calcutta

and then by air to Singapore and Hong Kong. Lesser numbers also move overland from eastern India into Bangladesh. The majority of turtles from central and northern India are destined for the food markets of southern China. A fourth route leading from India and Nepal into southwestern China is suspected to exist but remains to be confirmed.

Myanmar. — An extensive trans-border wildlife trade between Myanmar and China is known to exist, but travel restrictions in frontier areas have greatly hampered investigation by outsiders. The turtle trade is centered on Mandalay, where a number of wildlife traders are based. From Mandalay turtles are moved overland into northeastern Myanmar, and then into southern China along the old Ledo Road. Extensive markets exist in the Chinese town of Ruili, where turtles and other wildlife are openly sold. Extensive wildlife trade routes link Myanmar with markets in Thailand, but whether turtles are moved along these routes remains undocumented.

Nepal. — Little is known regarding the turtle trade in Nepal. Some local market surveys have been conducted, and limited export to food markets in China is suspected but has not been investigated. Additional turtles may be sent southwards into Bangladesh and then on to southern China, but likewise, this remains to be investigated. A fairly extensive trade exists in decorated curio masks made from turtle shells.

STATUS AND EXPLOITATION OF TURTLES IN SOUTH ASIA

Trionychidae

Amyda cartilaginea

Bangladesh. — Does not occur in Bangladesh; however, softshells exported from Bangladesh are often purposefully misidentified and labeled as *A. cartilaginea.*

India. — Recently found to occur in the Mizoram border area, where it is used for local subsistence; trade is not documented.

Myanmar. — This species is collected for both local and export markets. *Amyda cartilaginea* is in great demand and commands a relatively high price from traders. Almost nothing is known regarding its distribution and status in the wild.

Aspideretes gangeticus

Bangladesh. — Limited survey data suggest this species remains common. Captured primarily for export markets. Buyers prefer turtles under 1 kg, as these are easiest to process and package. Larger individuals are generally slaughtered for local consumption. More expensive than *A. hurum*.

India. — This species was formerly widespread in the Ganges-Brahmaputra River system, but dramatic population declines have resulted from over-harvesting. All size classes are now being collected. About 10% of the catch is consumed locally and the remainder is smuggled out.

Aspideretes hurum

Bangladesh. — Remains common. Frequently exported to food markets.

India. — Remains common in Brahmaputra River. Little is known regarding exploitation. Melanistic individuals are worth more than normally colored specimens. Eggs are consumed locally. To obtain eggs, nesting areas are excavated or gravid females are captured and held until laying.

Aspideretes leithii

India. — Restricted to peninsular India, where limited survey data indicate it is comparatively rare in most areas. Little is known regarding trade. There does appear to be a small harvest for local consumption.

Chitra indica

Bangladesh. — This species was common in the trade prior to 1986, but is now largely absent. The reason for this remains unclear, but is possibly due to population declines resulting from sustained over-harvesting.

India. — Limited harvest for local consumption. Populations believed to be declining and very few sightings of wild turtles in recent years. Furthermore, no longer available in markets, suggesting commercial if not biological extinction.

Lissemys punctata

Bangladesh. — Widespread local consumption of *L. punctata andersoni*. Eggs are also consumed. Few are apparently exported.

India. — Constitutes the largest volume of any single species in the trade. Available in markets during at least 9 months of the year. Most are consumed locally,

although a limited number are smuggled out to Bangladesh. *Lissemys punctata* is not being exported to China at this time, but may be expected to enter the export trade as stocks of other Asian species decline and become unavailable. Populations are robust and *Lissemys punctata* appears to remain common in both countries.

Lissemys scutata

Myanmar. — Large numbers of this endemic species are captured for both local consumption and export to southern China. Small to medium sized individuals are preferred for local markets. The available accounts suggest this species remains common in a wide variety of habitats. Rapid growth, relatively large clutch size, and the ability to inhabit ruderal habitats probably allows *L. scutata* to sustain a higher level of harvest than other species of chelonians in Myanmar.

Nilssonia formosa

Myanmar. — This endemic species is restricted to the Ayeyarwady, Sittang, and Salween rivers, although few recent records are available. *Nilssonia formosa* are harvested for local consumption and sold for export to China. The extent of this trade has not been determined and the conservation status of this species remains undetermined.

Pelochelys cantorii

India. — Present in market surveys during the 1980s, but no recent records. *Pelochelys cantorii* populations no longer sustain an export trade.

Bataguridae

Batagur baska

Bangladesh. — Extremely rare. No recent nesting reported. Last survey found only four males remaining. Commands an exceptionally high price when present in local markets. Aphrodisiac properties attributed to consumption of meat. Apparently very few are exported, probably owing to its extreme rarity.

India. — Extremely rare, but no data on population trends. Known populations restricted to the Sunderbans. The few specimens that reach markets are consumed locally, rather than being exported.

Cuora amboinensis

Bangladesh. — Consumed locally and also exported.

India. — Collected for local markets only.

Myanmar. — Status and distribution remain ill defined. No recent records.

Cyclemys dentata complex

Bangladesh. — Rare, confined to upland hill areas. Subsistence use only.

India. — Common, confined to upland hill forests of northeastern India. Subsistence use only.

Myanmar. — Status and distribution remain poorly known. Some are collected for local consumption. Plastrons are also exported.

Geoclemys hamiltonii

Bangladesh. — Exported to food markets in China. Populations are probably declining. Long-time turtle collectors note that formerly (about 20 years ago), 6 to 8 turtles could be captured in one day, whereas now none are to be found.

India. — Present in markets, but most are consumed locally. A limited number are also exported, although this trade is poorly documented. Populations are believed to be declining, and sightings of wild turtles have recently decreased by approximately 50%.

Geoemyda silvatica

India. — It is likely a few turtles are consumed locally, but there are few available trade data. The species is recorded in at least six protected areas of the western Ghats. Other than low levels of exploitation, there does not seem to be any immediate threat to wild populations.

Hardella thurjii

Bangladesh. — Consumed locally and exported to food markets. Females are particularly sought as they attain a larger body size than males. Hatchlings are also exported to pet markets. Recent range reduction noted, suggesting populations are declining from over-harvesting. Furthermore, long-time residents of many areas have noted an increase in the effort required to capture turtles. Selective harvesting of females likely exacerbates the demographic effects of over-harvesting.

India. — Small-scale subsistence use, primarily in northeastern India. Occasionally found in Calcutta markets and a limited number are probably exported. Decline in number of turtles found in market surveys indicative of population declines.

Kachuga dhongoka

Bangladesh. — Very small numbers are exported; extremely rare.

India. — Extremely rare; regarded as critically endangered due to past over-harvesting. A few are consumed locally, but this species does not appear to be exported in significant numbers owing to its rarity. No recent market records.

Kachuga kachuga

India. — This species is regarded as critically endangered. Nonetheless, there is some local consumption of the few turtles remaining. Has not been encountered in recent market surveys.

Kachuga smithi

Bangladesh. — Collected for export and local markets.

India. — Large-scale local use, but apparently few are exported.

Kachuga sylhetensis

Bangladesh. — Extremely rare; present only in eastern region of the country. Few recent records. Local consumption only.

India. — Extremely rare and confined to northeastern Indian states, such as Assam, Arunachal Pradesh, Nagaland, and Meghalaya. Consumed locally, but not exported.

Kachuga tecta

Bangladesh. — Large numbers present in local food markets; also exported to food and pet markets. Populations declining and becoming rare in some regions. Low frequency of sightings along many rivers.

India. — Eaten locally and exported for pet market.

Kachuga tentoria

Bangladesh. — Consumed locally, but apparently only exported in small numbers for the pet trade.

India. — Consumed locally, but not exported.

Kachuga trivittata

Myanmar. — Very little information is available on this endemic species. Populations at mouth of the Ayeyarwady River are believed extirpated. Elsewhere, the species is still probably collected for local consumption. Some eggs may also be harvested.

Melanochelys tricarinata

Bangladesh. — Local consumption only.

India. — Local consumption, but some exported for pet trade.

Melanochelys trijuga

Bangladesh. — Local consumption only.

India. — Primarily consumed by certain hill tribes. The strong smell of the meat is objectionable to many people, and there is little demand for this species in local markets. This species is not exported.

Myanmar. — Apparently the species is rare in most areas. A few are consumed locally; live animals and plastrons are exported to China.

Morenia ocellata

Myanmar. — This endemic species is exploited for local consumption, but large numbers were also exported to markets in southern China. The status of wild populations is unknown, but based on the number of turtles in markets and temple ponds, it was probably common in many areas in the recent past.

Morenia petersi

Bangladesh. — This turtle was the second-most common species encountered in market surveys. Many are consumed locally, but significant numbers are also exported to food markets in China. Local hunters have reported that an increasing amount of effort is required to capture turtles in areas where they were formerly common.

India. — Very few records. Apparently not present in local or export trade.

Pyxidea mouhotii

India. — Likely some collecting for local markets, but very few records. This species is not exported.

Myanmar. — Few records, but has been recorded in local markets and almost certainly exported to food markets in southern China. Distribution and status remains virtually unknown.

Testudinidae

Geochelone elegans

India. — The only Indian tortoise species affected by trade. Extensive illegal collection in western India to supply European pet markets. Wildlife authorities consistently confiscate large shipments of these tortoises indicating the magnitude of this trade. Remains common in many areas, but many populations are undoubtedly being over-harvested. Little recruitment is occurring in many populations as smaller tortoises are selectively collected for the pet trade. Declines have also been noted among larger size classes in other populations. A status survey is urgently needed to assess the impacts of harvest levels. *Geochelone elegans* is also being collected in Sri Lanka and Pakistan for European and Asian pet markets.

Geochelone platynota

Myanmar. — This endemic tortoise occurs within the central dry zone of Myanmar, but its distribution remains ill defined. Large numbers are collected by locals for food, and exploitation has been accelerated by recent commercial demands of the pet trade. Few quantitative trade data are available. Populations have dramatically declined and the species is considered critically endangered.

Indotestudo elongata

Bangladesh. — Consumed locally, and some are also exported. Steady decline in the number of tortoises observed in markets probably indicates populations are being subjected to unsustainable levels of harvest. Additionally, smaller size classes are now entering the trade in larger numbers.

India. — Uncommon. Little evidence of export, although some local consumption.

Myanmar. — Widespread collection for local consumption and export. Both living tortoises and plastrons are exported. Field surveys indicate populations are declining in many areas as a result of over-collection.

Indotestudo travancorica

India. — Some exploitation for consumption by tribal inhabitants of the western Ghats. This species is not exported from India, and specimens of *I. travancorica / forstenii* reported from Chinese markets almost certainly originated from Sulawesi, Indonesia.

Manouria emys

Bangladesh. — Extremely rare. Last recorded in 1988. No recent exports, although the few remaining populations are undoubtedly harvested for local consumption.

India. — Occurs only in northeast India where there is some local consumption. No records of any recent exports.

Myanmar. — Extremely rare and extirpated from many areas. Very few recent records. These tortoises are eaten locally and plastrons are exported to China.

CONSERVATION LEGISLATION

Bangladesh

Wildlife Preservation Act of 1973. — This is the most important document concerning wildlife legislation in the country. It was amended in 1974. A proposal to revise the act was drafted about 10 years ago, but no action has since been taken. The act places all wildlife on one of three schedules. Schedule 1 species are not protected. These include *Indotestudo elongata* and *Aspideretes hurum*. Schedule 2 species are monitored and a permit is required from the Forest Department for trade. No turtles are listed on Schedule 2. Schedule 3 species are totally protected, and any trade or harvest is considered illegal. Four turtles are listed as Schedule 3 species; these are *Morenia petersi*, *Aspideretes gangeticus*, *Aspideretes nigricans*, and *Lissemys punctata*.

Enforcement. — Forest Officers are designated as wardens, who are responsible for enforcement of the Wildlife Protection Act. There are 21 Forest Divisions in Bangladesh, each commanded by a District Forest Officer designated as the area warden. Violators can be sentenced to up to two years in jail and fined up to US\$ 1000. Unfortunately, enforcement and sentencing has been lax, and violators often receive light sentences or are not prosecuted. There is currently a program underway to educate judges about the need for strict enforcement of protective wildlife legislation.

India

Wildlife Protection Act of 1972. — This is the major wildlife protection legislation in the country. The act was amended in 1972, and a new amendment is currently pending. Species are assigned to one of four schedules. The greatest degree of protection is afforded to Schedule 1 species. Both federal and provincial permission is required for any activity involving these species. A lesser degree of protection is afforded species on Schedules 2 and 3. Trade in these species is prohibited, although possession is allowed provided permits are obtained from provincial authorities. Local trade in Schedule 4 species is permitted, providing permission is obtained from provincial authorities.

Enforcement. — There are six Federal Wildlife Directorates in India. Each region is staffed by 6 to 10 wildlife inspectors who randomly check trade consignments. Furthermore, Provincial Forest Officers are responsible for enforcement of wildlife laws, and each province has 300 to 700 such officers. Additionally, Honorary Wardens can confiscate illegally held wildlife, although they are not allowed to prosecute cases.

Violations involving Schedule 1 species must be handled by Federal Courts, while other violations can be resolved by Forest Officers in local courts. Typically, violations involving Schedule 1 species carry penalties of two to six years imprisonment and fines. Fines are typically imposed for violations involving other species. The judiciary has been lenient in imposing penalties for cases involving violations of wildlife laws.

Myanmar

According to law, blanket protection is extended to all wildlife species. Furthermore, the Fisheries Department provides additional protection to all species of turtles. Enforcement of protective wildlife legislation is the responsibility of the Departments of Fisheries and Forestry. Violators face a US$ 1500 fine and up to two years in jail. Twenty-three people were sentenced to jail for turtle trading in 1998.

CONSERVATION RECOMMENDATIONS

Bangladesh

1. Comprehensive review of the distribution and status of all turtle species, impacts of harvesting, and condition and availability of habitat are needed. Particular efforts should be devoted to determining the conservation status of *Kachuga kachuga* and *K. dhongoka*. Formerly common, these species have disappeared from markets in recent years and may be commercially extinct. Other high priority species include *Batagur baska* and *Chitra indica.*

2. Conduct countrywide market surveys to determine levels of trade for each species.

3. Include turtles in future Environmental Impact Statements for development projects.

India

1. Determine the conservation status of *Kachuga kachuga* and *K. dhongoka* and develop plans for population recovery.

2. Determine the conservation status and effects of subsistence hunting on *Indotestudo travancorica* and *Geoemyda silvatica* in western Ghats.

3. Investigate subsistence harvest of turtles in northeastern India.

4. Conduct a countrywide market survey in 2002. Previous surveys were conducted in 1983 and 1993. Completion of a survey in 2003 will provide market data spanning a 20-year period.

Myanmar

1. Continue countrywide turtle biodiversity inventory and status survey. Special effort should be given to determining the status of endemic species, such as *Geochelone platynota*, *Heosemys depressa*, *Kachuga trivittata*, and *Nilssonia formosa.*

2. Market surveys are urgently needed to determine what species are involved in the trade and in what amount. Market surveys are particularly needed in Mandalay and the border region of northeastern Myanmar.

Regional Recommendations

1. Continue market surveys throughout the region. General conservation status surveys are urgently needed for almost all species in the region.

2. Monitor trade between India, Bangladesh, Myanmar, and Nepal. Furthermore, market surveys should also be initiated in Nepal, Pakistan, and Sri Lanka as there are currently almost no trade data from these countries.

3. Develop regional databases incorporating available trade data.

4. Review existing conservation and trade legislation, and amend if deemed necessary.

5. Develop regional turtle identification guides in local languages for Bangladesh, Myanmar, and Nepal.

6. Conduct workshops and compulsive in-service training in turtle identification and protective legislation for customs officials, border police, and others responsible for enforcing laws pertaining to wildlife trade.

7. Develop protocols for repatriation of confiscated turtles into nature reserves and other protected areas.

8. Importing countries should provide accounting to countries of origin. Accounts should be presented for each species.

9. Keep turtle trade issues at forefront of media.

10. Work with airlines to reduce trade by insisting on observance of animal shipping guidelines.

Freshwater Turtle and Tortoise Conservation and Utilization in Indonesia

Samedi[1] and Djoko T. Iskandar[2]

[1]*Directorate General of Nature Protection and Conservation, Ministry of Forestry and Estate Crops,*
Manggala Wanabakti Building, Block VII, 7th floor, Jl. Gatot Subroto, Senayan, Jakarta, Indonesia
[Fax: 62-21-572-0227; E-mail: sam.phpa@dephut.cbn.net.id];
[2]*Genetics Laboratory, Institute of Technology,*
Bandung Labtek XI, 2nd floor, Jl. Ganesa 10, Bandung 40132 Indonesia
[Fax: 62-22-250-0258; Email: iskandar@bi.itb.ac.id]

Freshwater turtles and tortoises are among the most important components of Indonesian biodiversity. However, they are not as well-known or popular as the sea turtles. Even though taxonomists have not reached consensus on the nomenclature of all freshwater turtles and tortoises, some scientific publications on the taxonomy of these species have been compiled in the Data Dictionary of the Wetland Database. About 29 described species have been recorded or suspected to be native to Indonesia (Table 1; Wibowo, 1999, updated). This means that the richness in species is quite high, containing 11.2% of the world's 260 species of freshwater turtles and tortoises (IUCN/SSC Tortoise and Freshwater Turtle Specialist Group, 1991).

Biological Parameters

Distribution. — As seen in Table 1, the distribution of freshwater turtles and tortoises is skewed with most species confined to the western Indonesian islands of Sumatra, Borneo, and Java. Some species, mostly from eastern Indonesia, are known to be endemic to Indonesia. These are *Chelodina mccordi* (Roti) (Fig. 1), *Heosemys yuwonoi* (Sulawesi) (Fig. 2), *Chelodina reimanni* (Irian Jaya), and *Elseya branderhorstii* (Irian Jaya). In addition, *Pelochelys bibroni, Chelodina parkeri, C. siebenrocki, Elseya novaeguineae,* and several additional undescribed species of the genus *Elseya* are endemic to the island of New Guinea, including Indonesian Irian Jaya and Papua New Guinea.

Habitat Availability. — Wetlands are an important habitat element for freshwater turtles and tortoises. The Wetland International Indonesia Program has compiled information in its Wetland Database (WDB) on 272 important wetland sites in Indonesia. From these sites, 24 locations (Table 2) have been identified as especially important habitats for 15 species of freshwater turtles and tortoises.

Population Status. — Information is limited on the status of most populations of freshwater turtles and tortoises in the wild. Table 1 shows the current population status of all the Indonesian species. Only 6 species are now totally protected in Indonesia. Even though many more species have been categorized by the IUCN 1996 Red List as Endangered or Vulnerable, they are not currently protected in Indonesia. Furthermore, *Chitra indica* probably does not occur in Indonesia, but this species is listed as an Indonesian protected species and records are included in the Wetland Database (Wibowo, 1999); this name is likely based on a misidentification and probably applies to *Chitra chitra* or perhaps *Pelochelys*.

Population Trends. — There is little scientific information on the population trends of freshwater turtles and tortoises in Indonesia. However, information from traders and hunters indicates that some species, such as *Orlitia borneensis, Indotestudo forstenii, Manouria emys,* and *Notochelys platynota* have declined considerably. The declines in populations have been indicated by considerable reductions in the numbers of animals caught and handled by hunters and traders in recent years. In the period 1999–2000, a number of reptile dealers in the pet trade have changed their profession because many reptile species are now unavailable. The species *Chelodina mccordi* (Fig. 1) is possibly extinct in its natural habitat and is considered commercially extinct by Indonesian pet traders. All specimens in the market were bought by a single Indonesian animal trader soon after the government issued a quota when the species was first available in the market after its initial description in 1994.

Threats. — The most significant threat to Indonesian freshwater turtle and tortoise populations is hunting for trade. Freshwater turtles and tortoises in Southeast Asia have long been utilized and traded for pets, food, and medicine. However, only a few ethnic groups in Indonesia actually utilize freshwater turtles and tortoises as food. During the last decade, the trade in these species has increased considerably. Some of this trade centers on domestic consumption, but most of the trade is for export to fulfill the substantial increase in demand from consumer countries in East Asia, particularly China.

The second major threat to the existence of Indonesian freshwater turtles and tortoises is habitat destruction. The habitat of these species is mainly in lowland areas. Unfortunately, these kinds of habitat are the most threatened by deforestation and conversion into intensive agriculture, settlements, transmigration areas, and logging. There is little representation of these types of habitat within the network of protected areas, which are established mainly in highland

Table 1. Distribution, conservation status, and legal status of freshwater turtles and tortoises in Indonesia.

No. Family Species	Distribution	Conservation Status	Legal Status
Carettochelyidae			
1 *Carettochelys insculpta*	Irian Jaya	Abundant locally, Vulnerable	Protected
Chelidae			
2 *Chelodina mccordi*	Roti	Nearly extinct, Endangered	-
3 *Chelodina novaeguineae*	South Irian Jaya	Rare, Vulnerable	Protected
4 *Chelodina parkeri*	South Irian Jaya	Rare, Vulnerable	-
5 *Chelodina siebenrocki*	South Irian Jaya	Uncommon	-
6 *Chelodina reimanni*	South Irian Jaya	Rare	-
7 *Elseya branderhorstii*	South Irian Jaya	Uncommon	-
8 *Elseya novaeguineae*	North Irian Jaya	Uncommon	Protected
9 *Elseya* new species 1	South Irian Jaya	Uncommon	-
10 *Elseya* new species 2	Central Irian (mountains)	Rare	-
11 *Elseya* new species 3	Birdshead Irian Jaya	Rare	-
12 *Emydura subglobosa*	South Irian Jaya	Abundant	-
Trionychidae			
13 *Amyda cartilaginea*	Sumatra, Java, Borneo, Sulawesi (?)	Common	-
14 *Chitra chitra*	Sumatra, Java	Rare	Protected under *C. indica*
15 *Dogania subplana*	Sumatra, Java, Borneo	Common	-
16 *Pelochelys bibroni*	South Irian Jaya	Uncommon	-
17 *Pelochelys cantorii*	Sumatra, Borneo, Sulawesi (?), Irian Jaya	Rare	-
18 *Pelodiscus sinensis*	Sumatra, Timor (?)	Introduced	-
Bataguridae			
19 *Batagur baska*	Sumatra	Rare, Endangered	CITES App. I; protected
20 *Callagur borneoensis*	Sumatra, Borneo	Rare, Endangered	CITES App. II
21 *Cuora amboinensis* (3 subspp.)	Sumatra, Java, Bali, Borneo, Sulawesi, Maluku, Sumbawa, Timor	Common	-
22 *Cyclemys dentata*	Sumatra, Java, Borneo	Common	-
23 *Cyclemys oldhami*	Sumatra, Java, Borneo	Common	-
24 *Geoemyda spengleri* *	Sumatra (?), Borneo (?)	Rare	-
25 *Heosemys spinosa*	Sumatra, Borneo	Rare	-
26 *Heosemys yuwonoi*	Sulawesi	Rare, Endangered	-
27 *Malayemys subtrijuga*	Sumatra, Java, Borneo (?)	Rare	-
28 *Notochelys platynota*	Sumatra, Java, Borneo	Uncommon	-
29 *Orlitia borneensis*	Sumatra, Borneo	Uncommon	Protected
30 *Siebenrockiella crassicollis*	Sumatra, Java, Borneo	Uncommon	-
Testudinidae			
31 *Indotestudo forsteni*	Sulawesi	Rare	CITES App. II
32 *Indotestudo elongata* (?)	Sumatra (?), Borneo (?)	?	CITES App. II
33 *Manouria emys*	Sumatra, Borneo	Rare	CITES App. II
Emydidae			
34 *Trachemys scripta elegans*	Sumatra, Java, Borneo, Sulawesi, Irian Jaya	Introduced	-
35 *Trachemys terrapen* **	Java	Introduced	-

Notes: Conservation status assessments were by the authors. "Protected" refers to Indonesian national legislation.
* The occurrence of *Geoemyda spengleri* is questionable and probably based on *Heosemys spinosa* (Mertens, 1942; Fritz, 1997). Considering that recent reports still mention this species from several places, its occurrence could not be ignored and might represent an undescribed species (McCord et al., 1995).
** This species is represented by a number of introduced specimens seen in the market or caught by turtle hunters.

regions. Another major cause of habitat destruction is forest fires, which occur mainly in lowland forests, including peat and swamp forests.

Utilization and Trade

Freshwater turtles and tortoises are mostly utilized and traded for human consumption. Meat and eggs are consumed for food and medicine. It is difficult to differentiate between turtle consumption merely for food and for medicine because of the Chinese community's belief that there is a medicinal effect from chelonian products such as blood, intestine, fat, eggs, and the shell. The consumption of chelonian products usually increases during the winter season. In addition, there is also an extensive trade in turtle plastra and turtle paste from Indonesia to East Asia, mainly from Sulawesi, but possibly including sources from a much wider range.

National Utilization. — There is little documented information on the domestic use of freshwater turtles and tortoises in Indonesia. It is believed that domestic use is much lower than the number of animals exported. A field study undertaken during August – September 1998 in Irian Jaya showed that despite the protected status of the species, exploitation of the eggs of the Fly River pig-nosed turtle (*Carettochelys insculpta*), was recorded at 84,000 eggs collected over just a two month period. Furthermore, villagers also caught juveniles and these were shipped out from the

Figure 1. Roti Island snake-necked turtle, *Chelodina mccordi*, described in 1994, occurs only in a very limited range and is already considered commercially extinct due to the pet trade. Photo by Anders G.J. Rhodin.

area through middlemen. Local authorities also issued a quota, even for protected species, because of the pressure from higher authorities as well as from local people. Although this species is protected, Indonesian legislation allows captive ranching programs. Hatchlings from eggs collected from the wild are considered ranched specimens. The program is undertaken mainly for species that have naturally low hatchling survival rates in the wild (e.g., crocodiles).

Legal International Trade. — Table 3 shows the exports of freshwater turtles and tortoises recorded by the Directorate General of Fisheries in 1997 and 1998 from some ports of export. The records do not identify the species, but it was reported that the species exported in greatest volumes were *Amyda cartilaginea, Callagur borneoensis*, and *Pelodiscus sinensis* (Suwelo, 1999). We believe that the identifications of the last two species must be erroneous and most probably apply to *Orlitia borneensis* (a protected species), *Siebenrockiella crassicollis, Notochelys platynota, Cuora amboinensis* (Fig. 3), and *Pelochelys* or *Chitra*.

The exports reported in Table 3 were undertaken by 40 exporters distributed in those ports of export. It was reported that five of the exporters were initiating captive ranching or rearing, however, there are no confirmed records of such operations in Indonesia.

Ranching or captive breeding of *Pelodiscus sinensis* in North Sumatra started in 1997. As the majority of Indonesian citizens are Moslems, turtles are rarely eaten and so 99% of the production is exported to China. They do not incubate turtle eggs, but import hatchlings from Taiwan or Thailand.

Illegal Trade. — For protected species such as *Carettochelys insculpta*, control is under the authority of the Ministry of Forestry and Estate Crops. In the regency of Merauke (near the border with Papua New Guinea), "illegal" collection of *Carettochelys* eggs is estimated to be 1,500,000 to 2,000,000 per year. The local government (sub-

regency) has recorded that in 1998, from the river bank of the Flinschap River alone, about 500,000 eggs were collected (J. Maturbongs, in prep.). The eggs were collected along with the nest sand, put in buckets, and then hatched in captivity. The young turtles were then shipped to Jakarta, Ujung Pandang, Surabaya, or Denpasar, from where they were illegally exported to Taiwan, China, or Singapore. The turtles were declared as fish when export was undertaken.

The actual export numbers of all species are essentially several times greater than those managed by the Indonesian authorities. The Province of Irian Jaya had been allocated a quota in 1997 for *Cuora amboinensis* as well as other reptile species that do not even occur in Irian Jaya. So the species that were declared to be shipped out from Irian Jaya might actually have been other species (Iskandar, pers. obs.).

Potential Trade Impacts. — With the growing human population and economic improvements in especially East and Southeast Asia, the demand for turtles and tortoises for pets, food, and medicine is increasing. Of the approximately 29 native species in Indonesia, only 9 are somewhat covered by protection (6 species are nationally protected and 4 species are included in CITES appendices). It can be predicted that without any further control on the trade these species will certainly decline, as trade still occurs even for protected species.

Conservation and Management

Legal Status. — Table 1 shows the legal status of the species in Indonesia. There are six freshwater turtle species that are listed in the national protection status based on Government Regulation No. 7 of 1999: *Batagur baska, Carettochelys insculpta, Chelodina novaeguineae, Chitra indica, Elseya novaeguineae*, and *Orlitia borneensis*. No utilization in any form is allowed for species listed in this protection status, except with special permission from the Minister and under the consent of the Scientific Authority for very special circumstances such as research and captive

Table 2. Freshwater turtles and tortoises recorded as occurring in some Indonesian wetlands. Source: Wetlands International Indonesia Program, Wetland Database. Although some of these records are questionable, it is inappropriate to change or eliminate them, so that they can be traced back to their source.

ISLAND SITES	IDENTIFIED SPECIES	HABITAT TYPES
SUMATRA		
Karang Gading Wildlife Reserve, South Sumatra	*Siebenrockiella crassicollis, Chitra indica*[1], *Batagur baska*	Estuarine mangrove in estuarine and sandy hummocks in forested beach
Kerumutan Baru Nature Reserve, Riau	*Siebenrockiella crassicollis, Amyda cartilaginea, Orlitia borneensis*	Intermittent freshwater swamp, forest
Berbak National Park	*Siebenrockiella crassicollis, Amyda cartilaginea, Orlitia borneesis, Chitra indica*[1], *Batagur baska, Pelochelys cantorii, Cuora amboinensis, Cyclemys dentata*	National Park protects a wetland habitat which comprises swamp forest, estuarine, peat forest, river, lake, mangroves, and lowland tropical rain forest
Lebak Ogan-Komering, South Sumatra	*Siebenrockiella crassicollis*	Grassland in intermittent swamp
Delta of Banyuasin-Musi rivers, South Sumatra	*Chitra indica*[1]	-
Lau Tapus	*Amyda cartilaginea*	Intermittent freshwater swamp
Giam-Siak Kecil Wildlife Reserve, Riau	*Amyda cartilaginea, Orlitia borneensis*	Lake
Padang Island and Tanjung Padang, West Sumatra	*Amyda cartilaginea, Heosemys spinosa*	Lake, fresh water swamp, peat forest
Singkarak Lake, West Sumatra	*Amyda cartilaginea*	Lake periphery
Blok Kluet, Leuser National Park	*Amyda cartilaginea* *	Forest along lake periphery
Taitai Wildlife Reserve, Siberut Island	*Geoemyda* sp.	-
KALIMANTAN (BORNEO)		
Lake Sentarum Wildlife Reserve, West Kalimantan	*Siebenrockiella crassicollis, Chitra indica*[1], *Manouria emys, Cuora amboinensis* *, *Cyclemys dentata, Heosemys spinosa, Malayemys subtrijuga, Orlitia borneensis, Pyxidea mouhotii*[2]	Freshwater swamp with aquatic vegetation and lowland rainforest associated with terrestrial wetland
Kembang island	*Amyda cartilaginea*	-
Pleihari Martapura Wildlife Reserve, South Kalimantan	*Amyda cartilaginea*	-
Paloh Nature Reserve	*Callagur borneoensis*	-
JAVA		
Rawa Danau Nature Reserve, West Java	*Amyda cartilaginea, Siebenrockiella crassicollis*	Freshwater swamp
Rawa pening, Central Java	*Amyda cartilaginea*	Lake
Leuweng Sancang Nature Reserve	*Amyda cartilaginea*	Lowland forest
SULAWESI		
Morowali Nature Reserve	*Indotestudo forsteni, Testudo* sp.[3]	- -
Rawa Aopa Watumohai National Park	*Amyda cartilaginea* *	-
Lake Tempe and Lake Buaya	*Cuora amboinensis*	-
Bunaken National Park	*Cuora amboinensis*[4]	-
EAST NUSA TENGGARA		
Lake Lebu (Taliwang)	*Cuora amboinensis*	-
IRIAN JAYA		
Wasur National Park	*Carettochelys insculpta, Emydura subglobosa, Chelodina* spp.; *Elseya* spp.*	- - -

[1] *Chitra indica* probably refers to *Chitra chitra*;
[2] *Pyxidea mouhotii* probably refers to *Geoemyda* cf. *spengleri* or *Heosemys spinosa*;
[3] Probably refers to *Cuora amboinensis*;
[4] It seems improbable that this area has a freshwater turtle, most probably marine turtles;
* Not reported but surely present.

breeding. It is also shown in Table 1 that at least four Indonesian species have been listed in CITES appendices, one species in Appendix I (*Batagur baska*) and three others in Appendix II (*Callagur borneoensis*, *Indotestudo forstenii*, *Manouria emys,* and *I. elongata* if it occurs in Indonesia). Indonesia acceded to CITES in 1978.

Species that are neither listed in the national protection status nor in CITES appendices are managed as a fishery resource. The fishery resource status can lead to over-exploitation because the management is then delegated to the Fishery Service, which is under the local (district) government where expertise in conservation is very limited.

Species Management. — The line of command for regulation of protected and wildlife species is simple and clear enough, but there are lots of weaknesses in the regulations. The Fisheries Department manages the species through issuing capture permits. For CITES-listed species and/or non-protected species, the Directorate General of Nature Protection and Conservation (DGNPC), as the CITES Management Authority, sets annual catch quotas based on recommendations from the Scientific Authority (Indonesian Institute of Sciences) for the whole country. This quota is then divided into provincial quotas and managed by the Local Office of the DGNPC. For the non-CITES species, the District Fishery Service issues capture and export permits, which in many cases are decided without considering the quota set by the DGNPC. Table 4 shows the catch quota set by the CITES Manage-

Figure 2. *Heosemys yuwonoi*, described in 1995, occurs only in a limited distribution in Sulawesi and has been significantly depleted by both the meat and pet trade. Photo by John B. Iverson.

ment Authority for 1998 for freshwater turtles and tortoises.

Management Problems. — There are several weaknesses and abuses concerned with species management:

1. There is no checklist of all potentially exploitable species occurring in each province.

2. The Forestry Department has no control over all of the protected species, essentially because of the high number of species that have to be identified (this includes all plants and animals). Nobody is able to identify all wild species (plants and animals). This is a major issue, because Indonesia is so rich in biodiversity and the number of potentially exploitable species is unlimited.

3. It is impossible to set a quota for all potentially exploitable species (because of the above two reasons). On the other hand, traders have a tendency to export anything that has an economic value.

4. The basis for quota establishment is somewhat questionable, depending on data availability as provided by the District Fishery Service, Local Office of the Directorate General of Nature Protection and Conservation, discussion with NGOs, and scientists working on the species.

5. Many local traders give a scientific name of a species that is permissible to be exported according to the local authority (District Fishery Service or Local Office of the Directorate General of Nature Protection and Conservation), but nobody is able to confirm its identity.

6. Some provinces erroneously have a quota for a species that does not occur in the region. Because such an empty quota means less income, the quota will be abused for shipments of other species.

7. The difficulty in combatting this illegal trade is caused mainly by current laws, such as Act No. 10 of 1995 concerning Customs and Excise, by which customs officers are not permitted to open packages unless there is intelligence information that the package contains illegal goods.

8. Turtles are regarded as a fishery resource, according to Act No. 12 of 1985. This means that all management of the resource is under the authority of the Fisheries Department, which has no power and expertise in conservation.

9. There is confusion in the Wildlife section of the Government Regulation No. 8 of 1999. According to Chapter III, Article 7, eggs as well as juveniles of species with naturally low hatchling survival rates (e.g., crocodiles and turtles) may be collected from the wild for captive breeding, and may afterwards be exploited as a commodity after the second generation. But Chapter XI, Article 44, allows the possibility to use any captive-bred species for trade. Although harvested from the wild, such specimens already meet the status as captive-bred specimens. For this reason, some protected species have a quota, despite Government Regulation No. 7 of 1999 which stipulates that a protected species shall have no quota (see also Illegal Trade). The captive management section (Chapter 3) must be corrected according to international definitions of captive breeding and ranching.

10. Once a company has a captive breeding license, there is ample opportunity for false declaration in that wild specimens are reported as captive bred specimens.

Table 3. Export of freshwater turtles and tortoises (weight in kg and number of individuals) in 1997–98 from some Indonesian ports. Source: Directorate General of Fisheries of Indonesia.

Province (port of export)	1997 Weight (kg)	Ind.	1998 Weight (kg)	Ind.
Java	118,271	29,147	109,305	28,635
North Sumatra (Medan)	—	238,912	—	150,405
South Sumatra (Palembang)	270,781	42,332	308,900	80,024
Riau (Pekanbaru)	45,138	20,628	82,400	58,170
South Kalimantan (Banjarmasin)	234,392	69,320	317,379	55,496
West Kalimantan (Pontianak)	—	22,243	—	22,240
East Kalimantan (Balikpapan)	2,071	518	7,302	525
Bali	—	—	2,737	1,194
Total	670,653	423,100	828,032	396,719

Figure 3. *Cuora amboinensis*, exported in huge numbers from Indonesia to East Asia. Photo by Peter Paul van Dijk.

Habitat Conservation. — Some of the wetland areas which are important habitat for freshwater turtles and tortoises have been included in the network of protected areas in the forms of National Parks, Wildlife Reserves, and Nature Reserves. Table 2 lists some protected areas which have been identified as maintaining suitable habitat for freshwater turtles and tortoises. There is growing concern in Indonesia that lowland areas are under-represented in the network of protected areas. The challenge to conservation of biodiversity in the lowland areas is to integrate management of lowland production forest, mangrove, and other wetland sites with conservation of biodiversity, including freshwater turtles and tortoises.

Control Measures. — In order to lessen the occurrence of illegal trade, some programs of control measures should be undertaken. The programs are not always specifically designed for turtles but for general wildlife conservation and trade monitoring and control. These include:

1. Undertaking consistent law enforcement, especially for protected and CITES-listed species which are under the responsibility of the Ministry of Forestry. The Special Forestry Police posted in the regional offices must be specifically trained in conservation of biological resources.

2. Undertaking closer coordination with Fisheries Department at Central and Local Levels in conservation management of non-protected and non-CITES species, especially in quota setting and capture and trade permits issuance.

3. Undertaking closer coordination and cooperation with law enforcement agencies such as customs, police, and also quarantine through regular coordination meetings and establishment of networking with NGOs concerned with trade monitoring. A network of NGOs called "Jaringan PANTAU" has been established in 1998 and is currently working.

4. Undertaking training for field officers of Customs, Police, Quarantine, and Forest Police in control of wildlife trade including CITES, species identification, and general conservation.

5. Undertaking education and extension for the general community concerning conservation of turtles.

6. Reviewing current legislation to accommodate ongoing developments in conservation of wildlife and trade monitoring.

LITERATURE CITED

FRITZ, U. 1997. Zur Vorkommen von *Heosemys spinosa* (Gray, 1831) auf den Philippinen (Reptilia: Testudines: Bataguridae). Faunistische Abhandlungen, Staatliches Museum für Tierkunde Dresden, Vol. 21 (7): 131-134.

IUCN/SSC TORTOISE AND FRESHWATER TURTLE SPECIALIST GROUP. 1991. Tortoises and Freshwater Turtles. IUCN. Gland. Switzerland.

IUCN (INTERNATIONAL UNION FOR THE CONSERVATION OF NATURE AND NATURAL RESOURCES). 1996. 1996 IUCN Red List of Threatened Animals. IUCN, Gland, Switzerland, 448 pp.

MATURBONGS, J.A. In prep. Report on Pignose turtle (*Carettochelys insculpta*) trade from Friendschap river, Suator district, Merauke county Irian Jaya 23 August-23 Sept 1999. (in Indonesian) WWF IP Sahul.

MCCORD, W.P., IVERSON, J.B., AND BOEADI. 1995. A new batagurid turtle from northern Sulawesi, Indonesia. Chelonian Conservation and Biology 1(4):311-316.

MERTENS, R. 1942. Zwei Bemerkungen über Schildkröten Südost-Asiens. Senckenbergiana 7(2):49-54.

SUWELO, I.S. 1999. Export of Freshwater Turtle (in Indonesian language). Paper presented in the One Day Seminar of Reptile and Amphibian Diversity Conservation in Indonesia. Bogor, 4 November 1999.

WIBOWO, P. 1999. Indonesian freshwater turtles and tortoises: Data status in Wetland Database (WDB) in supporting the conservation. (in Indonesian language). Paper presented in the One Day Seminar of Reptile and Amphibian Diversity Conservation in Indonesia. Bogor, 4 November 1999.

Table 4. 1998 export quotas set by the CITES Management Authority for freshwater turtles and tortoises in Indonesia. Source: Directorate General of Nature Protection and Conservation.

Species	Individuals
Chelodina mccordi[1]	450
Chelodina parkeri	270
Chelodina reimanni	270
Chelodina siebenrocki	1,935
Callagur borneoensis	450
Cuora amboinensis	90,000
Cyclemys dentata[2]	21,450
Dogania subplana	13,500
Elseya branderhorstii	3,800
Elseya novaeguineae	450
Elseya schultzei[3]	1,300
Emydura albertisii[4]	3,590
Emydura subglobosa	1,200
Heosemys spinosa	7,200
Indotestudo forstenii	450
Manouria emys	450
Total	146,765

[1] *Chelodina mccordi* is now considered extinct in the trade.
[2] No efforts were made to distinguish members of the *Cyclemys dentata* complex.
[3] *Elseya schultzei* is a synonym of *Elseya novaeguineae* (a protected species).
[4] *Emydura albertisii* is a synonym of *Emydura subglobosa*.

Asian Turtle Trade: Proceedings of a Workshop on Conservation and Trade of Freshwater Turtles and Tortoises in Asia
P.P. van Dijk, B.L. Stuart, and A.G.J. Rhodin, Eds.
Chelonian Research Monographs 2:112–119 • © 2000 by Chelonian Research Foundation

Export of Live Freshwater Turtles and Tortoises
from North Sumatra and Riau, Indonesia: A Case Study

Chris R. Shepherd[1]

[1]*TRAFFIC Southeast Asia, M19B Jalan Pasar (1/21), 46000 Petaling Jaya, Selangor, Malaysia*
[E-mail: tsea@po.jaring.my; Shepherd7@hotmail.com]

ABSTRACT. – Freshwater turtles, tortoises, and softshell turtles are exported from a few locations in Sumatra in large quantities. The trade involves all species native to Sumatra and two exotic species. This study found that more than 25 tons of live turtles are exported each week to China, Hong Kong, and Singapore from two exporting companies surveyed in the provinces of North Sumatra and Riau. Actual figures would be higher but no records were available of export by sea from Medan. Two additional exporting companies were not surveyed. According to government statistics, these two provinces exported approximately half of the softshell turtles exported from the entire country in 1998. While laws are in place to protect some of the species, monitoring and enforcement is inadequate and ineffective. According to all dealers interviewed during this study, wild populations of all species are declining. Trappers bring in fewer turtles, resulting in export volumes that have dropped to about half of what they were two or three years ago.

The island of Sumatra in Indonesia is extremely rich in wildlife. Originally part of mainland Southeast Asia, Sumatra shares many species of wildlife with Peninsular Malaysia and Thailand. However, habitat loss and over-harvesting are taking their toll on many species. Numerous species are harvested for commercial export and to a much lesser extent for local consumption and the pet trade. Among the most heavily traded animals are the freshwater turtles and tortoises. Thirteen species of native freshwater turtles and tortoises are found in or reported from Sumatra. An additional two exotic species were also found in trade during this survey. The species and their English names as well as the Indonesian names used in North Sumatra and Riau are listed in Table 1. Turtles, tortoises and softshell turtles are collected and exported alive in large quantities, mostly to China, Hong Kong, and Singapore. There are virtually no field data on how this trade may be affecting the wild populations.

This case study focused on the trade in two important exporting provinces: North Sumatra and Riau. These two locations were chosen as both have international ports and airports. Both are major centers well known for the export of freshwater turtles and tortoises. Marine turtles are not included in the scope of this report. The study examined the species in trade, the volumes being exported, and the laws controlling the trade. Information was gathered through field observations, interviews, and literature and government record searches.

Protection Status

Several species of turtles and tortoises are given protection in Indonesia through both national legislation and through the Convention on International Trade in Endangered Species of Wild Fauna and Flora (CITES). The historical development

that has led to the protection of particular species is uncertain. A complete list of species protected in Indonesia and therefore prohibited from export is found in Table 2.

Only two species occurring in Sumatra are prohibited from export: the river terrapin, *Batagur baska*, and the Malaysian giant turtle, *Orlitia borneensis* (Table 3).

The two Sumatran species listed on CITES Appendix II, *Callagur borneoensis* and *Manouria emys*, both have capture quotas and export quotas (Table 3). Capture is only permitted in certain provinces. Each of the provinces where capture is permitted has its own capture quota. Capture and export quotas are set by the Indonesian Institute of Science (LIPI), which is the Scientific Authority in Indonesia.

Capture of *Callagur borneoensis* is only permitted in South Sumatra where 300 may be taken, and in West Kalimantan, where 200 can be taken. Capture of *Manouria emys* is confined to North Sumatra and Riau where 150 can be taken from each province and another 200 from South Kalimantan. While export quotas for each of these two species is set at 450, capture quotas are set at 500. This is presumably to allow for some local use as well as to take into account that some of the animals captured will die before being exported. Capture of these species in provinces that do not have set capture quotas is prohibited.

Trade Statistics

This study found that the two provinces surveyed are very significant in the trade of live softshell turtles. From Fisheries Department statistics, these two provinces combined are the largest exporters of softshell turtles in the country. These official figures were only available for 1996 to 1998 and are presented in Table 4. These figures are supposed to be for only one species, the Asiatic softshell turtle, *Amyda cartilaginea*. However, from observations and interviews, it is apparent that other native species of softshell turtles are included in these shipments but are not declared. Observations also suggest that these figures are very likely to be underestimates.

The numbers exported from Medan indicate a significant drop in numbers for each of the years. Although trade in Riau has increased (more than doubled) by approximately 27,000 specimens in 1998, the drop in Medan is reflective of the entire export of softshell turtles from Indonesia for these three years.

Capture Methods

In Sumatra, turtles are collected from plantations, forests, and other suitable habitats, including those within protected areas. Trappers use a variety of methods to collect turtles. Softshell turtles are captured using traps, nets, baited fishing lines, and with electric current. Electricity is shot into the water using a pair of poles attached to a car battery, carried in a backpack by the trappers. The stunned softshell turtles surface and are captured. The most frequently used methods of catching these animals involve the use of baited fishing lines and traps. Steel traps are placed in the water in strategic locations with a freshly slaughtered animal inside as bait. An average trap usually can hold between five and ten turtles. Terrestrial species are collected manually from the forests and agricultural and plantation areas.

Trade Structure

Turtles are captured throughout the island of Sumatra as well as some of Sumatra's satellite islands such as Nias. Turtles from the provinces of Aceh, West Sumatra, North Sumatra, and parts of Riau are brought to Medan for export.

Turtles in the southern parts of the island are exported from Tembilahan and Palembang (Palembang was not included in the scope of this study). There are three levels to the trade structure in Sumatra: trappers, middlemen, and exporters (Fig. 1).

Trappers

Trappers today rarely catch turtles as a full-time occupation as was the case in the past. The reasons given were that prices have decreased and that it is becoming increasingly difficult to find substantial quantities of turtles. Turtle collectors are usually fishermen, plantation workers, farmers, and other rural workers who supplement their income. According to one exporter in Tembilahan, Riau, thousands of people bring in turtles to his location per month (at least 20 people were observed bringing in small amounts of turtles during the author's two-hour visit). A trapper catching turtles in Sinkil, Aceh, claimed that there were at least 100 people catching turtles in the Sinkil area alone.

Middlemen

There are various middlemen who link the trappers and the large exporting companies. Middlemen usually operate in areas without shipping locations. Turtles and tortoises are purchased from the trappers by middlemen who in turn resell them to the large exporting companies. Trappers close to exporting centers do not go through the middlemen but sell directly to the exporters. Middlemen are more common in Riau due to the greater distances from the capture sites to the export locations.

There is only one middleman operating in Medan. Approximately 10 years ago this operation was an exporter, shipping turtles by sea. Since then other companies have

Table 1. Freshwater turtles and tortoises reported in the literature to occur in Sumatra and their English and local names.

Species Name	English Name	Local Name
Bataguridae		
Batagur baska	River terrapin	Tungtung
Callagur borneoensis	Painted terrapin	Tuntung semangka (Watermelon terrapin – so named because the lines on the back resemble the lines on a watermelon)
Cuora amboinensis	Asian box turtle	Kura
Cyclemys dentata *	Asian leaf turtle	Kura-kura ninja – B (Ninja turtle – B)
Cyclemys oldhami *	Asian leaf turtle	Kura-kura ninja – B (Ninja turtle – B)
Heosemys spinosa	Spiny turtle	Kura-kura mas or Baneng mas (Gold turtle)
Malayemys subtrijuga	Malayan snail-eating turtle	
Notochelys platynota	Malayan flat-shelled turtle	Kura-kura ninja – B (Ninja turtle – B)
Orlitia borneensis	Malaysian giant turtle	Tungtung or Biuku
Siebenrockiella crassicollis	Black marsh turtle	Kura-kura ninja – A (Ninja turtle – A)
Testudinidae		
Manouria emys	Asian brown tortoise	Baneng
Trionychidae		
Amyda cartilaginea	Asiatic softshell turtle	Labi-labi biasa (Common softshell turtle)
Dogania subplana	Malayan softshell turtle	Labi-labi batu (Stone softshell turtle)
Pelochelys cantorii	Asian giant softshell turtle	Labi-labi pasir (Sand softshell turtle)
Exotic Species		
Trachemys scripta elegans	Red-eared slider	Kura-kura ninja hijau / Kura-kura ninja Brazil (Green ninja turtle/Brazilian ninja turtle)
Pelodiscus sinensis	Chinese softshell turtle	Labi-labi Taiwan (Taiwanese softshell turtle)

Sources: Iverson (1992), Pritchard (1979). * - Note that no distinction is made between *Cyclemys dentata* and *C. oldhami* in this report.

Table 2. Legal decrees and the turtle species they prohibit from export from Indonesia. Source: List of Turtles Prohibited from International Trade in Indonesia, 1995 (Department of Fisheries, 1999). English names and distributions taken from Iverson (1992).

Species Name	Common Name	Local Name	Distribution in Indonesia
Ministry of Agriculture 327/1978			
Chitra indica	Narrow-headed softshell turtle	Labi-labi Besar	Java
Carettochelys insculpta	Pig-nosed turtle	Kura-kura Irian	Irian Jaya
Orlitia borneensis	Malayan giant turtle	Kura-kura Gading	Sumatra and Kalimantan
Batagur baska	River terrapin	Tuntong	Sumatra
Ministry of Agriculture 716/1980			
Elseya novaeguineae	New Guinea snapper	Kura-kura Irian Leher Pendek	Irian Jaya
Chelodina novaeguineae	New Guinea snake-necked turtle	Kura-kura Leher Panjang	Irian Jaya
CITES Appendix I			
Batagur baska	River terrapin	Tuntong	Sumatra
Trionyx ater	Black spiny softshell turtle	-	Not present
T. gangeticus	Indian softshell turtle	-	Not present
T. hurum	Indian peacock softshell turtle	-	Not present
T. nigricans	Black softshell turtle	-	Not present
CITES Appendix II			
Lissemys punctata	Indian flapshell turtle	-	Not present

started up and, with more capital, export most of the turtles by air. The original exporters, not able to compete, began operating as middlemen. However, most trappers now sell directly to the exporters themselves, as the price is higher than that paid by the middlemen. The middleman in Medan now buys and sells turtles as a sideline business to a more profitable reptile skin business. This location only receives approximately 50 freshwater turtles and tortoises per day.

Middlemen were visited in the cities of Pekan Baru, Duri, and Kandis in the province of Riau. There is only one middleman in Pekan Baru. This company deals solely in turtles and does not deal in reptile skins. This location reportedly receives approximately 1.5–2 tons of freshwater turtles and tortoises per week. The turtles are sent from here to exporters in Medan. In past years shipments were flown directly from the airport in Pekan Baru to Singapore, but this has ceased as the amount of turtles brought in has apparently decreased significantly.

There is only a single middleman in Duri, Riau. The trade of turtles is a sideline business to a larger snake and monitor lizard skin shipping operation. The middleman in Duri reportedly sells approximately 2–3 tons per week of freshwater turtles and tortoises to exporters in Medan and less often to Tembilahan. Three years ago shipments from this operation were made up of approximately 4 tons of softshell turtles and 3 tons of hard-shelled turtles per week. According to staff, the decline is largely due to the increasing scarcity of turtles.

There are four middlemen operating in the town of Kandis in Riau. At least two of these operations are owned by the same person. These companies all operate as sideline businesses to reptile skin operations. Shipments from this location are sent to Medan. Less than 500 kg of turtles per month (25% of which are softshell turtles) are brought in.

Exporters

Export companies are located in cities with major seaports and/or airports. Trappers and middlemen bring freshwater turtles and tortoises to these locations from throughout Sumatra. There are at least two large exporting companies in the city of Medan and at least two more in Tembilahan in Riau. There is at least one other large exporter in Sumatra, found in the southern province of Palembang. This last location was not visited during this survey, but is said to be one of the largest exporters on the island.

Medan. — There are at least two exporting companies in Medan, both apparently of similar size. Only one of these was visited during this survey (Table 5). The company visited in Medan keeps their turtles at two separate locations to handle the sheer volumes. All specimens brought into these locations are sorted by species upon arrival and weighed (Figs. 2 and 3). When there is enough to make up a shipment, they are packaged and exported (Fig. 4). Handling of the turtles between this location and the airports or seaports is done by cargo agencies. According to the Department of Fisheries in Medan, there are 22 cargo agencies involved in the trade in North Sumatra alone. According to staff, shipments by air usually average 3–5 tons and are sent approximately 2 or 3 times each week. Cargo agencies in Medan which handle the shipping stated that as much as 30 tons are exported each week. Shipments by sea are at least as frequent

Table 3. Tortoise and freshwater turtle species listed in the CITES Appendices and species prohibited from export in Sumatra, 1999.

Species	Protected Status	Capture Quota	Export Quota
Batagur baska	CITES I	0	0
Callagur borneoensis	CITES II	500	450
Manouria emys	CITES II	500	450
Orlitia borneensis	Nationally Protected	0	0

Table 4. Indonesian softshell turtle export figures for 1996–98 (numbers of animals). Source: Directorate General of Fisheries, Agriculture Department, Indonesia.

Location	1996	1997	1998
Medan	271,673	238,912	150,405
Riau	21,067	20,628	47,795
Indonesia (total)	715,192	423,100	358,927

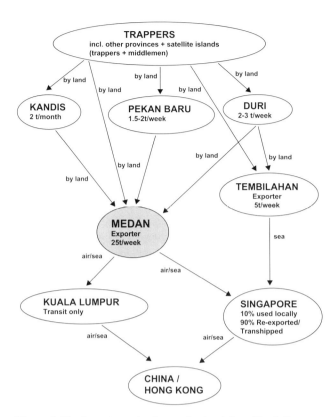

Figure 1. Trade routes and volumes (t = tons) from North Sumatra and Riau, September 1999.

Table 5. Turtles observed at an exporting company in Medan, Sumatra, on 24 September 1999.

Common name	Species name	Quantity (individuals)
Painted terrapin	*Callagur borneoensis*	9
Asian box turtle	*Cuora amboinensis*	ca. 1350
Asian leaf turtle	*Cyclemys dentata*	ca. 150
Spiny turtle	*Heosemys spinosa*	ca. 450–500
Malayan flat-shelled turtle	*Notochelys platynota*	40
Malaysian giant turtle	*Orlitia borneensis*	ca. 250
Black marsh turtle	*Siebenrockiella crassicollis*	ca. 400
Asian brown tortoise *	*Manouria emys*	0
Asiatic softshell turtle	*Amyda cartilaginea*	ca. 80–100
Malayan softshell turtle	*Dogania subplana*	ca. 50–100
Asian giant softshell turtle *	*Pelochelys cantorii*	0

* Staff confirmed that although they were not observed on this particular visit, both the Asian brown tortoise and the Asian giant softshell turtle are traded.

but the average weight of these was not given. Shipments leave Medan by air on both Malaysian and Singapore Airlines as well as on Indonesian freight planes. Shipments are sent by sea from both seaports near Medan: Belawan and Tanjung Balai. Usually softshells are sent by air and hard-shelled turtles by sea, as the hard-shelled turtles tend to be hardier. However, hard-shelled turtles are often sent by air as well. Staff at this exporting company claimed that as much

as 4–5 tons of live turtles were received daily; however, this figure could not be confirmed.

Tembilahan. — This city is located approximately 10 hours by vehicle southward of Pekan Baru, along the east coast of Riau. There are apparently two large turtle exporting companies in Tembilahan. One of these operations was visited in October 1999. The second location was not visited during this study, but is, according to locals, of similar size to the first.

Turtles are collected from all around the region and brought to this operation. Sales are brisk with a continual flow of people bringing in turtles as well as pythons and monitor lizards. The majority of these people are plantation workers who collect turtles opportunistically.

The operation visited in this town is located near the port of Tembilahan. Turtles are exported by ship to Singapore, which lies 16 hours away by cargo ship. It should be noted that the port of Tembilahan is not included in the list of ports of entry and exit for specimens listed on CITES Appendices

Figure 2. Daily shipment of hundreds of *Cuora amboinensis* awaiting export to East Asia from a holding facility in Medan, Sumatra, September 1999. Photo by Chris R. Shepherd/TRAFFIC Southeast Asia.

Figure 3. Daily shipment of hundreds of *Orlitia borneensis* awaiting export to East Asia from a holding facility in Medan, Sumatra, September 1999. For a close-up, see the front cover photograph of this monograph. Photo by Chris R. Shepherd/TRAFFIC Southeast Asia.

as designated by the Indonesian CITES Management Authority. Not only are *Manouria emys* exported from this location but also various species of CITES-listed snakes and monitor lizards, in direct violation of CITES Notification No. 1999/79 (CITES Secretariat, 1999).

    According to the owner of this company, the demand in China for turtle meat is highest in the winter months. During the slow season an average of 20 tons of turtles are exported from this operation per month. Shipments are sent once per week and average 5 tons each. According to the owner, in 1997 shipments ranged from 20 to 80 tons per month. The decrease in shipment size is due to the fall in prices and the

increasing difficulty in obtaining large quantities of turtles. According to this dealer, Hong Kong is not receiving any softshells from Indonesia. Currently all shipments of hard-shelled and softshell turtles from this location are being sent to Singapore. According to the Management Authority in Singapore, only approximately 10% of the turtles imported into Singapore are used domestically. The rest are re-exported or trans-shipped to other countries.

    Additionally a large collection and export business located in Palembang, the province south of Riau, often sells some of their turtles to this dealer in Tembilahan. According to various dealers in Riau, the business in Palembang is very

Table 6. Middlemen and exporter purchasing prices (in Rupiah, Rp/kg; ca. 8,900 Rp = US $1) for all species in trade in North Sumatra and Riau, Indonesia, in September 1999. * In many instances prices are not given or are very low. This is because those species are rarely or never brought into that particular location. Apparently there are far fewer species found in the Riau area than in the North Sumatra area. Note that few species are mentioned in the Medan middleman column, as most trappers deliver directly to the exporters.

Species name	Size Class	Middlemen purchasing prices			Exporter purchasing prices		
		Medan	Pekan Baru	Duri	Kandis	Medan	Tembilahan
Batagur baska		*	*	*	*	*	*
Callagur borneoensis		*	*	*	*	13,000/kg	*
Cuora amboinensis		10,000/kg	7,000/kg	6,000/kg	7,500-10,000/kg	17,000/kg	12,000/kg
Cyclemys dentata		10,000/kg	*	*	*	15,000/kg	9,000/kg
Heosemys spinosa		*	*	4,000/kg	5,000/kg	25,000/kg	10,000+/kg
Malayemys subtrijuga		*	*	*	*	*	*
Notochelys platynota		*	*	4,000/kg	*	10,000/kg	9,000/kg
Orlitia borneensis		*	7,000/kg	8,0000/kg	5,000/kg	13,000/kg	9,000/kg
Siebenrockiella crassicollis		10,000/kg	7,000/kg	5,000/kg	8,000/kg	10,000/kg	9,000/kg
Manouria emys		*	*	*	*	10,000/kg	9,000/kg
Amyda cartilaginea	A.3: 0-1.5 kg	30,000/kg	20,000/kg	Not accepted	15-18,000/kg	50,000/kg	20,000/kg
	A.2: 1.5-3 kg	Less	15,000/kg	15,000/kg	15-18,000/kg	50,000/kg	Less
	A.1: 3-5 kg	Less	12,000/kg	12,000/kg	15-18,000/kg	Less	Less
	B: 5-10 kg	Less	9,000/kg	9,000/kg	15-18,000/kg	Less	Less
	C: 10-15 kg	Less	7,000/kg	9,000/kg	8,000/kg	Less	Less
	D: 15-20 kg	Less	75,000 ea.	9,000/kg	8,000/kg	Less	Less
	E: 20-30 kg	Less	75,000 ea.	9,000/kg	8,000/kg	Less	Less
	F: 30-40 kg	Less	75,000 ea.	9,000/kg	8,000/kg	Less	12,000/kg
Dogania subplana	0-1.5 kg	8,000/kg	*	*	*	20,000/kg	*
	1.6 and above	5,000/kg	*	*	*	*	*
Pelochelys cantorii		*	*	*	*	8,000/kg	*

Figure 4. Interior of warehouse in Medan, Sumatra, where thousands of turtles have been packed and are awaiting immediate export via air cargo to East Asian markets, September 1999. Photo by Chris R. Shepherd/TRAFFIC Southeast Asia.

large, exporting approximately 40 tons of turtles per month. When prices are high, the Palembang location sometimes sells large quantities to the dealers in Tembilahan. The Palembang company exports their turtles from the port in Tembilahan as well.

In Tembilahan, *Cuora amboinensis* is the most numerous species brought into this operation, followed by *Orlitia borneensis* and *Siebenrockiella crassicollis*. The list of turtles traded and prices paid are listed in Table 6. *Cyclemys dentata* and *Heosemys spinosa* apparently do not occur in this region but are occasionally brought in by collectors from the neighboring province of West Sumatra. *Heosemys spinosa* are the most valuable, after *Amyda cartilaginea*. *Notochelys platynota* are also rarely brought in, and usually these

originate from the province of West Sumatra. *Manouria emys* are commonly brought in, including some very large specimens. No large specimens of softshell turtles were accepted as Hong Kong was not buying these at the time, for unknown reasons. According to the owner of this operation, there is only one species of softshell found in this region, *Amyda cartilaginea*.

A few red-eared sliders, *Trachemys scripta elegans*, are occasionally brought in. These are generally not accepted as there is no market for them. According to this dealer, specimens of this species captured in the wild are animals released by people who tired of keeping them as pets.

Prices have dropped considerably over the past year. According to the owner, prices paid for *Cuora amboinensis*

Figure 5. *Callagur borneoensis* breeding males being exported to East Asian markets from Medan, Sumatra, September 1999. Photo courtesy TRAFFIC Southeast Asia.

in 1997 ranged from Rp. 17,000 to 18,000 per kg, compared to the current price of Rp. 11,000 to 12,000 per kg. Similarly the price paid for the small specimens of *Amyda cartilaginea* has dropped from Rp. 60,000 to Rp. 20,000 per kg.

Species in Trade

Of the 13 species of freshwater turtles and tortoises recorded from Sumatra, 10 were observed in trade during this survey. Two of the three Sumatran species not observed, *Batagur baska* and *Pelochelys cantorii*, are apparently traded but in low volumes. No *Malayemys subtrijuga* were observed during this survey. People involved in the trade at all levels were shown pictures and questioned about this species but none had ever seen it. Apparently *Malayemys subtrijuga* is not traded in Sumatra, and it is questionable whether the species even occurs in Sumatra.

Exporters in Medan and Tembilahan stated that the most numerous species received are *Cuora amboinensis* (Fig. 2) and *Orlitia borneensis* (Fig. 3). *Heosemys spinosa* are also received in large quantities in Medan. *Notochelys platynota* is the least expensive species due to its high mortality rate, reported to be approximately 10% even before they are shipped. Many dead specimens were observed on site. No small specimens of this species were observed. Staff claimed they very rarely receive the young of this species, as they die very quickly after capture.

Manouria emys is usually common and numerous at these locations in the trade. Staff at the exporting company in Medan claimed that this species is quite popular locally for food, as the meat is "hot" and thought to promote blood circulation. They also acknowledged that this was a protected species and that export of it was illegal.

Interestingly traders do not accept *Trachemys scripta elegans*, which are therefore very rarely brought in. The reason for this is that their meat is apparently very poor in quality. Occasionally one or two may be added into a shipment if they are given freely but the business does not pay for these.

Turtles of all sizes were observed, including hatchlings of at least three species, *Cuora amboinensis*, *Heosemys spinosa,* and *Cyclemys dentata*, as well as some very small *Orlitia borneensis*. It is interesting to note that eggs are often laid by various species in the holding pens and in transport crates. Apparently *Orlitia borneensis* most often lays eggs here. Staff members reported that there have never been any requests for the eggs, and so the eggs are discarded.

Softshell turtles are more valuable commercially than are the other species. The smaller the specimen, the higher the price, as the meat quality of smaller softshell turtles is apparently higher (Table 6) These are brought to the Medan center and are exported almost daily. *Amyda cartilaginea* is the most common and numerous softshell turtle in trade in Sumatra and is apparently the only species found in the Tembilahan area. According to the owner of the exporting company in Medan, specimens of the striped giant softshell turtle, *Chitra chitra,* are occasionally brought in. This species has not yet been confirmed to occur in Sumatra (Pritchard, 1979; Iverson, 1992).

The Chinese softshell turtle, *Pelodiscus sinensis,* is occasionally brought in to Medan. According to the trader, these are refused as it is illegal to export this species and they would be fined at the quarantine station if they contravene the law. Only licensed softshell farms can trade in this species.

It was reported that specimens of *Dogania subplana* suffer a higher mortality rate than do the other softshell species, as they are more susceptible to infected scratches and cuts inflicted upon them by the claws of other turtles with which they are often packed in sacks when brought in. Upon arrival at this location, they are separated into individual plastic tubs. According to the staff, the softshells, especially *Amyda cartilaginea*, often lay eggs in the holding containers. These eggs are often eaten by the staff but are not sold.

According to staff in Medan, average daily quantities of softshell turtles brought in by middlemen and trappers to the Medan exporter are as follows: *Amyda cartilaginea*, approximately one ton per day; *Dogania subplana*, approximately 200 kg per day; and *Pelochelys cantorii,* less than 50 kg per day. The latter is not brought in daily, but the other two species are.

Prices of the species of softshells vary according to the quality of the meat, with *Amyda cartilaginea* being the best quality and therefore the most expensive and *Pelochelys cantorii* the poorest in quality and therefore the least expensive (Table 6).

Discussion

Combined shipments from Medan and Tembilahan amounted to as much as 25 tons of turtles per week. As only half of the export locations in these two provinces were investigated, figures are likely to be twice that. Official records show that the number of softshell turtles exported from these two provinces amounts to approximately half of the entire country's export. Is trade of these proportions sustainable? More work needs to be done to clarify and analyze figures. The impacts of trade in these quantities occurring over any length of time is difficult to measure until there has been solid baseline data collected on wild populations.

It has become clear from this survey that almost all species of freshwater turtles and tortoises found in Sumatra are captured for export. Two of these species, *Batagur baska* and *Orlitia borneensis,* are protected and trade of these species is prohibited. Another two species, *Callagur borneoensis* and *Manouria emys,* are listed by CITES on Appendix II and therefore require permits for export and must follow a strict quota. This survey found that *Orlitia borneensis* is one of the two most heavily exported species and was observed in great numbers at all locations surveyed (Fig. 3). All export of this species is illegal. Although no

Batagur baska were observed during this survey, they have been observed upon arrival in China in consignments from Medan.

Both species listed on Appendix II, *Callagur borneoensis* and *Manouria emys*, were also commonly observed in export. CITES certificates were not used nor were quotas respected. According to the exporter in Medan, approximately 10 *Callagur borneoensis* are received every day (Fig. 5). Shipments containing these two species did not declare them. It was observed that all shipments from each of the ports of export were falsely labeled. All invoices, records of trade, and quarantine records declared that only three species were exported: *Cuora amboinensis*, *Amyda cartilaginea*, and the giant Asian pond turtle, *Heosemys grandis*. The latter has not been recorded from Sumatra.

Management authorities and enforcement bodies are either not aware of the problem or are not equipped to monitor and control it. The ability of authority staff to identify the various turtle species is a concern.

As there are relatively few large exporters and ports of export, enforcement of existing regulations should be focused on these. Stopping the illegal trade at these points will have a chain-reaction effect down to the trappers. If there is no opportunity to export protected species or to exceed quotas, exporters will not buy these species from the trappers and middlemen. Additionally, airlines should be carefully monitored. Shipments containing illegal species should be stopped. Smuggling by ship may continue but mortality rates will make it much less profitable for the dealers.

Several activities which will contribute to better control and understanding of the trade should be carried out. These include:

• Species identification training and materials should be made available to enforcement agencies responsible for regulating and controlling the export of turtles.

• These agencies as well as the government must be motivated and encouraged to take the necessary steps needed to control this trade.

• Surveys of the status of freshwater turtles and tortoises in the wild must be carried out. Without these baseline surveys, it will be difficult to monitor impacts of the trade on wild populations.

• Quotas should be reviewed and enforced.

• The port of Tembilahan is not legally permitted to export CITES-listed species. Authorities should be made aware that such protected turtles are being exported.

Acknowledgments. — TRAFFIC Southeast Asia thanks WWF-Germany for funding to carry out this field investigation in Sumatra.

LITERATURE CITED

CITES SECRETARIAT. 1999. Notification to the Parties, No. 1999/79, Indonesia – Ports of entry and exit of CITES specimens. Geneva, Switzerland.

IVERSON, J.B. 1992. A Revised Checklist with Distribution Maps of the Turtles of the World. Earlham College. Privately Printed. Richmond, Indiana, USA.

JENKINS, M.D. 1995. Tortoises and Freshwater Turtles: The trade in Southeast Asia. TRAFFIC International, United Kingdom.

PRITCHARD, P.C.H. 1979. Encyclopedia of Turtles. T.F.H. Publications, New Jersey.

SHEPHERD, C.R. 1999. Live Turtle and Tortoise Export from North Sumatra and Riau, Indonesia. In prep. TRAFFIC Southeast Asia. Petaling Jaya, Malaysia.

Asian Turtle Trade: Proceedings of a Workshop on Conservation and Trade of Freshwater Turtles and Tortoises in Asia
P.P. van Dijk, B.L. Stuart, and A.G.J. Rhodin, Eds.
Chelonian Research Monographs 2:120–128 • © 2000 by Chelonian Research Foundation

Freshwater Turtle and Tortoise Utilization and Conservation Status in Malaysia

DIONYSIUS S.K. SHARMA[1] AND OSWALD BRAKEN TISEN[2]

[1]*Animal Species Conservation Unit, WWF Malaysia,*
Locked Bag No. 911, Jalan Sultan P.O., 46990 Petaling Jaya, Malaysia
[E-mail: DSharma@wwfnet.org];
[2]*National Parks and Wildlife Office, Sarawak Forest Department,*
Wisma Sumber Alam, Petra Jaya, 93660 Kuching, Sarawak, Malaysia

Malaysia consists of eleven mainland states, forming West or Peninsular Malaysia, plus the states of Sarawak and Sabah covering the northern and northwestern parts of Borneo. The total area is about 328,550 km². The country is inhabited by about 21 million humans. Malaysia also supports a total of 18 species of tortoises and freshwater and estuarine turtles (Table 1). All species occur in the Peninsula, but some of them do not range to Sarawak or Sabah.

Malaysia is entirely located in the tropics and experiences warm temperatures and rainfall throughout the year. Major hill and mountain areas in the center of the Peninsula and in Sarawak and Sabah have cooler conditions at higher altitudes. Virtually all of Malaysia was originally covered by forest. Strong and steady economic development has replaced much of these natural forests with plantations of rubber trees and oil palms, agricultural lands, and industrial and housing estates. The remaining forests continue to be under pressure from the powerful logging industry, whose practices continue to include both selective logging and clearcutting. A number of protected areas have been declared, including extensive areas such as Belum, Taman Negara, and Endau-Rompin in the Peninsula, and Mulu and Kinabalu National Parks in Sarawak and Sabah. In the Peninsula, forest-dwelling tribal people, known as "orang asli," continue to live from subsistence hunting and gathering in these remaining large forested areas.

LEGAL CONSERVATION AND MANAGEMENT

Federal Legislation

At the national level, two federal Acts are the primary legislation for the protection of wildlife and fisheries: the Protection of Wild Life Act 1972 and Fisheries Act 1985. The former, applicable only to Peninsular Malaysia, affords protection to wild animals listed in its extensive schedules of mammals, birds, reptiles, and insects under several categories of protection. Inexplicably absent from these federal schedules are all species of chelonians, and this means that they are extremely vulnerable to exploitation. Responsibility for implementation and enforcement of the Protection of Wild Life Act 1972 rests with the Department of Wildlife and National Parks of Peninsular Malaysia.

In contrast, the Fisheries Act 1985 specifically states in its preamble, "An Act relating to fisheries, including the conservation, management and development of maritime and estuarine fishing and fisheries, in Malaysian fisheries waters, to include turtles and riverine fishing in Malaysia and matters connected therewith or incidental thereto." The Act also clarifies that matters relating to maritime and estuarine fisheries, excluding turtles, are enumerated in the Federal and Concurrent Lists, whereas turtle hunting and riverine fishing are under the State List. This means that provisions of the Act "insofar as they relate to turtles and riverine fisheries in any State in Malaysia shall not come into operation in that State until they have been adopted by law made by the Legislature of the State."

Whether or not individual States have adopted the Fisheries Act 1985, their fisheries resources are automatically afforded legal protection by virtue of these matters being on the Concurrent List of the Constitution, but turtles are specifically excluded from this legal mandate. Thus, the onus lies on each State to formulate effective legislation to protect both marine and non-marine turtles. Unfortunately, this circumstance has led to either a lack of standardized legal protection for most turtle species inhabiting the Peninsula, or lack of protection whatsoever.

Part VII of the Fisheries Act 1985 deals with turtles and inland fisheries and promotes development and rational management by state authorities in consultation with the Director General of the Department of Fisheries. This allows the states to make rules for proper conservation and regulation of turtles, their eggs, and inland fisheries, inclusive of licensing, fishing methods, dam construction, and sand removal. In areas beyond the jurisdiction of the States, the Director General has the power to make regulations. It is unclear as to whether the terminology used in the legislation intended to include only marine turtles, or provides means to protect freshwater terrapins as well.

The import and export of turtle eggs are subject to the restrictions stated in the Customs (Prohibition of Imports) Order 1988 and Customs (Prohibition of Export) Order 1988; however, there is confusion over the exact meaning of the terms used in the legislation. Under the First Schedules, the importation and exportation of "the turtles eggs" from or to any country are absolutely prohibited. Under the Second Schedules, "eggs of testudinate (terrapin and the like) excluding turtle eggs" may not be imported or exported from or to any country without license. Unfortunately, the terminology is not well defined in the legislation, which may

Table 1. Native freshwater turtles and tortoises in Malaysia (18 species).

Trionychidae	
Asiatic softshell turtle	*Amyda cartilaginea*
Malayan softshell turtle	*Dogania subplana*
Asian giant softshell turtle	*Pelochelys cantorii*
Southeast Asian striped giant softshell turtle	*Chitra chitra*
Bataguridae	
River terrapin	*Batagur baska*
Painted terrapin	*Callagur borneoensis*
Malaysian giant turtle	*Orlitia borneensis*
Giant Asian pond turtle	*Heosemys grandis*
Spiny turtle	*Heosemys spinosa*
Asian leaf turtle	*Cyclemys dentata*
Asian box turtle	*Cuora amboinensis*
Yellow-headed temple turtle	*Hieremys annandalii*
Malayan flat-shelled turtle	*Notochelys platynota*
Malayan snail-eating turtle	*Malayemys subtrijuga*
Black marsh turtle	*Siebenrockiella crassicollis*
Testudinidae	
Asian brown tortoise	*Manouria emys*
Impressed tortoise	*Manouria impressa*
Elongated tortoise	*Indotestudo elongata*

result in various interpretations. It is widely assumed that "turtle eggs" means those of marine turtles only, while the "eggs of testudinates (terrapin and the like)" refer to all other species, since all turtles, terrapins, and tortoises are considered testudinates.

State Legislation

Peninsular Malaysia. — Existing legislation at the State level in Peninsular Malaysia concentrates on matters related to regulated exploitation, licensing for egg collection, and possession or killing of marine turtles, but not terrapins or tortoises (Gregory and Sharma, 1997).

Of the eleven peninsular States, only six, excluding Perak's River Rights Enactment 1915, currently have legislation pertaining to protection and exploitation of turtles and three States (Pahang, Penang, and Perak) have a draft document under review. However, two States (Perlis and Selangor) do not have any legislation whatsoever to safeguard chelonians.

In 1915, Perak implemented the River Rights Enactment, which granted exclusive rights to take turtle eggs along specified areas of the Perak River to be vested in the Ruler of the State. During five months of the year, setting traps was prohibited and at no time could anyone kill any turtle without permission. Still in effect today, this enactment claims turtles as those reptiles of the genera *Orlitia, Callagur, Batagur,* or *Hardella,* which include the painted terrapin, river terrapin, and the Malaysian giant turtle. New legislation is currently being drafted in Perak to provide more effective protection for turtles.

Legal measures for turtle conservation were initiated in Terengganu and Kedah in 1951 and 1972, respectively, where legislation pertaining to reptiles was based on local names instead of using taxonomic criteria. These two States rely on Malay language terms such as "tuntung" and "penyu," which are generic names for terrapins and marine turtles, for

identification of species. Disjointed phrasing in the Kedah Enactment seems to imply that only reptiles known as "penyu" and "tuntung" known as *Callagur picta* (painted terrapin = *Callagur borneoensis*) are covered by the legislation.

Legislation from Johor, Kelantan, and Negeri Sembilan uses the phrase "any reptile belonging to Order Chelonia" in its interpretation. However, Malacca's legislation restricts its coverage to five species listed in the First Schedule, although it qualifies turtles as being any reptile belonging to the Order Chelonia, which technically mean all 18 local species (Table 1).

Sabah and Sarawak. — Upon their entry into the Federation in 1963, the States of Sabah and Sarawak were granted special rights and powers, not provided for peninsular States, to enact legislation autonomously. Therefore, two main pieces of legislation form the basis of protection for some of East Malaysia's marine and non-marine species, i.e., the Fauna Conservation Ordinance 1963 and Wild Life Protection Ordinance 1998.

In Sabah, the Parks Enactment 1984 provides blanket protection of all animals, including reptiles, from exploitation within the boundaries of Sabah's parks. Under the Wild Life Enactment 1997, only *Manouria emys* and *Orlitia borneensis* are listed in the Protected Species List, but no other freshwater turtles are included.

In Sarawak, *Orlitia borneensis* and *Callagur borneoensis* are listed as "Totally Protected Species" and all freshwater turtles and tortoises are listed as "Protected Species" under the Wild Life Protection Ordinance 1998. Enforcement of this protection is the responsibility of the Wildlife, National Parks and Wildlife Office of the Sarawak Forestry Department.

International and Regional Conventions and Agreements

Malaysia is a party to the Convention on Wetlands of International Importance Especially as Waterfowl Habitat (i.e., the Ramsar Convention), the Convention on International Trade in Endangered Species of Wild Fauna and Flora (CITES), and the Convention on Biological Diversity (CBD). Malaysia has refrained from signing the Convention on the Conservation of Migratory Species of Wild Animals (Bonn Convention) and Convention Concerning the Protection of World Cultural and Natural Heritage (World Heritage Convention). Though the CBD does not contain lists of threatened species, it encourages nations to value their diverse genetic resources and implement policies to safeguard wild plants and animals.

Utilization and Trade of Turtles in Malaysia

National Utilization. — Use of turtles through subsistence hunting, pet and meat trade has been discussed by Sharma (1999). A summary is presented in Table 2.

Legal International Trade. — Limited information is available from the Department of Wildlife and National Parks on the legal trade in freshwater turtles (Table 3). The

Table 2. Utilization of freshwater turtles and tortoises in Malaysia and potential population impacts resulting from trade

Scientific name	Known use	Potential population impacts resulting from trade
Amyda cartilaginea	Eggs as food, pet trade, meat source, medicinal use, zoo exhibit	Reduced numbers in freshwater systems where over-harvested
Dogania subplana	Eggs as food, medicinal source, zoo exhibit, meat source	Not significant
Pelochelys cantorii	Eggs as food, medicinal use, zoo exhibit	Unknown
Chitra chitra	?	Unknown
Pelodiscus sinensis	Meat source, pet trade, medicinal use	Not applicable
Batagur baska	Eggs as food, medicinal use, zoo exhibit	Trade impacts are mainly from local use of the eggs
Callagur borneoensis	Eggs as food, medicinal use, zoo exhibit	Trade impacts are mainly from local use of the eggs
Orlitia borneensis	Zoo exhibit, pet trade, meat source	Possibly localized reduction in numbers in over-harvested areas
Heosemys grandis	Pet trade, meat source, zoo exhibit, religious use	Reduction in numbers localized
Heosemys spinosa	Pet trade, meat source, medicinal use, religious use	Population reduction outside protected areas
Cyclemys dentata	Pet trade, meat source	Not significant
Cuora amboinensis	Pet trade, meat source, zoo exhibit, religious use, medicinal use	Reduction in numbers in multiple locations due to extensive collection
Hieremys annandalii	Religious use	Unknown
Notochelys platynota	Pet trade, meat source	Not significant
Malayemys subtrijuga	Meat source	Reduction in numbers localized
Siebenrockiella crassicollis	Pet trade, meat source	Reduction in numbers localized
Manouria emys	Eggs as food, pet trade, meat source, zoo exhibit	Populations unlikely severely impacted by trade alone. Reduction in numbers likely only outside protected areas
Manouria impressa	Pet trade, meat source	Populations unlikely severely impacted by trade alone. Reduction in numbers likely only outside protected areas
Indotestudo elongata	Pet trade, meat source, zoo exhibit	Populations unlikely severely impacted by trade alone. Reduction in numbers likely only outside protected areas

source of *Pelodiscus sinensis* (= *Trionyx sinensis*) and *Trachemys scripta elegans* were recorded as "captive bred." All native species were recorded as wild-caught animals. Trade volumes are large and are cause for concern.

Records of live turtles exported into Hong Kong from Malaysia and Singapore between 1993 and 1996 are presented in Table 4. Legal international trade for CITES listed species of tortoises for 1990, 1991, and 1993 is presented in Table 5.

Illegal Trade and Potential Trade Impacts. — Illegal trade is probably present since it is unlikely that local management authorities, including Wildlife Department and Customs staff, are able to identify all turtle species that are traded. It is likely that CITES listed species of tortoises are shipped out together with non-CITES species. Juvenile *M. emys* and *M. impressa* may be easily misidentified as *H. spinosa*. It is noteworthy that no *D. subplana, C. dentata, H. spinosa,* or *M. subtrijuga* are listed in the official export data records for Peninsular Malaysia for 1999. All these species

were observed on the premises of a trader in Perlis in early 1999 who reported that the turtles were mainly for the export market. A summary of trade utilization and potential trade impacts are presented in Table 2.

ACCOUNTS OF TURTLE SPECIES

Status in Peninsular Malaysia –
Data not Available for Sarawak or Sabah

Amyda cartilaginea. — Asiatic softshell turtle.

Distribution: Widespread in Peninsular Malaysia, occurring in rivers, streams, ponds, lakes, and various man-made freshwater habitats (e.g., rice fields and irrigation canals).

Habitat availability: There is ample habitat for this species to breed. This includes numerous large rivers on the east coast of the Peninsula (e.g., Terengganu, Dungun, Pahang, Setiu, Paka, and Kelantan rivers) and the west coast (e.g., Perak, Linggi, Melaka, Muda, Bernam rivers). Several protected areas including Taman Negara, Krau Wildlife Reserve, and Kuala Selangor Nature Park provide pristine habitat for the species. Additionally there are still relatively large areas of *Melaleuca* swamps on the east coast that constitute good habitat for the species.

Population status: No estimates of populations have been made for the species, although it appears to be fairly common throughout the country. Adults and juveniles are still easily captured from most rivers and swamps.

Population trends: Possibly still abundant where it occurs in protected habitats (forest reserves and state or national parks) but populations likely to be reduced where trappers (including orang asli) frequent. This may include most rivers that are easily accessible by road.

Table 3. Export of freshwater turtles from Peninsular Malaysia from January to October 1999 (source: Department of Wildlife and National Parks, Peninsular Malaysia).

Scientific name	Quantity	Source
Amyda cartilaginea	8,773	Wild
Pelochelys cantorii	4,300	Wild
Cuora amboinensis	456,541	Wild
Siebenrockiella crassicollis	135,121	Wild
Heosemys grandis	325,325	Wild
Orlitia borneensis	21,972	Wild
Notochelys platynota	12,300	Wild
Pelodiscus sinensis	1,253,712	Captive bred
Trachemys scripta elegans	251,460	Captive bred
Total	2,469,504	

Table 4. Imports of live turtles into Hong Kong from Malaysia and Singapore between 1993 and August 1996 (in kg). Source: Lee (1996).

Country	1993	1994	1995	1996 (8 mo)
Malaysia	560	-	25,196	15,818
Singapore	-	8,498	30,622	7,412

Table 5. Total exports of tortoises from Peninsular Malaysia from 1990, 1991, and 1993 to the USA and Japan.

Species	USA	Japan	Total
Manouria emys	484	703	1,187
Manouria impressa	235	556	791
Indotestudo elongata	1,639	3,090	4,729
Total	2,358	4,349	6,707

Threats: It is captured from the wild for the meat trade and is the most common softshell offered in Chinese restaurants and in wet markets. Unable to eat the meat of this species due to religious reasons, the predominantly Muslim communities along rivers nevertheless catch this species and sell to middlemen traders for the food trade. In some places, even orang asli trap these turtles and sell them to middlemen traders. Middlemen pay between RM 8–12 per kg (US$ 2.10–3.20 per kg) of turtle. Local trade in this species appears to be rampant throughout the country. Additionally, the Department of Wildlife and National Parks (DWNP) reports that between January to October 1999, 8773 wild-caught animals were exported from Peninsular Malaysia (Table 3).

Dogania subplana. — Malayan softshell turtle.

Distribution: Widespread in Peninsular Malaysia where it is found mainly in forest streams and fast-flowing rivers (including waterfall pools).

Habitat availability: Most areas still under forest cover (forest reserves or parks) would constitute good habitat. The conversion of lowland forests to rubber plantations during British administration of the country and to oil palm plantations under the present government has reduced many lowland forest habitats. The forested mountains of the Main Range (Banjaran Titiwangsa) are predominantly intact and are likely to be so for the most part due to steep terrain. Forestry regulations and current laws will prevent excessive degradation of the Main Range forests.

Population status: No estimates of populations have been made for the species although it appears to be common in protected areas and forest reserves.

Population trends: Possibly still abundant where it occurs in protected habitats (forest reserves and state or national parks), but populations likely to be reduced where trappers (including orang asli) frequent. This may include rivers and streams that are easily accessible by both old and operational logging roads.

Threats: It is captured from the wild for the meat trade and is the second most common softshell offered in Chinese restaurants and in wet markets. As with the Asiatic softshell

turtles, this species is caught by Muslim riverine communities and sold to middlemen traders for the food trade. Middlemen pay between RM 8–12 per kg (US$ 2.10–3.20 per kg) of turtle. Eggs are also collected and eaten when these are encountered. Selective harvest of timber, although potentially disrupting forest hydrology and stream flow, appears to be a lesser threat compared to the access created by logging roads. Large parties of Chinese trappers and their orang asli guides, hunting for both edible frogs and softshell turtles, have been encountered in Kelantan and Terengganu in 1998 and 1999. Access to remote forests is by 4-wheel drive vehicles and through logging roads. The illegal use of poisons and explosives to catch fish in upriver areas is of concern. The continuous and illegal use of these methods by forest communities in Krau Wildlife Reserve recently has apparently wiped out fish and softshells in a major river.

Pelochelys cantorii. — Asian giant softshell turtle.

Distribution: Not as well known as *D. subplana* or *A. cartilaginea*. Nevertheless, the species has been collected from both east and west coast rivers of the Peninsula, and appears to be found throughout the country.

Habitat availability: As with other Peninsula softshells, rivers are the main habitat, although this species is more common in the lower reaches, and mainly areas under tidal influence. Estuarine areas of most Peninsula rivers are still intact and provide good habitat for the species.

Population status: Population estimates of this species in the Peninsula have not been attempted. Nevertheless, based on interviews with local fishermen, anglers, and personal experience, it is safe to say that this species is still found in fair numbers. Based on the number of animals captured by anglers (and often released) on the Setiu River, Terengganu, good populations must still be found.

Population trends: There is no reason to believe that there may be alarming population declines. This species is not sought after by local Chinese communities for the food trade (the flesh is considered inferior to *D. subplana* and *A. cartilaginea*) and likewise, riverine communities often release this species when caught on the hook.

Threats: The eggs are collected and eaten when encountered. This has been observed on the Dungun and Setiu rivers in Terengganu and the Perak River in Perak. Egg collection and consumption is likely to happen throughout the country. Anglers often kill these animals when captured on the hook (observed on the East Coast states), mainly out of frustration, as the entire hook is swallowed. Estuarine pollution from the maritime industry and chemicals from agricultural drainage potentially pose a threat to the species and its prey. Traditional riverine fishing methods such as the "belat" (small mesh net set parallel to the riverbank), "rawai" (longline with multiple hooks set across the river), and "bubu" (baited traps) have all been observed to kill softshell turtles in estuarine areas. Although no specimens have been observed in the pet or meat trade locally, the DWNP reports that between January to October 1999, 4300 individuals were exported from Peninsular Malaysia (Table 3).

Chitra chitra. — Southeast Asian striped giant softshell turtle.

Distribution: Unknown. Historical records are from Taman Negara.

Habitat availability: The availability of suitable habitat for this species in Malaysia is unknown.

Population status: Unknown. Research and interviews with locals conducted in several rivers over the last few years (1993–97) have not been successful in finding specimens nor obtaining information on this species.

Population trends: No population trends available; historical abundance equally unknown. The lack of specimens available in trade from the 1970s to early 1990s suggests that even if there were small localized populations, these were wiped out long before modern-day pressures were exerted on turtle populations by international commercial trade.

Threats: Some of the threats that apply to softshell turtles generally must be valid for *C. chitra*. It is likely that this species may be or has been hunted out well before any surviving populations can be identified.

Batagur baska. — River terrapin.

Distribution: Throughout the Peninsula, from the northern state of Kedah to at least Selangor in the south. Occurs mainly in large rivers and is noticeably absent in small rivers that can support the painted terrapin (*Callagur borneoensis*).

Habitat availability: While most large rivers are still intact and provide both nesting and feeding grounds, the construction of dams upriver disrupts river flow and destroys nesting banks. Nesting banks on the Terengganu, Perak, and Setiu rivers have been severely degraded or totally destroyed.

Population status: The Perak River has the largest population in the country, where the Department of Wildlife and National Parks (DWNP) runs a breeding program and hatchery for wild-harvested eggs. Nesting populations have been reported to be gradually declining at some nesting banks. The DWNP also runs hatcheries in Terengganu and Kedah. Hatchlings are kept until they are 2–3 years old before being released. Some animals are kept for a captive breeding program. DWNP keeps records of annual nesting and juvenile releases for all their programs.

Population trends: The species used to be much more abundant in the Perak River based on historical accounts, but suffered losses during the Japanese occupation. In spite of well-intentioned conservation efforts, the species appears to be in decline in several rivers. The best nesting populations are managed by DWNP where both captive breeding and egg collection and incubation are conducted. The Perak, Muda, and Dungun rivers still have populations that produce more than 100 clutches, of 15–20 eggs each, per year.

Threats: Dam construction, egg harvest and consumption, removal of riparian vegetation, poisoning of rivers for fish capture, disruption of upriver sandbanks by sand mining, and incidental drowning in fishing gear are some of the major threats to the species.

Callagur borneoensis. — Painted terrapin (Fig. 1).

Distribution: From the north of the Peninsula in the state of Penang to the south in the Endau and Muar rivers. Occurs even in smaller rivers that are not inhabited by *B. baska*.

Habitat availability: There are still several rivers that can provide both nesting and feeding grounds, both on the east and west coasts of the Peninsula. Some nesting grounds, both coastal and upriver, continue to be lost to coastal and riverine development. This is particularly true for the east coast populations. Mega-development projects are planned for the Setiu lagoon and the coasts of Melaka. Both of these pose a serious threat to *C. borneoensis*. The nesting beaches at Paka-Kertih have also been degraded due to the development of the petrochemical industry.

Population status: Populations with more than 100 females nesting per year are found in the Setiu, Paka, and

Figure 1. Painted terrapin, *Callagur borneoensis*. Male showing faded post-breeding colors. Photo by Peter Paul van Dijk.

Linggi rivers. Hatcheries have been set up by the Department of Fisheries Malaysia and WWF Malaysia. Eggs are collected or purchased from licensed egg collectors for incubation purposes. All hatchlings produced are released back into the river of parental origin.

Population trends: The species is now absent from several rivers on the east coast where locals report that the species used to nest some 10–15 years ago. This may have been due to over-harvesting of eggs for human consumption coupled with coastal development. Data gathered between 1990–97 indicated that total egg productions on the Setiu, Linggi, and Paka rivers are on the decline. The Department of Fisheries Malaysia monitors nesting populations on several other rivers, but data gathered are largely reliant on information provided by licensed egg collectors.

Threats: Dam construction, egg harvest and consumption, removal of riparian vegetation, poisoning of rivers for fish capture, disruption of estuarine sandbanks by sand mining, incidental drowning in fishing gear, and beachfront development are some of the major threats. There are also incidental accounts of animals offered for sale in pet shops and occasionally being captured for food. Poaching of eggs from licensed and unlicensed nesting beaches occurs, and enforcement needs to be improved in some states.

Orlitia borneensis. — Malaysian giant turtle.

Distribution: Appears to be restricted mainly to the southern parts of the Peninsula, although no systematic surveys for this species have been conducted. Occurs in rivers, but also known from inland freshwater bodies.

Habitat availability: The freshwater swamps and natural lakes in the south provide ample habitat for the species. All rivers south of the Bernam River that possibly harbor this species are still intact with low impact riverine development, mainly at estuarine areas.

Population status: No systematic surveys have been conducted on this species. Based on secondary information, it appears that there are good populations in a southeastern swamp of the Peninsula and a freshwater lake.

Population trends: No information available.

Threats: In some areas, orang asli hunt the species for food during cultural and religious celebrations. Swamp habitats are burned to force the animals out of hiding. The sustainability of harvest by orang asli has not been studied. The species has not been observed in the pet trade or in the local food trade.

Heosemys grandis. — Giant Asian pond turtle.

Distribution: Mainly in the northern parts of the Peninsula where populations appear to be denser.

Habitat availability: The northern states of Kedah and Perlis, and the numerous rice fields, network of irrigation canals and natural lowland grass swamps provide ample habitat for the species. Swamps in northwestern Perak also provide good habitat. On the northeast coast, the swamps of Kelantan and Terengganu currently also provide adequate habitat to support viable populations.

Population status: Interviews with locals in the north indicate that the species is still captured in fair numbers in the above-mentioned habitats. The impacts of capture for the food-trade on wild populations have not been studied. It is the most common species killed on roads crossing rice fields and grass swamps. It was more abundant in so-called "pet stores" selling turtles for food 5–7 years ago; this species is now usually absent from stores in Kuala Lumpur.

Population trends: The species still appears to be abundant in Perlis and Kedah, where rice field habitats and grass swamps continue to provide habitat. The absence of the species from Chinese "pet stores," that sell the species for food, is of concern. Presumably there are actual declines in wild populations.

Threats: Capture of this species for the meat trade locally, and more recently in larger quantities for export to China (according to traders), is of concern. Two large operations, one in Perlis and another in Kedah, handle hundreds of animals of this species per week. Local trappers are employed to capture the specimens and are paid daily according to turtle weight. According to DWNP, 325,325 individuals were exported between January to October 1999 (Table 3). The east coast coastal swamps are continually being cleared for industrial and housing development projects while inland swamps are drained for agriculture. Inland human resettlement schemes are also encroaching on *H. grandis* habitats.

Heosemys spinosa. — Spiny turtle.

Distribution: Widespread in the country, from the lowland dipterocarp forests to the lower montane reaches of forested mountains.

Habitat availability: Forest reserves, forested state land and parks or sanctuaries still provide ample habitat for the species. Taman Negara, Krau Wildlife Reserve, Perlis State Park, and the Bukit Cerakah Agriculture Park provide adequate lowland habitats for the species. Nevertheless, much lowland habitat and hills have over the years given way to human settlement and agriculture.

Population status: It can still be found in fair numbers in unlogged forest reserves and protected areas if sampling intensity is high. Good populations are expected to occur in Taman Negara, Krau Wildlife Reserve, and the Endau-Rompin State Park, largely due to the size of these areas.

Population trends: No data available on population trends.

Threats: Selective logging of forests disrupts forest hydrology and may have impacts on this semi-aquatic species. The network of roads also allows for easy access for trappers and middlemen traders. Trappers are illegally operating in some forest reserves and parks, and *H. spinosa* are collected among other turtle species and edible frogs. The species is rarely encountered in oil palm plantations. Large-scale conversion of logged-over forests to oil palm plantations and other land uses rapidly diminishes available habitat. Capture of this species for the local pet trade is no longer significant; specimens are hardly seen in pet stores compared to past years. The DWNP turtle export records for January to October 1999 does not contain *H. spinosa* on its list.

Cyclemys dentata. — Asian leaf turtle.

Distribution: Widespread in the country and mainly in lowland areas.

Habitat availability: The species occurs in forest streams, ponds and freshwater bodies around limestone areas in the north of the Peninsula. Taman Negara, Krau Wildlife Reserve, Endau-Rompin State Park, and Perlis State Park provide adequate habitat for the species. The species is also common in oil palm and rubber plantations where streams and ponds are found.

Population status: Appears to be fairly common in available habitats and is the most common species encountered when sampling is intense and in diverse habitats in northern Peninsular Malaysia.

Population trends: No data available to show population stability or declines in the wild.

Threats: Chemicals (pesticides, fertilizers, etc.) from agriculture are carried into streams and other water bodies and impacts on this species have not been studied. Captured in large quantities for the meat trade locally, where it has been recorded in wet markets and "pet stores," and more recently for export, according to traders. One trader in Perlis was estimated to have bought approximately 100–150 animals from trappers in a week. Occasionally sold in pet stores in Ipoh, Kuala Lumpur, and Penang, but always in small quantities. Subsistence hunting of this species by orang asli is also common in Perak and Perlis.

Cuora amboinensis. — Asian box turtle.

Distribution: The most widespread of Peninsular Malaysian turtle species and is found in diverse habitats from the lowlands to hill forests.

Habitat availability: The species occurs in rice fields, irrigation canals, *Melaleuca* swamps, freshwater swamps, lakes and ponds, rubber and oil palm plantations, and riparian habitats. Due to its diverse habitat types, there appears to be ample habitat for the species.

Population status: Appears to be abundant in most states that still have swamps and man-made wetland habitats such as rice fields, irrigation canals, and ponds.

Population trends: The capture of animals from the wild will undoubtedly contribute to population reduction, particularly in areas where harvesting is regular and in large quantities. Because the species is not protected by state or federal wildlife laws, capture in agriculture areas (oil palm and rubber estates) is legal and will certainly lead to localized depletion.

Threats: The species is intensively captured for the meat trade locally. Traders in Kelantan and Perlis buy hundreds of individuals from trappers weekly. Five trappers working for

a Chinese middleman in Perlis were observed bringing in approximately 50–70 animals from ricefields in a single day's effort. This is the most common semi-aquatic species sold in wet markets and Chinese "pet stores" in Kuala Lumpur, Ipoh, and Melaka. In more recent months there appear to have been large quantities trapped locally and exported. In September 1999, one exporter in Perak reported buying more than 800 turtles per day from middlemen for export to Shenzhen, China. DWNP records show that between January to October 1999, 456,541 individuals were exported (Table 3). The *Melaleuca* swamps of the east coast are continually being cleared for coastal development projects.

Hieremys annandalii. — Yellow-headed temple turtle.

Distribution: Restricted to northern Peninsular Malaysia.

Habitat availability: Encountered in black-water swamps and associated *Malaleuca* forests in Terengganu and possibly Kelantan. This species is unknown from other habitat types in the Peninsula but likely to be encountered in irrigation canals and ricefields in the same states.

Population status: No data available. The species is rare in the Peninsula.

Population trends: No data available.

Threats: The black-water swamps in Terengganu and Kelantan are likely to be drained in the years to come as more and more swamps are identified for drainage and land development. The species has not been observed in pet stores or wet markets and therefore is unlikely threatened by local sale and consumption. DWNP export records for 1999 also do not list the species.

Notochelys platynota. — Malayan flat-shelled turtle.

Distribution: Widespread in the Peninsula and occurring mainly in lowland forest streams with sandy beds.

Habitat availability: Large protected habitats that will be able to support viable populations would include Taman Negara, Krau Wildlife Reserve, Endau Rompin State Park, Perlis State Park, and Belum State Park. Additionally, forest reserves under state jurisdiction would provide ample habitat for the species.

Population status: There have been no population assessments for this species. Nevertheless, it is frequently found in forest streams when herpetological surveys are conducted.

Population trends: The absence of this species from the local pet and meat trade is potentially an indication of its low abundance in non-forested habitats. Other species like *Cuora amboinensis* and *Cyclemys dentata* are more easily caught, as they occur in man-made habitats and therefore feature more prominently in local trade. It is largely unknown if over-harvesting in some non-protected forests (e.g., state land forests) have had detrimental impacts on the species.

Threats: Selective logging of forests disrupts forest hydrology and may have impacts on this semi-aquatic species. The network of roads also allows for easy access for

Figure 2. Malayan snail-eating turtle, *Malayemys subtrijuga*. Photo by Peter Paul van Dijk.

trappers and middlemen traders. Trappers are illegally operating in some forest reserves and parks, and *N. platynota* are collected among other turtle species. Large-scale conversion of logged-over forests to oil palm plantations and other land uses rapidly diminishes available habitat. Capture of this species for the local pet trade is not significant, as specimens are hardly seen in pet stores compared to past years. It may be the case that more are caught for the international trade. The DWNP turtle export records for January to October 1999 reports that 12,300 wild caught specimens were exported from Peninsular Malaysia (Table 3).

Malayemys subtrijuga. — Malayan snail-eating turtle (Fig. 2).

Distribution: Restricted to the northern parts of the Peninsula, in the states of Perlis and possibly Kedah and along the east coast *Melaleuca* swamps in Terengganu and possibly Kelantan.

Habitat availability: The species is commonly caught in rice fields in Perlis and has been captured in *Melaleuca* swamps in Terengganu. State or federal habitat protection laws do not protect either of these habitats. Rice fields in Perlis and Kedah are extensive and will remain so, but the east coast swamps are continually being drained and cleared for other land uses. The single *Melaleuca* swamp habitat protected in the country is at Jambu Bongkok Recreational Forest in Terengganu.

Population status: Data unavailable.

Population trends: Data unavailable.

Threats: The black-water *Melaleuca* swamps in Terengganu and Kelantan are likely to be drained in the years to come as more and more swamps are identified for drainage and land development. The capture of this species in large quantities in Perlis for the export market is of concern. An exporter in Perlis, who was seen to have

approximately 40–60 animals in a single pen, reported that the animals were to be exported to China. Interestingly, the species was not listed by DWNP on their export data sheets for trade between January to October 1999.

Siebenrockiella crassicollis. — Black marsh turtle.

Distribution: Widespread in the Peninsula and inhabits mainly freshwater and *Melaleuca* swamps, rice fields, and irrigation canals.

Habitat availability: Both natural and man-made habitats for this species are still abundant.

Population status: No assessments have been made on populations. Nevertheless, the species appears to be commonly caught by trappers in Kelantan, Terengganu, and Perak. It often is offered for sale in pet shops and wet markets, and supply is reported to come from the north of the Peninsula (presumably Kelantan and Terengganu).

Population trends: No data available. The species is currently not as common as *C. amboinensis* both in the pet and meat trade, but data on availability in the past are unrecorded.

Threats: As with other species inhabiting freshwater swamps, draining of coastal and inland swamps and conversion to other land uses is potentially a major threat. Capture for the international meat trade is equally important. DWNP reports that between January to October 1999 135,121 wild caught specimens were exported (Table 3).

Manouria emys. — Asian brown tortoise.

Distribution: Widespread in the Peninsula and appears to be more abundant in lowland dipterocarp forests. Unknown in rubber or oil palm plantations.

Habitat availability: Taman Negara, Krau Wildlife Reserve, and Endau Rompin all contain good lowland dipterocarp forests. In addition, some selectively logged forest reserves in Kelantan, Pahang, and Terengganu have good habitat for the species.

Population status: No population estimates have been made. Surveys done in Terengganu in early 1998 indicate that there are still good numbers in lowland forests.

Population trends: There are no data to support or deny that harvest of wild animals may have impacts on population numbers. At least for the three largest protected areas in the Peninsula, populations of these species are assumed to be stable.

Threats: Captured for the international pet trade. Selective logging may have impacts on the species. The accessibility created by logging roads in the lowlands and hills make it easier for trappers with 4-wheel drive vehicles to reach otherwise inaccessible areas.

Manouria impressa. — Impressed tortoise.
Distribution: Restricted to the highland forests of the Main Range and on the mountains in Kelantan. Not recorded on very high altitudes as in the Cameron Highlands.

Habitat availability: Much of the forested mountains of the Main Range remain intact and provide ample habitat for the species.

Population status: No population estimates. Some recent work continues in Fraser's Hill and the lower reaches of Cameron Highlands and results are yet to be analyzed.

Population trends: No data available.

Threats: Captured for the international pet trade. Highland development as observed in Cameron Highlands, Genting Highlands, and Fraser's Hill might have impacts on the species. Orang asli hunt this species for food but also for sale to middlemen traders.

Indotestudo elongata. — Elongated tortoise.
Distribution: Largely restricted to the northern parts of the Peninsula although there are published accounts of the species in Negeri Sembilan in the south. Also found in rubber plantations in Perlis, the northernmost state in the Peninsula.

Habitat availability: Much of the lowland forests of the north parts of Peninsular Malaysia have been converted to rice fields and rubber. The best-protected areas for the species are in the north, i.e., the Perlis State Park and several forest reserves.

Population status: No population assessments have been made, but based on recent surveys in the north of the country, it appears that the species occurs in fair numbers in lowland forests of the Nakawan Range and also in rubber estates.

Population trends: There have been no observations on changes to population numbers but declines can be expected outside protected areas where harvesting for the pet trade is unrestricted.

Threats: Captured for the international pet trade and perhaps food trade.

LITERATURE CITED

GREGORY, R. AND SHARMA, D.S.K. 1997. Review of legislation affecting marine and freshwater turtle, terrapin and tortoise conservation and management in Malaysia: recommendations for change. WWF Malaysia Project Report MYS 343/96.

LEE, S.K.H. 1996. In litt. to the German Scientific Authority for CITES.

SHARMA, D.S.K. 1999. Tortoise and freshwater turtle trade and utilisation in Peninsular Malaysia. TRAFFIC Southeast Asia, Petaling Jaya, 39 pp.

Asian Turtle Trade: Proceedings of a Workshop on Conservation and Trade of Freshwater Turtles and Tortoises in Asia
P.P. van Dijk, B.L. Stuart, and A.G.J. Rhodin, Eds.
Chelonian Research Monographs 2:129–136 • © 2000 by Chelonian Research Foundation

Conservation Status of Freshwater Turtles in Papua New Guinea

Anders G.J. Rhodin[1] and Vagi R. Genorupa[2]

[1]*Chelonian Research Foundation, 168 Goodrich Street, Lunenburg, Massachusetts 01462 USA*
[Fax: 978-582-6279; E-mail: RhodinCRF@aol.com];
[2]*Department of Environment and Conservation, P.O. Box 6601, Boroko, NCD, Papua New Guinea*
[Fax: 675-325-0182]

The island of New Guinea represents one of the world's last great wilderness areas where native peoples still rely to a great extent on the natural resources and biological diversity present in their environment. Freshwater turtles are an integral part of that environment, and their utilization by native peoples constitutes an age-old relationship. However, with an increasing human population and advancing development and westernization, all natural resources, including turtles, are increasingly threatened in New Guinea.

Much of the turtle diversity present in New Guinea has only recently begun to be understood, and the number of recognized taxa is increasing steadily, with many new species yet to be described. For analysis of patterns of distribution and systematics, the turtles of Papua New Guinea (PNG) in eastern New Guinea are best understood by also documenting their distribution in the adjacent Indonesian province of Irian Jaya in western New Guinea.

Freshwater turtles are distributed throughout most of the lowland areas of New Guinea, being separated into primarily northern vs. southern distributions by the central mountain ranges, where no turtles are known to occur. The eastern end of the island is relatively depauperate in terms of freshwater turtles, with diversity being the greatest in the central southern lowlands.

There are at least 13 species of freshwater turtles currently recognized to occur on the island of New Guinea (Table 1), of which 11 are named and 10 occur in PNG itself. As of 25 years ago, only 6 species of freshwater turtles were recognized to occur in New Guinea: *Carettochelys insculpta* (Ramsay, 1886), *Pelochelys bibroni* (Owen, 1853), *Emydura subglobosa* (Krefft, 1876), *Elseya novaeguineae* (Meyer, 1874), *Chelodina siebenrocki* (Werner, 1901), and *Chelodina novaeguineae* (Boulenger, 1888). Other named taxa of turtles from New Guinea have previously been synonymized under these taxa: *Emydura albertisii* (Boulenger, 1888) under *E. subglobosa*; *Elseya schultzei* (Vogt, 1911) and *Elseya branderhorsti* (Ouwens, 1914) under *E. novaeguineae*.

Over the last quarter century, 3 new species of New Guinea turtles have been described: *Chelodina parkeri* (Rhodin and Mittermeier, 1976), *Chelodina reimanni* (Philippen and Grossmann, 1990), and *Chelodina pritchardi* (Rhodin, 1994a). In addition, 2 New Guinea species have recently been recognized as consisting of 2 or more taxa. The giant softshell turtle, *Pelochelys bibroni*, has been formally split into 2 species: *P. bibroni* in the south and *P. cantorii*

(Gray, 1864) in the north (Rhodin et al., 1993; Webb, 1995). Whether the northern form referred to as *P. cantorii* is the same taxon as the widespread southeast Asian form of the same name is not known — in fact, they are most likely different species, with the northern New Guinea form probably an isolated and undescribed species. The New Guinea snapping turtle, *Elseya novaeguineae*, has recently been recognized to consist of at least 4 distinct taxa: *E. novaeguineae* in the northern lowlands, *E. branderhorsti* in the southeastern Irian lowlands, an undescribed *Elseya* sp. 1 in the southern lowlands, and an undescribed *Elseya* sp. 2 in northwestern Irian (Rhodin, unpubl. data in prep.).

In addition, another species of snake-necked turtle of the Australasian faunal realm, *Chelodina mccordi* (Rhodin, 1994b), has recently been described from Roti Island in eastern Indonesia, where it is isolated, endemic, extremely restricted, and already critically endangered (Rhodin, 1996; Samedi and Iskandar, this volume). Although specimens of *C. mccordi* have recently sold for up to US$2000 each by western pet retailers, the species is now considered commercially extinct by Indonesian wildlife traders who can no longer obtain it (D. Iskandar, *pers. comm.*); the species has gone from description to near-extinction in only 5 years, an indication of the extreme pressures the pet trade can place on isolated and rare species.

Freshwater Turtles in Papua New Guinea

We now summarize information on the distribution, status, and trade of the 10 species of freshwater turtles known to occur in Papua New Guinea. These results are summarized in Table 2.

Carettochelys insculpta

The pig-nose turtle (Fig. 1) is probably the most distinctive of New Guinea's turtles. Sole surviving member of the family Carettochelyidae, the species is an isolated and relictual form of a previously wide-spread family with an extensive near-global fossil record.

The distribution of *C. insculpta* in the New Guinea region includes northern Australia where it occurs in the Daly River and other drainages of Northern Territory (Georges and Rose, 1993). In New Guinea it is found in the southern lowlands from the Purari River region of central PNG in the east to at least the Timika region of Irian in the west, possibly occurring as far west as the Lake Yamur

Table 1. Species of freshwater turtles in the greater New Guinea (NG) region, including Papua New Guinea (PNG), Irian Jaya, Indonesia, and Roti Island, Indonesia.

Family	Species	Common Name	Occurrence PNG	Irian	Distribution
Carettochelyidae	*Carettochelys insculpta*	Pig-nose turtle	X	X	southern NG lowlands
Trionychidae	*Pelochelys bibroni*	New Guinea giant softshell turtle	X	X	southern NG lowlands
	Pelochelys cantorii	Asian giant softshell turtle	X	X	northern NG lowlands
Chelidae	*Emydura subglobosa*	Red-bellied short-necked turtle	X	X	southern NG lowlands
	Elseya novaeguineae	New Guinea snapping turtle	X	X	northern NG lowlands
	Elseya branderhorsti	White-bellied snapping turtle	–	X	southeastern Irian
	Elseya sp. 1	Red-bellied snapping turtle	X	X	southern NG lowlands
	Elseya sp. 2	Serrated snapping turtle	–	X	northwestern Irian
	Chelodina siebenrocki	Siebenrock's snake-necked turtle	X	X	southern NG coastal
	Chelodina parkeri	Parker's snake-necked turtle	X	X	southern NG inland
	Chelodina novaeguineae	New Guinea snake-necked turtle	X	X	southern NG lowlands
	Chelodina pritchardi	Pritchard's snake-necked turtle	X	–	southeastern PNG
	Chelodina reimanni	Reimann's snake-necked turtle	–	X	southeastern Irian
	Chelodina mccordi	Roti snake-necked turtle	–	–	endemic to Roti

region. It is most commonly found inland in primarily riverine habitat (Liem and Haines, 1977), but also occurs along the coast where it occasionally enters the sea to nest on marine beaches (Rhodin and Rhodin, 1977).

Populations in New Guinea have historically been abundant throughout the range, but appear to have suffered declines over the last few decades (Rose et al., 1982; Georges and Rose, 1993; Georges et al., in press). The species is widely and heavily exploited in New Guinea for its meat and eggs and is an important component of the subsistence economies of local peoples (Pernetta and Burgin, 1980; Rose et al., 1982; Mambai, 1997). Over 20,000 eggs were harvested and sold in Kikori markets over a 5-month period in 1981–82 (M. Rose, unpubl. data). The species is especially vulnerable due to its nesting habits which are partially synchronous and somewhat predictable on exposed sandbanks and shores of rivers and other water bodies, similar in many respects to the nesting habits of marine turtles.

Local subsistence consumption continues today, as does legal trade to local regional food markets. In addition, illegal trade in the species apparently occurs along the southern PNG – Irian border, where villagers living close to the border stockpile specimens and then trade or barter these animals along the coast with seafaring traders from Merauke in southeastern Irian. These specimens are primarily intended for the international pet trade and huge numbers of the species are exported from Merauke to Jakarta and then internationally to multiple distribution centers (Samedi and Iskandar, this volume). What percentage of the enormous Merauke trade in *C. insculpta* represents animals from PNG is not known.

Pelochelys bibroni

The New Guinea giant softshell turtle (Fig. 2) is the largest and most beautifully patterned turtle from New Guinea, reaching shell sizes of over 1 meter in length. Originally assumed to be simply an isolated population of the wide-spread Asian species originally carrying the same name, Rhodin et al. (1993) demonstrated that the southern New Guinea population was different and distinct. Webb (1995) formalized this distinction and restricted the name *P. bibroni* to this southern New Guinea population, referring the wide-spread Asian species to the previously described *P. cantorii*.

Pelochelys bibroni is endemic to New Guinea, but its distribution includes both Irian Jaya, Indonesia, and Papua New Guinea. Its distribution extends across the southern lowlands of New Guinea, from the Port Moresby region in the east, to the southern lowlands of Irian Jaya, where its western extent is not well documented, but reaches at least as far as the Timika region. It appears to be most abundant

Table 2. Population status and trade threats for species of freshwater turtles in Papua New Guinea. Conservation status reflects actual or proposed status according to IUCN Red List criteria (IUCN, 1996).

Species	Population Status	Trade Threats	Conservation Status
Carettochelys insculpta	Relatively abundant, becoming depleted	Regional food markets, illegal export for pet trade	Vulnerable
Pelochelys bibroni	Uncommon	Regional food markets	Vulnerable
Pelochelys cantorii	Relatively scarce	Regional food markets, curio masks for export	Endangered
Emydura subglobosa	Abundant	Regional food markets	Lower Risk: Least Concern
Elseya novaeguineae	Abundant	Regional food markets, curio masks for export	Lower Risk: Least Concern
Elseya sp. 1	Abundant	Regional food markets, illegal export for pet trade	Lower Risk: Least Concern
Chelodina siebenrocki	Common, restricted	Illegal export for pet trade	Lower Risk: Near Threatened
Chelodina parkeri	Uncommon, restricted	Illegal export for pet trade	Vulnerable
Chelodina novaeguineae	Relatively common	Illegal export for pet trade	Lower Risk: Least Concern
Chelodina pritchardi	Scarce, restricted	Illegal export for pet trade	Endangered

Figure 1. The pig-nose turtle, *Carettochelys insculpta*, from the Fly River region, Western Prov., PNG. Photo by Jeffrey W. Lang.

in the trans-Fly region of Western Province in PNG, especially in the Lake Murray and Fly River drainage, but is relatively uncommon, being encountered much less frequently than the more common *C. insculpta*.

The species is apparently exploited whenever encountered, being prized both for its eggs and meat, and is consumed locally or sold in local or regional food markets. There is no evidence of international pet trade in this species from PNG.

Pelochelys cantorii

The Asian giant softshell turtle is also a large species, but without the dramatic shell pattern found in *P. bibroni*. Whether the northern New Guinea populations here referred to as *P. cantorii* are distinct from the widespread Asian form of the same name is not known, but

Figure 2. The New Guinea giant softshell turtle, *Pelochelys bibroni*, for sale in a market at Debapare, Strickland River, Western Prov., PNG. Photo by Jeffrey W. Lang.

preliminary work indicates this may indeed be an undescribed isolated and restricted species endemic to New Guinea (Rhodin et al., 1993).

The distribution of *P. cantorii* in New Guinea includes the northern lowlands as far east as Madang, including both the Sepik and Ramu drainages of PNG. Its western extent into to the northern lowlands of Irian Jaya includes the Jayapura region, the Mamberano drainage, and the Nabire region on the southern shore of Cenderawasih Bay. Whether there is sympatry, allopatry, or intergradation with southern *P. bibroni* in the far western lowlands of New Guinea is not known. The species appears to be scarce throughout its range.

Exploitation of *P. cantorii* is similar to that for *P. bibroni*, with significant local consumption and local market trade for food and eggs. In addition, the bony carapaces of *P. cantorii* are used for the production of ornamental curio turtle masks manufactured primarily in the Sepik region (notably the Chambri Lakes area) for sale to the tourist industry (Rhodin et al., 1993). Large numbers of these masks, usually made from shells of the smaller hard-shelled turtle, *Elseya novaeguineae*, but also including significant numbers of *P. cantorii*, are sold as artifacts at many tourist locations both in northern PNG and in Port Moresby. The full extent of this trade is not known, but appears to be quite robust, with hundreds if not thousands of masks available for sale at any given time. There is no evidence of international pet trade in this species from PNG.

Emydura subglobosa

The red-bellied short-necked turtle (Fig. 3) is a beautiful small species of hard-shelled turtle that occurs throughout the lowland regions of southern New Guinea. It is probably the most common and abundant turtle species in New Guinea.

The distribution of *E. subglobosa* includes the entire southern lowlands of PNG and Irian Jaya. The eastern extent reaches to the Kemp Welch River basin east of Port Moresby (Rhodin, 1993), and it reaches as far west as the Lake Yamur

Figure 3. The red-bellied short-necked turtle, *Emydura subglobosa*, from the Kemp Welch River area, Central Prov., PNG. Photo by AGJR.

region of Irian Jaya. It is the most widely distributed species in southern New Guinea, extending further east than the southern *Elseya* sp.

Despite apparent records to the contrary (Iverson, 1992), the species does not occur naturally in northern New Guinea. Most northern records of *E. subglobosa* represent misidentified *Elseya novaeguineae*. However, there appear to be scattered populations of introduced *E. subglobosa* in various northern locations, probably representing escaped or released animals from the domestic food market trade. For example, specimens of *E. subglobosa* have been recorded from high elevations in the central mountains at Goroka, and from the northern island of New Britain where no natural populations of freshwater turtles are known to occur, but where the huge natural foods market in Rabaul probably deals occasionally in freshwater turtles imported from mainland PNG.

Local subsistence consumption of *E. subglobosa* is common, with many villagers keeping animals alive in villages for a short time awaiting slaughter for special occasions. Legal trade to local and regional food markets also occurs. In addition, illegal trade in the species apparently occurs along the southern PNG – Irian border, where villagers living close to the border stockpile specimens and then trade or barter these animals along the coast with seafaring traders from Merauke in southeastern Irian, as for *C. insculpta*. These specimens are primarily intended for the international pet trade and large numbers of the species are exported from Merauke to Jakarta and then

internationally to multiple distribution centers (Samedi and Iskandar, this volume). What percentage of the Merauke trade in *E. subglobosa* represents animals from PNG is not known. Legal export from PNG occurs only rarely, with only a single animal of this species documented over the last 3 years.

Elseya novaeguineae

The New Guinea snapping turtle is a wide-spread species of relative abundance that occurs throughout the lowland regions of northern New Guinea. Previously considered to be distributed throughout New Guinea, the southern populations are in fact at least two separate species (Rhodin, unpubl. data in prep.).

The species is distributed from the Popondetta region of northeastern PNG in the east, all the way to the Vogelkop Peninsula of northwestern Irian in the west, making it the most widely distributed chelonian in New Guinea. The systematic relationships of the various populations in this wide distribution have not yet been elucidated, and further taxonomic study is clearly necessary. The type locality for *E. novaeguineae* is on the southwestern shore of Cenderawasih Bay on the southeastern Vogelkop. The previously described species *Elseya schultzei* from the Tami River near Jayapura might possibly represent a distinct taxon, as may the northwestern Vogelkop populations from around Sarong. There is also a possibility that the Sepik and eastern PNG populations are distinct. An isolated population on Waigeo Island might well be distinct. The species has also been recorded extra-limitally in the Palau Islands (Aoki, 1977) where it may have been introduced but was not found in recent surveys (Crombie and Pregill, 1999). The species may also occur as an introduction on Malaita, Solomon Islands (Dahl, 1986).

Trade in the species includes extensive local consumption and local and regional food markets, especially promi-

Figure 4. Eggs and adults of the New Guinea snapping turtle, *Elseya novaeguineae*, for sale in a market at Angoram, Sepik River, East Sepik Prov., PNG. Photo by Jeffrey W. Lang.

Figure 5. Curio mask made from shell of the New Guinea snapping turtle, *Elseya novaeguineae*, for sale in tourist store in Port Moresby, Central Prov., PNG. Photo by AGJR.

nent in the Sepik River region (Fig. 4), but we have seen it for sale in food markets all over northern PNG. In addition, as for *P. cantorii*, there is a robust trade in *E. novaeguineae* shells used in the ornamental curio trade (Fig. 5) for sale as artifacts to tourists. Hundreds if not thousands of these shell masks are readily available for sale to tourists all over northern PNG and in Port Moresby.

There does not appear to be any significant illegal trade in this species across the northern PNG – Irian border between Vanimo and Jayapura, primarily due to fairly rigorous local border controls. The international pet trade in this species appears to emanate primarily from Sorong on the Vogelkop Peninsula in northwestern Irian.

A few shipments of this species have also appeared in the international food markets of Hong Kong and southern China, but the animals seen were in poor shape due probably to lengthy travel from northern PNG or Irian (P. Crow, *pers. comm.*). As of now, the Chinese food market trade does not yet appear to have impacted turtles of New Guinea. However, as populations of heavily traded species in southeast Asia are depleted, the export routes for the pet trade currently emanating from New Guinea will probably convert and begin to trade increasing amounts of turtles primarily for the food trade.

Elseya sp. 1.

The red-bellied snapping turtle is a still undescribed species representing the southern populations of what was previously considered to be *E. novaeguineae* (Rhodin, unpubl. data in prep.). The species is distinguished from northern *E. novaeguineae* by a combination of characters including a striking red plastron in juveniles and sub-adults and a generally rounder carapace, with *E. novaeguineae* having a yellow plastron and more oval shell.

The species is distributed from the Purari River region of PNG in the east to at least the Timika region of Irian Jaya in the west. Further west in the Berau Gulf region of Irian it appears to be replaced by *Elseya* sp. 2, a second undescribed species distinguished by a prominently serrated and keeled shell. In the southeastern Irian lowlands around Merauke, the species appears to occur sympatrically with *E. branderhorsti*, a large species with limited distribution characterized by a white plastron. Animals of this species complex have also been recorded from the Aru Islands of Indonesia on the Sahul shelf between New Guinea and Australia, but whether these represent a new species or not is not known. The species appears to be relatively abundant, with similar population levels as *E. novaeguineae* and *E. subglobosa*.

Local subsistence consumption of *Elseya* sp. 1 is common, with many villagers keeping animals on hand for special occasions. Legal trade to local and regional food markets also occurs. In addition, illegal trade in the species apparently occurs along the southern PNG – Irian border, where villagers living close to the border stockpile specimens and then trade or barter these animals with traders from

Figure 6. Parker's snake-necked turtle, *Chelodina parkeri*, from the Western Prov., PNG. Photo by AGJR.

Merauke in southeastern Irian, as for *C. insculpta* and *E. subglobosa*. These specimens are primarily intended for the international pet trade and large numbers of the species are exported from Merauke to Jakarta and then internationally to multiple distribution centers (Samedi and Iskandar, this volume). What percentage of the Merauke trade in *Elseya* sp. 1 represents animals from PNG is not known.

Chelodina siebenrocki

The snake-necked turtles occur only in the southern lowlands of New Guinea, with the relatively large, non-descript Siebenrock's snake-neck turtle being restricted to the southern coastal areas of Western Province in PNG and adjacent southeastern Irian. Its inland distribution is markedly limited, being replaced there by *C. parkeri*.

There is limited local consumption of *C. siebenrocki*, but in general snake-necked turtles are not a highly desired food item and do not appear to be present in the regional food market trade (the relatively strong musk odor and snake-like appearance contribute to the reluctance of people to eat them). Populations of *C. siebenrocki* appear to be relatively robust, although the limited distribution may make the species vulnerable to continued exploitation. Some illegal trade in the species may occur along the southern PNG – Irian border destined for the international pet trade, but the species is very common in the Merauke area and most international shipments probably consist primarily of locally-caught Irian animals. In addition, the species is not very valuable or desired on the pet market, which also lessens demand for illegal export from PNG.

Chelodina parkeri

Parker's snake-necked turtle (Fig. 6) is among the most beautifully patterned of all the snake-necked turtles of either New Guinea or Australia. As a result it has become heavily exploited by the international pet trade and commands extremely high retail prices by western reptile dealers. It has a very limited distribution which also renders it vulnerable.

The species is distributed in the inland areas of the trans-Fly region of Western Province in PNG, notably Lake Murray and the Fly and Aramia rivers. The species probably also occurs in inland southeastern Irian portions of the Fly River watershed, however, no actual localities have been documented there yet. It does not occur in coastal areas where it is replaced by *C. siebenrocki*. It is relatively uncommon within its area of distribution, and has only a limited area of occurrence.

As with *C. siebenrocki* there is no significant trade in the species to local or regional food markets, but it may occasionally be eaten locally. In view of the high demand for the species there is probably illegal trade occurring across the PNG – Irian border, especially inland and west of the Lake Murray region, with the animals destined for the international pet trade for export from Merauke in southeastern Irian. How many of the animals exported from Merauke represent illegal PNG specimens vs. legal Irian animals is not known, but it is suspected that most animals of supposed Irian origin are probably illegally exported from PNG.

Chelodina novaeguineae

The New Guinea snake-necked turtle is a small and relatively non-descript species that does not appear to figure prominently in either the local food or illegal pet trade. It was the first snake-necked turtle to be described from New Guinea, with its type locality in southern coastal Western Province of PNG. Subsequent discovery of other populations of similar animals throughout the Australasian faunal region led to an apparently huge expansion of its range to eventually include most of southern New Guinea, most of northern Australia (Iverson, 1992), and Roti Island west of Timor in Indonesia (Lidth de Jeude, 1895). With subsequent systematic analysis of these various widespread populations, however, *C. novaeguineae* itself has come to be restricted to southwestern PNG and possibly southeastern Irian with other populations previously referred to as "*C. novaeguineae*" representing separate species: *Chelodina reimanni* (Philippen and Grossmann, 1990) from the Merauke region of southeastern Irian, *C. pritchardi* (Rhodin, 1994a) from the Kemp Welch River area of southeastern PNG, and *C. mccordi* (Rhodin, 1994b) from Roti Island, Indonesia. The northern Australian populations of "*C. novaeguineae*" are also distinct and have previously received the invalid name *C. rankini* (Wells and Wellington, 1985), and are now in the process of being formally described (W.P. McCord and S.A. Thomson, in review).

Chelodina novaeguineae now appears restricted to the Western Province of PNG from about the Bamu River in the

Figure 7. Pritchard's snake-necked turtle, *Chelodina pritchardi*, from the Kemp Welch River area, Central Prov., PNG. Photo by AGJR.

east to approximately the PNG – Irian border, although it may possibly occur in southeastern Irian as well. To the west it appears to be replaced by, or possibly intergrade with, *C. reimanni*, which has not yet been recorded from PNG; to the east it does not appear to extend to the central Gulf Province and a large range discontinuity occurs between *C. novaeguineae* and *C. pritchardi* further to the east. *Chelodina novaeguineae* occurs both inland (notably the Lake Murray region) and coastally, encompassing to a certain extent the combined distributions of inland *C. parkeri* and coastal *C. siebenrocki*.

There is limited local consumption of *C. novaeguineae*, but in general snake-necked turtles are not a highly desired food item and do not appear to be present in the regional food market trade. Populations appear to be relatively robust. Some illegal trade in the species may occur along the southern PNG – Irian border destined for the international pet trade.

Chelodina pritchardi

Pritchard's snake-necked turtle (Fig. 7), a distinctive member of the *C. novaeguineae* complex closely related to *C. longicollis* of Australia (Rhodin, 1994a), is PNG's only documented endemic turtle species, with no occurrence in Irian Jaya or Australia. It has an extremely limited distribution and has only been recorded from three known localities in the Kemp Welch River basin southeast of Port Moresby in southeastern PNG (Rhodin, 1994a). Its range is isolated and discontinuous from other members of its species complex, and it may represent a relictual species of previous Australian origin occurring on the periphery of a widely distributed pre-"*C. novaeguineae*" ancestor (Rhodin, 1994a).

There is limited local consumption of *C. pritchardi*, but in general snake-necked turtles are not a highly desired food item and do not appear to be present in the regional food market trade. The species appears to be relatively scarce within its range, which it shares with only the relatively common *E. subglobosa* (Rhodin, 1993). There has been no legal export of *C. pritchardi* except for the holotype at the time of the species description. All animals present in the international pet trade have been exported illegally and continued trade in this threatened species poses a major risk to its continued survival. It is highly endangered due to its restricted range, limited known localities, and continued illegal trade for the pet industry. In many respects the status of *C. pritchardi* parallels the biology and potential fate of the even more critically endangered *C. mccordi*.

General Comments

Trade in turtles from PNG is strictly regulated by law as proscribed by the Fauna (Protection and Control) Act (Parker, 1981) (this Act is currently in the process of being amended). Papua New Guinea is also a CITES signatory since 1975. All exports of all turtles require permits to be issued by the Conservator of Fauna (currently the Dept. of Environment and Conservation). No turtles are listed by PNG as Protected Species, which would limit legal permitted export to at most 4 animals to legitimate approved zoological institutions. However, all marine turtles and two freshwater turtles, *C. insculpta* and *P. bibroni* are listed as Restricted Species, with narrow guidelines limiting any legal export to only a few animals for legitimate scientific purposes. The rest of the non-protected and non-restricted turtle species may be exported only with issued export permits, and then only for approved legitimate scientific and zoological purposes. Export of curios incorporating wildlife parts (e.g., turtle shell masks) also requires export permits.

At least on paper, PNG protects its wildlife and turtle resources fervently from export, with proper concern for their continued utilization at the local level by the native population. Unfortunately, control and enforcement of these regulations is badly lacking, and very few export permits for turtles are actually issued. A search of permits issued during the last 3 years yielded evidence of only a single specimen of *E. subglobosa* exported to Hawaii in 1996. Permits were also previously obtained in 1987 for export of one *C. novaeguineae* (actually *C. pritchardi*), and in 1977 for a few specimens each of *C. siebenrocki*, *C. novaeguineae*, *E. subglobosa*, and *E. novaeguineae*, with only one specimen each of *C. insculpta* and *P. bibroni* (AGJR, pers. obs.).

Trade in New Guinea turtles at present appears to be restricted primarily to the international exotic pet industry.

There appear to be significant levels of illegal export trade along the southern PNG – Irian border, as described above for the different species traded along this route. Some of this trade may pass through Daru, an off-shore regional port and air facility with a long history of illegal wildlife trade and also a major regional market for the sale of marine turtle meat. No similar trade appears to occur along the northern PNG – Irian border. The reasons for the difference reflect the higher levels of border control present along the northern border. Illegal export via air or ship from major ports such as Port Moresby probably also occurs, especially for vulnerable species like *C. pritchardi* which occurs close to Port Moresby. The Dept. of Environment and Conservation has inadequate manpower and resources to inspect and control these probable avenues of illegal trade.

As mentioned above for *E. novaeguineae*, the international food trade does not yet appear to have significantly impacted populations of turtles in New Guinea. However, as populations of heavily traded species in southeast Asia are depleted, the export routes for the pet trade currently emanating from New Guinea will probably convert and begin to trade increasing amounts of turtles primarily for the food trade.

If the freshwater turtle fauna of Papua New Guinea is to continue to survive as a viable and sustainable resource base for utilization by the native population, and if we are to avoid the consumption of this resource in international exotic pet and food markets, then stricter adherence to existing laws and necessary control and inspection at probable export sites needs urgently to be implemented.

LITERATURE CITED

AOKI, R. 1977. The occurrence of a short-necked chelid in the Palau Islands. Jap. J. Herpetol. 7(2):32-33.

BOULENGER, G.A. 1888. On the chelydoid chelonians of New Guinea. Ann. Mus. Civ. Stor. Nat. Genova (2)6:449-452.

CROMBIE, R.I., AND PREGILL, G.K. 1999. A checklist of the herpetofauna of the Palau Islands (Republic of Belau), Oceania. Herpetological Monographs 13:29-80.

DAHL, A.L. 1986. Review of the Protected Areas System in Oceania. IUCN Comm. Nat. Parks.

GEORGES, A., AND ROSE, M. 1993. Conservation biology of the pig-nosed turtle, *Carettochelys insculpta*. Chelonian Conservation and Biology 1(1):3-12.

GEORGES, A., ROSE, M., AND DOODY, J.S. In press. *Carettochelys insculpta* Ramsay, 1886, Pig-nose turtle. In: Pritchard, P.C.H., and Rhodin, A.G.J. (Eds.). The Conservation Biology of Freshwater Turtles. Chelonian Research Monographs.

GRAY, J.E. 1864. Revision of the species of Trionychidae found in Asia and Africa, with the descriptions of some new species. Proc. Zool. Soc. London. 1864:76-98.

IUCN. 1996. 1996 IUCN Red List of Threatened Animals. Gland, Switzerland: IUCN, 378 pp.

IVERSON, J.B. 1992. A Revised Checklist with Distribution Maps of the Turtles of the World. Richmond, IN: Privately printed, 363 pp.

KREFFT, G. 1876. Notes on Australian animals in New Guinea with description of a new species of fresh water tortoise belonging to the genus *Euchelymys* (Gray). Ann. Mus. Civ. Stor. Nat. Giacomo

Doria 8:390-394.

LIDTH DE JEUDE, T.W.V. 1895. Reptiles from Timor and the neighbouring islands. Notes Leyden Mus. 16:119-127.

LIEM, D.S., AND HAINES, A.K. 1977. The ecological significance and economic importance of the mangrove and estuarine communities of the Gulf Province, Papua New Guinea. In: Petr, T. (Ed.). Purari River (Wabo) Hydroelectric Scheme Environmental Studies, Volume 3. Waigani, Papua New Guinea: Office of Environment and Conservation, pp. 1-35.

MAMBAI, B.V. 1997. The risk to the Irian tortoise: utilization and population degradation. New Guinea Tropical Ecology and Biodiversity Digest 3:1-2.

MEYER, A.B. 1874. Eine Mittheilung über die von mir auf Neu-Guinea und den Inseln Jobi, Mysore und Mafoor im Jahre 1873 gesammelten Amphibien. Mber. Akad. Wiss. Berlin 39:128-140.

OUWENS, P.A. 1914. List of Dutch East Indian chelonians in the Buitenzorg Zoological Museum. Contrib. Faune Ind. Neerl. Buitenzorg 1:29-32.

OWEN, R. 1853. Descriptive catalogue of the osteological series contained in the Museum of the Royal College of Surgeons of England. Vol I. Pisces, Reptilia, Aves, Marsupialia. London: Taylor and Francis, 350 pp.

PARKER, F. 1981. Collecting, export, import, research and filming involving wildlife in Papua New Guinea. Wildlife Pap. New Guinea Wildl. Publ. 81(2):1-58.

PERNETTA, J.C., AND BURGIN, S. 1980. Census of crocodile populations and their exploitation in the Purari area (with annotated checklist of the herpetofauna). Purari River (Wabo) Hydroelectric Scheme Environ. Stud. 14:1-44.

PHILIPPEN, H., AND GROSSMANN, P. 1990. Eine neue Schlangenhals-schildkröte von Neuguinea: *Chelodina reimanni* sp. n. (Reptilia, Testudines, Pleurodira: Chelidae). Zoologische Abhandlungen Staatliches Museum Tierkunde Dresden 46(5):95-102.

RAMSAY, E.P. 1886. On a new genus and species of freshwater tortoise from the Fly River, New Guinea. Proc. Linn. Soc. New South Wales (2)1(1887)[1886]:158-162.

RHODIN, A.G.J. 1993. Range extension for *Emydura subglobosa* in Papua New Guinea. Chelonian Conservation and Biology 1(1):47-48.

RHODIN, A.G.J. 1994a. Chelid turtles of the Australasian Archi-

RHODIN, A.G.J. 1994b. Chelid turtles of the Australasian Archipelago: II. A new species of *Chelodina* from Roti Island, Indonesia. Breviora 498:1-31.

RHODIN, A.G.J. 1996. Status and conservation of *Chelodina mccordi*, an isolated and restricted freshwater turtle from Roti Island, Indonesia. In: Devaux, B. (Ed.). Proceedings – International Congress of Chelonian Conservation. Gonfaron, France: Editions SOPTOM, p. 67.

RHODIN, A.G.J., AND MITTERMEIER, R.A. 1976. *Chelodina parkeri*, a new species of chelid turtle from New Guinea, with a discussion of *Chelodina siebenrocki* Werner, 1901. Bulletin of the Museum of Comparative Zoology 147(11):465-488.

RHODIN, A.G.J., AND RHODIN, S.D. 1977. Iakttagelser från en herpetologisk samlingsresa till Papua New Guinea. Snoken - National Swedish Herpetological Association 7(2/3):65-72.

RHODIN, A.G.J., MITTERMEIER, R.A., AND HALL, P.M. 1993. Distribution, osteology, and natural history of the Asian giant softshell turtle, *Pelochelys bibroni*, in Papua New Guinea. Chelonian Conservation and Biology 1(1):19-30.

ROSE, M.R., PARKER, F., AND RHODIN, A.G.J. 1982. New Guinea plateless turtle or pitted shell turtle (Fly River or pig-nosed turtle), *Carettochelys insculpta* Ramsay 1886. In: Groombridge, B. (Ed.). The IUCN Amphibia - Reptilia Red Data Book, Part 1. Testudines, Crocodylia, Rhynchocephalia. Gland: International Union for Conservation of Nature and Natural Resources, pp. 243-246.

SAMEDI, AND ISKANDAR, D. 2000. Turtle utilization and conservation in Indonesia. This volume.

VOGT, T. 1911. Reptilien und Amphibien aus Neu-Guinea. Sber. Ges. Naturf. Freunde, Berlin 9:410-414.

WEBB, R.G. 1995. Redescription and neotype designation of *Pelochelys bibroni* from southern New Guinea (Testudines: Trionychidae). Chelonian Conservation and Biology 1(4):301-310.

WELLS, R.W., AND WELLINGTON, C.R. 1985. A classification of the Amphibia and Reptilia of Australia. Austr. J. Herp. Supp. Ser. 1:1-61.

WERNER, F. 1901. Ueber Reptilien und Batrachier aus Ecuador und Neu-Guinea. Verh. Zool. Bot. Ges. Wien. 51:593-603.

pelago: I. A new species of *Chelodina* from southeastern Papua New Guinea. Breviora 497:1-36.

Asian Turtle Trade: Proceedings of a Workshop on Conservation and Trade of Freshwater Turtles and Tortoises in Asia
P.P. van Dijk, B.L. Stuart, and A.G.J. Rhodin, Eds.
Chelonian Research Monographs 2:137–144 • © 2000 by Chelonian Research Foundation

Conservation Status, Trade, and Management of Tortoises and Freshwater Turtles in Thailand

PETER PAUL VAN DIJK[1,3] AND THANIT PALASUWAN[2]

[1]*Biology Department, Science Faculty, Chulalongkorn University, Phaya Thai Road, Pathumwan, Bangkok 10330, Thailand;*
[2]*Forest Protection Division 1 (Central Region), Forest Protection Office, Royal Forest Department,*
61 Phahonyothin Road, Bangkhen, Bangkok 10900, Thailand [E-mail: wildlifept@hotmail.com];
[3]*Present Address: TRAFFIC Southeast Asia, M19-B (2nd Floor), Jalan Pasar (1/21),*
46000 Petaling Jaya, Selangor, Malaysia [E-mail: pptsea@po.jaring.my]

Thailand covers 513,517 km² at the center of mainland South-East Asia, stretching some 1600 km north to south and about 780 km east to west at its widest point. It encompasses a wide variety of hills, mountains, plains, rivers, seacoasts, and other geographical features. Thailand experiences a distinct seasonal monsoon climate in its mainland northern part, and a more uniform wet climate in the peninsular region. Correspondingly, there is a rich diversity of natural vegetation types and agricultural landscape types, inhabited by a multitude of animal and plant species as well as over 60 million humans. A total of 3 tortoise species, 15 freshwater turtles, and 5 marine turtles are native to the country and its coastal waters, with an additional 4 freshwater turtles reported as occurring but unconfirmed, and 2 exotic freshwater turtle species established in the country.

Legal Status

All 26 species of turtles that are considered native to Thailand are protected from exploitation under the WARPA law (Wild Animals Reservation and Protection Act B.E. 2535) which was revised in 1992. This law controls hunting, trade, possession, import, export, and commercial breeding of wildlife. Thailand is a signatory to CITES, whose provisions are implemented through WARPA. The WARPA law also enables the exclusive protection of areas of land as Wildlife Sanctuaries, and limited protection for Non-Hunting Areas. The National Parks Act of 1961 protects areas to be "preserved in its natural state for the benefit of public education and enjoyment."

The Royal Forest Department is the management authority for protected areas and the conservation of terrestrial species, including tortoises, while the Fisheries Department acts as management authority for aquatic species, including freshwater turtles. The Scientific Authority is formed by a committee of experts.

National Parks and Wildlife Sanctuaries are legally protected from all forms of removal, release, disturbance, or other impacts on all plants, animals, and the habitat as a whole. Development, management measures, or other impacts may only be carried out by the Government, through the Royal Forest Department or its designated agents, after wide consultation. Supervised recreational tourism is only permitted and encouraged in the National Parks.

Species Management

Species management, in the form of captive breeding projects, exist for *Batagur baska*, *Callagur borneoensis*, *Chitra chitra*, *Platysternon megacephalum*, and the marine turtles. These have varying degrees of success, but none could be considered particularly successful.

Habitat Conservation

Thailand has gazetted over 100 protected areas, together covering over 67,000 km² or 12% of the country's surface, where collecting or other forms of disturbance of any plant or animal are prohibited. In practice, the protected areas are fairly well to very well protected. Not all native turtle species are confirmed to occur in protected areas in significant populations.

In addition, various Non-Hunting areas also represent turtle habitat, but their often intensive use by the local population (including fishing with monofilament nets) intentionally or accidentally impacts freshwater turtles.

Control Measures

Enforcement efforts are made to stop exploitation and trade in protected species and to prevent incursions and encroachment in protected areas. These efforts are restrained by a lack of manpower and identification skills and the complications arising from different responsibilities and authorities of the various departments involved in enforcement.

During 1998 and 1999, the enforcement division of the Royal Forest Department prosecuted more than 60 cases on all Thai wildlife, including 5 cases involving turtles. In the past three years, over 2200 turtles were confiscated. The seizures included 5 species; more than half were snail-eating turtles (*Malayemys subtrijuga*), the others were yellow-headed temple turtles (*Hieremys annandalii*), Asian box turtles (*Cuora amboinensis*), black marsh turtles (*Siebenrockiella crassicollis*), and Asian leaf turtles (*Cyclemys dentata* group). More than 600 of these turtles were destined for export to Guangzhou, China. They were mixed with farmed Chinese softshell turtles (*Pelodiscus sinensis*), which may be exported legally, together with protected and illegal snakes. The remaining turtles were confiscated from temple sellers or fresh markets. Most of the market turtles were intended for release to gain religious merit and long life; only a small percentage is thought to be used for food.

National Trade and Use

Subsistence use of wild-collected turtles, particularly of tortoises, still occurs among rural people living in or near forest areas throughout the country. They are collected and maintained alive until required for consumption.

Some regional trade of wild-collected freshwater turtles for consumption exists; some show up in markets throughout the country, but presumably the majority are traded unseen to specialized restaurants or perhaps to wholesale exporters. The lower Mae Klong region and the hills of western Thailand seem most favored with collectors.

Some small native turtles are still offered at markets for release in temple ponds and other places, in connection with religious beliefs. Significant markets in this category include Nakhon Sawan (Fig. 1), Nakhon Pathom, other provincial markets, and a variety of neighborhood markets in Bangkok.

Some trade in small turtles of a wide variety of species (native and exotic) occurs as pets, particularly at Chatuchak market in Bangkok but also in pet shops (aquarium shops) elsewhere.

There is a substantial but undocumented trade in farmed hatchlings of Chinese softshell turtles (*Pelodiscus sinensis*) from breeder farms to smaller rearing operations and to

Figure 1. Selling *Malayemys subtrijuga* in the Nakhon Sawan market, primarily for religious release. Photo by PPvD.

Table 1. Trade in live freshwater turtles (number of individual animals) between Thailand and the rest of the world, based on statistics from the Fisheries Department of Thailand. No data available pre-1994; data for 1998 are for January – July only.

Year	Exports	Imports
1994	469,578	38,962
1995	3,394,842	28,120
1996	6,045,667	8,049
1997	4,832,346	6,503
1998 (7 mo)	472,130	90,500

exporting wholesalers. Some Chinese softshell turtle hatchlings are offered in the pet trade, but only a few raised adults appear in the domestic consumption markets, either fresh, on ice, or as prepared dishes.

International Trade

Thailand exports great volumes of farmed Chinese softshell turtles (*Pelodiscus sinensis*), mainly to East Asia (Hong Kong, mainland China, Taiwan, and possibly Japan; Table 1).

Illegal exports of protected native species may happen in an incidental or somewhat organized manner. Wild-collected turtles are occasionally mixed in with shipments of farmed Chinese softshell turtles, but this is a risky activity for the exporter and rarely involves great numbers of animals.

Other Comments

Thailand has seen a massive increase in environmental awareness and sympathy towards conservation of its natural heritage in the past decade. Thailand is prosperous enough not to need exploitation of minor natural resources to feed its people or develop its economy. Thailand continues to industrialize and develop rapidly, and with this comes an increasing trend to buy plastic-wrapped food in supermarkets instead of local fresh produce.

Scientific research, including ecological studies, distribution surveys, and applied aquaculture practices, is carried out through a multitude of relatively small projects of the Fisheries Department, the Technical Division of the Royal Forest Department, and the academic sector.

Conservation of turtles is not a great priority for conservation authorities and NGOs in Thailand at this time. More support for Royal Forest Department enforcement efforts and increased public awareness are necessary for effective conservation of turtles.

SPECIES ACCOUNTS

Family Testudinidae

Indotestudo elongata. — Elongated tortoise, yellow tortoise.
     Distribution (Thailand): Most forested hill areas.
     Habitat availability: Extensive, much of it included in protected areas.

Figure 2. *Manouria impressa* from Thailand. Photo by PPvD.

Population status: Uncommon (probably long-term depleted).

Population trends: Apparently fairly stable, but recruitment apparently compromised by dry-season fires even in protected areas.

Threats: Collection for consumption and pet trade; habitat degradation and loss; effects of forest fires.

National utilization: Adults collected for subsistence consumption and local trade; small animals occasionally sold as pets.

Legal international trade: None — the species is specifically protected from exploitation under the WARPA law and listing on CITES appendix II.

Illegal trade: Local consumption trade. Unquantified trade in plastrons and other shell parts used in TCM exists. Some juveniles exported as pets. Animals in domestic pet trade (alleged to originate from Myanmar) lack import documents. Shells made into masks and other curios (manufactured in Nepal) are sold without import documents.

Potential trade impacts: Modest but locally serious impacts from local trade.

Manouria emys. — Asian giant tortoise.

Distribution (Thailand): Forested hill areas of western and peninsular regions.

Habitat availability: Moderate, generally restricted to isolated patches of evergreen forest; many of these are included in protected areas.

Population status: Rare, presumably depleted.

Population trends: Unknown.

Threats: Subsistence consumption, habitat degradation and loss, pet trade.

National utilization: Popular for subsistence consumption because it provides so much meat; modestly popular as a pet.

Legal international trade: None — the species is specifi-

cally protected from exploitation under the WARPA law and listing on CITES appendix II.

Illegal trade: Some trade in juveniles and adults as pets.

Potential trade impacts: Modest compared to consumption impacts and habitat effects.

Manouria impressa. — Impressed tortoise (Fig. 2).

Distribution (Thailand): Localized in mountain areas of north, northeast, and western regions, perhaps also in southeast and peninsular regions.

Habitat availability: Modest; habitat requirements not well understood, areas of occurrence scattered, partly included in protected areas.

Population status: Rare even in suitable habitat; fragmented small populations at best, presumably depleted.

Population trends: Unknown, presumed depleted and in further decline.

Threats: Subsistence consumption, pet trade, habitat degradation and loss.

National utilization: Subsistence consumption whenever encountered; some animals are traded as pets but few, if any, survive for more than a few months.

Legal international trade: None — the species is specifically protected from exploitation under the WARPA law and listing on CITES appendix II.

Illegal trade: Modest turnover in pet trade, some of which may originate from Laos and other countries.

Potential trade impacts: Potentially serious when considered together with habitat and subsistence impacts on limited populations.

Family Platysternidae

Platysternon megacephalum. — Big-headed turtle (Fig. 3).

Distribution (Thailand): Mountains of northern, northwestern, and north-north-eastern areas.

Habitat availability: Substantial, most areas of occurrence are included in protected areas.

Population status: Uncommon to locally fairly common.

Population trends: Unknown, presumed stable where not (no longer) exploited, encouraging proportions of juveniles.

Threats: Collection for consumption in relation to TCM, for pet trade and *ex situ* captive breeding programs; habitat degradation.

National utilization: Modest collection for pet trade and captive breeding attempts.

Legal international trade: None — the species is specifically protected from exploitation under the WARPA law.

Illegal trade: Unknown; the potential for collection to supply the TCM demand to the north is undeniable.

Potential trade impacts: Potentially severe, given the limited size of individual populations and the difficulty to re-colonize depleted areas.

Family Bataguridae

Batagur baska. — River terrapin, mangrove terrapin.

Distribution (Thailand): Historically, most estuarine areas.

Habitat availability: Limited, but a few smaller rivers and mangrove areas are relatively intact; the Thale Sap system may still be suitable if appropriate nesting sites still exist.

Population status: Extinct in the wild; about 100–150 animals of various Thai origins are maintained at a single facility in the natural range.

Population trends: Extinct in the wild.

Threats: Mismanagement, disease, accidents, theft.

National utilization: None at present.

Legal international trade: None — the species is specifically protected from exploitation under the WARPA law and listing on CITES appendix I.

Illegal trade: Hatchlings, allegedly imported from Malaysia but lacking documentation, are occasionally offered in the domestic pet trade.

Potential trade impacts: Negligible, unless trade inspires theft.

Callagur borneoensis. — Red-crowned terrapin, painted terrapin (Fig. 4).

Distribution (Thailand): Historically, in the mangrove and lower river sections of southern peninsular Thailand.

Habitat availability: Limited, but a few smaller rivers and mangrove areas are relatively intact.

Population status: Extinct in the wild; about 150–200 animals of various Thai origins are maintained at a single facility in the natural range.

Population trends: Extinct in the wild.

Threats: Mismanagement, disease, accidents, theft.

National utilization: None at present.

Legal international trade: None — the species is specifically protected from exploitation under the WARPA law and listing on CITES appendix II.

Figure 3. Juvenile big-headed turtle, *Platysternon megacephalum*, from Phu Luang, Thailand. Photo by PPvD.

Illegal trade: Animals, allegedly imported from Malaysia but lacking documentation, are occasionally offered in the domestic pet trade.

Potential trade impacts: Negligible, unless trade inspires theft.

Cuora amboinensis. — Southeast Asian box turtle.

Distribution (Thailand): Throughout the country.

Habitat availability: Vast areas of potential habitat remain, although it is unclear how secure these are from incidental collection, risk of accidental capture by fishermen, entanglement in discarded nets, habitat degradation, and pollution. Small populations are confirmed from protected areas.

Population status: Uncommon.

Population trends: Unknown.

Threats: Collection for pet trade and especially sale for pious release at temple ponds; accidental capture by fishermen, entanglement in discarded nets; habitat degradation, loss and pollution.

National utilization: Collection for sale for religious release at temple ponds and pet trade.

Legal international trade: None — the species is specifically protected from exploitation under the WARPA law.

Illegal trade: Modest domestic trade, and small numbers of animals in the pet trade allegedly imported from other countries.

Figure 4. Female *Callagur borneoensis* from Thailand. Photo by PPvD.

Potential trade impacts: Modest in comparison to habitat effects.

Cyclemys complex (*oldhami,tcheponensis,atripons,dentata*). — Stream terrapins, Asian leaf turtles (Fig. 5).

Distribution (Thailand): Widespread, probably throughout the country except the agricultural plains.

Habitat availability: Extensive, and much of it included in the protected areas system.

Population status: Locally fairly common and with generally good proportions of young animals.

Population trends: Presumed stable.

Threats: Incidental capture of adults for subsistence consumption and juveniles for pet trade; habitat degradation.

National utilization: Incidental capture of adults for subsistence consumption.

Legal international trade: None — the species is specifically protected from exploitation under the WARPA law.

Illegal trade: Little evidence of domestic pet or consumption trade or of illegal exports in recent years.

Potential trade impacts: Slight at present.

Heosemys grandis. — Asian giant pond turtle.

Distribution (Thailand): Mainly southeastern and peninsular regions but probably in wet lowland areas throughout the country.

Habitat availability: Reasonably good, including large areas of protected areas, some of which contain confirmed populations.

Population status: Uncommon to rare, presumed depleted in most areas.

Population trends: Unknown, likely declining further outside protected areas.

Threats: Capture for consumption of adults; habitat loss.

National utilization: Capture of adults for subsistence consumption, as well as to supply specialized restaurants. Few individuals appear in the food markets, for religious release, or

the pet trade.

Legal international trade: None — the species is specifically protected from exploitation under the WARPA law.

Illegal trade: The supply trade to restaurants is apparently fairly intensive and organized. There is no evidence of an international component.

Potential trade impacts: Potentially serious given the depleted populations and the likelihood that organized teams of collectors probably trespass into protected areas.

Heosemys spinosa. — Spiny turtle.

Distribution (Thailand): Forested areas of peninsular region, from Chumphon southwards.

Habitat availability: Reasonable, much of it inside protected areas of substantial size.

Population status: Uncommon to rare.

Population trends: Unknown.

Threats: Subsistence consumption of adults; collection of young animals for pet trade; habitat degradation and loss.

National utilization: Modest levels of consumption; modest numbers in the pet trade.

Legal international trade: None — the species is specifically protected from exploitation under the WARPA law.

Illegal trade: Animals in the pet trade, which continue to sell clandestinely for substantial sums, may originate from Malaysia or Indonesia.

Potential trade impacts: Modest if the protected areas system remains effectively implemented.

Hieremys annandalii. — Yellow-headed temple turtle.

Distribution (Thailand): Lowland wetlands of central and peninsular regions.

Habitat availability: Worrisome; most suitable habitat has been converted to agricultural land and watercourses are regulated. Not confirmed to occur inside appropriate protected areas.

Population status: Uncommon, presumed depleted in most areas.

Figure 5. Hatchling *Cyclemys* sp. from Huai Kha Khaeng W.S., western Thailand. Photo by PPvD.

Population trends: Unknown, likely in continuing decline.

Threats: Capture for consumption of adults; loss and degradation of lowland wetland habitat; entanglement in nets; pollution.

National utilization: Capture of adults for subsistence consumption, as well as to supply specialized restaurants. Few individuals appear in the food markets, for religious release, or occasionally the pet trade.

Legal international trade: None — the species is specifically protected from exploitation under the WARPA law.

Illegal trade: The supply trade to restaurants is apparently fairly intensive and organized. There is no evidence of an international component.

Potential trade impacts: Potentially serious given the depleted populations and absence of securely protected populations

Malayemys subtrijuga. — Snail-eating turtle, ricefield turtle.

Distribution (Thailand): Lowlands throughout the country.

Habitat availability: Suitable habitat appears widespread, but it is unclear how severely animals are affected by the use and abandonment of monofilament fishing nets and water pollution. Not confirmed to occur in any great numbers inside protected areas.

Population status: Not uncommon to reasonably common.

Population trends: Apparently stable or in modest decline.

Threats: Modest collection; habitat degradation; accidental drowning in (abandoned) fishing nets; physical injury from agricultural machinery.

National utilization: Collection for sale to religious people who will release the animals in temple ponds and elsewhere; collection (for subsistence and local or regional sale) of large females for consumption; localized collection of eggs for local consumption and sale; manufacture of stuffed tourist curios.

Legal international trade: None — the species is specifically protected from exploitation under the WARPA law.

Illegal trade: Local and regional domestic trade; little to no international trade reported.

Potential trade impacts: Presumed modest in view of the size of populations and the ability of the species to reproduce before it reaches a size that is attractive for consumption.

Melanochelys trijuga. — Indoburmese pond turtle.

Distribution (Thailand): Allegedly in a small area in the extreme west.

Habitat availability: Alleged area of occurrence is close to a wildlife sanctuary and if the records are genuine it might inhabit this protected area.

Population status: Unconfirmed, at most a small population.

Population trends: Unknown.

Threats: Presumably incidental consumption of adults.

National utilization: No animals claimed to originate from Thailand are known to have appeared on the market in recent years.

Legal international trade: None — the species is specifically protected from exploitation under the WARPA law.

Illegal trade: Some animals brought in from Myanmar for the pet trade.

Potential trade impacts: None postulated for Thailand.

Notochelys platynota. — Malayan flat-backed turtle.

Distribution (Thailand): Forested areas of the peninsular region, from Surat Thani southwards.

Habitat availability: Substantial areas of suitable habitat exist inside protected areas.

Population status: Presumed uncommon.

Population trends: Unknown.

Threats: Collection, habitat loss.

National utilization: Subsistence consumption and some rural trade.

Legal international trade: None — the species is specifically protected from exploitation under the WARPA law.

Illegal trade: None reported.

Potential trade impacts: Probably modest to insignificant relative to habitat and local effects.

Pyxidea mouhotii. — Keeled box turtle.

Distribution (Thailand): Allegedly in parts of the far north-north-east.

Habitat availability: Unknown; not known to occur inside protected areas.

Population status: Not confirmed to occur in Thailand; at most a small population.

Threats: None reported in Thailand beyond general forest degradation and perhaps incidental consumption.

National utilization: None reported.

Legal international trade: None — the species is specifically protected from exploitation under the WARPA law.

Illegal trade: Some animals are offered in the domestic pet trade, these are said to originate from Laos, Vietnam, or China.

Potential trade impacts: None envisaged for Thailand at this time.

Siebenrockiella crassicollis. — Black marsh turtle.

Distribution (Thailand): Lowlands of central and peninsular regions, possibly throughout the country.

Habitat availability: Suitable habitat appears widespread, but it is unclear how severely animals would be affected by the use and abandonment of monofilament fishing nets, bait-fishing, and water pollution. Not confirmed to occur inside protected areas.

Population status: Not uncommon.

Population trends: Apparently stable or in modest decline.

Threats: Some collection; habitat degradation; accidental catch by fishermen, drowning in abandoned nets.

National utilization: Possibly the least desirable turtle for consumption because of its smell; some animals traded for release at temple ponds.

Legal international trade: None — the species is specifically protected from exploitation under the WARPA law.

Figure 6. Hatchling *Chitra chitra,* Kanchanaburi, Thailand. Photo by PPvD.

Illegal trade: Occasionally, juveniles are traded as pets; animals of any size may be sold for release at temple ponds.

Potential trade impacts: Probably modest to insignificant compared to habitat degradation and fishing impacts.

Family Trionychidae

Amyda cartilaginea. — Southeast Asian softshell turtle.

Distribution (Thailand): Throughout the country in suitable habitat.

Habitat availability: Reasonable; much lost to or made unsuitable by agriculture, settlement, and resultant exploitation pressures, as well as abandoned monofilament nets; suitable habitat occurs in several protected areas in various parts of the country.

Population status: Uncommon; less uncommon in a few protected areas.

Population trends: Depleted in exploited areas; populations deep inside protected areas probably stable and approaching carrying capacity in a few places.

Threats: Subsistence consumption; monofilament nets; water pollution; attainment of maturity at a late age and large size (likely to be caught before reproductive maturity).

National utilization: Very popular for subsistence consumption wherever it occurs; eggs presumably collected for consumption, but not in any great numbers.

Legal international trade: None — the species is specifically protected from exploitation under the WARPA law.

Illegal trade: Some live animals are thought to be exported to East Asian consumption markets among shipments of farmed Chinese foftshell turtles or labeled as "seafood." Visible local trade has become minimal in recent years.

Potential trade impacts: Trade, subsistence consumption, and habitat degradation together are likely to eliminate the species from most areas of occurrence.

Chitra chitra. — Southeast Asian striped giant softshell turtle (Fig. 6).

Distribution (Thailand): Mae Klong basin of western Thailand.

Habitat availability: Modest; the Khwae Noi still provides good habitat but is not protected from alteration; the protected section of upper Khwae Yai is probably too small to harbor a viable population.

Population status: Uncommon to rare; certainly depleted.

Population trends: In severe decline.

Threats: River alteration and pollution, sand dredging, effects of dam construction; collection of adults and juveniles as pets (perished animals for consumption); egg collection (no longer worthwhile); captive breeding programs.

National utilization: Adults are prized as status symbol pets; captive breeding programs have taken in dozens of animals but not produced a single captive-bred hatchling.

Legal international trade: None — the species is specifically protected from exploitation under the WARPA law.

Illegal trade: Animals are traded domestically and smuggled into the international pet trade, destined mainly for Japan.

Potential trade impacts: Potentially severe, given the combination of a small, depleted natural population and very high prices paid for live animals (currently over US$ 2500 for adults, US$ 1000 for hatchlings).

Dogania subplana. — Stream softshell turtle (Fig. 7).

Distribution (Thailand): Western and peninsular Thailand.

Habitat availability: Large areas containing suitable streams exist in protected areas of western and southern regions.

Population status: Not uncommon.

Population trends: Thought stable inside protected areas, presumably depleted outside.

Threats: Subsistence hunting, pet trade collection, habitat degradation.

National utilization: Some subsistence hunting; some animals, mainly juveniles, sold as pets.

Legal international trade: None — the species is specifically protected from exploitation under the WARPA law.

Illegal trade: Occasional animals in the pet trade, either from domestic or foreign (Malaysian or Indonesian) origin.

Potential trade impacts: Limited, probably less severe than subsistence consumption impacts.

Lissemys scutata. — Burmese flapshell turtle.

Distribution (Thailand): Allegedly in a few minor streams in the extreme west.

Habitat availability: Very limited, but partly located inside a wildlife sanctuary.

Population status: Unconfirmed, at most a small population.

Population trends: Unknown.

Threats: Collection for consumption and pet trade.

National utilization: Presumably local consumption of adults; capture of animals for the pet trade ("local Thai" animals command a higher price).

Legal international trade: Some animals brought in from Myanmar for the pet trade. Legal status unclear, as species is generally covered by Myanmar wildlife laws, not covered under the WARPA law, and apparently excluded from CITES II listing of *Lissemys punctata*.

Potential trade impacts: Unknown, potentially severe because population is thought to be small.

Nilssonia formosa. — Burmese peacock softshell turtle.

Distribution (Thailand): Not known to occur in Thailand, but could inhabit the section of the Salawin (Salween or Thanlwin) river that forms the Thai-Myanmar border.

National utilization: Not reported in trade in Thailand.

Legal international trade: None — the species is specifically protected from exploitation under the WARPA law.

Pelochelys cantorii. — Frog-faced giant softshell turtle.

Distribution (Thailand): Currently restricted to rivers of the peninsular region; occurrence in Thai part of Mekong unconfirmed.

Habitat availability: Limited, most areas of known or suspected occurrence are intensively used by humans.

Population status: Scarce and depleted; locally extinct from Chao Phraya and Mae Klong systems and probably from other, minor river basins.

Population trends: In decline, probably strongly.

Threats: Subsistence hunting, pet trade collection, habitat degradation (infrastructure development, aquaculture, pollution, disturbance).

National utilization: Some subsistence hunting where it still occurs; some animals traded as pets.

Legal international trade: None — the species is specifically protected from exploitation under the WARPA law.

Figure 7. *Dogania subplana* from Khao Luang, Thailand. Photo by PPvD.

Illegal trade: Most pet animals are said to originate from Cambodia.

Potential trade impacts: Unknown.

Pelodiscus sinensis. — Chinese softshell turtle.

Distribution (Thailand): Non-native; widely cultured in farms across the country.

Habitat availability. Suitable habitat for introduced population exists almost throughout the country.

Population status: Unknown; individuals have been found in many places.

Population trends: Presumably established as an invasive species in the early 1990s.

Threats: Popular for consumption.

National utilization: Millions of animals farmed annually; a modest part of farm production is marketed locally.

Legal international trade: Annual exports of a few million farmed individuals (Table 1), plus some imports of founder stock and hatchlings.

Illegal trade: None (the species is not protected or otherwise regulated in Thailand).

Potential trade impacts: Additional animals for potential release in Thailand; genetic pollution of native populations if escaped or released back into native range.

Family Emydidae

Trachemys scripta. — Red-eared slider.

Distribution (Thailand): Non-native; widespread in parks and temple ponds in major cities, a few populations apparently established in the countryside.

Habitat availability: Reasonable to good.

Population status: Locally common.

Population trends: Increasing.

Threats: None.

National utilization: Some local consumption of adults; some release into temple ponds.

Legal international trade: Numerous hatchlings imported as pets.

Illegal trade: None (not protected or regulated).

Potential trade impacts: Additional animals for potential release.

Asian Turtle Trade: Proceedings of a Workshop on Conservation and Trade of Freshwater Turtles and Tortoises in Asia
P.P. van Dijk, B.L. Stuart, and A.G.J. Rhodin, Eds.
Chelonian Research Monographs 2:145–147 • © 2000 by Chelonian Research Foundation

Turtle Trade in Southeast Asia: Regional Summary
(Indonesia, Malaysia, Papua New Guinea, and Thailand)

Peter Paul van Dijk[1], Djoko T. Iskandar[2], Thanit Palasuwan[3],
Anders G.J. Rhodin[4], Samedi[5], Dionysius S.K. Sharma[6],
Chris R. Shepherd[7], Oswald Braken Tisen[8], and Vagi R. Genorupa[9]

[1]TRAFFIC Southeast Asia, M19-B (2nd Floor), Jalan Pasar (1/21), 46000 Petaling Jaya, Selangor, Malaysia
[Fax: 60-3-7784-7220; E-mail: pptsea@po.jaring.my];
[2]Dept. of Biology, Bandung Institute of Technology, 10 Jalan Ganesha, Bandung 40132 Java, Indonesia
[Fax: 62-022-250-0258; E-mail: Iskandar@bi.itb.ac.id];
[3]Royal Forest Department, Phaholyothin Road, Bangkhen, Bangkok 10900, Thailand
[Fax: 66-2-579-3004; E-mail: wildlifept@hotmail.com];
[4]Chelonian Research Foundation, 168 Goodrich Street, Lunenburg, MA 01462 USA
[Fax: 1-978-582-6279; E-mail: RhodinCRF@aol.com];
[5]Protected Wildlife Captive Breeding Section, Directorate General of Nature Protection and Conservation,
Ministry of Forest and Estate Crops, Jl. Gatot Subroto, Senayan, Jakarta, Java, Indonesia
[Fax: 62-21-572-0227; E-mail: sam.phpa@dephut.cbn.net.id];
[6]WWF Malaysia, 49 Jalan SS 23/15, Taman SEA, 47301 Petaling Jaya, Malaysia
[Fax: 60-3-703-5157; E-mail: DSharma@wwfnet.org];
[7]TRAFFIC Southeast Asia, M19-B (2nd Floor), Jalan Pasar (1/21), 46000 Petaling Jaya, Selangor, Malaysia
[Fax: 60-3-7784-7220; E-mail: shepherd7@hotmail.com];
[8]National Parks and Wildlife Office, Sarawak Forest Department, Wisma Sumber Alam, Petra Jaya, 93660 Kuching,
Sarawak, Malaysia [E-mail: oswald@pd.jaring.my];
[9]Dept. of Environment and Conservation, P.O. Box 6601, Boroko, NCD 111, Papua New Guinea [Fax: 675-325-0182]

Patterns of Trade

Two fundamentally different types of non-marine turtle trade operate in the Southeast Asian subregion, which in this regional summary means Indonesia, Malaysia, Papua New Guinea, and Thailand (and also Singapore). These are the high value, moderate volume trade in rare and unusual animals for the international pet market, and the high volume commodity trade in turtles as a food item. Most of the food trade involves animals collected from nature for export, though some is for local consumption. The trade in farmed exotic Chinese softshell turtles represents a significant proportion of the overall food trade. The proportion of local use is very small in western Indonesia, but is significant in Irian Jaya, Papua New Guinea, and Thailand.

The food trade exports high volumes of wild-caught turtles, mainly from Sumatra, Kalimantan, Java, and Sulawesi, to the consumer markets of East Asia. The trade from Sulawesi is routed through Kalimantan. Much of the documented trade, particularly of softshell turtles, occurs by air; an unknown proportion of the trade goes by sea. Only a limited number of airports handle turtle shipments, dependent primarily on the available routes and schedules of airline connections to East Asia. For example, previously turtles were shipped directly from Padang to Kuala Lumpur and onwards, but when the regional economic collapse forced closure of the Padang – Kuala Lumpur air link, the turtle trade re-routed through Medan. At present, the main regional airports involved in export and/or transit are Medan, Jakarta, Surabaya, Denpasar, Kuala Lumpur, Singapore,

Bangkok, and possibly Kuching. The relative importance of sea routes is not clear; mortality rates during sea transport are much higher, but shipping costs are lower and inspection and enforcement at sea ports are deficient, making overseas shipping an economically feasible alternative. The importance of the Philippines as a source region and trans-shipment area is unknown.

The source regions of the trade in captured wild turtles for consumption have shifted every few years over the past decade. In the early 1990s, the largest volumes were exported from Kalimantan; a few years later Sumatra became a larger exporter. Within Sumatra there has been a similar shift in greatest trade volume from northern to southern regions.

Farming of non-native Chinese softshell turtles (Pelodiscus sinensis) is widely established in the Southeast Asian subregion. Large closed-cycle farms exist in Thailand, and rearing farms which raise hatchlings imported from Taiwan or Thailand exist in at least Peninsular Malaysia, Sarawak, and Sumatra. Virtually all raised animals are exported by air to East Asia, directly from Bangkok and Kuala Lumpur, and from Kuching and Medan via Singapore or Kuala Lumpur.

The trade in turtle parts and derivatives is poorly known. There are indications of a significant trade in turtle plastra from Indonesia, particularly Sulawesi, to East Asia where these are used as traditional Chinese medicine (TCM) ingredients. It also appears that at least some processing of turtle shells into turtle paste or jelly is carried out in Sulawesi; shells are obtained from other parts of Indonesia and the paste is shipped to China, Taiwan, or Hong Kong. This reduces storage and shipping expenses and makes identification impossible, which creates problems for trade controls and enforcement and provides opportunities for mislabeling of the end-products.

The pet trade, in contrast, is most significant in Irian Jaya, with some sources reaching back into Papua New Guinea and possibly northern Australia. Legal export of turtles from Papua New Guinea is strictly controlled and insignificant; instead illegal trade apparently occurs along the southern Papua New Guinea – Irian Jaya border, with animals possibly being exported from Daru to Merauke. Some illegal trade appears also to filter across from Australia's Cape York Peninsula to Daru, and from Darwin in Australia's Northern Territory to Kupang on Timor. Pet turtles from Papua New Guinea and Irian Jaya are processed and shipped from Merauke (and Sorong to a lesser extent) by air to Jakarta and onwards into the international pet trade. Because the pet trade tends to focus on particular species, there is little indication of shifting source areas, except as occurs after a new species has been described, when the pet trade quickly focuses on obtaining specimens of the newly described species. This pattern has already led to commercial extinction of *Chelodina mccordi* from Roti Island, described in 1994, and contributed to the severe impacts on *Heosemys yuwonoi* from Sulawesi, described in 1995. Some hatchlings or juvenile turtles collected in other parts of the Southeast Asian subregion also enter the pet trade, but their numbers are relatively low.

It is worth noting that the "four-inch rule" imposed by several western countries as a measure to limit mass trade in potentially *Salmonella*-bearing farmed hatchlings, and thus reduce impulsive purchases, clearly obstructs trade in hatchlings. This makes captive breeding for the pet trade economically unattractive and thus shifts the pet trade to wild collection of half-grown and adult animals larger than four inches in size.

Species in Trade

The consumption trade in the Southeast Asian subregion is not particularly species-specific, but generally takes in all animals found by collectors. *Amyda* softshell turtles fetch the highest prices per kg and are consequently more intensively searched for. The primary native species (i.e., excluding farmed *Pelodiscus sinensis*) in the food trade, by number of individuals, are *Cuora amboinensis* and *Amyda cartilaginea*; lesser but still high numbers are traded of *Siebenrockiella crassicollis*, *Heosemys grandis*, and *Orlitia borneensis*. The next most numerous species in subregional consumption trade are *Notochelys platynota*, the *Cyclemys dentata* complex, *Malayemys subtrijuga*, *Indotestudo forstenii*, *Hieremys annandalii*, *Manouria emys*, *Indotestudo elongata*, *Pelochelys cantorii*, and *Dogania subplana*. It is worth pointing out that certain species are relatively less desirable to traders, such as *Notochelys platynota* which has an exceptionally high mortality rate during transport, and *Dogania subplana* whose meat is considered of inferior

quality and consequently in low demand from consumers.

In New Guinea (combining Irian Jaya and Papua New Guinea), by far the most exploited species is the pig-nosed turtle, *Carettochelys insculpta*. Adults and eggs of this species are esteemed for local consumption, and up to 2 million eggs are collected annually in limited areas of Irian Jaya. A proportion of these eggs are incubated and the hatchlings enter the pet trade.

Other species are also exploited by a combination of local consumption and international pet trade, legal from Irian Jaya and illegal from Papua New Guinea. These are, in decreasing order of number of individuals traded, *Emydura subglobosa*, *Elseya* sp. (southern lowlands), *Chelodina parkeri*, *Elseya novaeguineae*, *Chelodina siebenrocki*, *Chelodina reimanni*, *Pelochelys cantorii*, *Pelochelys bibroni*, and *Chelodina pritchardi*.

Effects of Trade on Native Turtle Populations

The importance of impacts of trade on individual species is very different from the proportional numbers of animals traded. The species of the whole subregion whose populations are known or suspected to be most seriously impacted by the food trade are *Batagur baska*, *Callagur borneoensis*, *Orlitia borneensis*, *Chitra chitra*, and *Heosemys yuwonoi*. The species identified as most seriously impacted by the pet trade are *Chelodina mccordi*, *Heosemys yuwonoi*, and *Chitra chitra*. It is significant to note that these species are either large riverine species or extremely restricted-range species, or both.

The effects of farming non-native Chinese softshell turtles on the exploitation of native turtle populations are unclear and can be interpreted differently. Whether farming eases the pressure on wild populations or creates an increased demand for turtles and increased pressure on wild populations remains unknown and debatable. Farming also represents a potential invasive species problem, and may additionally serve as a possible conduit for laundering illegally caught wild animals. The topic deserves further study, but this should not proceed at the expense of studies of native populations. It should be kept in mind that farming is profitable and that economic factors tend to outweigh ecological concerns.

The introduction and spread of invasive species is clearly facilitated by international trade in turtles. Exotic species are introduced to regional countries as pets and some are released, while some farmed softshell turtles escape and may establish feral populations. The views of the delegates diverged on the actual and potential impacts of exotic species introductions, and it was agreed that the topic deserves further study but is not a top priority.

Current Regulations and Controls

• Thailand, Malaysia, Indonesia, and Papua New Guinea afford adequate legal protection to their native turtle species, at least on paper, except for Peninsular Malaysia.

• The responsibility for implementation and enforcement of legal protection rests with several agencies in most countries, and coordination of efforts is not optimal.

• Conservation authorities have conflicting interests from utilization authorities, frequently involving economic factors.

• Enforcement of existing legislation is seriously hampered by administrative complications as well as lack of manpower, species identification skills, and other resources.

• The IATA guidelines governing the transport of live animals by air are appropriate but are insufficiently implemented. Increased inspection, compliance, and discriminating acceptance of shipments are required at points of export and of trans-shipment, by the airlines and by airport and other government authorities in places where the IATA guidelines are legally binding.

• Systematic inspection of turtle shipments is spotty and inadequate. The reasons behind this are lack of facilities, resources, incentive, and the generally low profile of wildlife trade.

• Enforcement at trans-shipment points is particularly lacking, despite the fact that trans-shipment points are obliged to enforce CITES provisions.

Priority Projects

Improved implementation and enforcement of existing legislation is essential. We suggest that a small number of airports in our area be selected to begin inspecting trade. We suggest the selection of these airports on criteria including offering the best cooperation and chances of success and high trade volumes based on available information. These airports are Medan, Kuala Lumpur International Airport, Bangkok, Kuching, and Singapore. Sea ports are considered a lesser priority at this moment. The group members in collaboration with (fellow) authorities resolved to take responsibility for implementing a plan of action:

• Medan Airport, Indonesia: provide identification materials and training in species identification and build incentive.

• Kuala Lumpur International Airport, Malaysia: systematic monitoring, enforcement assistance, and capacity building through training and identification materials.

• Bangkok International Airport, Thailand: working with responsible authorities, species identification assistance, checks on compliance with IATA guidelines.

• Kuching Airport, Sarawak, Malaysia: assist with implementation and enforcement, species identification, and a characterization of the turtle trade through Kuching airport.

• Singapore Airport: cooperation and encouragement by working with local graduate students and NGOs.

The delegates from the Southeast Asian subregion noted that every single turtle species of this area is heavily affected by trade and strongly recommend that every Southeast Asian turtle species be included in at least Appendix II of CITES, and that *Callagur borneoensis*, *Heosemys yuwonoi*, *Chitra chitra*, *Chelodina mccordi*, and possibly *Orlitia borneensis* be considered for inclusion in Appendix I of CITES.

The delegates also made recommendations that the following specific projects be carried out:

• An investigation into the actual areas of origin of *Orlitia borneensis* in trade.

• Investigation of the level of illegal turtle trade from Papua New Guinea to Irian Jaya and onwards, with specific monitoring of exports from Port Moresby, Daru, and along the southern border.

• Continual monitoring of export shipments, trans-shipment points, and consumer markets.

• Urgent evaluation of the status of *Chelodina mccordi* on Roti Island and development of a recovery plan including consideration of *ex-situ* breeding.

• Case studies on and recovery plans for species proposed for inclusion on CITES Appendix I (*Callagur borneoensis*, *Heosemys yuwonoi*, *Orlitia borneensis*, *Chitra chitra*, and *Chelodina mccordi*), plus *Batagur baska* which already is on CITES I.

• Taxonomic study and identification characteristics of *Indotestudo* tortoises.

• Ecological study of the effects and impacts of invasive turtle species (lesser priority).

• Study of the socio-economic effects of softshell turtle farming and its effects on exploitation levels and trends of native softshell turtles (lesser priority).

Asian Turtle Trade: Proceedings of a Workshop on Conservation and Trade of Freshwater Turtles and Tortoises in Asia
P.P. van Dijk, B.L. Stuart, and A.G.J. Rhodin, Eds.
Chelonian Research Monographs 2:148–155 • © 2000 by Chelonian Research Foundation

Conclusions and Recommendations from the Workshop on Conservation and Trade of Freshwater Turtles and Tortoises in Asia

ASIAN TURTLE TRADE WORKING GROUP[1]

[1]*Authorship of this document is by the Asian Turtle Trade Working Group,*
which consisted of the following participants at the
Workshop on Conservation and Trade of Freshwater Turtles and Tortoises in Asia:

Gary Ades, Chris B. Banks, S. Bhupathy, Kurt A. Buhlmann, Bosco Chan, Hsien-Cheh Chang, Tien-Hsi Chen,
B.C. Choudhury, Chul Thach, Chun Sophat, James Compton, Paul Crow, Peter Paul van Dijk, Vagi R. Genorupa,
Fahmeeda Hanfee, Heiko Haupt, Douglas B. Hendrie, Heng Kimchay, Rohan Holloway, Hout Piseth, Djoko T. Iskandar, Kalyar,
Raymond Kan, S.M. Munjurul Hannan Khan, Jo-Yen Lai, Michael Lau, Lieng Sopha, Hua-Ching Lin, Prak Leang Hour,
Thanit Palasuwan, Steven G. Platt, S.M.A. Rashid, Anders G.J. Rhodin, Samedi, Dionysius S.K. Sharma, Chris R. Shepherd,
Shi Haitao, Bryan L. Stuart, Robert J. Timmins, Oswald Braken Tisen, and Touch Seang Tana

Recognizing the rapidly growing number of Asian turtle species that are considered threatened, it is clear that prompt action is necessary to prevent extinctions.

A combination of immediate and longer-term measures will be needed for the conservation of Asian turtles. The exploitation of populations in nature must be reduced to sustainable levels. This must be achieved by a collaborative coordinated strategy involving improved enforcement of existing legislation and regulations as well as improvement of current laws, raising public awareness and concern, the effective protection of natural habitats, the establishment of *in situ* and *ex situ* conservation breeding programs, and perhaps promotion of commercial farming operations. The immediate aim is to reduce or eliminate collection from wild native populations and reduce demand in consumer countries.

Patterns of Exploitation and Trade, Species in Trade, and Trade Impacts on Natural Populations

Two main types of trade in turtles occur in Asia. One is a high-volume, commodity-type trade in turtles or turtle parts for consumption, both for food and traditional medicine; the other is the pet trade, which involves smaller numbers of animals, and often smaller animals, with high individual value. From a conservation perspective, the consumption trade can be further divided into the trade in commercially farmed turtles and the trade in turtles captured from nature. Each of these trade segments gives cause for concern, but the mass exploitation of wild-caught turtles for consumption is the more significant.

Consumption Trade

The trade in turtles for consumption generally originates in the source countries of Southeast and South Asia and terminates in the consumer countries of East Asia. A certain proportion of turtles captured, in some locations a substantial proportion, is consumed locally for subsistence and in the restaurant trade, but the greater portion of capture is exported. Local consumption of turtles, or refusal to eat turtles, is often related to religion and ethnic culture. The intensity of exploitation of natural populations in source countries varies among countries and regions, depending on the quality and degree of enforcement of national legislation, status of turtle stocks, and the available methods and routes to transport captured turtles. In Asia, traded turtles represent a luxury food, not a source of protein for the poor.

Which turtle species are actually collected for the food trade depends on which species occur in the region. In general, all turtles encountered are collected and traded; professional turtle hunters as well as plantation workers who incidentally come across turtles take all species of all sizes. Softshell turtles are preferred because they command a higher price per kilogram, which may be six times the price of lamb or chicken in India. Small softshells are preferred over large animals, because they have a higher proportion of cartilage and gelatinous skin – the most valuable parts. In addition, small whole softshells are preferred as restaurant servings, compared to parts of a large animal. The only constraint on which species are traded is the refusal by some traders to accept certain species because they are in very low market demand or are perceived to create problems when discovered in a shipment. Overall, almost every Asian species is traded; only a very few turtle species have not (yet) been reported in trade; these are exceptionally rare and in some cases sacred or probably extinct species.

A recurring pattern is for collection and export operations to become established at a particular location, collecting turtles through an extensive network of trappers, hunters, and middlemen. Collection efforts and capture and export volumes increase rapidly, reach a peak, and then decline as accessible populations become depleted and collectors need to venture into new, more distant areas. There is also a corresponding decline in the average size of animals that are traded. Such "boom-and-bust" cycles at particular locations were noted for species such as *Callagur borneoensis*, *Indotestudo forstenii*, *Manouria emys*, and *Cuora amboinensis* in Indonesia and *Morenia petersi, Geoclemys hamiltonii, Hardella thurjii,* and *Indotestudo elongata* in Bangladesh.

Trade routes for wild-captured turtles for food are varied, complex, and ever-changing, but can be summarized by the observation that almost every available transport route between source and consumer countries is used. Transport by air is preferred, because the quality and survival rate of the traded turtles is optimal. Land routes are used where trails, roads and border crossings exist, and some shipments are made by river boat or by sea. Consequently, a map of turtle trade routes will show routes along all existing air, land, and sea routes from South and Southeast Asia to East Asia, converging at the major airports, border crossings, and sea ports of the source countries, and diverging from the major airports and sea ports of the consumer countries.

Softshell Turtle Farming

Large and small commercial operations to farm Chinese softshell turtles, *Pelodiscus sinensis*, exist in Thailand, Malaysia, and Indonesia. The Chinese softshell is native to temperate East Asia but grows and breeds rapidly in tropical climates, making it the most productive and economically attractive species to farm there. The species is also extensively farmed in mainland China and Taiwan. At present, farms produce an estimated 5000 to 10,000 metric tons per year, approximately matching or exceeding the amount of wild-caught softshells in trade. Farmed Chinese softshells are rarely marketed on the domestic markets of Southeast Asia; virtually the entire production is shipped by air to East Asian markets. While softshell turtle farming obviously contributes to meeting demand and thus may help relieve pressure on wild populations, it also has negative effects on wild turtle populations when native populations of Chinese softshells are exploited for additional founder stock. In areas where the species is farmed outside its natural distribution, there is the likelihood that escaped animals will establish invasive populations, with unknown effects on the local ecosystem, while mixing of genetically different stocks (i.e., genetic pollution) is a risk of farming within the range countries. Farmed softshell turtles are raised on a high-protein diet and their production actually represents a net protein reduction to satisfy a luxury demand. Wild-caught animals command much higher prices in the food trade and a market for wild-caught turtles will continue to exist alongside a market for farmed turtles.

Turtle Shell

In addition to live turtles as food, turtle shell is also traded to supply the Traditional Chinese Medicine (TCM) industry. These shells are usually by-products from the consumption of turtles, but there have been some reports of the specific collection of turtle plastrons, after which the rest of the animal was discarded (Jenkins, 1995) or perhaps used as food in crocodile farms. The limited quantitative data available suggest that the amount of turtle shell imported to Taiwan alone exceeds 100 metric tons per year, and the total trade may add up to several times this amount. Turtle shell represents about 5–20% of the weight of an average turtle; if the shell trade concerns plastrons only, shell trade figures should be multiplied by a factor of 20 to estimate the total weight of animals affected. Turtle shell is used for the production of turtle jelly, a glue-like residue produced by long-term boiling of turtle shells and concentrated by evaporation. There are indications that this jelly is also manufactured outside East Asia in Indonesia and perhaps other source countries. This jelly is transported as a high-value, low-volume product, and it is impossible to check its composition. This creates problems for customs inspections, as well as consumer concerns about genuine content.

Pet Trade

The collection of turtles as pets is an entirely different trade issue. The preferred species in the pet trade from Asia are rare and unusual species, such as Indian star tortoises, *Geochelone elegans*, Australasian snake-necked turtles of the genus *Chelodina*, and pig-nosed turtles, *Carettochelys insculpta*. In addition, hatchlings and juveniles of other species from throughout the region are traded internationally in large numbers. Because pet turtles have a particular value per specimen, pet traders prefer small specimens that are easier and cheaper to ship.

The total numbers of Asian turtles traded specifically as pets are difficult to estimate, because their proportion is so small compared to the massive numbers of red-eared slider (*Trachemys scripta*) hatchlings in the trade and data are rarely collected on a species-by-species basis. The market for the relatively expensive Asian species and very expensive Australasian species is limited and partly illegal, but still involves hundreds to thousands of individuals for certain species per year, and may be significantly higher for hatchling pig-nosed turtles.

Because prices in the pet trade are directly related to the rarity of a species, the pet trade poses a particularly significant risk to rare species. Meanwhile, captive breeding of such species as pets becomes less attractive economically because of the "four-inch-rule" imposed by the United States, Canada, and some European Union countries. These regulations make the import of hatchlings or juveniles under 10 cm shell length illegal and thus force the pet trade to deal in larger, wild-collected animals.

Species in the pet trade follow relatively consistent trade routes that depend on the area where the species occurs. Nearly all transport occurs by air, although some shipments are transported by land and sea routes to the main centers of the pet trade in Jakarta, Singapore, and Bangkok. From these locations most animals enter the global pet trade, while a small proportion are sold locally. Correspondingly, these cities are also the main distribution points for the mass trade in other exotic species (i.e., birds, mammals, and other reptiles) for the international and Southeast Asian domestic pet markets.

In recent years, there has been a high-profile trade in turtles known or thought to represent new species. Such animals, usually known only from very few individuals, command prices of several hundred to several thousand US dollars per animal. It has generally been assumed that this high-end pet trade in potentially new species was a matter of traders' agents picking out unusual animals from large shipments of food turtles. However, traders also send agents to remote source areas to purchase rare turtles from local villagers. This not only causes the depletion of the target species, but also other chelonian species as the locals often cannot tell the turtle species apart. Once the links are established, the trade continues until yet another source area has been vacuumed of its turtles.

Accuracy of Available Trade Data

While some data are available for the numbers or shipment weights of turtles traded, the available data are incomplete, making it difficult to form a precise picture of the trade. Under-reporting is common practice, species are incorrectly identified, some countries do not compile statistics for certain categories, and some of the trade is carried out illegally. The data on trade in farmed Chinese softshell turtles are reasonably accurate, while data on wild-caught turtles for food are more likely to be underestimates, and data on the pet trade in native and unusual species is buried within the mass trade in red-eared sliders farmed in North America and in the region.

Effects of Trade on Native Turtle Populations

The paucity of trade data, natural history data, and particularly long-term status data makes it difficult to judge the precise effects of trade on native turtle populations. It is clear, though, that trade is at least a contributing factor in the decline of most species and in many cases it is the main cause. The workshop participants spent two evenings evaluating the current conservation status of the region's tortoises and freshwater turtles and found that trade was a factor in the threatened assessment for 52 species. Of 88 species evaluated, it was recommended that 63 species should be considered as threatened following the IUCN Red List criteria.

Legislation, Regulations, and Other Controls on Turtle Trade

Existing Legislation. — At present, every country in the region has national legislation that affords at least some protection to at least some turtle species. In addition, all countries except Bhutan and Laos are signatories to the Convention on International Trade in Endangered Species of Wild Fauna and Flora (CITES), the provisions of which should be implemented through national legislation. Over-all, the scope and extent of the existing laws are adequate to protect most turtle species, though not all.

Enforcement. — By contrast, enforcement of existing legislation and regulations is frequently insufficient. One representative referred to his country's conservation laws as a "paper tiger." In every country, the inability of customs officers, wildlife enforcement agency staff, and others to identify turtle species with any accuracy is a serious obstruction to effective enforcement. Without being able to identify animals in trade, it is nearly impossible to determine which species are traded legally and which are illegal. This problem is exploited by traders, who intentionally misidentify and make false declarations of the contents of shipments.

Five key recommendations for improvement of the legal protection of turtles and control of the turtle trade emerged in almost every country presentation and discussion session:

• Increased enforcement of existing legislation and regulations;

• Provision of turtle identification materials in local languages;

• Training of customs, law enforcement, and wildlife conservation personnel;

• Review and, where necessary, clarification and improvement of national legislation;

• Monitoring and regular review of quotas and other regulations.

Capacity building is essential if enforcement is to be improved. Providing additional resources such as staff, office and equipment facilities, and improved funding for work outside the office are primarily the responsibility of the respective governments. Other organizations have an important role in organizing and providing training, preparing and distributing identification materials, and giving other practical assistance.

The International Air Transport Association (IATA) has detailed guidelines for the transport of live animals by air, including precise shipping requirements for live turtles. These regulations, which were recently updated, are rarely observed when shipping live turtles for the food trade. Enforcement of IATA cargo regulations on carrier airlines is strongly recommended and should be encouraged significantly by pressure from airline business partners, authorities, and the general public.

The existing mechanisms to impose fines and other penalties on those individuals, companies, and organizations who knowingly breach laws and regulations should be implemented. A proportion of the fines resulting from confiscations and prosecutions could be transferred directly to the budget of the specific enforcement agencies, with a possibility of bonus pay, which would provide a very effective incentive for improved enforcement. In countries where there is a shortage of funds to hire the necessary staff and provide the facilities needed to enforce the legislation and regulations, a tax on the cross-border trade of turtles can be imposed to supplement funding for the enforcement authorities.

Enforcement training for the turtle trade could also be incorporated in general wildlife enforcement programs; the relatively low charismatic value of turtles (compared to mammals or birds) and resultant lesser priority could be balanced by access to more funding for general programs. The importance of turtle conservation as a priority for enforcement should be emphasized in training programs and general awareness development.

Confiscated Turtles. — Practical difficulties result from confiscation of large shipments of live turtles. Authorities usually do not have the necessary facilities and resources to house and care for the animals. The options available for placing or relocating confiscated turtles should be investigated and discussed, and collaboration with government or NGO rescue centers and facilities is recommended. The eventual destiny of the animals should be decided with reference to the IUCN Draft Guidelines on Placement of Confiscated Animals. Some confiscated animals could contribute to conservation breeding programs. The IUCN Guidelines for Re-introduction should be applied if turtles are repatriated to their country of origin, particularly if return to the wild is anticipated. It is reasonable to insist that those responsible for illegal or inappropriate shipments should cover the costs of efforts to solve these problems.

Clarification of Legislation. — Enforcement is hampered by overlapping, competing, or undefined responsibilities of different government authorities. Such overlapping authorities may involve species conservation and protected areas management divisions of forestry departments, aquaculture and fisheries departments, veterinary health departments, coastal management authorities, and security forces. Certain authorities may be assigned specific jurisdiction over certain species, while another authority is responsible for its habitat management and yet another authority has exclusive control over trade in the species. In many countries, the specific details may not be spelled out in law, leading to different interpretations of authority. Where such complications exist, review of national legislation is urgently recommended to clarify the precise duties and responsibilities of various authorities, and procedures should be developed to increase cooperation between these authorities.

In addition, existing laws that restrict trade in, and shipment of, farmed turtles under 10 cm shell length need to be critically re-examined for their indirect impact on the conservation of wild populations. These regulations were passed either to reduce the risk of humans contracting salmonellosis from turtles carrying the *Salmonella* bacteria, or as animal welfare measures to curb the trade in "toy turtles."

Other Legislation Concerning Turtles. — Clearly, regulation of the trade in turtles is only one aspect of the overall legislation that affects turtles. Legislation establishing and implementing Protected Areas is essential for the survival of populations of turtles and other organisms in their natural habitat. These laws must be implemented to the maximum extent and expanded where appropriate. Restraining or preventing infrastructure development in remaining natural areas will reduce accessibility and consequently reduce exploitation pressure for trade and subsistence. However, it will also impede enforcement efforts.

Trade Monitoring. — There is an urgent need for more data on turtle trade. Information is needed on species and volumes of turtles shipped from different regions, and species composition and volumes traded in consumer markets. Information on the extent of hard-shelled turtle farming in China is also necessary. Equally important is knowledge of the use of turtle parts and products, the places of manufacture and trade routes, and the volumes traded. It would probably be most effective if a single organization could coordinate the compilation and analysis of the trade data collected. At the same time, status surveys of native populations by field scientists, NGOs, and other conservation groups are recommended, as are studies of the ecology and biology of turtle species. All these are essential components towards identifying trends in the trade and the impacts of trade on species.

Other Priority Projects and Next Steps for Turtle Conservation

Improved enforcement of existing and updated legislation is a key component of efforts to conserve tortoises and freshwater turtles in Asia. Much more needs to be done, however, if the ultimate goal – the survival of secure populations of all regional turtle species in their natural habitats – is to be achieved. A variety of projects and topics for consideration are presented below.

CITES Listing of Asian or All Turtles

The workshop participants support the current proposal by Germany and the United States to include all species of Asian box turtles (genus *Cuora*) in Appendix II of the Convention on International Trade in Endangered Species of Fauna and Flora (CITES) [successfully passed at the 11th CITES Conference of the Parties in April 2000]. A groundswell of support formed among the workshop participants for the concept of listing all turtle species native to the Indomalayan, eastern Palearctic, and Australasian Realms in at least Appendix II of CITES. There was also support for the concept of listing all turtle species of the world in at least Appendix II of CITES. This support was tempered by the acknowledgment that this would include many turtle species beyond the evaluation of the workshop and currently not involved in the East Asian food trade.

The justification for at least Appendix II listing of all regional species is two-fold: the non-discriminatory nature of the food trade, and look-alike reasons.

All available trade data indicate that the turtle food trade has shifted its source regions and the species traded several times during the past decade. While this results in relatively stable (though high) long-term overall trade, the effect on the turtle populations of particular regions is devastating. The country reports and regional overview discussions documented several species whose trade volumes in successive years showed sharp increases followed by even sharper declines, indicating the overexploitation and subsequent commercial extinction of particular species. Such patterns are most obvious in restricted-range species such as *Heosemys yuwonoi* and the *Morenia* species, and are less obvious in widespread species like the Southeast Asian softshell turtle *Amyda cartilaginea*. Correspondingly, available information from source regions consistently shows declines in number and average size of animals supplied to traders, which may amount to 50% in three years.

Country and regional presentations consistently noted the inability of personnel of supervisory and enforcement authorities to identify turtle species in trade. This inability leads to virtually unrestrained trade in species protected under the CITES Appendices as well as under national legislation. Evidence was presented of ongoing illegal trade in every CITES-listed tortoise and freshwater turtle species in the region, except for the black softshell turtle, *Aspideretes nigricans*, which occurs only in a single temple pond in Bangladesh. Annex 2b of CITES Res. Conf. 9.24 states that a species should be included in Appendix II if it resembles a species which is included in Appendix II because of threats from trade, or a species included in Appendix I, and the resemblance is such that a non-expert, with reasonable effort, is unlikely to be able to distinguish between them.

The justification for listing all the world's turtle species in at least CITES Appendix II is based on the same criteria of trade shifts in source regions and species identification issues. Given the history of the turtle food trade and the continuing demand for turtles for consumption, it is highly likely that any regional reduction in turtle trade effected by CITES regulations will be compensated for by new sources developed beyond the Asian region. Identification problems will only become more complicated when source regions become more diverse. By listing all turtles in at least CITES Appendix II, every traded turtle will need to be accompanied by appropriate documentation, and it becomes much easier for the authorities of both source and consumer countries to insist on the required documents.

Several precedents exist for listing an entire group in a CITES Appendix – all primates, all wild cats, all owls and raptors, all parrots, all crocodiles, all marine mammals, and all hard corals are included in the appendices. Within turtles, all tortoises and all sea turtles are already listed, leaving only the freshwater turtles without complete listing protection. Two of twelve families, Testudinidae and Cheloniidae, are included as a whole in the appendices, and two more families are essentially included completely by the listing of their single species, the leatherback turtle *Dermochelys coriacea* and the Central American river turtle *Dermatemys mawii*.

CITES listing of all turtles will not solve the turtle trade problem on its own. It would, however, result in a clarified and simpler protocol for inspection and enforcement authorities: if turtles are traded, they would all need documentation. Identification of Appendix I species in commercial trade is much more likely when every shipment of turtles is documented and inspected.

The workshop participants recognized that each of these suggestions would lead to the inclusion in CITES Appendix II of species that are farmed in economically important quantities and are traded internationally. Concern was expressed that inclusion of these species in CITES would generate administrative delays and constraints on legitimate farming operations. These concerns need to be addressed, either by certification of farms and streamlining the administrative procedures in the trading nations, or by excluding a small number of farmed turtle species from CITES Appendix II. In the latter case, the identification problem would persist, but in a more manageable form, whereby inspecting authorities would only need to positively recognize the few species actually farmed.

The appropriateness of proposing some species for inclusion in CITES Appendix I was discussed. A substantial number of species was considered to meet the IUCN criteria for Critically Endangered in part or exclusively through exploitation for international trade. However, it was also recognized that the stronger protection afforded by inclusion in Appendix I could be counterbalanced by the practical constraints it would impose on the international movements of animals as part of *ex situ* conservation breeding and recovery programs. It was decided that further consideration of this issue is needed, as a consultation process between the CITES scientific authorities and the IUCN/SSC Tortoise and Freshwater Turtle Specialist Group.

Traditional Chinese Medicine

Great quantities of turtle shell are used as an ingredient in Traditional Chinese Medicine (TCM). For example, Taiwan declared that 940 tons of hard-shelled turtle bone and 200 tons of softshell turtle bone were imported from 1992 to 1998; prices remained stable throughout this period. The great majority of turtle bone used in TCM prescriptions is plastron. This use of plastron is based on centuries of traditional custom, tracing back to a time when available quantities of turtle shell led to a preference among TCM practitioners for roasted plastron bone that had been used in divination ceremonies. A TCM scientist participating in the workshop, however, argued that there is no difference in utility and efficacy between plastron and carapace bone. Acceptance and use of both plastron and carapace bone would reduce the number of turtles required to make a certain amount of TCM prescriptions by at least 50%.

Current TCM research also suggests that there is no difference in the pharmaceutical effects of bone from animals produced in farms compared to animals captured in nature. Farm production of turtle bone for TCM or as a by-product from farming for consumption appears feasible. Finally, herbal or other ingredients may be identified through continuing TCM research as alternatives to turtle bone. Gaining acceptance for such alternatives among TCM practitioners and pharmacists, who work in a very old and stable tradition, will be critical to success. If these alternative ingredients can be harvested sustainably, they represent an encouraging possibility to eliminate or at least reduce the demand for turtle bone. Whether western industrial pharmacology or homeopathy can contribute alternatives to prescriptions containing turtle bone should be explored in a culture-sensitive dialogue between the various interest groups. These groups include the TCM establishment, the pharmaceutical industry, turtle and other conservationists, and consumer groups.

Pharmaceutical properties of turtles claimed by some traders, such as the alleged cancer-curing effects of the three-striped box turtle *Cuora trifasciata*, should be examined and tested scientifically. If turtles do possess such properties, industrial synthesis of the active compounds, alternative herbal medicine, and turtle farming should be explored to reduce the demand for animals from the wild. If such claims are ill-founded, a publicity campaign should be launched together with TCM practitioners to provide the general public with accurate information.

Conservation Breeding Programs for Endangered Turtle Species

Given that current levels of trade directly threaten a number of turtle species with extinction in their natural range, it is essential that species recovery programs be formulated. Such programs are likely to involve both *in situ* and *ex situ* conservation breeding efforts. Many details of such recovery programs ranged beyond the scope of the workshop. However, it was noted that the space, care, and other resources available in zoos and dedicated, organized amateur circles represented a valuable component in genetic management of endangered turtle species. Indeed, studbook programs and other initiatives have already taken shape in Europe and the US, and there has been extensive communication between zoo and conservation personnel in Europe, Australia, the United States, and Vietnam over the past two years to explore coordinated recovery programs. Exchange of animals between breeding groups inside and outside range countries will inevitably be affected by the proposed tightening of legal protection, but should remain possible through the appropriate channels.

Commercial Farming of Freshwater Turtles

Commercial farming of freshwater turtles to provide luxury food, animals for the pet trade, and for local religious release is well established and represents a large proportion of the regional and global trade in turtles. While farming is an economic activity undertaken for financial gain and is often a closed-cycle production process, it is not without effects on native turtle populations. Farming of species within their native range is likely to create pressure on natural populations as additional founder stock is collected. Farming non-native species carries the inherent risk of escape and establishment of exotic species. On the positive

side, a substantial and reliable supply of farmed turtles is likely to keep market prices stable and may thus lead to a correspondingly stable maximum price for wild-collected turtles, which will likely be higher than for farmed turtles. Once a price ceiling is established, wholesale prices and the prices paid to collectors should remain stable. In turn, this would prompt a local hunter to make an economic decision whether it is worthwhile spending a certain amount of time to capture a turtle, or pursue an alternative income-generating activity. Depending on local conditions, a point is reached where it is no longer profitable to spend great amounts of time looking for the very last individuals of a depleted population, or to travel vast distances from roads or middleman depots. The result should be the survival of some populations of turtles in some inaccessible regions, in contrast to the current situation with regard to the three-striped box turtle *Cuora trifasciata* where it is still profitable to spend a whole year searching for a single animal. In addition, the possibility exists that organized turtle farmers would push for a ban on trade in wild-caught turtles.

Farming of Chinese softshelled turtles *Pelodiscus sinensis* has grown rapidly in recent years and is well enough developed that it could obviate the need for mass collection of softshells from nature. Red-eared sliders *Trachemys scripta*, native to the United States but now with established populations in Asia, are similarly farmed in massive numbers, and animals could be raised to supply the food trade and the demand for turtle bone as a TCM ingredient. Another promising hard-shelled species for farming operations to produce turtles for the food and TCM trade is the Chinese striped-necked turtle *Ocadia sinensis*; in some farms in Taiwan up to 50,000 hatchlings are produced per year. The decision to farm particular hard-shelled turtle species would need to consider consumer preferences for or against particular species, as well as husbandry practices.

Commercial turtle farming is a complex issue that has great potential to relieve the exploitation pressure on wild populations, but also has the potential for significant negative impacts on native populations. More study and discussion of the issue is required.

Availability of Turtle Population and Natural History Data, Increased Scientific Expertise, and Encouragement in Range States

The necessity to survey the distribution and monitor the status of known populations and to study the ecology of turtle species in their natural habitat emerged from all presentations and discussions. Survey work inside protected areas is particularly appropriate as these areas generally offer some reprieve from collection for subsistence and trade. Surveys of species coexisting with humans in stable agricultural landscapes or man-made waterbodies are also useful to identify species with adequate populations and thus of lesser conservation concern. Field studies are essential components of species management plans and recovery programs. Field study data directly contribute to the success of *ex situ* captive maintenance, while observations of captive animals will suggest new avenues for field research. The successful reintroductions of species from *ex situ* conservation programs will require knowledge of the species' native distributions, habitats, and basic ecology.

Much of this survey work would be best carried out by local scientists and wildlife authorities. International organizations have a significant capacity-building role to play by participating in joint fieldwork and providing training and expert skills, as well as by contributing literature, equipment and other resources and establishing and maintaining a communications network. A turtle conservation website can be a very rich source of information, though not all turtle conservationists have access to the internet.

Taxonomic studies of particular groups of turtles are needed, because they have a direct bearing on the identification of priority species. Whether the Sulawesi population of the tortoise *Indotestudo forstenii* is taxonomically identical to the *Indotestudo* tortoise population of south-western India (formerly recognized as a separate species, *I. travancorica*) determines whether there is one species considered "Vulnerable," or two species respectively considered "Endangered" and "Vulnerable" under the IUCN Red List criteria. Similar cases of widespread species groups of low conservation concern, which likely include one or more currently unrecognized taxa of much higher concern, include the *Cyclemys dentata*, *Pelochelys cantorii*, and *Pelodiscus sinensis* complexes. At the same time, the recognition of a particular population as a separate species may increase collection pressure for the pet trade. In the case of at least one restricted-range species, the Roti snakeneck turtle *Chelodina mccordi*, this pressure was intense enough that traders now consider it commercially extinct and conservationists suggest moving the species from "Vulnerable" in 1996 to "Critically Endangered" in the present Red List.

Public Awareness of the Extent and Impacts of the Turtle Trade

Public awareness and education are important tools in any long-term conservation strategy. Awareness of the trade in turtles and other wildlife works at different levels. Unsustainable trade leads to the loss of a group of species from peoples' daily lives, customs, and conceptual world, thus leaving a culturally and emotionally poorer world for their children. Financially, short-term exploitation of a limited resource with very slow recovery is inappropriate, particularly since local collectors gain very little financial benefit from selling off their resources and compromise their options for sustainable developments like eco-tourism or perhaps wildlife ranching. Ecologically, the role of Asian turtles is almost unknown, and it will be close to impossible to ever obtain that knowledge or restore this role once a species has disappeared from the wild. Turtles can serve as a focal point in general conservation awareness programs. Conservation can be presented on television and integrated in global marketing and donor aid programs. Turtles must be portrayed as a conservation priority, as animals with an intrinsic value to share the Earth, not just a commodity to be exploited. Culture-sensitive information can contribute greatly to turtle conservation in source and consumer countries.

RECOMMENDATIONS

The delegates at the workshop formulated the following official recommendations based on the data and discussions presented in the various country reports, regional summaries, plenary sessions, and consensus conclusions presented above.

1. The delegates recognize that legislation and regulations to protect turtles from harvest and trade exist in Asian countries. This legislation is often adequate, but its enforcement is usually inadequate. The delegates strongly urge all local, state, and national governments to enforce, at all levels and as expeditiously as possible, the existing legislation concerning the conservation of turtles.

2. The delegates recognize that national legislation in some countries leaves gaps or creates overlapping responsibilities for enforcement authorities. The delegates support efforts to review, clarify, and improve national legislation for effective protection of turtles in the region.

3. Recognizing that transport by air is the most significant method of shipping turtles, the delegates request that all national governments implement and enforce IATA guidelines as a high priority.

4. The delegates realize that placement of confiscated turtles will be a significant issue when increased enforcement takes effect, and request the IUCN/SSC Tortoise & Freshwater Turtle Specialist Group to develop guidelines and realistic solutions to assist authorities to adequately deal with confiscated turtles.

5. The delegates strongly recommend that each and every turtle species native to the Indomalayan, eastern Palearctic, and Australasian biogeographic realms be listed in at least CITES Appendix II (having evaluated 93 regional species at the workshop and noting that some species are already listed on CITES Appendix I where they should remain and some others should be proposed for inclusion in Appendix I).

6. Considering the regular shifts in source countries to supply the Asian mass turtle trade, and enforcement staff often not being able to easily identify many turtle species, the delegates recommend an examination of the value and feasibility of a proposal to list all species of freshwater turtles worldwide in at least CITES Appendix II (all tortoises and all marine turtles already being listed).

7. The delegates recognize that trade is the major concern for the conservation of tortoises and freshwater turtles in the region, and therefore recommend further and continuing studies in the following topics:

a. Trade of tortoises and freshwater turtles in both source and consumer countries.

b. Status and distribution, with particular attention to protected areas in which they occur.

c. Natural history and ecology, with particular reference to species management plans.

d. Systematic studies of the tortoises and freshwater turtles of the region, especially those where taxonomic status has a direct bearing on conservation status.

These studies would contribute both directly and indirectly to identification of priority species and areas, as well as understanding the conservation needs of the region's tortoises and freshwater turtles.

8. The delegates specifically recommend further and continuing collection of market and field data in China to make the need for tortoise and freshwater turtle conservation clear to Chinese authorities.

9. The delegates recognize that *in situ* and *ex situ* conservation breeding programs exist. We support these efforts and encourage their expansion to assist in preserving maximum genetic diversity as a contribution to collaborative coordinated programs to preserve species in their natural habitats.

10. The delegates support the concept of freshwater turtle farming as part of a package of conservation measures, but recognize that farming needs to be investigated comprehensively for its actual and potential impacts, positive and negative, on native populations of turtles and other organisms. The delegates also recognize that farming needs to be regulated and monitored.

11. The delegates are encouraged by the efforts made in Traditional Chinese Medicine (TCM) research to develop herbal alternatives for turtle shell as a TCM ingredient, with due concern for the sustainability of collection of all ingredients used. Until effective substitutes for turtle shell in TCM are found, the delegates urge that turtle shell be produced sustainably through farming, subject to Recommendation 10, and ensuring no detrimental impacts, either real or potential, on wild turtle populations. The delegates further suggest that recent claims of cancer-curing potential of turtles should be investigated scientifically. Results of such studies should be used in a manner that will not harm turtle populations, by either chemical synthesis of potential pharmaceutically active compounds or by working with the TCM establishment to dispel false claims.

12. The delegates recognize that outreach programs need to be developed to highlight the magnitude of the turtle trade and its consequences to the global community. We recommend collaboration with media, schools, and other institutions, to develop popularized market campaigns that boost awareness in all sectors of the community and generate financial returns to support the conservation of native turtle populations. It is imperative that levels of awareness be raised within both source and user countries, notably at the local community level.

Acknowledgments. — The delegates gratefully acknowledge the assistance and support of the organizers and sponsors of the workshop: Wildlife Conservation Society (WCS); TRAFFIC; World Wildlife Fund (WWF); Office of Scientific Authority, U.S. Fish and Wildlife Service; Chelonian Research Foundation (CRF); Kadoorie Farm & Botanic Garden; the German Federal Agency for Nature Conservation, Ministry of Environment, Nature Conservation and Nuclear Safety; and Kari and Andrew Sabin.

LITERATURE CITED

JENKINS, M.D. 1995. Tortoises and Freshwater Turtles: The Trade in Southeast Asia. TRAFFIC International, United Kingdom, 48 pp.

Asian Turtle Trade: Proceedings of a Workshop on Conservation and Trade of Freshwater Turtles and Tortoises in Asia
P.P. van Dijk, B.L. Stuart, and A.G.J. Rhodin, Eds.
Chelonian Research Monographs 2:156–164 • © 2000 by Chelonian Research Foundation

Recommended Changes to 1996 IUCN Red List Status of Asian Turtle Species

IUCN/SSC TORTOISE AND FRESHWATER TURTLE SPECIALIST GROUP

AND

ASIAN TURTLE TRADE WORKING GROUP[1]

[1]*Authorship of this document is by these two groups,
which for the purposes of this document consisted of the following participants and subsequent contributors at the
Workshop on Conservation and Trade of Freshwater Turtles and Tortoises in Asia:*

S. Bhupathy, Kurt A. Buhlmann, Bosco Chan, Tien-Hsi Chen, B.C. Choudhury, Indraneil Das, Peter Paul van Dijk,
Fahmeeda Hanfee, Douglas B. Hendrie, Djoko T. Iskandar, Raymond Kan, S.M. Munjurul Hannan Khan, Michael Lau,
Hidetoshi Ota, Thanit Palasuwan, Steven G. Platt, S.M.A. Rashid, Anders G.J. Rhodin, Dionysius S.K. Sharma,
Chris R. Shepherd, Shi Haitao, Bryan L. Stuart, Robert J. Timmins, and Yuichirou Yasukawa

This document summarizes the recommendations for revised IUCN Red List status for 90 Asian non-marine turtle species as determined by members of the IUCN/SSC Tortoise and Freshwater Turtle Specialist Group and the Asian Turtle Trade Working Group during meetings in Phnom Penh, Cambodia, on 2–3 December 1999. The attendants at the meeting identified a number of species where further information was deemed necessary, and this was solicited from additional colleagues and sources after the meeting.

Participants in the evaluations and follow-up consultations were S. Bhupathy (IN), Kurt Buhlmann (US), Bosco Chan (CN-HK), Tien-Hsi Chen (TW), B.C. Choudhury (IN), Indraneil Das (IN, BN, MY), Peter Paul van Dijk (TH), Fahmeeda Hanfee (IN), Doug Hendrie (VN), Djoko Iskandar (ID), Raymond Kan (CN-HK), S.M. Munjurul Hannan Khan (BD), Michael Lau (CN-HK), Hidetoshi Ota (JP), Thanit Palasuwan (TH), Steve Platt (ID, MM), S.M.A. Rashid (BD), Anders Rhodin (PN, US), Dionysius Sharma (MY), Chris Shepherd (ID), Shi Haitao (CN), Bryan Stuart (LA), Rob Timmins (LA), and Yuichirou Yasukawa (JP), representing 15 regional countries and territories and global perspectives.

Information on a species' status in a particular country was based on the assessments by the representatives of that country at the meeting, with reference to national Red Lists where available, whose information and status was updated and refined where appropriate. National status is therefore not attributed to individuals. National Red Lists and assessments are available for Bangladesh (IUCN-Bangladesh, 1999), China (Zhao, 1998), India (CAMP/BCPP, in Hanfee, 1999), and Thailand (OEPP, 1997). Some information was specifically attributed to individuals, as indicated in the following document. Most attention by the group was focused on the levels of international trade in the various species from their countries of origin; data on wild population levels were utilized as available.

The accounts below summarize the existing listing in the 1996 IUCN Red List, the proposed revised listing in the 2000 IUCN Red List, the change between the current and proposed listing, and brief supporting statements. Two of the 90 Asian species were not evaluated by the group: *Testudo horsfieldii* and the introduced North American *Trachemys scripta*. Evaluation results are summarized in Tables 1 and 2. The group determined that nearly three fourths (74%) of all Asian turtle species were threatened, with over half (51%) endangered, constituting a major deterioration of their survival status as compared to the previous 1996 Red List.

These recommendations were subsequently reviewed by the Tortoise and Freshwater Turtle Specialist Group Steering Committee and the Species Survival Commission and were accepted in July 2000 for inclusion in the 2000 IUCN Red List.

Table 1. Summary of evaluation results and proposed IUCN Red List category levels for Asian non-marine turtle species.

Categories	Number of Species	Percent of Asian Species
Extinct (EX)	1	1.1
Critically Endangered (CR)	18	20.0
Endangered (EN)	27	30.0
Vulnerable (VU)	21	23.3
Lower Risk, near threatened (LR:nt)	6	6.7
Lower Risk, least concern (LR:lc)	9	10.0
Data Deficient (DD)	6	6.7
Not evaluated	2	2.2
Total	90	100.0

Table 2. Summary of proposed IUCN Red List status category changes for Asian non-marine turtle species.

Proposed Category Change	Number of Species	Percent of Asian Species
Unchanged	24	26.7
Up 1 category	24	26.7
Up 2 categories	6	6.7
Up 3–5 categories	4	4.4
Down	0	0.0
New evaluations (including previous DD and LR:lc)	30	33.3
Not evaluated	2	2.2
Total	90	100.0

Family Testudinidae

Geochelone elegans
IN, LK, PK
1996 Red List: —
Proposed: LR: lc   unchanged
The CAMP/BCPP (in Hanfee, 1999) evaluations considered the species VU in IN.

Geochelone platynota
MM
1996 Red List: CR A1cd+2cd, C2a
Proposed: CR A1cd+2cd, C2a unchanged
The species is rare and heavily exploited in MM, confirmed by recent field surveys.

Indotestudo elongata
BD, KH, CN?, IN, LA, MM, MY, NP, TH, VN
1996 Red List: VU A1acd
Proposed: EN A1cd+2cd   + 1 category
Considered EN in BD, KH, LA, MM, MY; CR in VN; VU in TH (though not listed in OEPP Red List); LR:nt in IN (CAMP/BCPP).

Indotestudo forstenii
ID
1996 Red List: VU A1cd
Proposed: EN (A1cd+2cd) + 1 category
Assessment refers to Sulawesi population only (see note under *I. travancorica*). ID has an annual quota of 450 for the Sulawesi population (S. Platt). Animals occur in substantial numbers in both the food and pet trade.

Indotestudo travancorica
IN
1996 Red List: VU A1cd
Proposed: VU A1cd   unchanged
This species was originally described as endemic to the Western Ghats of India; more recently *I. travancorica* was synonymized with *I. forstenii*, but has recently been resurrected as a full species (Pritchard, 2000). The Indian population was assessed as LR:nt in the CAMP/BCPP workshops and as VU by the Indian delegates at the Phnom Penh meeting.

Manouria emys
BD, CN?, ID, IN, KH?, MM, MY, TH
1996 Red List: VU A1cd
Proposed: EN A1cd+2cd   +1 category
Populations of the southern subspecies *M. e. emys* were considered EN in ID and VU in TH (OEPP, 1997) and peninsular MY, and no data available for Sarawak and Sabah; populations of the northern subspecies *M. e. phayrei* were considered CR in BD and EN in IN (after an earlier CAMP/BCPP assessment as VU), MM, and TH. The validity of the two subspecies was called into question (S. Bhupathy).

Manouria impressa
CN, LA, KH?, MM, MY, TH, VN
1996 Red List: VU A1acd, B1+2acd
Proposed: VU A1acd, B1+2acd   unchanged
Listed as EN in TH (OEPP, 1997); considered VU in LA and VN.

Testudo horsfieldii
CN, central Asia
1996 Red List: VU A2d
Proposed: not evaluated
This species was left without evaluation by the group and instead the information about status in China could be incorporated into a regional assessment for the turtles of the Middle East and Mediterranean regions. The species is considered EN in CN, where the species has declined. In the early 1960s, the average density was more than 4000 ind./km^2 and the distribution area was 300 km^2. In the early 1980s, the average density was only 60 ind./km^2; the distribution area was 270 km^2; in the early 1990s, the average density was only 6 ind./km^2; the practical distribution area was 180 km^2. Reports of severe declines of density in Kazakhstan were also presented (high-density sites declining from 15,000–20,000 in 1956 to 1070–1510 in 1988 per km^2) (Shi Haitao).

Family Bataguridae

Batagur baska
BD, ID, IN, KH?, MM?, MY, SG?, TH?, VN?
1996 Red List: EN A1bcd
Proposed: CR A1cd   +1 category
Considered EN in peninsular MY and ID; CR in BD and IN, populations very small; EW in TH (considered CR in OEPP, 1997); no recent data and presumed EX in MM, KH, VN, and SG. Illegally exported from ID and traded in substantial numbers in CN despite CITES I listing. Overall situation at least as serious as that of *Callagur borneoensis*.

Callagur borneoensis
BN, ID, MY, TH?
1996 Red List: CR A1bcd
Proposed: CR A1bcd unchanged
Listed as CR in TH (OEPP, 1997).

Chinemys megalocephala
CN
1996 Red List: —
Proposed: EN A1d+2d   new
Argued to be a distinct taxon (Guo et al., 1997). Seriously threatened by domestic consumption trade (R. Kan).

Chinemys nigricans
CN
1996 Red List: DD
Proposed: EN A1d+2d   new
Restricted-range species, generally disappeared from food markets several years ago, presumed commercially extinct

though occasional animals still appear in the markets (R. Kan, M. Lau, P.P. van Dijk).

Chinemys reevesii
CN, JP, TW
1996 Red List: —
Proposed: EN A1cd   + 3 categories
Previously the commonest Chinese turtle species, now completely disappeared from markets, not found during field surveys in CN; increasingly threatened small populations exist in parts of TW (Lue et al., 1999) and JP.

Cuora amboinensis
BD, ID, IN, KH, LA, MM, MY, SG, TH, VN
1996 Red List: LR:nt
Proposed: VU A1d+2d   + 1 category
Considered EN in BD, KH, LA, VN; considered VU in ID, IN, MY, TH (not listed by OEPP, 1997); no information available for MM; presumed stable in SG (small population). Subspecies: *C. a. amboinensis*, *C. a. couro*, *C. a. kamaroma*, *C. a. lineata*.

Cuora aurocapitata
CN
1996 Red List: DD
Proposed: CR A1d+2d   new
Considered commercially extinct; species has very high value in trade.

Cuora flavomarginata
CN, JP, TW
1996 Red List: VU A2c
Proposed: EN A1cd+2cd   +1 category
Taiwan population (*C. f. flavomarginata*) VU A1c, has declined in recent decades due to expansion of agricultural lands, remnants now stable or slightly recovering (T. Chen); mainland CN population (*C. f. sinensis*) probably CR. In CN and TW combined, the species was considered EN (Zhao, 1998, in China Red Data Book). Ryukyu populations (JP: *C. f. evelynae*) are small but relatively well protected and rated as VU in the 1999 Japanese Red List (Matsui and Ota, 1999; Ota, in press).

Cuora galbinifrons
CN, KH?, LA, VN
1996 Red List: LR:nt
Proposed: CR A1d+2d   + 3 categories
Species considered CR in LA, VN; considered EN in CN (Hainan). Conservation situation made even more acute by the diversity of subspecies: *C. g. bourreti*, *C. g. galbinifrons*, *C. g. picturata*, *C. g. serrata*.

Cuora mccordi
CN
1996 Red List: DD
Proposed: CR A1d+2d   new
Considered commercially extinct; species has very high value in trade.

Cuora pani
CN
1996 Red List: DD
Proposed: CR A1d+2d   new
Considered commercially extinct; species has very high value in trade.

Cuora trifasciata
CN, VN, LA
1996 Red List: EN A2d
Proposed: CR A1d+2d   +1 category
Species is extremely valuable in trade (most expensive Asian turtle in markets) and subject to exceptionally high exploitation pressures; EW is to be expected within years.

Cuora yunnanensis
CN
1996 Red List: DD
Proposed: EX   new
Not recorded since 1906 despite intensive specific searches and the massive general market trade (recent market records almost certainly derive from misidentification). One of two known sites of past occurrence has disappeared under expanding urbanization of Kunming.

Cuora zhoui
CN
1996 Red List: DD
Proposed: CR A1d+2d   new
Considered commercially extinct; species has very high value in trade.

Cyclemys dentata
BD, BN, CN?, ID, IN, KH, LA, MM, MY, NP, SG, TH, VN
1996 Red List: —
Proposed: LR:nt   +1 category
Widespread and locally reasonably common species, but occurs in substantial numbers in the food trade. Until recently, the various forms of this species complex were thought to represent just a single species, *C. dentata*, but are now recognized as representing a complex of up to 5 full species: *C. atripons* (KH, TH), *C. dentata* (BN, ID, TH, MY, SG), *C. oldhamii* (ID, IN, LA, MM, MY, TH), *C. pulchristriata* (VN), and *C. tcheponensis* (LA, TH, VN). Their conservation status has not been assessed because the taxonomy and distribution remain unclear. It is likely that some taxa will be VU.

Geoclemys hamiltonii
BD, ID, NP?, PK
1996 Red List: LR:nt
Proposed: VU A1d+2d   + 1 category
Considered EN in BD; VU in IN; no information available for NP or PK. Traded in some numbers in international consumption trade despite listing on CITES Appendix I.

Geoemyda japonica

JP

1996 Red List: EN A1c, B1+2c

Proposed: EN A1ce, B1+2c   unchanged

Endemic to no more than three islands of the central Ryukyus, JP. Continued to be listed as VU in the 1991 and 1999 Japanese Red Lists (Ota, in press). Populations were judged to be badly declining on Okinawajima, with two small isolated populations on Kumejima, and no status data for Tokashikijima (Yasukawa and Ota, in press). Hybridization threat (A1e) added based on Matsui and Ota (1999).

Geoemyda silvatica

IN

1996 Red List: EN B1+2c

Proposed: EN B1+2c   unchanged

Curiously, the CAMP/BCPP evaluations considered the species only VU in IN.

Geoemyda spengleri

CN, VN

1996 Red List: —

Proposed: EN A1cd+2cd   + 3 categories

Considered EN by the group based on levels of trade and scarcity.

Hardella thurji

BD, IN, NP, PK

1996 Red List: LR:nt

Proposed: VU A1cd A2cd   + 1 category

The CAMP/BCPP evaluations considered the species VU in IN. Considered EN in BD Red Data Book. No data available on status in PK. Subspecies: *H. t. indi, H. t. thurji.*

Heosemys depressa

MM

1996 Red List: CR A2cd, B1+2c

Proposed: CR A2cd, B1+2c   unchanged

Recent rediscovery of a few specimens in markets in MM and across the border in CN confirm the rarity and endangered status of this rarely-seen species.

Heosemys grandis

KH, LA, MM, MY, TH, VN

1996 Red List: LR:nt

Proposed: VU A1d+2cd   + 1 category

Considered VU A1d+2d in KH, LA, and VN; considered VU A2cd in MY; limited data for MM and TH (currently not listed - OEPP, 1997) suggest at least VU A1d.

Heosemys leytensis

PH

1996 Red List: EN B1+2c

Proposed: CR A2d, B1+2c   +1 category

Known from 3 specimens reported in 1921 allegedly collected in Leyte, and a single animal found in 1988 in northern Palawan. Proposed to be upgraded from EN to CR based on the fact that no further animals have been found despite intensive specific searches of both regions. Its mythical reputation will make any further animals extremely valuable in the pet trade. No data are available to make statements on extent of occurrence, but presumed either extremely rare or restricted to one or very few small localities.

Heosemys spinosa

BN, ID, MM?, MY, PH, SG, TH

1996 Red List: VU A1bd

Proposed: EN A1bcd   +1 category

Detailed monitoring of trade and status is urgently required; known trade volumes of the species have declined by about 50% in ID recently despite high demand in the food trade (C. Shepherd) and the species is considered CR in ID (D. Iskandar). In TH, the species is VU (OEPP, 1997) to EN and restricted to small, isolated populations. Populations in BN, MM, SG, and PH are considered to be small and low density, while only those of SG and BN may be moderately secure. Information for MY is scarce, but VU was suggested for Borneo and Peninsular Malaysia (I. Das, D. Sharma). Given the numbers in trade, the lack of confirmed extensive populations occurring inside adequately protected areas, the known low reproductive output, and the wide-ranging status assessments summarized here, the species is proposed as EN.

Heosemys yuwonoi

ID

1996 Red List: DD

Proposed: CR A1cd+2cd, C1   new

Trade in the species in East Asian markets, discovered among shipments in the early 1990s, peaked at an estimated annual level of 2000–3000 animals in 1998 and collapsed to 100 animals in 1999 (R. Kan, B. Chan).

Hieremys annandalii

KH, MM?, MY, TH, VN

1996 Red List: VU A1acd+2cd

Proposed: EN A1cd+2d   +1 category

Considered EN due to trade exploitation in KH, LA, and VN; present status in TH poorly known, likely VU or EN (though not listed in 1997 OEPP Red List); population in MY is marginal and very small. Habitat loss remains a contributing factor throughout its range.

Kachuga dhongoka

BD, IN, NP?

1996 Red List: LR:nt

Proposed: EN A1cd+2cd   + 2 categories

Considered EN in IN due to disappearance from much of former range, though a number of stable populations are known; formerly VU in the CAMP/BCPP evaluations. Considered CR in BD.

Kachuga kachuga

BD, IN, NP

1996 Red List: EN A1cd

Proposed: CR A1cd +1 category
Upgraded to CR due to continuing disappearance over much of its range, from VU in the CAMP/BCPP evaluations.

Kachuga smithi
BD, IN, PK
1996 Red List: —
Proposed: LR:nt new
The CAMP/BCPP evaluations considered the species LR:lc in IN. Subspecies: *K. s. pallidipes, K. s. smithi.*

Kachuga sylhetensis
BD, IN
1996 Red List: DD
Proposed: EN B1+2c new
Extremely rare species known from only a few animals; apparently occurs scarcely in scattered localities. Forest stream habitat impacted by conversion to tea plantations. The CAMP/ BCPP evaluations considered the species CR in IN, but the available data are insufficient to justify CR across the range.

Kachuga tecta
BD, IN, NP, PK
1996 Red List: —
Proposed: LR:lc unchanged
The CAMP/BCPP evaluations considered the species LR:nt in IN.

Kachuga tentoria
BD, IN
1996 Red List: —
Proposed: LR:lc unchanged
The CAMP/BCPP evaluations considered the species LR:nt in IN. Subspecies: *K. t. circumdata, K. t. flaviventer, K. t. tentoria.*

Kachuga trivittata
MM
1996 Red List: EN A1c
Proposed: EN A1c unchanged
Actually a candidate for CR or EX, considering that no animals have been reliably recorded since 1935 despite mass trade of riverine turtles from MM to CN.

Malayemys subtrijuga
ID, KH, LA, MY, TH, VN
1996 Red List: —
Proposed: VU A1d+2d + 2 categories
Considered VU in KH, LA, VN; populations in ID and MY small and restricted; status in TH not uncommon, not listed in OEPP 1997 Red List, but here suffers from habitat impacts.

Mauremys annamensis
VN
1996 Red List: LR:lc
Proposed: CR A1d+2d + 5 categories

Should never have been de-listed from 1994 Red List. Extremely scarce and endangered in VN.

Mauremys iversoni
CN
1996 Red List: DD
Proposed: DD unchanged
No new field or trade data available since 1996.

Mauremys japonica
JP
1996 Red List: —
Proposed: LR:nt new
Quoting and paraphrasing a manuscript by Yasukawa, Yabe, and Ota: "...the turtle is often observed in high density in various areas... Even so, however, it is highly likely that many populations have recently suffered a decline." Threats include habitat conversion, land development, waterway engineering, collection as pets, and possibly competition from introduced *Trachemys scripta*. One habitat area is protected, no other conservation measures are in effect. This suggests a Red Listing as LR:nt.

Mauremys mutica
CN, JP, TW, VN
1996 Red List: —
Proposed: EN A1cd+2cd new
Considered EN in VN and CN; corresponding decline observed in market supply (B. Chan, R. Kan, M. Lau); considered VU A1c in TW (T. Chen). Considered VU in the southern Ryukyus, JP (*M. m. kami*) (Yasukawa et al., in press). Subspecies: *M. m. kami, M. m. mutica.*

Mauremys pritchardi
CN, MM?
1996 Red List: DD
Proposed: DD unchanged
No field or trade data available for the species in either reported range country; taxonomy unclear.

Melanochelys tricarinata
BD, IN, NP
1996 Red List: VU B1+2c
Proposed: VU B1+2c unchanged
Considered EN in BD and NP, but only LR:lc (CAMP/ BCPP) to currently VU in IN, its main range state.

Melanochelys trijuga
BD, IN, LK, MM, MV, NP
1996 Red List: DD
Proposed: LR:nt new
Considered EN in BD (*M. t. indopeninsularis*). Population in MM (*M. t. edeniana*) DD but presumed VU or EN. Common in IN and NP. The CAMP/BCPP evaluations considered the subspecies *M. t. trijuga* as LR:lc, *M. t. coronata* as VU, Indian population of *M. t. indopeninsularis* as LR:nt, and Indian population of *M. t. thermalis* as EN. No

data were available for LK, and overall the species was considered fairly secure.

Morenia ocellata
MM
1996 Red List: LR:nt
Proposed: VU A1d+2d   + 1 category
Listing based on market trends; food market turnover was 10 tons per day during peak season in 1996–97, but then disappeared from markets in 1998 (B. Chan, R. Kan).

Morenia petersi
BD, IN
1996 Red List: LR:nt
Proposed: VU A1cd+2cd   + 1 category
Considered VU in BD, where it is the most commonly traded species; also LR:nt or VU in IN. In East Asian food markets, supply reached peaks of 30 tons per day in April–May of 1996–97, but disappeared from markets by 1998 (B. Chan, R. Kan).

Notochelys platynota
BN, ID, MY, MM?, TH, SG
1996 Red List: DD
Proposed: VU A1cd+2cd   new
In ID, declined from extremely common in late 1980s to reasonably common at present. In MY, trade volume has increased while habitat has decreased. In TH considered at least VU (OEPP 97). Traded in East Asian food markets in 1999 at levels of 2–3 tons per day (B. Chan, R. Kan), after proportionally very high mortality during transport.

Ocadia glyphistoma
CN
1996 Red List: DD
Proposed: DD   unchanged
No new information available since 1996.

Ocadia philippeni
CN
1996 Red List: DD
Proposed: DD   unchanged
No new information available since 1996.

Ocadia sinensis
CN, TW, VN
1996 Red List: LR:nt
Proposed: EN A1cd   + 2 categories
Considered EN in mainland CN (greatest part of range); modest population of VN considered VU; population on TW (which possibly represents a separate taxon) is considered LR:lc and is farmed in substantial numbers (T. Chen).

Orlitia borneensis
ID, MY
1996 Red List: LR:nt
Proposed: EN A1cd+2cd   + 2 categories

Considered VU A2cd in peninsular MY, status in Sarawak unknown; considered EN in ID and exported in large quantities despite official protection. Traded in East Asian food markets in huge numbers of animals of all sizes (B. Chan, R. Kan, M. Lau).

Pyxidea mouhotii
CN, IN, LA, MM, VN
1996 Red List: —
Proposed: EN A1d+2d   new
Considered EN in each of its range states, though only considered LR:nt in the CAMP/BCPP evaluations in IN. Subspecies: *P. m. mouhotii, P. m. obsti.*

Sacalia bealei
CN
1996 Red List: VU B1+2c
Proposed: EN A1d+2d   + 1 category
Uncommon and declining in its restricted range.

Sacalia pseudocellata
CN
1996 Red List: DD
Proposed: DD   unchanged
No new information available since 1996.

Sacalia quadriocellata
CN, VN, LA
1996 Red List: VU B1+2c
Proposed: EN A1d+2d   + 1 category
Considered EN in CN; modest to small populations in LA and VN considered VU.

Siebenrockiella crassicollis
ID, KH, MY, MM, SG, TH, VN
1996 Red List: —
Proposed: VU A1cd+2cd   new
Considered EN in KH and VN mainly due to direct exploitation, VU in ID, MY, and TH due to both exploitation and habitat conversion and loss (though not listed in 1997 OEPP Red List for TH). Official records of 135,000 animals exported from MY in the first 10 months of 1999 (D. Sharma).

Family Emydidae

Trachemys scripta elegans
[introduced]   not evaluated

Family Platysternidae

Platysternon megacephalum
CN, LA, MM, TH, VN
1996 Red List: DD
Proposed: EN A1d+2d   new
Considered EN due to specific trade demand in LA and VN; either VU or EN in CN (main range state); small populations in TH are VU (OEPP, 1997); situation in MM is DD.

Family Trionychidae

Amyda cartilaginea
BN, ID, IN, KH, LA, MM, MY, SG, TH, VN
1996 Red List: VU A1cd+2cd
Proposed: VU A1cd+2cd   unchanged
Security of wide distribution and occurrence in protected areas offset by specific demand for the species in the consumption trade, currently traded at levels of tons per day. Not listed in TH 1997 OEPP Red List.

Aspideretes gangeticus
BD, IN, PK
1996 Red List: —
Proposed: VU A1d+2d   new
Considered EN in BD and VU in IN, its main range state; previously traded in East Asian markets at volumes of 30–40 tons per week.

Aspideretes hurum
BD, IN
1996 Red List: —
Proposed: VU A1cd+2d   new
Considered EN in BD and LR:nt to VU in IN, its main range state; previously traded in East Asian markets at volumes of 60–80 tons per week.

Aspideretes leithii
IN
1996 Red List: LR:nt
Proposed: VU A1c   + 1 category
Distribution range reduced in IN due to river alteration and other habitat impacts.

Aspideretes nigricans
BD
1996 Red List: CR B1+2a
Proposed: CR B1+2a   unchanged
Still restricted to a single temple pond.

Chitra chitra
ID, TH, MY?
1996 Red List: CR A1cd, B1+2c
Proposed: CR A1cd+2d   unchanged
Criteria for CR altered. Discovery of second area of occurrence, in Java, offset by fact that this population is intensively exploited for food and international pet trade. In addition, Javan population may not be taxonomically identical to Thai species. Listed in 1997 OEPP Red List for TH as CR.

Chitra indica
BD, IN, MM, PK
1996 Red List: VU A1cd
Proposed: EN A1cd+2cd   + 1 category
Considered CR in BD, uncommon (between EN and VU) in IN; disappeared from Indian domestic trade in 1986–87.

Dogania subplana
ID, MM, MY, SG, TH
1996 Red List: —
Proposed: LR:lc   new
Locally common in ID, MY, and TH; habitat preference coincides with major protected areas. Exported in some numbers from ID and MY, but this is the least favored softshell species in the food trade.

Lissemys punctata
BD, IN, LK, MM, PK, NP
1996 Red List: —
Proposed: LR:lc   new
The CAMP/BCPP evaluations considered the species LR:nt in IN.

Lissemys scutata
MM, TH?
1996 Red List: DD
Proposed: DD   unchanged
Traded in substantial numbers in East Asian food markets; candidate for VU, but field data are completely lacking.

Nilssonia formosa
MM
1996 Red List: VU A1acd+2cd, B1+2c
Proposed: EN A1cd+2d, B1+2ce   + 1 category
Traded in some numbers in the East Asian food trade; uncommon to rare in the wild; not known to inhabit effectively protected areas; life history particularly sensitive to exploitation of adults.

Palea steindachneri
CN, VN, [MU, US]
1996 Red List: LR:nt
Proposed: EN A1cd+2cd   +2 categories
Considered EN in both natural range states; highly valuable in food trade. Security of introduced populations [MU, US] critical for survival of species.

Pelochelys bibroni
ID, PN
1996 Red List: VU A1cd
Proposed: VU A1cd+2cd   criteria altered
Revised taxonomy since 1996 Red List, now restricted to southern New Guinea; significant local consumption trade occurs in PN.

Pelochelys cantorii
BD, CN, ID, IN, KH, LA?, MM, MY, PH, PN, TH, VN
1996 Red List: VU A1cd+2cd
Proposed: EN A1cd+2cd   + 1 category
Considered CR in CN, KH, LA, VN, and CR (P.P. van Dijk) or EN (OEPP, 11997) in TH due to direct exploitation and habitat loss. The CAMP/BCPP evaluations considered the species LR:nt in IN. In BD found in all markets in coastal areas during market surveys. Consid-

ered VU A1cd+2cd in peninsular MY; considered VU in PN but may represent a separate taxon; DD in ID, presumed VU or EN and traded at low but steady levels; situation in PH is DD but presumed EN or CR. Conservation assessment complicated by the conviction that the current taxonomic designation hides a complex of several different species.

Pelodiscus sinensis
CN, JP, TW, VN, [TH, US]
1996 Red List: —
Proposed: VU A1d+2d   new
While this species is commercially farmed in vast numbers (several millions per year) for the food trade, the wild populations continue to be exploited for food and possibly farm founder stock, resulting in a decline in abundance throughout its wide range. The category status assessment was made with respect to the natural populations only. The taxonomic and genetic diversity of the taxon (several component species have been described or resurrected in recent years) have been confused and compromised by the mixing of animals of different origin in farms, and the escape of farmed animals into wild populations.

Rafetus swinhoei
CN, VN?
1996 Red List: —
Proposed: CR A1cd+2cd   new
Only confirmed area of occurrence seriously impacted by pollution; animals intensively exploited for food trade and would be for pet trade if captured alive. Status and taxonomic identity of the animals in northern VN unclear.

Family Carettochelyidae

Carettochelys insculpta
AU, ID, PN
1996 Red List: VU A1bd
Proposed: VU A1bd   unchanged
Exported in large numbers for the international live animal trade from southern Irian Jaya in ID; heavily exploited and locally consumed in PN; endangered by habitat loss and degradation in AU.

Family Chelidae

Chelodina mccordi
ID
1996 Red List: VU D2
Proposed: CR A1d, B1+2e   + 2 categories
Occurs only in 3 separate populations on a single small island (Roti); total available habitat 70 km² (A. Rhodin). Collected exclusively for the pet trade, where it commands high prices due to its status as a distinct, restricted-range endemic; now considered commercially extinct by ID traders (D. Iskandar).

Chelodina novaeguineae
ID, PN, AU
1996 Red List: —
Proposed: LR:lc   new
Taxonomy is in the process of being revised, AU populations are distinct from ID and PN. Local consumption occurs to a minor degree in PN.

Chelodina parkeri
ID, PN
1996 Red List: VU D2
Proposed: VU D2   unchanged
International live animal trade in this attractive species has led to probable illegal trade from PN to ID and western pet markets.

Chelodina pritchardi
PN
1996 Red List: VU D2
Proposed: EN B1+2e   + 1 category
The species is the only endemic turtle in PN and restricted to a small range close to an urban center. It is illegally exported to the international pet market where it commands high prices due to its status as a distinct, restricted-range endemic (A. Rhodin).

Chelodina reimanni
ID, PN?
1996 Red List: DD
Proposed: LR:nt   new
The international live animal trade has placed some pressure on this restricted-range species.

Chelodina siebenrocki
ID, PN
1996 Red List: —
Proposed: LR:nt   new
The international live animal trade has placed some pressure on this restricted-range species, especially in ID; there is also some local consumption in PN, where it does not appear to be seriously threatened at this time.

Elseya branderhorstii
ID
1996 Red List: —
Proposed: VU B1+2e   new
Recognizable species (previously considered part of *E. novaeguineae*) with restricted range; utilized for local consumption and the international live animal trade.

Elseya novaeguineae
ID, PN
1996 Red List: —
Proposed: LR:lc   new
Abundant species in northern New Guinea, heavily exploited in PN for local consumption and local trade, with shells being utilized for the international curio trade; not presently at risk,

but a few shipments of animals appearing in the East Asian food trade suggest possible future threat (A. Rhodin).

Emydura subglobosa
   ID, PN
   1996 Red List: —
   Proposed: LR:lc   new

Abundant species in southern New Guinea, exploited in PN for local consumption and local trade, with some trade emanating from ID for international pet markets, but most of the current pet trade demand appears to be satisfied by captive breeding in Europe.

Elseya species (southern New Guinea lowlands)
   ID, PN
   1996 Red List: —
   Proposed: LR:lc   new

Recognizable species, as yet undescribed. Since listing as LR:lc will hardly contribute to increased protection and museum specimen numbers are not provided, it does not actually satisfy the taxonomic criteria for listing.

Country codes: AU - Australia; BD - Bangladesh; BN - Brunei Darussalam; CN - P.R. China; CN-HK - Hong Kong; ID - Indonesia; IN - India; JP - Japan; KH - Cambodia; LA - Laos; LK - Sri Lanka; MM - Myanmar; MU - Mauritius; MV - Maldives; MY - Malaysia; NP - Nepal; PH - Philippines; PK - Pakistan; PN - Papua New Guinea; SG - Singapore; TH - Thailand; TW - Taiwan; US - U.S.A.; VN - Vietnam.

LITERATURE CITED

GUO, C.-W., NIE, L.-W., AND WANG, M. 1997. The karyotypes and NORs of two species of *Chinemys*. In: Zhao, E. (Ed.). Chinese Chelonian Research. Chinese Society for the Study of Amphibians and Reptiles, Herpetological Series No. 9, Sichuan J. Zool. 15 (Suppl.):97-104.

HANFEE, F. 1999. A WWF India Field Guide to Freshwater Turtles and Tortoises of India. TRAFFIC-India/WWF-India, 27 pp. Contains 1996 CAMP/BCPP (Conservation Assessment and Management Plan – Biodiversity Conservation Prioritisation Project).

IUCN-BANGLADESH. 1999. Bangladesh Red Book of Threatened Animals. Part 3: Amphibians and Reptiles. IUCN-Bangladesh, Dhaka, Bangladesh.

LUE, K.Y., TU, M.C., AND SHANG, G. 1999. Field Guide of Amphibians and Reptiles in Taiwan. Taipei: Society for Wildlife and Nature, 343 pp.

MATSUI, M., AND OTA, H. 1999. Amphibians and Reptiles. In: Endangered Wildlife of Japan, Red Data Book 2nd ed., Japan Agency of Environment, Tokyo.

OEPP (OFFICE OF ENVIRONMENTAL POLICY AND PLANNING). 1997. Proceedings of the Conference on the Status of Biological Resources in Thailand, 29-30 May 1996. Ministry of Science, Technology and Environment, Bangkok, 52 pp. [in Thai].

OTA, H. In press. Current Status of the Threatened Amphibians and Reptiles of Japan. Population Ecology.

PRITCHARD, P.C.H. 2000. *Indotestudo travancorica*...a valid species of tortoise? Reptile and Amphibian Hobbyist 5(6):18-28.

YASUKAWA, Y., AND OTA, H. In press. *Geoemyda japonica* Fan, 1931, Ryukyu Black-breasted Leaf Turtle. In: Pritchard, P.C.H. and Rhodin, A.G.J. (Eds.). Conservation Biology of Freshwater Turtles, Vol. 1. Chelonian Research Monographs.

YASUKAWA, Y., YABE, T., OTA, H., AND IVERSON, J.B. In press. *Mauremys mutica* (Cantor, 1842), Asian yellow pond turtle. In: Pritchard, P.C.H. and Rhodin, A.G.J. (Eds.). Conservation Biology of Freshwater Turtles, Vol. 1. Chelonian Research Monographs.

ZHAO, E. 1998. China Red Data Book of Endangered Animals. Vol. 3. Amphibia and Reptilia. Science Press, Beijing, 330 pp.